Service Quality in Leisure and Tourism

Service Quality in Leisure and Tourism

Christine Williams

Department of Tourism and Leisure Management
University of Central Lancashire
Preston
UK

and

John Buswell

Faculty of Environment and Leisure
University of Gloucestershire
Cheltenham
UK

CABI *Publishing*

CABI *Publishing* is a division of CAB *International*

CABI Publishing
CAB International
Wallingford
Oxon OX10 8DE
UK

Tel: +44 (0)1491 832111
Fax: +44 (0)1491 833508
E-mail: cabi@cabi.org
Web site: www.cabi-publishing.org

CABI Publishing
44 Brattle Street
4th Floor
Cambridge, MA 02138
USA

Tel: +1 617 395 4056
Fax: +1 617 354 6875
E-mail: cabi-nao@cabi.org

A catalogue record for this book is available from the British Library, London, UK.

Library of Congress Cataloging-in-Publication Data

Williams, Christine, 1951–
    Service quality in leisure and tourism / Christine Williams, John
    Buswell.
      p. cm.
    ISBN 0-85199-541-1 (alk. paper)
    1. Tourism.   2. Leisure industry.   3. Quality assurance.
I. Buswell, John.   II. Title.
G155.A1W488   2003
910′.68′4--dc21

2002010655

ISBN 0 85199 541 1

Typeset by AMA DataSet Ltd, UK.
Printed and bound in the UK by Cromwell Press, Trowbridge.

Contents

Introduction

The past 20 years have seen a total change in the way the leisure experience is delivered and consumed

(LIW News, 1999)

The careful management of the tourist experience is an absolutely vital and complex requirement . . . service quality will continue to be a major component of the future shape of tourism provision

(Page *et al.*, 2001)

Leisure and tourism managers need to know more than how to manage, and even how to manage quality. There is a product involved and the service shapes the way it is delivered; quality management is also the process of ensuring that it is delivered with as few mistakes as possible and as close as possible to customer requirements. Knowledge and understanding of the consumer and of the concepts of leisure and tourism, including the way they are consumed and experienced, are becoming increasingly important and even represent the difference between success and failure. They are integral to service quality, and its management, in leisure and tourism and help to contextualize the application of quality management tools and techniques to the specific contexts addressed by this book.

The book's approach incorporates several important elements:

- While its substance is certainly factual, in order to inform, it also raises issues, different views and theories, and attempts to present a structured and ordered overview of the study of service quality in its specific application to leisure and tourism from an academic perspective.
- Its essence, therefore, lies in the nature of the leisure and tourism product and, particularly, the consumption experience.
- It emphasizes the human dimension and the characteristics of both consumer behaviour and organizational response.
- A distinctive feature is a synthesis of the human and social elements with the more mechanistic aspects of service quality.

The book acknowledges the growing literature that enables the practitioner and the student to develop their knowledge and understanding of trends and issues in leisure and tourism management and in consumer behaviour, and the very concepts and theories that help to define the fields of enquiry. The book also recognizes the great strides made in the last decade in developing the subjects of service management, service operations management and service quality. There are many excellent texts and journals in both areas. However, the aim of this text is to integrate key points and principles from both areas to establish the particular requirements of managing service quality in an industry that has some distinctive features and challenges. The book's approach is to offer an understanding of the underpinning theory of service quality as well as informing the reader of the practical application of service quality management tools and techniques in the context of the leisure and tourism industry and its specific demands. A diverse range of quality management tools and techniques are included. Some will be applicable to many organizations (e.g. ISO 9000 2000), while others have been devised for a specific service provision (e.g. QUEST for leisure centres).

Case studies are used throughout the book that draw on a range of contexts and organizations in leisure and tourism, and further reading can be selected from the list of references at the end of the text.

The book is divided into three parts: (1) Understanding Quality in Leisure and Tourism; (2) Designing Quality; and (3) Achieving or Delivering Quality. It is expected that practitioners and students will access the various sections as and when required rather than reading them in their entirety. The three parts link with other aspects of management, service operations management/service management, marketing and human resource management. They reflect the importance of combining a deep knowledge and understanding of consumers and their lifestyles with management skills and the ability to identify and meet customer requirements.

Part 1: Understanding Quality in Leisure and Tourism

Part 1 sets out to establish the background to service quality in leisure and tourism and, particularly, to develop an understanding of the concepts and theories that underpin the application of quality management methods, tools and philosophies. Chapter 1 contextualizes the development and diversity of the leisure and tourism industry and its products, and shows how it is increasingly driven by consumer requirements and the competitive edge. Chapter 2 outlines the theoretical developments in service quality that have influenced the thinking behind such customer-led strategies. Chapter 3 briefly outlines the typology of consumer characteristics and motives, which needs to be understood in order to appreciate fully the complex nature of service quality in leisure and tourism and the role of the consumer

or customer. Chapters 4 and 5 extend this understanding by examining the concept of quality and the core theories that shape our understanding of service quality and customer satisfaction, especially the theories of the original quality management proponents such as Juran, Deming and Crosby. The validity of these ideas and theories in the context of the leisure and tourism industry is appraised. The final chapter in Part 1 builds on the work of the earlier chapters in evaluating the distinctiveness of leisure and tourism services, which lies in their experiential consumption and complex mix of motives and attributes.

Part 2: Designing Quality

While Part 1 establishes the challenges facing leisure and tourism managers in achieving service quality, Part 2 examines the skills and techniques of translating the understanding of consumers, quality and the nature of leisure and tourism experiences into appropriate products and services. This section will enable the reader to understand the complexity of designing a service package to meet customers' expectations. The characteristics of services such as perishability and heterogeneity pose questions for the management of service quality, and are discussed in Chapter 7, as is the issue of whether a leisure and tourism service is customized or standardized. Such characteristics are not always apparent to the customer or to the observer of leisure and tourism services.

It can also be difficult for some people to comprehend that a quality product or service is nothing to do with it being a five-star hotel, for example. Customer satisfaction can be achieved whether a room costs £30 or £1000 per night. Low cost is no excuse for poor service design or delivery. Chapter 8 tackles an underdeveloped aspect of the literature on service quality in leisure and tourism services. This aspect is concerned with 'doing the right thing' as well as 'doing things right' but is based on understanding the concept of the product/service, its features, attributes and identified standards and the system required to deliver products and services. The service design process is complicated for the reasons outlined in Part 1 and in Chapter 7, and the techniques and tools for analysing and refining this process are evaluated in Chapter 8. Service design raises questions about the flow of people through the service process and its relationship with the deployment of resources. The final chapter in Part 2 considers some fundamental issues of managing capacity in leisure and tourism operations and their implications for service quality. The uneven demand for, and usage of, facilities and services require an understanding of aspects such as yield management and queuing and how they can be managed to achieve both productivity and customer satisfaction.

Part 3: Achieving or Delivering Quality

The first two parts focus on topics that are not always considered important, but without that background knowledge it is difficult to make informed judgements on the selection of the most appropriate service quality management techniques for a particular scenario. Service quality and its delivery have to be designed, but where customer expectations also include 'right first time' and overall reliability, there are wider implications for the achievement of service quality. Part 3 takes the management of service quality beyond the design of services into the management of systems and procedures and the overall

philosophy of organizations in their approach to quality.

Chapter 10 highlights the importance of organizational culture to the achievement of quality but also reflects on the difficulties in changing the culture so that quality management is embedded in all areas and functions of the organization.

The next two chapters investigate the introduction and implementation of specific service quality management systems, tools and techniques in all sectors of the leisure and tourism industry. Whilst there is awareness in the industry of some of these tools and methods, the debate that should surround them has not always taken place. Most of these elements are concerned with quality improvement but, to be effective, require knowledge and understanding of what customers really think. While Part 1 demonstrated the complexity of customer requirements and expectations, Chapter 13 examines the difficulty of measuring them and the extent of customer satisfaction and the scope of methods such as SERVQUAL and the critical incident technique.

Part 3 concludes with a chapter on quality and human resource management, emphasizing the key role that staffing plays in the delivery of service quality. It highlights how staff and their interaction with customers (which is central to many contexts) can be managed and enhanced and returns to the exposé of the features and attributes of the leisure and tourism product in the very first chapter.

Part 1

Understanding Quality in Leisure and Tourism

Introduction

The first six chapters identify the context of managing quality in the leisure and tourism industry and establish a conceptual framework, which reflects the different management environments of the public, commercial and voluntary sectors. Parts 1 and 2 represent the more familiar, mechanistic aspects of service quality and quality management; the tools, techniques and methods of quality management are important and these sections of the book address these requirements.

However, it is also necessary to examine the concept of quality in services, particularly leisure and tourism services, in order to develop an understanding of the context in which the application of tools, techniques and methods occurs. As Chapter 1 points out, many of the issues and concerns are no different than those of the global service sector. Aspects such as competitive edge, changing demographics and consumer expectations, technological developments and a dynamic external environment apply across the board. It is also necessary to define and understand the nature and scope of the leisure and tourism industry and its range of products and services and this is the purpose of Chapter 1.

Part 1 is also concerned with establishing the distinctiveness of leisure and tourism, and their challenges for the management of service quality, and the last chapter takes this understanding further and explores the experiential properties of leisure and tourism. It concludes that leisure and tourism services are concerned not merely with products and services but with offering and enhancing a consumer experience, whether in a theme park, a holiday resort or a health club.

Chapters 2 to 4 illustrate the progression in understanding these characteristics and provide the link from Chapter 1 to Chapter 6. Chapter 2 highlights the strategic issue facing all leisure and tourism organizations, which is the competitive edge and the need to develop consumer-led strategies. Many quality theorists conclude that the only goal to aim for is continuous improvement to satisfy internal and external consumers as well as other stakeholders. The chapter debates the underpinning theories to such strategies and concludes that the key is the understanding of consumers and their characteristics.

Chapter 3 provides a wide-ranging framework for understanding the leisure and tourism consumer as well as other stakeholders involved. The leisure and tourism industry contains a wide range of interested groups, irrespective of the sector, and their interrelationships are an important factor in understanding the dynamics of managing service quality. It is sometimes difficult for practitioners to recognize the importance of each group or stakeholder, and the need to prioritize their needs and wants. It can involve conflicting and dialectical views and interests and such tensions have to be managed and reconciled. For example, customers want lower costs (as in package holidays) whilst employees may want higher wages and salaries.

Quality enhancement is increasingly being viewed as the key concept in the service quality and service management literature and Chapter 4 is concerned with the underpinning theories of service quality and quality management. The chapter describes the two schools of service quality management (North American and Scandinavian) and provides a critical appreciation of the origins of quality theory in the manufacturing sector. The chapter also highlights the recent emergence of service quality literature and emphasizes the need to be critical and informed, as practitioners and academics, in synthesizing and analysing all concepts and theories.

One significant strand of the recent literature has been the examination of what service quality really means to the customer and has provided an important paradigmatic development in the subject. The terms 'service quality' and 'customer satisfaction' are central to such an emerging theoretical framework and, although there is an aetiological dimension to debate, it has pragmatic implications for the work of the practitioner as well as the discourse of the academic. The meaning of each term is important but so too is the relationship, perhaps symbiotic, between the two terms and the chapter offers some pragmatic viewpoints. For example, it has been suggested that there has been an overreliance on quantitative measures (e.g. answering the telephone within a certain number of rings) rather than a focus on the qualitative impact on individual customers, or that customers can be satisfied without, perhaps, quality really being achieved. In other words, it is not easy to define what is meant by quality – especially in the context of leisure and tourism services, which offer a product with distinctive features and attributes (as the final chapter illustrates).

In such a way, Part 1 provides the opportunity to connect theory with practice and to demonstrate that the successful management of quality in leisure and tourism services demands an informed knowledge and understanding of key concepts and theories. On completion of Part 1, the reader will have an in-depth understanding of the nature of the leisure and tourism industry, the environment within which it operates and the influence of this on the ability to theorize service quality practice, and as Parts 2 and 3 indicate, the ability to deliver and achieve service quality.

1

The Leisure and Tourism Product

In order to examine service quality in leisure and tourism, it is useful to consider the nature of the leisure and tourism industry and, indeed, developments in the leisure and tourism product. The leisure and tourism industry is no different from any other in that the main strategic issue facing all organizations is achieving customer-perceived service quality.

On completion of this chapter it is expected that you will be able to:

- contextualize the growing importance of service quality within recent developments in the leisure and tourism industry;
- understand the nature of the leisure and tourism product and its implications for the management of service quality;
- analyse trends and issues in leisure and tourism markets that have implications for service quality;
- appreciate the relationship between service quality and product and service development in the leisure and tourism industry.

The Leisure and Tourism Industry

The leisure and tourism industry grew inexorably in the second half of the 20th century and for many nations, both industrialized and developing, represents a key element of the national economy figures. Annual expenditure on leisure and tourism in the UK in 2001 was £64.2 billion (Office for National Statistics, 2002) with 3.5 million people employed in 223,000 businesses (ILAM, 1998). It is an industry with a major impact on the quality of life of people and communities. It is a global industry embracing both cross-cultural development and the rise of multinational corporations that are a part of this development. It is an industry that covers a wide range of contexts and opportunities. It is an industry that invokes passion and emotion in people because of its perceptual nature and its human interaction. It represents both participation and consumption; it can be passive or active, creative or vicarious, educationally and culturally enriching or merely entertaining. It invites scrutiny and criticism since we can all relate to its purposes and functions and are acutely conscious of any shortcomings because of their immediacy and their impact on feelings of well-being.

Several key reports and studies published in recent years have illustrated the importance of quality for the future of the industry. One such report was published by the UK government (DCMS, 1999, p. 4) and set out its aspirations for tourism (including aspects of leisure):

> The Government is ambitious for Britain and British tourism. We are proud of what this country has to offer and want to make the most of it . . . We will only achieve this if we can guarantee a consistent high-quality experience for tourists whether from home or abroad.

The report contains a 15-point action plan of the Department for Culture, Media and Sport (see Box 1.1), which encapsulates many trends and developments in the tourism industry and highlights in particular changing expectations of tourists, the importance of sustainability, technology and training and the impact of recognized grading and classification schemes.

The report also suggests that as the tourist market becomes more experienced and discerning, greater importance will be attached to quality and value for money. Furthermore, as competition grows around the world, British tourism must raise its standards in facilities and service in order to compete. The report recommends the regeneration of traditional resorts, improving the range and quality of visitor attractions, improving the quality of tourism accommodation and developing new products, which promote Britain's culture, heritage and countryside.

The Relationship between Leisure and Tourism

A perennial issue is the scope and extent of the leisure and tourism industry and how it is defined. The relationship between leisure and tourism (Fig. 1.1) is an important factor in establishing the parameters of the industry and the perspectives from which it can be analysed. Clearly, much of the tourism sector is concerned with the actual circulation and movement of people and the hospitality associated with overnight stays. An economic perspective is important because of the impact on towns and cities and, indeed,

---

Box 1.1.   Government plan for tourism. (Source: DCMS, 1999, p. 5.)

Fifteen action points are at the core of our plan and together they form the basis of a coherent strategy to make our industry a world leader. They are:

- a blueprint for the sustainable development of tourism to safeguard our countryside, heritage and culture for future generations;
- initiatives to widen access to tourism for the 40% of people who do not take a long holiday;
- more money for a more focused and aggressive overseas promotion programme to bring in more overseas people;
- new Internet systems to deliver more worldwide tourist booking for Britain and to provide information on attractions and travel options;
- new computerized booking and information systems to make it easier for people to book accommodation and travel;
- a major careers festival and image campaign to raise the profile, and promote the image, of careers in the hospitality industry;
- a hospitality industry programme to sign up 500 employers to work towards Investors in People standard to help raise the quality of training in the industry;
- a new strategic national body for England to provide leadership to the English tourism industry;
- a new grading scheme for all hotels and guesthouses to give holidaymakers and business travellers consistent quality they can rely on;
- new targets for hotel development in London and further £4.5 million for marketing to exploit its potential as a premier location for business travellers and holidaymakers and as a gateway to Britain;
- more integrated promotion of our wonderful cultural, heritage and countryside attractions to enable visitors to enjoy a full range of what Britain has to offer;
- the development of innovative niche markets such as film tourism and sports tourism, to unlock the full potential of Britain's unique cultural and natural heritage;
- encouraging the regeneration of traditional resorts to allow leisure and business visitors to enjoy high-quality amenities and services;
- more central government support for the regions to give each part of the country better resources to develop their own identity and strengths; and
- a high-profile annual Tourism Summit bringing together industry and government to monitor progress, plan future action and keep all sides working in partnership towards the same objectives.

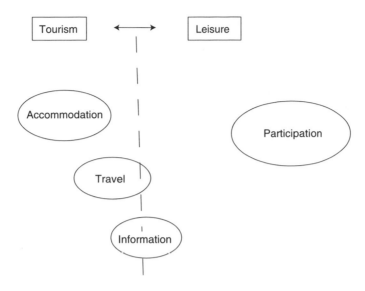

Fig. 1.1. The relationship between leisure and tourism.

regions or countries, with global tourism generating receipts in excess of £270 billion (DCMS, 1999). The tourism process might be viewed in terms of the three elements of: (i) travel; (ii) accommodation; and (iii) participation in activities at the destination, with an additional dimension involving its impact, from social, economic and environmental perspectives. These three elements make up the tourism system. The parameters of this book do not really account for the fourth dimension, although it has implications for quality of life, and the book is principally concerned with the first three elements.

For the purposes of the book, tourism is viewed as leisure consumption and participation with travel and accommodation. Some observers (Cooper et al., 1993; Ryan, 1997; Page et al., 2001) argue that tourism is a subset of leisure and that travel has its own forms of recreation, unless it is viewed as a necessary chore by the tourist. Undoubtedly, there is a blurring between the two concepts of leisure and tourism markets, as recent developments have demonstrated. For example, more holidays and tourist experiences have leisure activities incorporated into them or are based on them (e.g. trekking in the Himalayas). Cooper et al. (1993) viewed tourism as having three broad categories of purpose: (i) leisure and recreation, including holidays

and social visits; (ii) other tourism, including educational and health reasons; and (iii) business, including conferences, meetings and exhibitions.

The leisure industry is less easy to define than the tourism sector, because of the definitional problems with leisure as a concept and phenomenon. Leisure can be viewed in terms of residual time, activity, function, state of mind or, as shown in Chapter 6, an experience. It has already been stated that the leisure and tourism industry, for the purposes of the book, comprises managed contexts for activity, services and opportunities for activity. The contexts for leisure activities can range from purpose-built facilities such as leisure centres and theatres to resources such as national parks or urban open space, which may not involve a service encounter with staff, or mixed developments that may combine retailing with leisure opportunities and environments.

It is important to distinguish between the leisure industry and the leisure market, which embraces home-based leisure and the production of 'leisure goods' such as magazines, cameras and leisure wear. Finally, although food and drink in a social context account for an important element of leisure expenditure within the leisure market, and many contexts in the industry contain food and beverage operations, the book is not directly concerned with the hospitality sector, though there will be some references.

The common factor, therefore, is the encounter, or interface, between consumers (whether they are described as customers, participants or guests) and the context in the guise of staff, systems, procedures, information and technology. Service quality is now such a key strategic and operational issue because of the potential for variation and variability of service in the different contexts and, as shown in the next section, the growing importance of leisure and tourism to the individual and to society.

The Growing Importance of Service Quality to the Leisure and Tourism Industry

There are several reasons for the significance of service quality to the leisure and tourism industry. They are concerned with the competitive edge, social trends, consumer behaviour and demand, and technology.

New social structures

Harris (1999, p. 46) contended that 'ubiquitous connectivity and globalization will help to create a new social structure with important implications for leisure'. He considered the distinction between the following groups: the 'New Wealthy', who have the education or intelligence to make use of the new opportunities that they see complementing and fitting into their busy schedules; the 'New Purveyors', who can identify the needs of the 'New Wealthy' and can offer high-priced, quality services that maximize the use and value of limited leisure time; and the 'Service Army', who will either be front-line employees of the 'New Purveyors' or work directly for the 'New Wealthy'. Indeed, the UK's consumer expenditure on leisure is now 16% higher than the EU average, with the average UK household spending an annual £3410 on its leisure and holidays (Oxford Economic Forecasting, 2001).

Hyperreality

A factor of increasing importance in managing the quality of leisure and tourism services is the blurring of the distinction between reality and the replication of the real world. Museums and heritage centres represent past events and eras; theme parks recreate different parts of the world on one site and some attractions, of course, are based on fictional characters or television series and films. Rojek considered the relationship between postmodernism, with its emphasis on imagery, symbolism and technology, and hyperreality to be an increasingly significant one in the development of leisure and tourism products. He pointed to the effects of globalization and electric forms of communication and suggested that 'leisure experiences become dominated by spectacle and sensation' (Rojek, 1993, p. 285). Brown argued that hyperreality is manifest in the fantasy worlds of theme parks, hotels, airlines and shopping malls and many other contexts and he refers to the 'illusory, slightly phantasmagorical quality' of such experiences (Brown, 1995, p. 115). In other words, the rather sanitized and anodyne features of theme parks such as Disney are what consumers now expect in addition to high standards of provision and customer care. He also suggested that, in some respects, such facilities create their own reality with consumers expecting little variation. For these reasons the consumerism of postmodernism has considerable implications for the provision and management of leisure and tourism service quality.

Increasing expectations

The leisure and tourist industry is, therefore, affected as much as any other industry, if not more, by ever-increasing customer requirements and expectations. The Henley Centre (1999) highlighted the explosion in the quantity and quality of goods and services on the high street and showed how the range of goods in supermarkets compared with food outlets in the 1950s has increased 40 times; it also pointed to products on offer in financial services, which can now number tens of thousands. The leisure and tourist industry is no different. The growing diffusion of lifestyles and the higher priority given to leisure pursuits and holidays in their lifestyles by individuals can be juxtaposed with the opportunities for innovation and service development provided by technological advances and better education and training of staff, as shown by the case study in Box 1.2.

Value for time and money

It was shown earlier how consumers in the UK especially are spending a high proportion of income (1% in 2001) on leisure and tourism, but in an increasingly frantic way. Linder's 'harried classes' of the 1970s have

given way to Schor's 'accelerating leisure' (Schor, 1998), in which many consumers are transferring their work values into their leisure activities and are never slowing down. According to Mintel (2001):

> Britain has longer working hours than almost any other European country. Consequently, consumers are finding it increasingly difficult to achieve a balance between work and leisure.

Bailey and Hall (1998) also showed how value for time and money are important factors. The offerings in holidays or leisure activities not only have to appeal to a diffuse and discerning market but also, through their promotion and delivery, have to convince that the benefits are worth the investment in time, effort and money by the individual. As those in work appear to be under greater pressure or are working longer hours, leisure time and

---

Box 1.2.   Case study: cinemas.

Cinemas provide a useful example of a sector of the leisure industry that has recognized the developments in consumer preferences and expectations and their need to innovate and provide a quality experience. Attendances have increased from the lowest point, in 1984, of 54 million per year, to 112 million in 1996 (Henley Centre, 1997) and reflect the improvements made in both design and delivery of the consumer experience. The Henley Centre showed how cinema owners began to realize that consumers had a variety of entertainment options and therefore required a real motive and desire to go to the cinema, to experience not only the core product on offer (well-made films designed to appeal to a wide audience), but also the way it was provided. Analysis of the sector shows how cinemas were eventually perceived as old, out-of-date and uninviting facilities that did not offer an attractive alternative to television. The 'multiplex' revolution in the 1980s provided new and modern facilities containing several screens and appealing to different needs; today's complexes can contain bars and cafés, shops, 'high-tech' screens and much greater comfort. Virgin has introduced the 'Business Class' concept into cinemas and is offering waitress service and exclusive seating at an additional cost. Kingston (1998, p. 36) confirmed the progress being made by cinema operators: '. . . paramount in the drive to attract audiences is improved quality of the cinema product. High quality seating, greater legroom and state of the art sound systems are minimum requirements.' She demonstrated how UCI is developing its 'black box' auditoria with the walls, ceilings and floors blacked out to enhance the screen image.
    Fraser (1998, p. 43) was even more effusive in his description of the innovative approaches of the leading operators:

> Their business is fantasy, their mission to deliver dreams to a sophisticated, international, technology-literate audience. They will engineer the merger of the leading digital production houses with the leading players in simulation technology, do deals with Intel, the world's largest computer manufacturer, bring in the head of virtual development from MITT. They will segment their business from mass, 10,000-person sensorama experiences in capital cities, to the corporate and schools market . . . right down to the personal in-house, deep immersion experiences which will go through the roof in the growing singles market. They will be in trains, planes, cars not to mention hospitals, universities and museums. They will create city entertainment centres which have retailers clamouring for space. They will have their own restaurants and bar brands which are good enough to stand alone and they do. They will form joint ventures with leading developers in each country and have shopping centre designs which place their cinemas at the heart of a world-class entertainment district.

activities become more precious, and people are seeking quality time with family and friends. LIW News (1999, p. 1) illustrated the point:

> As competition intensifies, the battle for customer loyalty is increasingly being fought in the service arena . . . All of this has to be seen against a background of changing consumer expectations. Research has shown that as customers feel they have less leisure time, they expect more from what time they have. They want high quality experiences, with a style of service that matches the occasion. They want to be able to book either by phone or electronically. They want not only to be safe, but also to feel safe. They want choice. And they want the whole thing to feel in some way special. They don't want every destination to feel the same.

Consumer behaviour

An additional trend in consumer behaviour is what is referred to as 'time deepening' in which the individual is involved in more than one activity at the same time. Many people in the home will combine activities such as watching television while ironing, or reading while listening to music; but there are similar trends in managed contexts as well. An increasing number of people are seeking holidays that have an activity as the focus, such as painting or wine tasting, but where they are still attracted by conventional attributes such as climate, scenery and culture. 'Edutainment', in which entertainment is combined with educational learning, is also apparent in theme parks, heritage centres and contemporary museums and other facilities that are incorporating educational benefits into their service package, such as Chessington World of Adventure, Tecniquest and as we saw in the Millennium Dome.

The Leisure and Tourism Market

The scrutiny of holiday operators and travel companies by consumer interest bodies like Consumers' Association and the media adds to consumers' experience and their expectations. The move to a greatly differentiated market based on multiple interests, including adventure activities, hobbies, education and skills and individualized packages, is both a determinant and an indicator of the growing complexity and expectancy of the maturing market. Page et al. (2001) referred to travel typologies or psychographic (lifestyle and interest factors) or interactional segmentation (different motives). According to Cooper et al. (1993, p. 269), the maturing of the tourist market is creating a 'new tourist' who can be characterized as experienced, sophisticated and demanding.

Laws (1995) also suggested that the increasing familiarity of holiday-takers with destinations is forcing operators and authorities to upgrade their facilities and amenities and to deliver higher standards of service. The same is true of leisure markets: customers and users of facilities and services are becoming more experienced and clearer in terms of industry benchmarks, and what should be expected at a certain price, as the example of the Wembley Company shows:

> The last few years has seen a real change in direction of our UK greyhound racing business. The expectations and demands of our customers are constantly evolving and we have to remain one step ahead. In recent years we have introduced quality dining facilities into many of our tracks. A sports bar has been trialled at one track which combines on-course, off-course and intertrack betting around a central licensed bar with fully integrated screens. A first for the UK.
>
> We aim to surpass our customers' expectations and deliver the ultimate experience through constant innovation of our services and approach.
>
> (Wembley plc *Annual Report and Accounts* 1998)

The difference between the leisure and tourism industry and other industries, including other services, is in the nature of its markets, which are becoming increasingly complex, sophisticated and differentiated. Research undertaken by Deloitte & Touche in 1998 in the visitor attractions market revealed that some consumers are becoming bored with what some establishments are offering and that the market is not as simplistic and predictable as it used to be. A similar point is made by Bailey and Hall (1998, p. 1):

> It has become evident over recent years that commercial leisure and hospitality operators not only have to be able to segment the market traditionally using methods such as demographic segmentation (eg by age or socio-economic category) or lifestyle classification (eg pre-family, family empty nesters and post- family), but also understand that other external forces, such as fashion and image, are influencing the values and attitudes of people in terms of their leisure choices.

Cooper *et al.* (1993) suggested that the future of tourism will not lie in the mass, standardized and packaged industry of recent decades but will become much more customized and integrated with emphasis on meeting individual needs and expectations and responsiveness as well as reliability. For example, many tour operators find it difficult to tailor their products to specific foreign markets, let alone the market segments within each country (March, 1994). Eurocamp Travel has managed to achieve such differentiation through its use of agents who understand each market. With agents in The Netherlands selling to Dutch and Belgian customers since 1984, German agents dealing with German, Swiss and Austrian customers since 1988 and Danish agents retailing all over Scandinavia, Eurocamp has been able to identify particular requirements and gear its operations to meeting them.

Seaton (1996) suggested that psychographics and lifestyle segmentation, based on personality traits, attitudes, motivations and activities, are relevant, particularly if they are product related rather than generic to the population. He highlighted the four kinds of American visitor to the UK, which were developed by the British Tourism Authority in the 1990s:

1. First-time visitor – mainly London and environs.
2. Traditionalist – time divided between London and established regional locations (e.g. Stratford, Oxford).
3. Explorer – who wants to get to know the country better.

4. The Britophile – who knows the country well and has friends or contacts.

Market segmentation helps to differentiate the market in terms of provision and the delivery of quality and age is clearly another variable in determining the approach to achieving service quality. Conaway (1991, p. 18) showed how innovation and added value are particularly important to this group:

> Seniors aren't so much price oriented as value oriented. They're more willing to try something new if it adds value to their life regardless of price. They have experienced profound social change in their lifetime. As a result they're willing to try new things.

Service Quality and Product Development

The industry has developed its products in recent years to match and, perhaps, occasionally shape consumer demand. Travel operators now offer more customized packages and are no longer confined to the traditional family holiday. Developments in facilities confirm this trend. The short activity break market shows operators such as Center Parcs and Oasis designing and offering high specification holidays and established operators such as Butlins, Pontins and Haven also upgrading their facilities and services. Likewise, health and fitness operators such as David Lloyd and Esporta are investing in expensive, 'high tech' facilities and equipment.

The multifaceted approach to provision and consumption has seen the development of mixed facilities to provide for both a range of market segments and the diverse needs of the same segment. The local leisure centre has demonstrated this since the 1970s; commercial operators are constantly mixing and remixing activities and facilities in their family entertainment centres or entertainment centres. For example, Alton Towers opened a hotel on the theme park site several years ago and in early 2000 Family Leisure announced that the fomer Segaworld attraction in the Trocadero building would include ten-pin bowling, adventure golf, rides and other entertainments as well as a sports bar.

The branded leisure and tourism product

Branding is another factor, with the development of the 'branded leisure experience' (Smith, 1999) and its impact on switching behaviour. The purpose of branding is not simply to retain existing customers but to attract new ones from competitors or non-participation with a consistent but distinctive and differentiated product and service. Whitbread in 1998 spent £460 million developing its assets and brands, including the David Lloyd leisure chain, its country club hotel group (making it the UK's largest golf club operator) and range of food operations (Wheat, 1998). Harpers Health and Fitness Clubs provide another example of branding. They have achieved this by an identical design for each site, apart from size. Each site has a basic layout with the Harpers logo omnipresent and similar equipment, facilities and changing rooms and standard procedures. Thomas Cook regards itself as the leader in the travel sales business and is committed to maintaining that standard in addition to using and promoting the brand image. Its mission statement, 'Exceptional service from exceptional people', is a clear and concise summary of its approach and, as seen in Chapter 15, its training and development of staff is a key element in its approach to branding. Furthermore, branding is a factor in any organization's developments and strategic thinking. In 1999 the Thomas Cook Group merged with Carlson to double the number of its retail shops and it also added JMC Airlines (formerly Flying Colours), Caledonian and Airworld. Virgin offers perhaps the most illustrative example of the impact of branding: a Virgin cinema will sell Virgin cola in its shops or restaurants; there will be Virgin CDs and videos sold in the lobby of their cinemas and Virgin radio will be heard throughout.

Apart from these examples and other large commercial operators such as Hyatt Hotels, McDonald's and Center Parcs developing the 'branded leisure experience', there are now examples in the public sector. Birmingham City Council direct service organization (DSO) operates 'Leisure Point', which is the UK's largest DSO for leisure management, as a part of its branding strategy and its approach to quality. The Leisure Point brands have been developed to simplify its marketing strategy by promoting specific facilities under individual brand names with easily recognizable logos and images (for example: Pulse Point for its fitness centres and exercise-to-music programmes; Strokes for its swimming courses; and Golf Link for its golf courses). Its Marketing and Service Development Manager, Mike Dickenson, believes that branding has helped it to concentrate on the needs of customers rather than on the policies, procedures and structures that constrain many organizations. It has found it much easier to set common standards for each activity and to achieve them through consistent service delivery.

To support this approach, Birmingham Leisure Point has also created brand development teams comprising front-line staff, managers and specialist staff (it refers to them as doers, deciders and experts) to manage the brands and develop its marketing. The teams make up the Brand Development Group, which coordinates efforts to improve the brands through: (i) evaluating and, where appropriate, developing ideas generated by customer and front-line staff feedback; (ii) producing the technical and service standards and creating a marketing strategy; (iii) training staff and implementing the concept; and (iv) monitoring quality through customer feedback and comparing service delivery with quality standards.

According to Smith (1999) organizations, in order to create a branded experience, have to: (i) adopt new criteria for targeting profitable customers; (ii) achieve a superior understanding of what customers value; (iii) apply that understanding to create truly different branded experiences; (iv) make everyone a brand manager; (v) make promises their processes can exceed; and (vi) measure and monitor. There are a number of criteria in this 'blueprint' for success, although they tend to reinforce the principles of quality management that this book highlights. They suggest the need for innovation and distinctiveness in service design and promotion, based on an understanding of customer wants, and then consistency of delivery, not necessarily standardization. An important part of this process is relationship marketing which, with real-time access to customers and potential customers, has clear implications for the future of service marketing and service quality. Relationship marketing is concerned with the network of relationships between the brand and the identified customers and impacts on aspects of the product and its delivery, as the next section examines.

The nature of the leisure and tourism product

The leisure and tourism product requires some analysis in order to examine the nature of service quality. Although 'service' is the generic term used because of the characteristics referred to in Chapter 6, the term 'product' also applies to certain facets. It is known that there are tangible elements or aspects of technical service quality that can be more aligned with the notion of a physical product, and what is provided, and that there are aspects of functional or interpersonal quality that are more concerned with the process and the way the service is delivered.

The leisure and tourism product, like the industry itself, represents a wide range of specialisms and is not easy to categorize but its analysis has implications for service quality. The industry includes purpose-built facilities, natural resources and services such as sports development and tourism information as well as transportation, travel operators and destination providers.

It might be useful at this point to consider what is meant by the term 'product' in the context of leisure and tourism. According to Kotler (1996):

> A product is anything that can be offered to a market for attention, acquisition, use or consumption that might satisfy a want or

need. It includes physical objects, services, places, organizations and ideas.

Others (Wylle, 1992; Smith, 1994) have suggested that a product is a collection of physical attributes together with symbolic associations that are expected to meet the needs of the customer and comprise not simply what is offered but how it is presented. Seaton (1996) agreed and suggested that leisure and tourism products have two broad features: the physical and the symbolic. A facility like the Millennium Dome would appear to illustrate this point. It had its clear physical features in the various zones but was also designed to present a message and an image (even if it is a little fragmented).

Chapter 7 differentiates the management of services from the management of products because of the different processes involved and describes the particular characteristics of services that impact on the management of service quality. Yet if the actual transaction being purchased and consumed is considered, the distinction between the product and the service is somewhat academic and even spurious. Cooper *et al.* (1993) used the term 'service product' in the context of tourism, hospitality and leisure and they highlighted the increasing demands on service providers to develop a deeper understanding of the consumer benefits being sought as well as the service delivery system itself.

The pertinent element as far as the consumer is concerned is the offering or the bundle of attributes and, in particular, the benefits being sought and achieved. Of course, any product, including a manufactured one, can be perceived in terms of its benefits and, indeed, marketed on this basis. An exercise bike is made of plastic and metal; it may have some gleaming features and look attractive but its benefits are associated with health and fitness and a certain lifestyle. Likewise, a deckchair is composed of wood and canvas; it may add some colour and brightness to the summer garden but its benefits are viewed in terms of relaxation, socialization and comfort. Many leisure and tourism products are a mix of both tangible and intangible features that are difficult to disentangle. A swim in a managed pool takes place in a facility with specialist equipment and a created ambience but also depends on the service provided by trained staff and the way they interact with customers. The activity of swimming takes place with the development of the skill of swimming an important consideration, but benefits such as relaxation, enjoyment, socialization, health and fitness are also apparent. A skiing holiday is greatly influenced by the natural context – location, scenery, contours and scale and the way it has been adapted and built upon. Tangibles such as the pistes and the lift system are vital, as is the infrastructure of mountain restaurants and resort bars, shops and accommodation. The service element is also crucial in enhancing the quality of the experience for the tourist, who will always be conscious of, and even assessing, the attitude, skills and competencies of instructors, lift attendants and hotel and chalet staff.

In describing the leisure and tourism product it is, therefore, important to acknowledge the relationship between the tangible product and the process as well the core and augmented products. Figure 1.2 attempts to explain the relationships in which, in some contexts such as fitness instruction or sightseeing, the very expertise and demeanour of the instructor or tour guide are almost part of the core product and may be more significant than the tangible product. The model shows how the product is underpinned by the service, including systems, procedures and

information, and the consumer benefits such as enjoyment are the outcomes of the mix.

In this way we extend the views of Kotler (1996) and Swarbrooke (1995), who applied Kotler's definition of the product to visitor attractions and felt that the core product was excitement and atmosphere, the tangible product included rides and safety and the augmented product included the weather and car parking.

Another way of viewing tourism locations is to distinguish between the primary and secondary features (Laws, 1995). Primary features make up the natural attractiveness of a context, including climate, terrain, vegetation and culture. Secondary features comprise the infrastructure for tourism, including transport, accommodation, activities and information services.

It is also necessary to distinguish between provision that is supply led and that which is demand led. It could be argued that much tourism is more influenced by supply, in that it is shaped by the natural resource: its physical location, such as the scenery of the Canadian Rockies or the climate of the Caribbean; or its historical development, such as the heritage of Stratford or the culture of Florence. At the other end of the continuum, some leisure activities are really demand led in that the industry is responding to consumer trends and patterns of behaviour. Health and fitness is one of the boom sectors of the

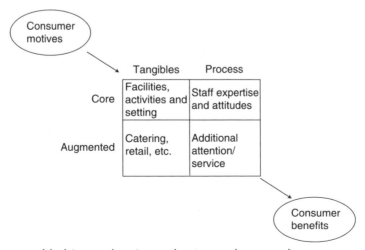

Fig. 1.2. The nature of the leisure and tourism product (core and augmented).

leisure industry and is buoyant because of the motives and needs of an increasing number of people. It could be argued, of course, that the industry is also helping to raise awareness and is constantly modifying its product to maintain interest, but provision is influenced by local demand, is purpose built and reflects the wish of more and more people to exercise in well-equipped, upmarket and relaxing facilities.

This illustrates another fundamental difference between some leisure and tourism activities. It could be argued that whereas tourism is constantly developing and offering new products, because of the uniqueness of the location or culture, there is little in leisure activities that is really new; many forms of provision are modified or adapted activities, as in health and fitness. Cinemas are experiencing a revival but the product is largely the same; it has simply become more sophisticated and technological. Day-to-day leisure activities are much more homogeneous. It can be difficult to be distinctive in terms of the core product. The competitive edge can possibly be distinguished in the way the product is delivered.

An important feature of activities such as holidays is the fact that the product is purchased before viewing. The consumer's decision will be greatly influenced by marketing material, and the significance of PZB's gap 4 in Zeithaml *et al.* (1990) gap model (examined in Chapter 13) becomes apparent here. The public and the industry are more conscious of the need for realistic promises or accurate information, and the wider study of service quality underlines the impact of image and 'top of the mind' awareness of a particular organization or holiday destination. It is significant that a number of Mediterranean resorts, once promoted and experienced as cheap and rather perfunctory ones, are being rebuilt and upgraded with the desire to make them more upmarket and dignified locations.

The technical quality of many leisure and tourism products, therefore, depends on constant improvement and innovation. Theme parks such as Alton Towers and Disney are committed to introducing new rides and attractions on a regular basis (indeed, it is

part of the Alton Towers strategy). Butlins and Pontins have invested millions of pounds in recent years in their holiday camps, to meet changing consumer requirements and to fight the competition of Center Parcs and Oasis. Marshall (1998, p. 12) illustrates the point:

> The challenge is to keep one step ahead of the public. They go to leisure premises for excitement, innovation and to see something different. There is a constant demand on a leisure business to take the customer one level beyond. Staying in line with the customer or one step behind means you fall behind your competitors and customers get bored with your offer. You must exceed customer expectations; it's a hackneyed phrase but it's true. With the technology available these days, people can walk into a shopping centre or down the high street and have leisure experiences. For people running cinemas, nightclubs, holiday centres or bingo halls, it means you have got to be something exceptional.

When considering the quality of leisure and tourism operations, it is important to analyse the relationship between the features of the core product and the secondary features or augmented product. As Laws (1995) suggested, the challenge to operators is to add value to the core offering through retailing, food and beverages, although in some contexts, such as hotels, restaurants and holiday centres, the distinction can become blurred. There is not always a clear relationship between the marketing of hotel beds and of additional facilities, especially in places such as Center Parcs, or Port Zeland in The Netherlands or Amelia Island Plantation in Florida, which combine activities with accommodation rather than the converse.

Thus, it is possible to apply the three levels of product – core, tangible and augmented – identified by Kotler (1996), but the relationship between the levels is less obvious than it is in manufacturing industry or in some services. The core product can be viewed as the main activity whether it is the whole holiday package or being transported from point A to point B, viewing a film in a cinema, playing badminton in a sports hall or sitting in a white-knuckle ride in a theme park. A clear augmented product can also be identified in many instances where there is food and drink and retailing; it is also known that the augmented product, or secondary spend, can generate more income than the core activity, as in some local authority leisure centres. Travel agents are constantly looking at how they can augment the core product of travel and holiday packages through car hire, foreign currency, guide books and visa services; Thomas Cook, for example, relies heavily on its foreign currency exchange services for additional revenue.

Nevertheless, it is often easier in many aspects of the leisure and tourism industry to think in terms of the core and augmented product and the *process* of delivering them. As has been established, an important element of many leisure and tourism products is the way the activity is managed and delivered. In some cases it can be the means to consume; in others the service and human elements are seen as the main attributes to be purchased. It might even be useful to view the term 'product' as an all-embracing one that subsumes the notions of activities, the context or setting and the process or delivery system and that creates and influences the overall consumer experience, as Fig. 1.3 demonstrates. Chapter 6 elaborates on the experiential properties of the leisure and tourism product and Chapter 8 considers the planning and design of service delivery systems and incorporates the elements of Fig. 1.3 into its examination. The next section examines some of the elements in more detail.

Features of the product to consider in managing service quality

In addition to the generic characteristics referred to in Chapter 7, there are several other factors that are becoming increasingly important in managing the quality of the consumer experience, as Fig. 1.4 illustrates.

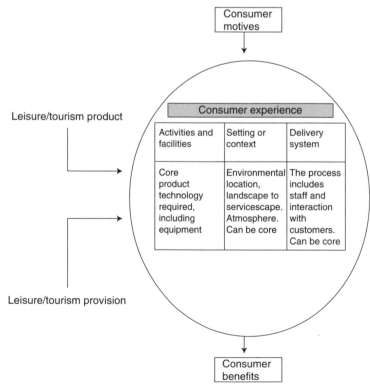

Fig. 1.3. The nature of the leisure and tourism product.

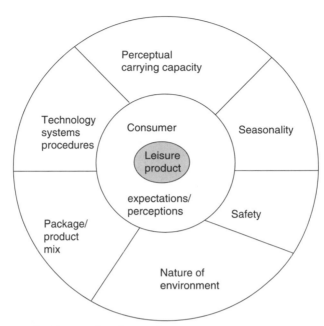

Fig. 1.4. Influences on the leisure and tourism product.

The carrying capacity of facilities and resources is one such factor. In any context, whether a national park or wilderness area or a swimming pool, there will be a perceptual carrying capacity and, possibly, physical capacity, which may be determined by fire and other safety regulations. Overcrowding can impair the enjoyment of consumers in a range of contexts and it is the task of providers to regulate numbers where they can. That can mean that a national park such as the Lake District can become full, with the capacity controlled by car parking numbers. Queuing is also a feature of some leisure facilities and can be built into the overall experience. For example, Futuroscope in Poitier employs staff to entertain the people queuing. Disney extends the theming approach into design features where people queue.

In local authority provision, a tourism officer's responsibility for a district will include some concern for the overall impact of visitors to the wider area and to individual sites. For example, the mountain of Snowdon in north Wales is regarded as a 'honeypot' to soak up about half a million visitors a year (many travelling by train). This has implications for the quality of the experience of those people, and especially those who walk up,

but is balanced against the need and desire to preserve the qualities of quieter, more ecologically sensitive sites in the same area. Clearly expectations, and the way they are created, are an important part of the managed process and the delivery of quality to tourists, trippers and locals.

Seasonality is another problem for many leisure and tourism operators and can test the capacity and the flexibility of locations. Theme parks attract most of their customers in the summer months with up to 35% of all customers attending in the months of July and August (Camp, 1997). Ski operators can be faced with many dissatisfied skiers during the February half-term holiday because of queuing and crowded pistes.

Safety is another factor that is at the forefront of consumers' minds. Activity holidays have had some bad publicity in recent years (e.g. deaths from white-water rafting in Austria in 1999). The safety records of public swimming pools and theme park rides are generally good but any death is highlighted by the media and raises awareness in the public.

The *environment* almost has a symbiotic relationship with service quality in leisure and tourism. Many activities or destinations are a result of the very beauty or attractiveness of the location but then risk impairing that beauty because of overuse. However, leisure and tourism, undoubtedly in some contexts, provide the stimulus for much investment in infrastructure and in maintaining the standard of provision of urban parks and town and city centres. An issue in Cheltenham for some time has been the amount of money spent on its hundreds of hanging baskets in the town centre. They look splendid and are part of the attraction for Americans and other tourists and visitors. It is likely that the same levels of money would not be spent on just the local population yet the quality of the town environment is also important for local residents enjoying shopping or simply moving through the town itself.

An important element of environmentalism is sustainability. Whereas technology is important to service quality because of its impact on service design and delivery, sustainable development can be seen as both a threat and an opportunity. Initiatives such as Agenda 21 and the general concern with the impact of leisure and tourism on the environment can be regarded as a constraint on existing operations and future developments. Yet the positive images associated with environmentalism and sustainable development can be utilized by organizations. Trends in social reporting by organizations demonstrate the attention paid by stakeholders and consumers to an organization's record and image and the standards of its operations. An example is provided by Center Parcs (see Box 1.3):

> At Center Parcs we aim to create and maintain the highest quality of landscapes and habitats . . . we aim to ensure that the health, safety and comfort of our guests and employees are safeguarded at all times and that all statutory requirements are met in full if not exceeded.

The *packaging of the product* can also be a factor where there are several elements that might have different standards. For example, some research by one of the authors found a source of dissatisfaction in a leisure centre to be the indifferent attitude of some staff compared with others in a different function.

Technology has a profound effect on product and service development and enhances both the product and the way it is delivered. The specification of many facilities and other resources is higher and the product has been greatly improved by certain developments and innovations. In-flight entertainment on long-haul flights is the norm; visitor attractions are technology led whether offering white-knuckle rides, audio visual interpretations, or cinematic effects such as 360-degree screens or three-dimensional films (multiplex and imax screens at cinemas have also contributed to their revival; the health and fitness sector also makes great use of technology in terms of training equipment).

Service systems have also been considerably improved, enabling the provider to improve booking systems, membership systems and ticketing. Computer reservation systems have had a particular impact on airlines, with developments in integrated systems involving tour operators and travel agencies.

New ways of obtaining information and making bookings are impacting on service quality. Seven million people, representing

---

Box 1.3.   Case study: Center Parcs and environmental quality.

An important element of the philosophy of Center Parcs is 'the care and development of the environment which guides and directs every aspect of the company's operations from the selection of new sites to its day to day procedures'. Center Parcs has shown that large tourism developments can be sensitively designed and even enhance the wildlife of an area. The positive aspects of Center Parcs' environmental policies and its interest in ecological matters have gained wide recognition, including a number of significant awards. For example, in 1988 Sherwood Forest Village received the Business and Industry Award and in 1990 the company received the English Tourist Board's inaugural Green Tourism Award. Center Parcs was also awarded the Business Commitment to the Environment Premier Award in 1993/94 in recognition of its human and social responsibility and environmental quality in respect of its development of its villages at Sherwood, Elvedon and Longleat Forests.

10% of the market in 1999, used teletext travel services (The Henley Centre, 1999). The increasing use of the Internet as a medium for booking packages, accommodation or flights is adding to the sense of competition in the high street and causing both operators and travel agencies to look critically at achieving a competitive edge through levels and standards of service. The traditional strengths of travel agents have been competitive pricing, access, and a customized, friendly and knowledgeable service; and to compete they will have to reaffirm the importance and benefits of the service encounter. The Henley Centre (1999) also contends that modern technology has created a real-time world for organizations and their customers through developments such as interactive databases that enable organizations to learn instantly who their customers are and what they want. It suggests that in the future organizations will need to: (i) be able to be contacted at all times; (ii) be able to respond instantly; (iii) have flexible systems, processes and people that can respond instantly; (iv) create true two-way dialogue with their customers; (v) truly respond to customer needs; and (vi) utilize modern technology to aid all of these.

Conclusions

In conclusion, it is known that leisure and tourism activities fulfill the normal features of service management but also contain particular dimensions that provide a challenge for the delivery of service quality. Tourism can often be a high-cost, high-risk business with a number of phases and operational functions involved in addition to the complex mix of emotions and perceptions on the part of the tourist. Control over the package can be complicated and difficult and the relations between travel agents, tour operators, airlines, rail and sea operators and destination and tourism authorities are crucial to the quality of the overall experience.

Evaluation by the customer and measurement of customer satisfaction by providers can be difficult, with no obvious conclusive moments of truth. The notion of the quality chain has particular application to complex holiday packages involving much travel and different elements, and the task of some tourist providers is to ensure seamless transition from one phase to the next. Other tourism providers will be more concerned with a particular element of the package, whether accommodation or activities, and will have more in common with many leisure providers, apart from the uniqueness of the experience and the expectations associated with a holiday.

Thus, there is a continuum of activities ranging from the holiday of a lifetime, with many phases and functions involved and based on the uniqueness and distinctiveness of the experience and its memories, to the several-times-weekly visit to a small local health club in which certain benefits, both short-term and long-term, are more apparent and the skill of relationship marketing over an extended period of time becomes more significant. There is less emphasis on the dreams and images associated with that special holiday and more concern with the motives for more mundane, everyday activities expressed by customers. These will involve socialization, health and fitness, education, relaxation and entertainment and, although less complex as an operation and package, require a subtle balance between familiarity and consistency, and enterprise and innovation, in order to encourage customer retention and loyalty.

Many contexts will occur between the two exemplars, with most managed leisure activities involving a less extended and complex package but with more implications for reliability and consistency, particularly where regular usage occurs. Some establishments may cater for both tourists and day trippers, or even local residents, such as a theme park, a museum or a theatre, though the operations do not really distinguish between them; others are quite simply local leisure facilities or resources for members or local inhabitants, such as the community centre or health club.

It might be useful, at this point, to summarize the trends identified by both leisure and tourist analysts, which have implications for service quality:

- Working patterns will become more varied, with leisure time more fragmented and spread across the population.
- As work becomes less physical and more cerebral, there will be greater interest in activities with sensory stimuli, either building on the use of mental faculties through interactive challenges, or in physical activities, with a compensatory function, which are exciting and time intensive, such as extreme sports or some keep-fit activities.
- Pressures on most people's time will continue and demand for a rich and distinctive experience will be judged on its ability to make people forget time momentarily.

- Developments in technology will be crucial and the use of computer simulations, virtual reality and sophisticated equipment will contribute to the competitive edge in many contexts.
- Branding will become an increasingly important element of service quality.

This chapter has considered the development of the leisure and tourism product and industry in relation to consumer requirements. It has examined the specific features of product development and the particular impact of technology on the management of the service encounter. Its focus on the customer and the relationship with the product and its attributes leads into the next chapter, which will examine in particular the implications of this for the significance of quality as a goal for many organizations.

2

Quality as a Goal

It is thought that organizations should emulate the best in their field, 'world class' as Dale (1999) calls them, but once they reach that level of service delivery the 'best' will have moved on. The response to the question, 'why?' is that their customers' needs are changing all the time and that the quality systems and culture they have in place enable them to respond much more quickly. Therefore following another organization's lead in terms of quality issues is not always the right strategy to adopt (Cutterbuck and Goldsmith, 1998). This is especially so in the context of the tourism and leisure industry, which is so diverse, not only in the services it offers but also in its variety of aims (i.e. social inclusion; improving the quality of life).

It is generally acknowledged that the only appropriate goal in the quality function of the organization is *continuous improvement* (Juran, 1988a). This is the concept of never being satisfied with what the organization is delivering and striving to do 'better' to meet customers' needs. This chapter will consider how this can be achieved.

- appreciate the extent of the evolution that an organization has to go through to strive towards its quality goal.

Excellent Service Quality

A number of writers, including Peters (1987), have suggested that if customer perception of a service is that it is 'excellent' and that it consistently meets their needs, the organization will establish a reputation for 'excellence' (e.g. Ritz Hotel or Disneyland). Peters (1987) described in his seven-step progression programme (Box 2.1) how an organization can achieve and deliver excellent quality. To instigate these concepts would require a change in organizational culture for many service providers. Peters was the only one of the early writers on quality (i.e. Juran, Deming, Crosby, etc.) to define quality in terms of excellence. Wyckoff (1992) also defined service quality by suggesting that it is

On completion of this chapter it is expected that you will:

- have an understanding of the factors in the development of an appropriate quality goal;
- recognize the importance of the need for continuous improvement, driven by the needs of customers and other stakeholders;
- be aware of the advantages and limitations of customer care concepts;

Box 2.1. Patterns of progression. (Source: Peters, 1987, p. 86.)

1. Quality within natural work group.
2. Quality with suppliers.
3. Quality with field sales/service.
4. Cross-functional teams.
5. Quality via system improvement.
6. Quality as close to the customer.
7. Quality as total customer responsiveness.

©CAB *International* 2003. *Service Quality in Leisure and Tourism*
(C. Williams and J. Buswell)

the degree of excellence intended, in meeting customer requirements.

Although many of those who write about service quality do not see excellence as a valid yardstick when assessing service quality, the one similarity that they all have in their views is that consistency of service is required at the level judged appropriate by the customers.

Having customers central to the organization, as Peters and Wyckoff stated, is also a strategy favoured by most of the service quality theorists. Mission statements of many of the most successful hotels demonstrate this. For Marriott Hotels it is 'The Spirit To Serve'.

One of the hardest concepts to understand is that excellent quality can be achieved and delivered by every organization and is not reliant on price. Some people think that quality only comes when a high price has been paid. This is represented by sayings such as 'you only get as good as you pay for' and 'cheap and nasty'. These are the perceptions that the budget airlines, such as Buzz and Easyjet, had to overcome when they were first established.

Although the expectation might be that a £19 bed-and-breakfast accommodation must give a poorer (worse) quality of service than a five-star hotel, in reality the food at each establishment has to be safe to eat, both are obliged to offer what has been advertised (e.g. en suite bathroom facilities), both require a fire certificate and the staff at both establishments should be courteous. Whilst the five-star establishment offers extras (e.g. a swimming pool, 24-h room service), both should offer a quality service within the confines of their respective customers' expectations, thus achieving customer satisfaction.

Crosby's Zero Defects

Another possible quality goal is Crosby's (1979) 'zero defects' concept, the main element of his five 'absolutes of quality management' (Box 2.2). Absolute 5 states, 'The only performance standard is zero defects' – the ultimate quality improvement goal, but this will not guarantee that customer needs have been met, only that the service has been

delivered to the specification set. Crosby also advocated celebrating 'Zero Defects Day' the first time that 100% conformance to the specification has been accomplished. This, in the opinion of many quality writers, has taken quality goals to the most extreme lengths and is appropriate for many tourism and leisure services where the benefit to the individual is the main reason for customers to participate (e.g. holidays; keep fit).

For organizations to work towards Crosby's five absolutes of quality management, a 14-step programme was devised. These steps (Box 2.3), which are said to ensure quality improvements and work towards Zero Defects Day, can be observed being implemented at many fast-food outlets.

Box 2.2. Crosby's five absolutes of quality management. (Source: Crosby, 1979, p. 131.)

1. Quality means conformance, not elegance.
2. There is no such thing as a quality problem.
3. There is no such thing as the economics of quality; it is always cheaper to do the job right the first time.
4. The only performance measurement is the cost of quality.
5. The only performance standard is zero defects.

Box 2.3. Crosby's fourteen-step quality improvement programme. (Source: Crosby, 1979, pp. 132–139.)

1. Management commitment.
2. Quality improvement team.
3. Quality measurement.
4. Cost of quality evaluation.
5. Quality awareness.
6. Corrective action.
7. Establish an *ad hoc* committee for the Zero Defects programme.
8. Supervisor training.
9. Zero Defects Day.
10. Goal setting.
11. Error cause removal.
12. Recognition.
13. Quality councils.
14. Do it over again.

Crosby's programme has similarities (continuous improvement and staff training) with other writers' quality improvement plans, especially those of Deming (1986), Feigenbaum (1991) and Juran (1988, cited in Dale, 1999), but the main difference is that it is focused on achieving Zero Defects Day – a phenomenon that some consider statistically impossible.

Services were not given special consideration by Crosby (1979), who did not differentiate between manufacturing and services, but his technique of the setting of performance indicators as a measure of conformance has been transferred to the public sector of the tourism and leisure industry (Audit Commission, 1994, 1998) (see Chapter 8).

Due to the extensive use of seasonal staff and poor retention rates of permanent workers in the leisure and tourism industry, Crosby's zero defects concept seems to be an unobtainable goal. Even without these added sector complications, zero defects does not always mean that an organization has achieved 100% customer satisfaction.

Continuous Improvement

This is known in some literature as a 'customer-orientated quality' whereby customers are central not only to the organization but to all aspects of the operational procedures and decision making. Knowing what customer needs are is of paramount importance to an organization working towards the ever-moving goal of continuous improvement of the services it provides.

This approach is not new, having being advocated by early quality gurus (Deming, 1986; Juran, 1988a) when they considered manufacturing. It was modified in the late 1980s to accommodate the theories of many service quality researchers, including Brown and Swartz (1989), Zeithaml et al. (1990), Bitner and Hubbet (1994) and Becker (1996). The later interpretation of this definition is based on the theory that customer satisfaction is achieved when their expectations of a service provider equal their perceptions of the service provided.

Edvardsson et al. (1994) advocated that a customer-oriented definition of service quality does not mean that organizations must always comply with their customers' needs and wishes. They did not reject the concept of the importance of the customers, but they did question the total reliance on customers' opinions. The public and voluntary sectors of the tourism and leisure industry have social objectives (e.g. social inclusion strategies) as part of their organizational aims; these may be in conflict with what their customers want. For example, initiatives have to be devised to induce the recreationally disadvantaged to use public sector leisure facilities. If more people are using the swimming pool at any one time, the existing customers may feel that their experience is not now as good and they are not satisfied with the service.

Rather than having the external customer as the focus of the service sector, Japanese manufacturing companies see that continuous improvement has an internal organizational concept known as *Kaizen*, based on the premise that everything can be improved upon. According to Oakland (1993, p. 315) the Japanese define *Kaizen* as 'a philosophy of continuous improvement of all the employees in an organization, so that they perform their task a little better each day'. Groups of employees known as *Kaizen Teians* implement quality improvement ideas, suggested by the staff. As Oakland (1993, p. 216) stated, continuous improvement 'cannot be achieved without specific opportunities, commonly called problems, being identified or recognised'; *Kaizen Teians* is one way of accomplishing this.

Both of the above concepts of continuous improvement mean that the norms and values of a traditional organizational culture cannot be preserved (Wilkinson and Willmott, 1995). The introduction of quality tools and techniques that can accomplish the cultural changes needed is advocated. These include business process re-engineering rather than tools that can maintain the status quo, such as quality circles (see Chapter 14).

Hill (1995) agreed, suggesting that a culture of continuous improvement needs to occur not only in the existing vertical structure of the organization but in the horizontal ones as well (i.e. across departments, divisions, etc.), mirroring Crosby's and Peters's quality improvement teams. Marriott Hotels have these in place. These are essential elements, together with the development of the notion that organizations seeking continuous improvements have internal as well as external customers. Hill listed the changes needed for a continuous improvement culture to evolve (see Box 2.4).

Cultural change is one of the hardest areas for an organization to achieve. If it can be accomplished, Edvardsson (1998) pointed out that there are three 'winners': the satisfied customers, the employees and the owners. Whilst 'owner' is not an appropriate term for many organizations, especially those operating in the voluntary and public sectors of the tourism and leisure industry, the notion of all stakeholders benefiting from a culture of continuous improvements is.

When the seasonal working environment of many leisure and tourism outlets means employees feel that there is no commitment from the organization, it is difficult for them to take ownership of these service quality ideals.

Quality Goal Evolution

Both Dale (1999) and Garvin (1988) wrote extensively on what they called the levels or eras in the evolution of quality management (Table 2.1). They both considered there to be four stages but Dale saw this as a progressive route that an organization moves through to total quality management (TQM), whilst Garvin considered the stages to be in a chronological order whereby new organizations now join at the later stages. The authors considered both views to be correct. There are more tourism and leisure organizations that have moved through Dale's levels, resulting in additional help for organizations new to service quality management principles. This enables them to introduce the more sophisticated or holistic approaches from the higher stages immediately. Some organizations, for various reasons including cost and lack of time, choose to start at the less sophisticated

> **Box 2.4.** Hill's quality culture. (Source: Hill, 1995.)
>
> - Internalization of quality.
> - Continuous improvement as a goal of all activities.
> - The absolute priority of customer satisfaction.
> - A systematic and rational approach to quality improvement.
> - More open communications, including front-line staff being listened to by senior managers.
> - Greatest involvement of a wider range of people in the decision-making process.
> - Creation of high-trust social relationships.

stages. These tend to be sole traders (health and fitness clubs) and voluntary sector organizations (sport, arts and youth organizations).

As long as organizations are aware of the limitations of the stage they are currently at, there would appear to be scope with either approach. The first three stages indicated in Table 2.1 can be considered as intermediate quality goals or stages along the path to total or strategic quality management. Many of the public sector leisure facilities have reached stage 3 (quality assurance).

TQM is a management philosophy that means that the whole of the organization is working towards meeting the needs and expectations of the customer. From past experience it has been observed that working to this goal is not only cost-effective for an organization but also enhances its external image. This results in new customers being attracted and, just as important, existing ones retained. Stage 4 in Table 2.1 is the most difficult to achieve as a change in organizational culture is required, an aspect that needs time. Very few service organizations have reached this level and those that have done so tend to have US parent companies (e.g. DHL courier service).

Dale (1994a) listed a very large number of barriers to achieving TQM, including: (i) lack of commitment from senior management to service quality, seen as a quick fix to a specific problem rather than a long-term cultural change; (ii) fear of the changes to work

Table 2.1.   Quality management goal evolution. (Adapted from Garvin, 1988; Dale, 1999.)

Stage	Characteristics of each stage
1. Quality inspection	Detection of non-conformance Methods used grading, sorting, inspection, etc. Quality the responsibility of the inspection department and solely an in-house activity Management still one of allocating blame, and compliance to specifications
2. Quality control	Systems devised to control processes (i.e. quality manuals) Methods used statistical process control, self-inspection Quality still an in-house activity A management culture that engages in quality inspection plus control in trying to solve or reduce problems
3. Quality assurance	Proactive approach to non-conformance via prevention Comprehensive planning and procedures used, with a range of measuring and monitoring tools. The introduction of externally accredited quality management systems (i.e. ISO 9000 series) to act as a framework for integrating the various quality tools Quality function devolved to all departments Management peripherally involved Customer needs and expectations sought Employees empowered to a limited extent to meet customers' needs
4. Total/strategic quality management	A philosophical approach to quality, holistic tools and techniques introduced (i.e. Business Excellence Model, benchmarking and business process re-engineering) Quality methods a mix of internal self-assessment and external verification Quality function devolved to everyone but with senior managers leading Empowerment of all employees, working as teams and extensively trained Organizational culture one of continuous improvement; building relationships with customers and suppliers important Customer needs and expectations central to decision-making process

patterns and processes, quality initiatives frequently used to downsize the workforce rather than redeploy them to improve service delivery; (iii) lack of resources (including staff), making service standards impossible to meet; (iv) no customer focus (decision making focused on the internal needs of the organization; other stakeholders such as shareholders take priority or financial factors such as profit or cutting subsidies are more important); and (v) poor data collection or analysis (e.g. invalid sampling frames used; only complaints data used).

To place this in the context of the UK tourism and leisure industry, development of quality initiatives is generally in the lower to middle stages of quality management evolution.

Most voluntary organizations are carrying out an assessment of a variety of quality tools and techniques with a view to implementation. Quality initiatives found are confined to those in the middle levels of the evolution process moving from quality control into quality assurance.

Within the commercial sector of the industry, in-house quality systems are the norm – mainly due to historical reasons of providing their own staff training. Whilst some organizations (e.g. Granada Group, Wembley Group) state that they are approaching a TQM culture, the majority are trying to emulate the quality cultures developed by McDonald's and Disney, a strategy we have previously discussed as not always being wise.

The most dynamic sector in terms of quality at the moment is the public sector. A number of culture changes are being forced on to local government by central government. These include monitoring their services under the Best Value regime, monitoring services that have been subjected to compulsory competitive tendering (e.g. leisure centre management, maintenance of outdoor sports facilities) from a period of stagnation whereby quality control has been the predominant goal to achieving a TQM culture. Local government services not regulated by compulsory competitive tendering (e.g. theatres, museums and art galleries) will be required to implement at least quality assurance initiatives, if they have not done so already on a voluntary basis.

The underlying philosophy of higher quality goals is for organizations to have or be developing a customer-centred approach, irrespective of whether they are internal or external to the organization. The care of all customers is paramount.

Customer Care?

The term 'customer care' has major connotations for practitioners. Generally it conjures up the image of 1-day courses that all staff are instructed to go on as part of their induction programme. Frequently it is a low-level course stating the importance of communications and how to handle complaints and enquiries. An example would be the Welcome Host course explained in Chapter 12. Unlike Welcome Host, which has a number of follow-up courses, many organizations do not provide additional training in this area.

The advantage of having an in-house course, apart from it being cost-effective, is that it can be customized to the organization's needs. A customer care course run by a London retail company instructs its staff on how to curtsy as it has royalty amongst its customers.

It should be an ongoing philosophy of the organization that customer care is a part of every decision, in all of the processes implemented as well as during service delivery. Even peripheral activities and services should have customer needs at their centre (e.g. staffing and location of the food outlets at a concert venue).

Lewis (1995) stated categorically that customer care strategies require 'substantial investments of time, money', including

'management commitment to customer care and the creation of an appropriate culture'. This echoes the factors that influence the development of a TQM culture.

The research of Zeithaml *et al.* (1990) indicated that the judgement of customers regarding service quality can be broken down into five dimensions: tangibles, empathy, assurance, responsiveness and reliability. This last dimension is the most important to customers as it is directly related to the care given.

Reliability is defined by Berry (1995) as 'the ability to perform the promised service dependably and accurately'. Howat *et al.* (1996) took this a stage further in saying that it 'assumes that there are no unpleasant surprises'. The fact that tourism and leisure customers are part of the service process exposes them immediately to any service failures and therefore the absence of reliability. Berry (1995) went on to suggest that the key for organizations being reliable is for them to want to be so. As Lewis (1995) pointed out, customer care is expensive and if financial efficiency is the main priority for an organization this can lead to conflicting organizational objectives.

Berry and Parasuraman (1994) also considered that some services are too technical for customers to know whether they have been carried out accurately and emphasized the importance of organizations being fair when offering very technical services (e.g. safety issues for airlines, ferries or football stadia). Berry (1995) and Grönroos (1990a) both discussed the notion of service fairness. According to Berry 'this is not a separate dimension . . . but part of all the others' and 'one perceived act of unfairness can destroy the company–customer relationship forever'. Ethical business practices need to be central to the organization for a culture of reliability and customer care to reign.

An example of an event that could be considered to be unfair, in the authors' opinion, was given on BBC Television's 1 o'clock news programme on Tuesday 23 December 1997.

> Wimbledon football team for the second time this season had a power failure resulting in the floodlighting going down. It was stated that the gate for the previous evening's game

was £250,000 and that a back-up generator would only cost £70,000. Away fans were contemplating going to court to gain compensation. The Football League spokesperson said that it would look into the situation but did not compel clubs to have back-up power.

It is interesting that the home fans were not going to sue for this lack of reliability despite what seems to be a clear case of unfairness. This is probably more to do with their relationship with their club, the 'fandom', as Bale (1989) calls it, than anything else. Loyalty such as this gives the home fans a wider tolerance (Parasuraman, 1995) about service failure at Wimbledon than one would expect from away fans, making them less likely to complain. The customers are considered in Chapter 3.

Whilst it is now known that the reason why the lighting failed at this and other football grounds was the result of tampering (to fix the match scores), if the football clubs had had back-up generators there would have been no reason for people to carry out these acts.

Hart et al. (1990) said: 'Think about the value of pleasing a customer – not the cost.' Having long-term relationships, with repeat transactions, is a more cost-effective strategy than constantly trying to generate new customers. Therefore all activities within the organization should be primarily customer driven and staff should be aware of the high priority that customers' needs have. The Institute of Leisure and Amenity Management's fact sheet on customer care (ILAM, 1996) sums this up by stating what should be obvious:

No customers
No business
No employment.

Conclusion

The above statement is a fitting conclusion to quality as a goal. The production of services without having a customer to purchase or use them is foolhardy. To examine quality as a goal requires an understanding of concepts such as 'excellence' and 'continuous improvement' in order to appreciate the factors that help to formulate an organization's approach to service quality management. This chapter has also demonstrated that the basis of these concepts is customer care – meeting customers' different and changing needs.

The next chapter takes the notion of customers a stage further and considers other groups of people who may benefit or are interested in the leisure or tourism provider. Buying and decision-making behaviour is also examined.

3

The Consumer

Although the title of this chapter is 'The Consumer', its contents take a wider perspective and focus on all customers of tourism and leisure services together with other groups with an interest in the provision of a specific service. These other interested parties tend to be known collectively as 'stakeholders'.

On completion of this chapter it is expected that you will be able to:

- understand the difference between consumers, internal customers and external customers and be able to apply these concepts to a range of organizations;
- analyse the importance of each of the above groups to specific tourism and leisure organizations;
- appreciate the need to develop relationships with suppliers;
- develop an understanding of the different stakeholders of public, private and voluntary sector tourism and leisure organizations;
- evaluate critically the benefits of tourism and leisure services to the consumers and customers;
- comprehend the decision-making process when applied to purchasing tourism and leisure experiences.

The Difference between Consumers, Internal Customers and External Customers

Many writers use the words 'consumer' and 'customer' to indicate one type of purchasing interaction with an organization. In service quality theory it is very rare that anyone writes about consumers; we are told that the needs of customers should be central to an organization's decision-making process. Whilst this approach may not be problematic for some sectors of the service industry, it does create a number of difficulties for the tourism and leisure industry. The reasons for this will be explained after the differences between these two concepts of consumer and customer are highlighted.

Consumers

Consumers can be defined as those people who directly purchase and then consume a service themselves.

There are many different types of consumer in the tourism and leisure industry but most are concerned with purchasing an admission ticket (e.g. to a concert or tourist attraction) or the use of a specific facility (e.g. a badminton court) or bundle of services (e.g. buying a place on a package holiday). Consumers are in a position to make immediate judgements on the quality of the service provided and will reconsider past experiences when deciding whether or not to make a further purchase.

Whilst service quality writers have left out the notion of consumers, legislation most certainly has not. The Consumer Protection Act, 1987 and its amendments set out to protect this group. This is achieved in a number of ways, one of which is to make sure that information given to potential consumers (e.g. price) is not misleading. Palmer (1998) states: 'This is important for services which are mentally intangible and for which many customers would be ill-equipped to make valid comparisons between competing suppliers.' This encompasses most of the services that the tourism and leisure industry provides. The Act also has the objective to ensure that products and services are safe and redress is available to anyone (not only a purchaser) if injured by them, and that this liability lasts for 10 years (Dale, 1994b).

Customers

Whilst the term customers can also encompass consumers, customers can be placed into two distinct groups: those that are either internal or external to the organization. Juran (1988a) was the first quality theorist to acknowledge these divisions.

External customers

An external customer is a person who purchases services from a provider but who, unlike a consumer, does not necessarily consume them. An example of this phenomenon would be the social secretary of a working men's club who arranges (purchases) day trips on behalf of the membership, or the treasurer of an amateur football team who books (purchases) the use of a football pitch from the local authority for the season. In each scenario the person may consume the service as well as purchase it but this is not necessarily the case.

To complicate the issue, other terms are often used to denote the external customer within the context of the tourism and leisure industry. A few examples are: tourist or traveller; visitor (e.g. to a museum or art gallery); concert goer; guest (of a hotel); participant (in sport); spectator (of sport); client (e.g. of a travel agency or fitness trainer); and user (of what is provided by public sector services). One of the authors, when

conducting a survey in an art gallery with no admission charge, was chastised for using the term customer and was told that 'patron of the arts' was more appropriate.

The lack of consensus as to a generic name for a user of facilities can cause confusion, especially to seasonal and new staff. Excessive labour turnover in tourism and leisure facilities ensures that there is always a high percentage of new employees. The importance of every external customer to the organization can be lost in the 'labelling' and inappropriate service may be delivered.

Internal customers

This term acknowledges that people working within an organization can be internal customers of each other. For example, the marketing department of a theatre is the internal customer of the creative director. Marketing requires information about the season's programme and the individual cast members so that the department can design the publicity leaflet and have it printed in time for the mailshot company to distribute. The marketing function is also the internal customer of the business director and equally requires the information on pricing structures for each event for the same reasons. Figure 3.1 illustrates how a marketing and box office department needs to meet its ticket sales targets as required by its internal customer, the business director.

In service quality management and customer care workshops, it is standard

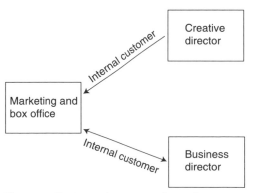

Fig. 3.1. The internal customer relationships in one area of theatre management: flow of information for publicity material production.

procedure for the facilitator to ask the participants to consider 'who are my customers?'
and 'who am I a customer of?' but it would be
better to differentiate between internal and
external customers. Many service organizations go to a lot of trouble to have a customer-centred organization but on analysis
this only refers to external customers. Juran
(1988b) considered that 'the first step in
quality planning is to identify who are the
customers.' Grönroos and Gummesson (1986,
cited in Burca, 1995) stressed that staff who are
not visible to the external customers are still
important to the overall quality of service
delivery, as their contribution influences the
outcome.

For the purpose of this text, as with most
others, in service quality the word 'customers'
is used generically to mean the three groups
defined above, as illustrated in the case study
in Box 3.1.

Whatever label is given to the 'customers', it is necessary to acknowledge their
importance to the organization. Their views
need to be sought, as their needs and expectations are always changing.

Suppliers and Contractors

Within a holistic service quality management
culture, the suppliers to an organization are
equally as important as the external and
internal customers. Of course, whether or not
they deliver (on time) the correct goods or
services can have a major impact on service
delivery quality and its outcomes. This inter-
relationship with the customers and suppliers is known as the *quality chain* (Oakland,
1993) or Juran's (1988a) *'spiral of progress in
quality'*.

In the past, suppliers were seen as a
necessary evil, to be dominated by the
organization's purchasing power. The main
objective was for the organization to look after
itself without any thought of the supplier and
to get the cheapest price (Juran, 1988a). This
adversarial approach was generally a recipe
for problems to occur.

Deming (1986) stated that price is not
a valid reason to award contracts. He took

> **Box 3.1.**   Case study: consumers, internal and
> external customers of a package holiday.
>
> Unlike the airline companies that are part and
> parcel of a vertically integrated holiday group,
> the hotel element of a package holiday tends
> to be owned by others. Therefore Table 3.1 is
> a good example of the difference between
> customers and consumers.

a more holistic approach when appraising
suppliers, considering the quality of goods
and services to be supplied. He suggested that
using only one supplier would eventually
reduce costs, but this may not always be
possible. A tourism and leisure facility, whilst
it may have one specific core service (e.g.
a museum or a golf course), may also have
a number of peripheral services attached
(e.g. food and beverage, merchandizing) and
multiple suppliers may be the only option.

The building of a relationship with
suppliers, whilst hinted at by Deming (1986),
was advocated by Feigenbaum (1991). He was
convinced that taking a holistic approach to all
aspects of quality management (total quality
control) includes building relationships with
the customers and the suppliers. This was
earlier supported by Peters (1987).

Gummesson (1993) made allowances for
occasional mistakes by suppliers, especially
major events outside the organization's control (such as strikes or earthquakes) that will
have a 'knock-on' effect on service delivery
quality. He suggested that if a quality prevention system is in place 'to give early warning
signs' of a potential problem or delays occur-
ring, alternative strategies may be put in
place. The only way for a supplier to 'admit'
that there are problems is if a trusting, supportive relationship has been developed. This
relationship will be based on a desire for both
organizations to be mutually successful.

Crosby (1984) took this concept a stage
further and went so far as to say that the
education of suppliers is appropriate, as well
as supporting them. He also advocated that
suppliers should be consulted using similar
methodologies as with customer audits (e.g.
focus groups, questionnaires; see Chapter 13),
in addition to the educational workshops. The

Table 3.1. The booking and consumption of a package holiday.

Supplier	Act	Definition
Travel agents (A)	Person (B) requests a holiday	B is a consumer of A's services
Travel agents (A)[a]	Books the holiday with tour operator (C)	A is an external customer of C's services B is a consumer of C's services
Airport (D)	Person (B) goes on holiday by aeroplane (C2)	B is a consumer of D's and C2's services
Tour operator's airline (C2)	Airport services (D)	C2 is a consumer of D's services C2 is also an internal customer of C and vice versa
Coach (E)	Transfer to the hotel and back Can supply coaches for day trips as well	B is a consumer of E's services C is an external customer of E's services
Hotel (F)	Accommodation for the duration of the holiday	B is a consumer of F's services C is an external customer of F's services
Hotel supplies (G)	Hotel has many suppliers (e.g. food, drinks, maintenance)	B is a consumer of G's services F is a consumer of G's services (i.e. the hotel staff will eat the food when on duty) and will be an external customer of other services (e.g. pool maintenance)
Attractions and hospitality venues (H)	Day trips arranged by tour operator (C)	B is a consumer of H's services C is an external customer of H's services
Airport (I)	Person (B) goes home by aeroplane (C2)	B is a consumer of I's and C2's services
Tour operator's airline (C2)	Airport services (I)	C2 is a consumer of I's services
Tour operator's representative (C3)	General information and problem solving	B consumes the services provided by C3 C3 is the internal customer of the tour operator's other departments (C) and airline (C2)

[a]If the travel agency is part of the same holiday group, the travel agency is an internal customer of the tour operator.

UK-based retailer, Marks and Spencer, was one of the first companies to adopt this approach; it is rarer for this to happen in the wider tourism and leisure industry than in the public sector.

This relationship culture between clients and contractors is inherent in public sector leisure management (parks, open spaces, leisure centres, etc.). The fact that many existing public sector employees won the contracts when compulsory competitive tendering of local government services was brought in, due to the formation of direct service organizations, meant that relationships of this nature were already formulated.

Another way of forming a relationship with suppliers/contractors is via the strategy of awarding long-term contracts (Dale and Boaden, 1994); this again was implemented when the public sector leisure services management contracts came up for renewal. On the first occasion they were awarded for 3 years; at renewal they were extended to 5–7 years.

Vendor rating

A systematic way of classifying different suppliers is by a technique known as vendor rating (Chaplin, 1982). This means that, after an in-depth appraisal of the supplier and its management systems, an organization is given a classification:

- Vendor rating A: continue with normal quality inspection of the goods or services it supplies.
- Vendor rating B: a more rigorous inspection is required.
- Vendor rating C: a reduction in inspection is appropriate.

Oakland (1993) saw this as time consuming on both parties and also costly. His method would be to expect suppliers to be certificated to an externally assessed quality system (e.g. ISO 9000, 2000, outlined in Chapter 11). He suggested that if this is achieved the suppliers will supply appropriate goods and services, and time can then be spent on building a 'partnership'. Audits and reviews in a much more concise form are still required from time to time.

Stakeholders

Another name for an organization's supplier could be 'stakeholder', as the supplier has a vested interest in the organization's present and future success. According to the *Concise Oxford Dictionary*, a stakeholder in an organization is someone who is 'materially concerned in its welfare'. This is the context appropriate to tourism and leisure organizations rather than the more familiar stakeholder definition appertaining to a gambler's 'wager on an event'.

Public sector stakeholders

The new management regime of '*Best Value*' (see Chapter 13) currently being implemented in public sector services requires that all stakeholders in a service are consulted about its delivery. Table 3.2 gives the list

Table 3.2. The range of stakeholders in a public sector heritage attraction. (Source: Davies and Girlder, 1998.)

Stakeholders	Definition and notes
Dedicated users	Those who use the facilities on a regular basis (e.g. local schools)
Direct users	Those with a direct interest (e.g. coach operators and tourists)
Indirect users	Those who benefit but do not use the service (e.g. local hoteliers)
Marginal users	Informal users (e.g. locals who only use the shop and café)
General public	Anyone who passes through the area and notices the attraction
Council taxpayers	Residential and businesses, financial stakeholders
Staff	Permanent and temporary
Elected representatives (councillors)	Those who represent some of the groups above
Grant-awarding organizations	(e.g. National Lottery)
Whole of the electorate	To which all councillors have to answer

of stakeholders concerned with a heritage attraction managed by the public sector.

Whilst this type of consultative process is expensive, recent research has shown that over 50% of responding leisure departments use a number of consultation methods and sample non-users as well as users (Guest and Taylor, 1999). One problem that may emerge is: whose opinions take priority if differing, conflicting views are given?

OMBUDSMEN.   Another set of stakeholders in the public sector not included in the list above is a number of bodies for its citizens to complain to known as ombudsmen, created by the UK government. Parliamentary or local government ombudsmen can investigate complaints about central or local government services. The complaint can be regarding either procedures or direct service provision. One area in which the ombudsmen will not get involved is pricing structures. Complaints of a financial nature can be taken to the National Audit Office (for government organizations) or the Audit Commission (in the case of local authorities).

NATIONAL LOTTERY COMMISSION.   Another commission directly related to the tourism and leisure industry is the one that oversees the running of the UK's National Lottery. Whilst the gaming side of the National Lottery has never been operated on a day-to-day basis by the State, having always been managed by the commercial company Camelot, this commission ensures that Camelot in its unique monopoly position does comply with the contract it has signed with the UK government.

Camelot does not award National Lottery grants but each week gives 28p in every £1 of its takings to the lottery grant-awarding bodies, Sports Councils, Arts Councils, Heritage Lottery Fund, Millennium Commission, National Lotteries Charities Board and the New Opportunities Fund, for distribution. Whilst it is very unusual for a lottery player to complain to the Lottery Commission, organizations have remonstrated with them about the way grants are awarded.

Stakeholders in the voluntary sector

The stakeholders of a voluntary organization (e.g. a choral society or an amateur athletic club) are very similar to those in the public sector. Whereas the decision-making process of public sector tourism and leisure facilities is carried out by elected councillors with advice from professional staff, in the voluntary sector many stakeholder representatives are part of the management team.

Handy (1988) states that a management team containing representatives from all stakeholders will generally comprise clients, the community at large and funding agencies, and is known as a *stakeholder democracy*.

Commercial sector stakeholders

Stakeholders in the commercial sector of the tourism and leisure industry include some of the categories above. For example, taking the 'community at large', the closure of large factories has shown how local economies can be dependent on a particular commercial operation (e.g. in Blackpool the whole of the economy is geared to tourism). Also the impact of major events (e.g. motor racing) on the community cannot be underestimated

(Burns *et al.*, 1986), not only economically but also environmentally.

Another stakeholder, similar to those previously mentioned, is represented by the funding agencies. Grant aid is available to the commercial sector and, whilst it cannot receive lottery funding, other grants are available especially in areas designated by central government as having 'assessed area status'. An additional source of income for commercial organizations is sponsorship. Although sports sponsors have some of the highest profiles, sponsorship can be found in tourist attraction, such as theme parks (e.g. Kodak at Disneyland Paris). The sponsors are another category of stakeholder.

The commercial sector is not made up of companies of similar size but needs to be divided into two sectors: (i) large commercial companies listed on the stock market (e.g. Granada Group, Manchester United Football Club); and (ii) smaller companies that are owned and managed by one or a few people, i.e. sole traders (e.g. small fitness clubs, restaurants).

STAKEHOLDERS OF LISTED COMPANIES.   As well as encompassing groups such as consumers, customers, staff and suppliers, the stakeholders of the large companies listed on the stock market must include the shareholders. Shareholders have specific rights to be involved in the decision-making process through a company's annual general meeting.

In 1999 a £623 million take-over bid for Manchester United Football Club was launched by BSkyB, the satellite television broadcasting company, and the smaller shareholders seemed to have very little power. The views of the owners of the major shares (i.e. the directors of the club and the financial institutions) outweighed those of the minority shareholders.

The minority shareholders are also the fans (consumers) of the team and passionately voiced their opposition to the take-over. This seemed to have very little effect and it was only averted by the intervention of the Department of Culture, Media and Sport, which referred the take-over decision to the Monopolies and Mergers Commission (MMC). The MMC decided that there would be a conflict of interest between owning the rights to broad-cast football matches if BSkyB also owned a team. At the same time, incidentally, Granada Group had a 9.9% shareholding in Liverpool Football Club at a cost of £22 million but the percentage was so low that it was not per-ceived to be a conflict of interest (Nisse and Snoddy, 1999).

Manchester United had controversially ignored their small shareholders and con-sumers by withdrawing from the 1999/2000 Football Association Cup to play in the World Club competition. This decision was made in consultation with the Football Association and the then Minister for Sport, Tony Banks, as it was felt that the team's presence might have persuaded FIFA to award the staging of the 2006 World Cup to Britain (Germany won the right to stage this event).

At one stage it was stated that it would be feasible to fly Manchester United's FA Cup opponents out to South America. The question was then asked whether or not the fans would be flown out as well.

The balance between the needs of various stakeholders and the consumers seems to have been upset. If a more in-depth analysis is carried out the 'spectators–consumers' are only a small percentage of the three consumer groups in the Manchester United case, the other two being purchasers of merchandise and the television viewers. Whilst success on the pitch is the foundation for the other business activities, the spectator–consumers only contribute a small percentage to the business.

STAKEHOLDERS OF SOLE TRADERS.   The second type of commercial organization is one that is owned and managed by a small number of people (e.g. personal trainers, dance studios, food and beverage outlets). Whilst the stake-holders will not include shareholders, other categories are relevant – especially any finan-cial institutions that have provided start-up capital.

Whilst the examples given above indicate small organizations, it must not be forgotten this is not always the case. For example, Blackpool Pleasure Beach, together with other major tourist attractions, is owned by the Thompson family.

To conclude, stakeholders in any of the three sectors of the leisure and tourism industry are a key variable in the management of service quality. Indeed, they must have their views solicited, as they have a legitimate interest in the organization and its ongoing success. The importance of all stakeholders in sustaining this development must not be overlooked but managers must decide which groups' views take priority within the context of service delivery. The authors would suggest that consumers and customers are normally the priority, because strategy and operations are geared towards their wants and needs and the extent to which the charac-teristics of consumer behaviour are identified and provided for.

Consumer/Buyer Behaviour

This section will not concentrate on tradi-tional services marketing activities, which can be found in many texts, but will investigate the reasons why one individual will select a particular activity or experience from a specific provider.

Many of the models of buyer behaviour are based on the whole of the consump-tion process (Fisk, 1981, cited in Palmer, 1998), including consumption and post-consumption phases. This section will only refer to the pre-consumption stage of the process. The evaluation of the service will be discussed in Chapter 4.

Swarbrooke and Horner (1999) examined a range of consumer behaviour models and carried out an analysis of them when applied to tourism. The consensus from the linear models of Mathieson and Wall (1992) and the more complex models of Andreason (1965) or Howard-Sheth (1969) (all cited in Swarbrooke and Horner (1999)) is that stimuli are required to make the potential customers aware of their needs. The stimuli sources can be advertisements, word of mouth from past customers, or customers' own previous experiences.

The move from needing something to par-ticipating will be modified by many influences, including social and economic. External factors will also play a part in the decision-making process: a war or natural disaster will make a destination inaccessible; the lack of a specific facility will also limit choice.

Time lags are not taken into account in many of the buyer decision-making models. Whilst a proportion of people will wait for a last-minute bargain break, many will make the decision many months before departure. The factors that are in place at the time that the decision is made may not be present when the event takes place (Swarbrooke and Horner, 1999).

Palmer (1998) simplifies the complex process of buyer decision-making by breaking it down into five steps: (i) need recognition; (ii) information search; (iii) evaluation; (iv) decision; and (v) post-purchase evaluation.

Need recognition

As the tourism and leisure industry provides such a diverse range of activities, the word 'benefits' is more appropriate than the phrase 'need recognition'. Exploring the benefits of a service provides an understanding of why individuals feel that they need these products and services.

Potential customers are attracted to a specific tourism and leisure product for different reasons. Benefits can be divided into: (i) extrinsic value – after consumption a definite known need has been fulfilled (e.g. meal in a restaurant) (Holbrook, 1994); and (ii) intrinsic – an experience that is good for its own sake (e.g. children's play). The main positive outcomes sought from tourism or leisure experience are satisfaction, enjoyment, sense of achievement and self-esteem.

Experiences that improve the individual's quality of life

Beard and Ragheb (1980) formally categorized 'quality of life' experiences into a leisure motivational scale. The six motivations or benefits of leisure are said to be:

- **Psychological** – a sense of freedom, enjoyment, involvement and intellectual challenge.

- **Educational** – intellectual stimulation and helps people to learn about themselves and their surroundings.
- **Social** – rewarding relationships with other people.
- **Relaxation** – relief from the stress and strain of life.
- **Physiological** – a means to develop physical fitness, stay healthy, control weight and otherwise promote well-being.
- **Aesthetic** – viewing the area in which people engage in their leisure activity as interesting, pleasing, beautiful and well designed.

Customers know what motivates them and will look for leisure and tourism opportunities to fulfil those needs. Examples are given in Table 3.3.

Experiences that give status

Customers can feel that buying a specific item of sports clothing or equipment (generally very expensive and endorsed by an existing champion) will give them a certain amount of kudos at the sports club. In the case of football club strips the feeling of belonging, and being part of a success story, provides some of the benefits. As the clothing is worn on many occasions not associated with being a football spectator, it shows the rest of the community what the customers are

Table 3.3. Example of 'quality of life' experiences.

Customer's needs	Experiences fulfilling the needs
Improve health	Relaxing holiday
	Visit to the gym
Improve looks	'Exercise will make you look good!'
Skill	Learn or improve an existing skill (e.g. landscape painting, fly fishing)
Emotional need	Classical concert
	Bungee-jumping type of activity
Educational need	Acquire knowledge via tour of overseas historical sites
Socialization	Directly (e.g. pub or club)
	Indirectly (e.g. when participating in another leisure activity)

passionate about, and with whom they wish to be associated. Swarbrooke and Horner (1999) demonstrated that status could be a motivator for visiting a specific tourist attraction (e.g. a theme park, but only if it has the reputation for having the best 'white-knuckle rides').

This phenomenon of status can be gained from becoming a member of an exclusive club (e.g. golf: anywhere the British Open Championship is staged; fitness: anywhere royalty or celebrities are members; gentlemen's clubs, generally found in London). In each example not only are the waiting lists long and membership and annual fees high, but also the ability to pay is not a criterion of eligibility to join, whereas knowing existing members is.

Although these exclusive clubs might have the best core and peripheral facilities, this is not always the case. It is not unknown for local authority leisure centres to be better equipped than, say, a fitness centre attached to a hotel. Within their locality a proportion of people will choose the more expensive hotel leisure club option because 'my sort of people go there' and 'you know you will not meet people who are on benefit'. These customers perceive that it is worth paying higher prices for the benefits received. Holbrook (1994) classified this value as 'self-oriented', which contrasts with an 'other-oriented value', where some people would rather be involved in an experience that benefits others (e.g. conservation holiday or scout leader).

Multiple benefits

Consumers do not always want one benefit at a time but seek a number of properties from the same experience. The possibility for conflict was highlighted by Swarbrooke and Horner (1999) as tourists generally look for more than one attribute from a holiday (e.g. an unspoilt destination but with things to do in the evening). Holbrook (1994) does not explain this in terms of conflict but as a matrix that will lead to the consumption of some experiences and a rejection of others. It is important to note that some buyer decisions are influenced by lack of opportunity (too costly, not accessible) rather than positive factors. For example, until recently there

was a lack of competition-level climbing walls in the UK, and elite climbers had to go to Belgium to practise.

Information search

The high percentage of intangible elements in the service package can mean that it is difficult for potential customers to gain objective information prior to purchase. Critiques of plays, films and restaurants offer their assessment, and television holiday programmes give extensive 'expert' advice. Both go some way to fill the information void but, just like the opinions of friends and family, they are only one person's perceptions of the experience.

Brand/image

A potential customer wants the service to be delivered with no problems – the 'right first time every time' approach of Crosby (1979). Accessing information from only organizations with reputable brands or image is one way of trying to reduce the risk of poor service. Word of mouth is one of the main ways of image building from a past to a potential customer but the Grönroos (1984) advocacy of traditional marketing activities to manage it actively is still supported by many people.

To reduce risk, some customers will remain loyal to multinational hotel chains and fast-food outlets, no matter where they are in the world. The brand conveys that the standards will be consistent and dependable, which simplifies customer decision making (Palmer, 1998).

Evaluation and decision

As can be seen from above, evaluation and decision are integrated into the information search. The process is a continuous loop with experiences and providers entering or being discarded as more information is received.

It is difficult to generalize as to what particular factors are going to make a person select a specific activity and provider, as the range of experiences on offer by the tourism and leisure industry is so diverse, but the following represent the main ones.

Price

Price is stated as a major element in the evaluation stage of the process but a number of writers, including Astbury (1998), have shown that this is not the most important factor. Reliability and responsiveness, not price, were frequently mentioned by Zeithaml *et al.* (1990) as the most important attributes of a service provider.

Convenience and accessibility

Services delivered at a time that suits the potential customer and that have the ability to reach the delivery location have been found to be a major factor in participation in leisure activities.

Retention, relationships and loyalty

The ideal scenario for an organization is for their customers to be completely satisfied, so that they wish to repeat the experience. Repeat business can be placed into a hierarchy of the level of involvement the customer has with the organization and the nature of the interaction.

RETENTION.   This interaction represents the customer repeating the purchase or experience as and when required, because they were previously satisfied. The customer will have very little involvement with the organization in the meantime and could be prone to switching to other providers if they felt it was advantageous.

RELATIONSHIPS.   The strategy of building a relationship with the customer, generally over time, requires an integrated holistic approach as advocated by the Scandinavian School of Service Quality Management (Grönroos, 1989). As previously discussed, building up a relationship with suppliers is also part of this holistic approach to service quality. Nevertheless, some marketers can be sceptical as to the effectiveness of relationship marketing,

seeing it as little more than database compilation (Palmer, 1998).

To achieve a relationship, it is necessary for organizations to know who their customers are and to have records of their addresses together with the number and type of transactions. As having a customer-oriented approach is central to this strategy, relationships need to be formed throughout the service exchange (Glynn and Lehtinen, 1995). Customers can also be invited to express their needs and expectations as well as opinions on the existing service delivery. This can be done via a range of techniques, including one-to-one interviews (see Chapter 13).

LOYALTY.   Both the retention and the development of relationships with customers results in repeat business; it can also lead to varying degrees of loyalty on behalf of the customers to the organization. Dwyer (1987, cited in Palmer, 1998) stated that there is a five-phase cycle to relationship building, from awareness to dissolution. Loyalty would be seen only in phase four (commitment), where an element of exclusivity can occur and the search for an alternative provider is minimal.

To build a loyal relationship, Lovelock (1992) advocated the strategy of trying to get the customers to perceive themselves as 'members' of the organization. Within the leisure industry this is easy to achieve, as most computerized booking systems have this facility, especially if someone books by credit card. Health clubs have membership systems and special offers; new services are easily circulated by mailshot to the members. Some clubs use every element of their members' details and will even send birthday cards.

The tourism industry tries to formulate 'membership' relationships by having loyalty cards. Most airlines and multinational hotel chains give free flights or stays after a number of points have been accumulated. Easyjet has advertised that these 'loyalty bonuses' create an artificial allegiance, especially when the consumers (i.e. business people) are not the customers. Easyjet suggests that having a captive consumer base enables the airlines to maintain artificially high prices.

Relationships can be instigated by encouraging people to pay for a whole course or series of sessions rather than on a 'pay as you go' basis. This is frequently encountered in the theatre or opera season. Whilst it is always sound practice for any organization to have money in advance, those purchasing tickets for the whole season ('subscribers') get not only an overall discount but also added the advantages of designated bars, lounges or car parking areas, etc.

Many leisure experiences are provided by clubs (e.g. golf clubs, choral societies, amateur dramatics) and most are run by the members for the membership. These types of organizations have an inbuilt loyalty system. The commercial sector has replicated this by opening up members-only health clubs, which are not only cost-effective for the organization but also tie the customer to one service provider. It is questionable whether or not this is considered a relationship in the truest sense, since what may be presumed to be loyalty on behalf of the customers could come about because there are no other suppliers available or it is too difficult or expensive to switch.

The underlying philosophy of building up relationships is to retain the customer base and to make it loyal to the organization, unlike the campsite owner in the case study given in Box 3.2. It is generally considered cheaper to retain existing customers than try to attract new ones but the culture of some UK organizations is seen by Astbury (1998) to reject this notion and persists in rewarding staff to attract new customers rather than to retain them. Barnes and Cumby (1995) pointed out that not all customers are of equal importance to an organization and there is a requirement to know which customers should be retained. They suggested that a cost/benefit analysis of all 'types' of customers ought to be conducted to ascertain this information (e.g. how many transactions over a given period; how many visits; how much the customer is spending with the organization).

The case study in Box 3.2 is an example of bad practice by an accommodation provider who did not understand that a relationship had developed and that loyalty had been forthcoming from his customers, which they had expected to be returned.

Box 3.2.   Case study: eclipse of the sun, Cornwall, 1999.

As over a million people were expected to travel to Cornwall for the eclipse of the sun on 11 August 1999, the local tourism industry decided to 'cash in' on the event by putting up accommodation charges. Two families had holidayed together in Cornwall for the previous 10 years, always staying for a month at the same campsite. In 1998 the charge per family was £15 per night, in 1999 during Eclipse Week, £30 per night was asked.

Outcome

One family continued as normal, paying the additional £105; the other decided not to go at all. Both felt that their 10 years of loyalty had been betrayed by the farmer; both suggested that, as long-term customers, they could have been charged as normal, believing that any levy should have been placed on new customers.

The short sightedness of the farmer lost a minimum of £450 in income that year and, additionally, the organization's image had suffered, all for the sake of £105. Whether the families returned is not known.

NOT-FOR-PROFIT SECTORS.   This section could give the impression that the decision to buy is purely a commercial transaction but a number of leisure facilities, especially in the public sector, have free admission (e.g. libraries, museums, parks and open spaces). The debate needs to be widened as participation in these activities brings in many benefits other than economic.

Torkildsen (1999) had three distinct groups of factors that influence leisure participation: (i) personal (age; gender; culture, etc.); (ii) social and circumstantial (occupation; income; car ownership, etc.); and (iii) opportunity (access and location; availability). Some of these will be a barrier to participation (e.g. the lack of a car if countryside recreational activities are required) and others a positive factor (e.g. more free time at retirement age). As previously shown, many of these factors are interrelated, producing a complex matrix of influences.

Many of the elements that are barriers to participation can be overcome if the organizations so wish; for example, concessionary admissions are widely available within the tourism and leisure industry. The debate on equity of leisure provision is relevant to the public sector of the industry, as community money is being used to subsidize the provision of a range of leisure facilities and the current government attempts to widen access and therefore participation (social inclusion).

Post-purchase evaluation

The final section of Palmer's buyer-decision model is post-purchase evaluation. Customers judge whether or not they were satisfied with a service both during the delivery process and after they have experienced the service. These subjective judgements influence the decision on whether to repeat the experience with the same provider. Unfortunately customers receiving the same service, even at the same time, can come to different conclusions, as they have differing needs and expectations. One factor that helps the tourism industry is that individuals of one nationality will expect similar but not the same service standards.

If the tourism or leisure provider is not aware of these factors, the post-purchase evaluation will be unfavourable and a high number of customers will not wish to repeat the experience with that particular organization. Swarbrooke and Horner (1999)

Box 3.3.   Las Vegas visitor study. (Adapted from Swarbrooke and Horner, 1999.)

- 10% of visitors found the people in Las Vegas rude and unfriendly.
- 8% thought it too expensive.
- 7% said it was too hard to get to.
- 4% felt it was too intense.
- 3% claimed it was dirty.
- Only 68% were satisfied and therefore may repeat the experience.

demonstrated these different conclusions in their study of Las Vegas visitors (Box 3.3).

Customer satisfaction and how to measure the phenomenon of post-purchase evaluation will be explored in more depth in Chapter 13.

Summary

Practitioners need to consider that customers of the leisure and tourism industry require that a provider not only fulfils or exceeds their expectations of a service but also meets the factors that motivate them to participate (or buy) their experience. The only solution for leisure and tourism organizations is to know what their customers' needs are but, because these are constantly changing in the long term and in depth, relationships need to be developed, the challenge to leisure and tourism managers is made even more demanding because of the difficulties in identifying and defining what quality means to individual consumers, as the next chapter demonstrates.

4

Concepts of Quality in Leisure and Tourism

This chapter examines the underpinning theories of quality and service quality management as applicable to the tourism and leisure industry and attempts to develop a conceptual framework within which the service quality literature can be analysed.

On completion of this chapter it is expected that you will be able to:

- appreciate that service quality theory has its foundation in manufacturing;
- critically evaluate the original quality theories when applied to the service context;
- be aware of the difficulty of defining quality and service quality and understand the thinking underpinning the many definitions;
- have an in-depth understanding of the service quality theorists of the two main schools of service quality management: the Scandinavian or Nordic school, and the North American school.

Quality Management Theories

The theories and concepts of quality and its management have percolated slowly into the service industry from manufacturing (Levitt, 1972). Rather than a paradigm shift taking place, the existing quality theories and tools were embraced in their entirety by parts of the service sector. The paradigm shift occurred when difficulties were experienced in the service sector by taking this route (e.g. the use of only qualitative data collection methods).

As the theories and concepts of the original quality gurus form part of the foundations of service quality management theory, it is important for leisure and tourism practitioners to have an understanding of them.

W.E. Deming and J.M. Juran have been the two major forces in the quality management movement for the global manufacturing industry since the Second World War, especially in Japan. One of their main quality techniques, *statistical process control* (SPC), was developed as early as 1931 by Shewhart. Dale (1994a) and Deming (1986) advocated SPC as the most appropriate method of detecting mistakes, known to quality practitioners as *'non-conformances'*.

Whilst the detection of non-conformances is very relevant to the tourism and leisure industry, the lack of statistical knowledge by its employees would make the wide-scale introduction of SPC very difficult. Even so, SPC is used in some fast-food outlets to aid their error detection.

W.A. Shewhart

Shewhart's (1931) development of the SPC technique is based on his concept of product quality: that products have qualities, rather than quality, and they can be partially measured. These qualities are classified into objective qualities, which can be measured by SPC, and subjective qualities, which cannot. Shewhart attempted to give objective values to the tangible elements (e.g. finished goods) and subjective values to the intangibles (e.g. attitude of the frontline staff). The realization that intangible elements are judged subjectively is very important to the leisure and tourism industry, which is trying to fulfil abstract and even elusive customer needs. For example, the 'dream holiday' can be one customer's dream but another one's nightmare, even when an identical experience has been offered.

In the 1950s Deming, Juran and Feigenbaum introduced quality management methods to the Japanese whilst being largely ignored in the USA, their own country (DTI, 1995).

W.E. Deming

Deming's (1986) overall theory was more complex than Shewhart's. As well as applying SPC to detect and prevent non-conformance, Deming suggested that the organization's culture needs to adapt as well. The 'Fourteen Points for Management' strategy (Box 4.1) gives an indication of how to achieve this.

Deming utilized Shewhart's concept of different qualities rather than quality and argued that these can be judged by a variety of scales. Price is considered a quality on which judgement will be made and Deming suggests that an appropriate strategy is 'to give satisfaction at a price that the user will pay' (Deming, 1986). Whilst the user is central to judging product qualities, Deming considers that 'it is not easy to comply with as consumers' needs are changing constantly'.

This is most noticeable in the tourism and leisure industry as fashions for free-time experiences come and go. Aerobics is but one instance where the experience has developed in a very short time to include aqua, step and slide aerobics. Each change has to be accommodated in the programming of a leisure centre if customer needs are to be met.

Deming suggested that this constant change is complex for organizations to manage, but he was looking from the manufacturer's perspective, where redesigning and

---

Box 4.1. Deming's 14 points for management. (Source: Deming, 1986.)

1. Create constancy of purpose towards improvement of product and service.
2. Adopt a new philosophy.
3. Cease dependence on inspection to achieve quality.
4. End the practice of awarding business on the basis of price tag. Instead, minimize total cost by working with a single supplier.
5. Improve constantly and forever every process for planning, production and service.
6. Institute training on the job.
7. Adopt and institute leadership.
8. Drive out fear.
9. Break down barriers between all staff areas.
10. Eliminate slogans, exhortations, and targets for the work force.
11. Eliminate numerical quotas on the factory floor and numerical goals for management.
12. Remove barriers that rob people of pride of workmanship. Eliminate the annual rating or merit system.
13. Institute a vigorous programme of education and self-improvement for everyone.
14. Put everyone in the company to work to accomplish the transformation.

---

retooling of a product can take 6–18 months. As long as the tourism and leisure industry is aware of the importance of monitoring customer needs on a regular basis, many elements of its services can be changed relatively quickly (e.g. the range of dishes on a menu).

In Deming's 'Fourteen Points for Management' strategy, only the internal processes are considered. This would leave major elements of tourism or leisure service delivery operations unaffected by cultural change, such as where the customer is present or performs some of the service delivery process.

Deming is an advocate of continuous improvement, a quality goal relevant to any industry. Oakland (1993) placed these concepts into Deming's 'Cycle of Continuous Improvement': PLAN DO CHECK ACT. Unfortunately, Deming did not suggest how a customer focus can be achieved. This is important, as it is one of the main strategies of managing the service delivery specification. Only customer feedback for the research and development department is mentioned by Deming (1986) and most leisure and tourism organizations do not have one. This approach also contradicts a continuous improvement organization culture, which requires feedback from both internal and external sources to all functional areas.

Although these theories were developed for application in the manufacturing sector, they have some relevance to the tourism and leisure industry as highlighted by the authors. However, Deming (1986) gave consideration to the differences between service and manufacturing industries (Box 4.2). According to Deming they mainly consist of the frequency and processing of transactions, which is equally applicable to manufacturing, rather than reflecting major differences.

It is stated that service industries have a captive market and are not competing head to head with foreign companies (Deming, 1986). This was true in the 1980s, when the globalization of services was generally a one-way flow from the USA to the rest of the world, as illustrated by Disney and McDonald's. However, this changed in the 1990s. American service companies have to compete, even in their home market, against foreign-owned companies (Segal-Horn, 1994).

Deming had taken a holistic approach to quality management but his focus became concerned with the internal organization: whilst acknowledging the needs of the end users, they are not central to his theory. This is a major limitation for the tourism and leisure practitioners. Attempts to develop the management plan model for the service sector have been left for others via anecdotal

---

Box 4.2.   Deming's service characteristics. (Adapted from Deming, 1986, p. 189.)

1.   Direct transactions with masses of people.
2.   Large volume of transactions.
3.   Large volume of paper involved in the main business.
4.   Large amount of processing.
5.   Many transactions with small amounts of money.
6.   An extremely large number of ways to make errors.
7.   Handling and re-handling of huge numbers of small items.

---

evidence and are very tentative (Deming, 1986). If adapted to contain additional customer-orientation elements, the model would have more relevance for the tourism and leisure industry.

J.M. Juran

Juran had a universal concept of quality, *'fitness for use'*, which can be applied to both goods and services (Juran and Godfrey, 1999). The fitness-for-use judgement is for the users to make and includes how beneficial the goods or services are to them.

Juran is therefore defining a user-based approach to quality management in which the customer is central; this is advocated by many service quality management theorists. It is also applicable to the tourism and leisure industry, as many experiences are marketed on the basis of the benefits they will give to the customer.

The concept of fitness for use is expanded upon by considering the parameters and characteristics that need to be met. These interrelated parameters are quality of design, quality of conformance, abilities, and field service. This has limitations for the tourism and leisure industry, even though a customer focus is being advocated, as the design process has to be driven by knowing their needs. The design specification is also needed so that judgements can be made as to whether 'conformance' or not has been achieved. The third parameter of abilities is not appropriate, as it is said to be applicable for long-lived products; the perishability of tourism and leisure services is well documented. The authors would also disagree with Juran on his inclusion of reliability as an example of an ability parameter; service quality research has shown that reliability is the most important dimension for customers (Zeithaml *et al.*, 1990).

The characteristic judgements to see if Juran's definition 'fitness for use' has been met are technological, psychological, time-oriented, contractual and ethical but it was suggested by Zimmerman and Enell (1988) that, to service industry customers, psychological, time-oriented and ethical characteristics are the most important of the five. Juran (1988a) considered that service industry users have a wide variety of needs, both psychological and physiological, including amusement, freedom from disagreeable chores, opportunity for learning and creativity. Juran's description seems to fit the tourism and leisure industry better than other sections of the service industry, such as banking and other financial services.

In order to meet the standards of the fitness-of-use concept, Zimmerman and Enell (1988) advocated that the performance of service industry professionals must surpass anything that their own clients could achieve if they tried to meet their own needs. This would be an ever-changing standard depending on the existing skill level of the client and would not be cost-effective or practical, especially for the leisure industry, as the upper extremes would have to be catered for.

Juran separates the 'fitness for use' theory into two further concepts. Firstly, end users can be internal as well as external to the organization (Juran and Godfrey, 1999). This principle has become standard to both manufacturing and service theorists. The impact of this concept is that it gives the basis to have a customer-oriented organization, which is continually seeking improvements to all processes. This approach is valid for the tourism industry, as 'bundles of services' make up a package holiday. The quality of the service given to internal customers will have a great impact on that delivered to the external ones. Juran's theory is hard for the tourism and leisure industry to put into practice as

it generally requires a cultural change, the hardest adjustment to undertake.

Secondly, quality is managed by three interrelated processes: quality planning, quality control and quality improvement. This is what is known as Juran's Trilogy (Juran, 1988b) (Table 4.1).

The Trilogy incorporates the concept of sporadic and chronic troubles. When sporadic troubles occur, they require immediate action to get back to quality levels normally in operation. Chronic troubles are constant defects that were built in at the planning stage of the system design; they are outside the control of the operational staff and are the responsibility of the managers (e.g. deliberately overbooking airline seats in the hope that some passengers will not show up).

This gives rise to Dale (1994a) stating that project management is now the focus of Juran's approach to quality management, based on a ten-point plan for quality improvement (Box 4.3). As with Deming, SPC monitoring methods are prominent.

Deming and Juran have a number of similar management approaches. They both identify training as being important and they advocate continuous improvement, but Juran is in favour of setting goals and monitoring scores, which is favoured by public sector leisure providers. Deming takes the opposite view: he advocates elimination of numerical quotas and goals along with targets and slogans. Whilst Juran has a more user-based approach than Deming, neither management plan acknowledges it. Although both have started to consider services, they do not do so

Table 4.1. Juran Trilogy diagram: the three universal processes of managing for quality. (Source: Juran, 1989, p. 22.)

Quality planning	Quality control	Quality improvement
Determine who the customers are Determine the needs of the customers Develop product features that respond to customer needs Develop processes able to produce the product features Transfer the plans to the operating forces	Evaluate actual product performance Compare actual performance to product goals Act on the difference	Establish the infrastructure Identify the improvement projects Establish project teams Provide teams with resources, training and motivation to: • diagnose the causes; • stimulate remedies; • establish controls to hold the gains

Box 4.3.   Juran's method. (Source: Dale, 1994a, p. 19.)

1. Build awareness of the need and opportunity for improvement.
2. Set goals for improvement.
3. Organize to reach the goals.
4. Provide training.
5. Carry out projects to solve problems.
6. Report progress.
7. Give recognition.
8. Communicate results.
9. Keep the score.
10. Maintain momentum by making annual improvement part of the regular system processes of the company.

in great detail. Juran (1989) classifies services by the output of any process: if the end product is a physical thing, it is classified as goods. If it is work performed for someone else, it is service. This seems naïve, as most processes are so specialized that they are all performed for someone else.

A.V. Feigenbaum

Feigenbaum's (1991) theory built upon the previous quality writers and requires the application of quality systems to manage the whole of the organization. Quality management is seen as a framework for all aspects of the business, including its culture, and is known as 'total quality management' (TQM). As tourism and leisure organizations were some of the last in the service sector to embrace quality management concepts, most are only just moving from implementing quality control and assurance tools and techniques (e.g. quality circles, quality manuals, error detection) to the more sophisticated holistic quality systems. If tourism and leisure organizations are to be successful in this transition, it is therefore important for them to be aware of the philosophies, such as Feigenbaum's, that underpin these holistic quality frameworks.

Feigenbaum agreed that customers determine quality by judging whether or not the goods or services purchased meet their requirements (Feigenbaum, 1991). This 'total customer satisfaction oriented' approach is the foundation of this theory but, unlike Deming's concepts, the differences between goods and services are not considered, as Feigenbaum (1991) defines quality as:

> The total composite product and service characteristics of marketing, engineering, manufacture and maintenance through which the product and service in use will meet the expectations of the customer.

Feigenbaum was one of the first writers on quality to distinguish between tangibles (the decor, uniforms of staff, etc.) and intangibles of service, stating that the service sector is 'heavily dependent upon human skills, attitudes and training' (Feigenbaum, 1991). This acknowledgement of the importance of the interaction between customers and staff is fundamental to managing quality in tourism and leisure services.

From Feigenbaum's TQM approach, it would be expected that issues of employees, quality costs, the use of SPC and development of organization-wide systems are addressed. These are found in 'Ten Benchmarks of Total Quality Control for the 1990s' outlined in Box 4.4. Unexpectedly, in point 10 the monitoring of customer needs is left with third parties such as dealerships or corporate buyers (Feigenbaum, 1991). As systems for direct measurement of the customers' needs, expectations and perceptions are omitted,

Box 4.4.   Feigenbaum's Ten Benchmarks of Total Quality Control for the 1990s. (Source: Feigenbaum, 1991.)

1. Quality is a company-wide process.
2. Quality is what the customer says it is.
3. Quality and costs are a sum not a difference.
4. Quality requires both individual and teamwork zealotry.
5. Quality is a way of managing.
6. Quality and innovation are mutually dependent.
7. Quality is an ethic.
8. Quality requires continuous improvement.
9. Quality is most cost-effective.
10. Quality is implemented with a total system connected with customers and suppliers.

Feigenbaum's theories would be difficult for tourism and leisure practitioners to put into operation. The lack of application is a continuing omission on the part of all the original quality gurus; this task was left for the service quality management theorists to resolve.

P.B. Crosby

The three writers quoted thus far were initiators of the quality management paradigm. In the 1970s Crosby devised his theory as a quality practitioner, implementing quality concepts of Deming and Juran.

Crosby (1979) stated that the entire concept of quality management is people-oriented. Peters (1987) suggested that Crosby's primary concern is with meeting technical requirements and refuted that his theories are people-oriented. This point of view is validated by Crosby's absolutes (see Chapter 5). They do not reflect customer needs but internalize by measuring non-conformance costs and trying to achieve conformance. Even his definition of quality is 'conformance to requirements' (Crosby, 1979), but how to solicit customer requirements directly is not addressed; only indirect methods are considered. This is again unhelpful to tourism and leisure practitioners.

Crosby has given quality management literature the most slogans, but Deming's view was that they should be eliminated. The slogans include: 'Quality is Free'; 'Zero Defects'; 'Right First Time Every Time' (Crosby, 1979). Unfortunately, tourism and leisure practitioners have been exposed to these maxims rather than the underlying concepts and so misunderstandings have occurred. The introduction of a quality culture can be initially very expensive for items such as training and fees for engaging quality management consultants and is far from free.

Crosby (1979) proposed two concepts: (i) non-conformance costs money and therefore it must be measured; and (ii) standards must be set throughout the company and performance indicators need to be included for corrective actions. It is interesting that the production of performance indicators as

a measure for monitoring public sector service standards is embedded in a number of government-devised quality management regimes (e.g. Service First, Best Value; see Chapters 12 and 13).

Although Crosby is not an advocate of SPC (unlike Deming, Juran and Feigenbaum), he does agree that most factors contributing to non-conformance are the responsibility of senior managers and outside the control of other employees.

Crosby devised a 14-step quality improvement programme for organizations to attain and work towards 'Zero Defects Day' – the first time when 100% conformance is accomplished (Box 4.5).

The programme has similarities with the previous writers' quality management plans, especially in the areas of continuous improvement and staff training. The main difference is the focus on achieving Zero Defects Day and measuring the cost of non-conformance. Even though this would mean that the service is delivered correctly each time, it does not help the tourism and leisure industry to create a customer focus because the service specification could be wrong, as the customer needs are not known.

Service is not given special consideration, as Crosby (1979) does not differentiate between manufacturing and service sectors. Crosby's associate, Kennedy (1991), applied

---

Box 4.5.   The 14-step quality improvement programme. (Adapted from Crosby, 1979, pp. 132–139.)

1. Management commitment
2. Quality improvement team
3. Quality measurement
4. Cost of quality evaluation
5. Quality awareness
6. Corrective action
7. Establish an ad hoc committee for the zero defects programme
8. Supervisor training
9. Zero defects day
10. Goal setting
11. Error cause removal
12. Recognition
13. Quality councils
14. Do it over again

these theories in the not-for-profit sectors, which are of major importance to the leisure industry. Although taking into account the reliance on volunteers in some organizations, Kennedy did not move away from Crosby's original theories. One exception is that he placed a larger emphasis on consultation with all interested groups (e.g. government, tax-payers), not only the users. Although quality management is still being introduced to many organizations within the voluntary sector of the leisure industry, Kennedy's consultation strategies have recently been incorporated into the public sector under the Best Value management regime (see Chapter 13).

T. Peters

Peters (1987) adopted a slightly different per-spective. Even though he had criticized Crosby on his lack of customer orientation, some of the observations that Peters and Waterman (1982) noticed when researching excellent US companies are directly related to Crosby's work – for example, trying to achieve limited defects and reduce the cost of rework.

Peters (1987) defined quality as 'the cus-tomer's perception of excellence'. From this abstract view of quality, Peters listed the excellent quality attributes as being: virtuous, practical, aesthetic, perceptual, subjective and above expectations. The not-for-profit sectors of the tourism and leisure industry would see giving a level of service above expectations as being costly and wasteful of community resources.

Peters is the only one of these early quality writers who defines quality in terms of excellence. Of the service quality writers, Becker (1996) considered this to be a trad-itional, philosophical view of quality but Zeithaml et al. (1990) agreed with this notion. In fact some of the most sophisticated service quality management systems, especially those that are based on the Business Excellence Model, follow the Peters definition and there-fore measure and monitor 'excellence' in all aspects of an organization.

Peters (1987) also takes a customer orien-tation of quality, associated with recognizing the importance of customer expectations and perceptions. This is central to managing a customer-focused tourism and leisure organization and many service quality theories (discussed later in this chapter) have devised methods to measure these factors. Peters (1987) is slightly sceptical as to the significance of customer perceptions of a service or a product, saying that they can have perverse perceptions; unfortunately he does not suggest how to manage this.

Summary

In relating the philosophies of the quality management gurus to the leisure and tourism industry, there is a need to be pragmatic. Deming and Juran, whilst they have laid the foundations for quality management theory, have also offered perceptions of service quality that are simplistic or limited. Additionally, Crosby is totally dismissive of any complex differences between goods and services. It must be remembered that the backgrounds of these writers as practitioners in the manufacturing industry gave them very little or no exposure to services in the working environment.

Apart from slight advances into service quality characteristics by Shewhart and Feigenbaum, very little had been achieved to contribute to a new paradigm until Peters offered the concept of customer expectations and perceptions as being fundamental to the assessment of quality.

Table 4.2 provides a comparative analysis of the main theories of the six quality theorists discussed so far in this chapter.

Service Quality Theory

Leisure and tourism practitioners require quality management tools and techniques to enable them to assess the outcomes of their management decisions, what is required by their customers and whether their customers are satisfied with the services or not. Before venturing into the management elements of service quality management, it

Table 4.2. Comparison of quality management principles and practices. (After Gillies, 1992; Oakland, 1993.)

	Shewhart	Deming	Juran	Feigenbaum	Crosby	Peters
Definition	Conformance to requirements	Predictable degree of uniformity and dependability at low cost	Fitness for purpose	Total quality control throughout the organization	Conformance to requirements	Customer perception of excellence
Senior management responsibility	–	Responsible for 94% of problems	Responsible for > 80% of problems	Leadership but with a quality manager	Responsible for quality	Should be passionate about quality
Performance standard	Various qualities can be measured	Many scales: use SPC, *not* zero defects	Avoid campaigns to exhort perfection	Continuous upward-moving targets	Zero defects; setting performance indicators	Measure everything
Judges of quality	Customers	Users	Benefits to users	Customers determine whether goods and services meet their requirements	Meeting of set standards	Customers
General approach	Detection of conformance or non-conformance	Reduce variability; continuous improvement	Emphasis on management of human aspects	Application of quality systems throughout the organization	Prevention	Total customer responsiveness giving rise to a quality 'revolution'
Structure	–	14 points	10 steps	10 benchmarks	14 steps (5 absolutes)	7 patterns
SPC	SPC must be used	SPC must be used	Recommends SPC, but cautions against tool-based approach	SPC to be used; ratio measures for productivity, effective views of timeliness of action	Rejects statistically acceptable level of quality	Sees the need for qualitative measurements as well

Continued

Table 4.2. *Continued.*

	Shewhart	Deming	Juran	Feigenbaum	Crosby	Peters
Basis for improvement	Meeting customers' changing needs	Continuous: eliminate goals	Project-based approach: set goals	Continuous improvement to have a total customer satisfaction orientation	A process, not a programme	Create a shadow quality organization in parallel, e.g. quality circles
Teamwork	–	Employee participation in decisions	Team/quality circle approach	Individual and teamwork zealotry, quality circles	Quality improvement teams: quality councils	Cross-functional teams
Costs of quality	–	No optimum, continuous improvement	Optimum, quality is *not* free	Quality is cost-effective throughout the process	Quality is free!	Poor quality costs and should be measured
Purchasing	–	Use SPC through strong cooperation	Complex problems, use formal surveys	Suppliers important in a total system	Supplier is extension of business	Suppliers important to quality process
Vendor rating	–	No	Yes, but work with suppliers	Yes	Yes	–
Single sourcing of supply	–	Yes	No	–	–	Few suppliers as possible
Service sector considered different	No	Yes	Yes	Yes	No	Yes
Service concepts	Concept of tangibles and intangibles	Seven points itemizing service characteristics	Defines service and service characteristics	Distinguishes between tangibles and intangibles of service. Importance of customer/staff interactions	–	Customer expectations and perceptions fundamental to assessment of quality

SPC, statistical process control.

is imperative that an understanding of the underpinning theories of the subject is developed.

Service quality defined

Defining the concept of service quality is as difficult for the service quality theorists as the multifaceted thoughts of the original quality gurus. Although Garvin (1988) lists five definitions of quality (Box 4.6) the majority of service quality writers concentrate on user-based and value-based approaches. This is a valid approach for the tourism and leisure industry.

User-based approach

This is known in some of the literature as a 'customer-oriented' quality whereby customers are central not only to the organization but also to all aspects of the operational procedures. Customer needs are paramount to the continuous improvement of a service, a factor that, if ignored by the tourism and leisure industry, could see customers moving to an organization's competitors.

This approach is not new; it was advocated by the early quality gurus but was later modified by Brown and Swartz (1989), Zeithaml et al. (1990), Bitner and Hubbet (1994) and Becker (1996). The later interpretation of this definition is based on the theory that service quality level is correct when customers are satisfied (Parasuraman, Zeithaml and Berry, 1985; Parasuraman, 1995). Customer satisfaction occurs when perception of the service received equals or exceeds expectations.

Perceived service quality exists along a continuum ranging from the customer's ideal

---

Box 4.6.   Garvin's five definitions of quality. (Source: Garvin, 1988.)

- Transcendent
- Product-based
- User-based
- Manufacturing-based
- Value-based.

---

quality to totally unacceptable, with a point along the continuum representing satisfactory quality. This is expanded into the theory of *'zones of tolerance'*, to be discussed in Chapter 5. The factors influencing the formation of this judgement, according to Zeithaml et al. (1990), are service providers' external communications, word of mouth from other clients as well as customers' personal needs and past experiences.

Edvardsson (1994) agreed that a customer-oriented definition of service quality does not mean that organizations must always comply with customer needs and wishes. The tourism industry's customers required low-priced packaged holidays, which led to a number of companies going out of business. This is why Zeithaml et al.'s continuum of service quality is valid.

These writers acknowledge the importance of the customers when defining service quality but, as can be seen in later in this chapter, there is no consensus as to whether service quality and customer satisfaction judgements are the same.

Service quality defined as excellence

According to Garvin (1988), this is a hybrid concept from the value-based definition of quality. One of the earliest theorists to consider quality in terms of excellence was Peters (1987).

Wyckoff (1992) also defined service quality by suggesting that it is the degree of excellence intended that meets customer requirements. This is recognized by the practitioner panels of the quality awards schemes, such as European Quality Award (Armistead, 1994), as being a valid approach.

Service quality management academics have not addressed the specific issue of quality in tourism and leisure services; therefore specific definitions of quality have not been attributed to this particular industry. Customer care and quality training materials, developed for tourism and leisure practitioners, tend to favour the user-based approach, stressing the need to gain customer feedback and to cater for customers' needs (Cantle-Jones, 1992; ILAM, 1992; English Tourist Board, undated).

Service quality schools

Defining service quality is a research activity comparable to that of the earlier quality researchers.

The application of quality management research specifically to the service sector commenced in the 1980s (Brogowicz *et al.*, 1990). The research developed into two separate schools: the Scandinavian school, with Grönroos and Gummesson as the main writers; and the North American school (Buttle, 1993), with research led by Zeithaml, Parasuraman and Berry.

Both sets of researchers come from marketing backgrounds and one of the main differences is in the definition of marketing. The American Marketing Association defined marketing as the four Ps (people, place, position and promotion) and by default stated what marketing is not (Grönroos, 1989). The Scandinavians took a holistic view of marketing of services, requiring an integrated approach based on building customer relationships (Grönroos, 1989).

Scandinavian school of service quality

Customer orientation is central to the thinking of this movement, which requires relationships to form throughout the service exchange (Glynn and Lehtinen, 1995). The Scandinavian school's models have a second orientation, the process, which is considered of equal importance (Gummesson, 1995). The models are based on the formula that customer satisfaction equals customer perception minus their expectation, and this is common to both schools. The Scandinavian school agrees with Shewhart (1931) that customer perceptions can be subjective as well as objective and that the subjectivity is a socio-economic-factor dependent (Gummesson, 1988).

The Scandinavian school is based on cooperation between academics and practitioners and the application of theories is a major focus for the researchers (Grönroos and Gummesson, 1985).

C. GRÖNROOS.   Grönroos is one of the founder members of this school of service quality and defined service as:

. . .an activity or series of activities of more or less intangible nature that normally, but not necessarily, take place in interactions between the customer and service employees and/or physical resources or goods and/or systems of the service provider, which are provided as solutions to customer problems.
(Grönroos, 1990a)

It is seen as important for tourism and leisure organizations to build relationships with customers, whose perceptions of a service are subjective and personal to themselves (Irons, 1994).

Grönroos (1990a) also supported the view that services are not homogeneous and made a distinction between whether or not individuals or organizations are receiving the service. This is important to the tourism and leisure industry, because many of their services are purchased by organizations for others to use (e.g. a school teacher taking a class to a museum).

Grönroos (1990a) stated that services are complicated phenomena and suggested along with Berry and Schneider (1994) that the service should be 'tangiblized', to remove as much risk as possible from the potential customer's mind when selecting a service provider. The tourism and leisure industry engages in these strategies by the selection of uniforms, decor of the facilities, etc. to create the image of reliability. Grönroos highlighted the importance of an organization managing its wider image (its general reputation), as this can also persuade the customer to select a particular service provider (Edvardsson, 1994).

He also suggested that the service package (Box 4.7) should have four elements (Payne and Clark, 1995). The notion of a core

---

Box 4.7.   Grönroos's service package.

1.   Develop the service concept to enable the core and support services to be designed.
2.   Develop an augmented service of interactions between provider and customers.
3.   Manage the image to support and enhance the augmented service.
4.   Decide on the degree of customers' participation and service accessibility.

and support service concept is an adaptation of Normann's (1991) core and peripheral services, which differs from augmented services. The example in Table 4.3 illustrates these concepts.

Due to the close relationship of the Nordic school of service quality with the industry, Grönroos (1990b) looked at service management principles in detail (Table 4.4).

Grönroos's six principles display a strong leaning towards the commercial sector of the service industry, but as tourism and leisure have a high percentage of facilities and attractions run by the public and voluntary sectors they would need some adaptation. To

encompass these sectors, minor changes such as less emphasis on profit would be required.

Grönroos (1990c) agreed with the empowerment of front-line staff, suggesting that the interaction between them and the customers can be used as 'moments of opportunities' to form relationships, to market the organization's services and to collect valuable data. Apart from forming relationships with customers, other methods for monitoring the service are not stated (see Table 4.4).

Grönroos (1994) reflected on the service delivery processes and suggested that the mass production and standardization of Taylorism are inappropriate, but many fast-food companies have successfully adopted these strategies.

Grönroos (1994) stated that services require 'Teamwork, interfunctional collaboration and interorganizational partnerships', for successful service delivery that satisfies the customers. He maintained that this is different from a TQM culture, as the marketing function is left out by that approach.

Grönroos's model (Fig. 4.1) is based on the impact of the technical quality (the 'what'), measured by customers in an objective

Table 4.3. Examples of core and support service concept: theatre services.

Service	Examples
Core service	Play, theatre building and seats
Support or peripheral services	Booking office, programmes, bar, car park
Augmented services	Pre-theatre dinner; or pre-production talk

Table 4.4. Six principles of service management. (Source: Grönroos, 1990b.)

Principle	Theme	Remarks
1. The profit equation and business logic	Customer-perceived service quality drives profit	Decisions on external efficiency and internal efficiency (cost control and productivity of capital and labour) have to be carefully integrated
2. Decision-making authority	Decision making has to be decentralized as close as possible to the organization–customer interface	Some strategically important decisions have to be made centrally
3. Organizational focus	Organization has to be structured and functioning so that its main goal is the mobilization of resources to support the front-line operations	May often require a flat organization without unnecessary layers
4. Supervisory control	Managers and supervisors have to focus on the encouragement and support of employees	As few legislative control procedures as possible, though some may be required
5. Reward systems	Production of customer-perceived quality has to be the focus of reward systems	All relevant facets of service quality should be considered, though all cannot always be built into a reward system
6. Measurement focus	Customer satisfaction with service quality has to be the focus of measurement of achievements	To monitor productivity and internal efficiency, internal measurement criteria may have to be used as well; the focus on customer satisfaction is, however, dominating

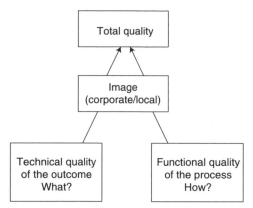

Fig. 4.1.   Grönroos model: two service quality dimensions. (Adapted from Grönroos, 1990a, p. 38.)

manner, and functional quality (the 'how'), measured by customers subjectively. Customers' interaction with staff and other customers has a crucial impact on their judgement (Grönroos, 1984). From Grönroos's empirical research, functional quality was found to be very important when customers judged the perceived service – unlike the third part of the model, image, which is secondary and affected by tradition, word of mouth and traditional marketing activities (Grönroos, 1984).

This model is very relevant to the tourism and leisure industry, as many of the services are performed in front of the customers (e.g. sports injuries clinic). The image will have helped them to formulate their expectations of the service but the technical and functional qualities will contribute to their perceptions.

Levitt (1972) and Wright (1995) proposed improving the total quality of service delivery

by the introduction of technology. Grönroos (1984) found that if this is done in isolation from the functional quality, customer perception of quality will not improve. Since the technical quality can be replicated by other companies, there is no competitive edge from this strategy.

Grönroos's original model of 1982 evolved into the 'total perceived quality' model (Fig. 4.2), which was developed further by other members of the Nordic school: Sandelin (1985) and Lehtinen (1985). The new model takes a holistic approach in which the expected quality is affected by external factors such as customer needs and word of mouth from others. The extended model is still appropriate to the tourism and leisure services.

This concept has similarities to the US school of service quality management (Zeithaml *et al.*, 1990) and Grönroos agreed with them that customers break down services into the following dimensions: *tangibles, reliability, responsiveness, empathy and assurance* (to be discussed later in this chapter); but he added a sixth dimension: *'recovery'* (Lewis, 1995), which is the ability of an organization to rectify mistakes in an appropriate way (as judged by the customer) and which can improve customer perceptions of the service provider. Tour operators have sometimes not appreciated the significance of appropriate service recovery strategies and have found themselves on television consumer programmes having to justify not only poor service but also insufficient compensation. Negative comments impinge on an organization's image, whilst a customer who has had a bad

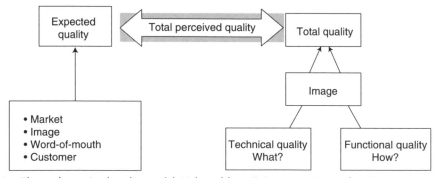

Fig. 4.2.   The total perceived quality model. (Adapted from Grönroos, 1988, cited in Grönroos, 1990a.)

experience but has been recompensed at an appropriate level will generally express positive comments to others. Potential customers feel that if there was a problem this is a company that would try to do something about it and are therefore not deterred from using that company.

In none of his work did Grönroos allude to the measurement of service quality, except to reiterate that a customer-oriented approach is needed (Grönroos, 1990b). Box 4.8 lists Grönroos's criteria for good service, which gives some indication of appropriate measurements and places them in relation to the total perceived quality model (see Fig. 4.2). The lack of a measurement tool was a criticism of the original quality writers by the authors and this can also be said of Grönroos.

E. GUMMESSON.   Grönroos's theory was not developed further on its own but became integrated with Gummesson's (Gummesson and Grönroos, 1987). Gummesson's 4Q model (Fig. 4.3), unlike Grönroos's, was transferred to the service sector from manufacturing (Payne and Clark, 1995). Gummesson (1988, 1989) devised his quality model to apply to goods as well as services, defining quality by uniting Crosby's 'conformance to requirements' with Juran's 'fitness for use'.

Gummesson (1988, 1993) gave three quality maxims, the first being 'quality pays', again echoing Crosby (1979) that poor quality costs money in reworking the task and therefore following Crosby's 'zero defects' theory. Gummesson was more realistic than Crosby, as the second maxim made allowances for occasional mistakes happening, especially those outside the organization's control. The third maxim was to have quality prevention systems in place 'to give early warning signs' of mistakes or delays.

According to Grönroos (1990a), Gummesson's 4Q model looks at quality from the view that everyone contributes to quality and there are a number of different sources of quality. The model combines customer orientation with process orientation, applicable to manufacturing as well as service delivery (Edvardsson, 1994). There are four sources of quality: (i) design quality: the goods or services are designed to meet the needs of the customer; (ii) production quality: referring purely to manufacturing aspects of the service production system such as those found in the fast- food industry (Gummesson, 1993); (iii) delivery quality: consistently meeting the standards promised to customers; and

---

Box 4.8.   Grönroos's criteria of good perceived service quality. (Adapted from Edvardsson, 1994, p. 86, cited in Grönroos, 1990b.)

Outcome-related criteria
1.   Professional and skills

Process-related criteria
2.   Attitudes and behaviour of contact staff
3.   Accessibility and flexibility of the service provider
4.   Reliability and trustworthiness for the best interest of the customer
5.   Recovery immediately when something goes wrong

Image-related criteria
6.   Reputation and credibility, value for money and good performance

---

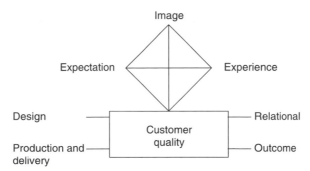

Fig. 4.3.   Gummesson's 4Q model. (Adapted from Edvardsson, 1994, p. 34.)

(iv) rational quality: this includes the inter-action between front-line staff and the cus-tomers, but Gummesson expands the concept to all interactions within the organization. As with Grönroos's theories, Gummesson expounded the virtues of TQM philosophy but without addressing the pragmatic issues that tourism and leisure practitioners would face when trying to manage facilities in line with these concepts.

Gummesson (1989) stated that the generic features of service quality manage-ment are production, delivery and marketing. He considered services to be the 'leftover' of production, whose productivity cannot be increased or automated with the introduction of technology and cannot be substituted for goods. He suggested (Gummesson, 1993):

> ...we can buy a CD player and a disc that will give us access to any world class orchestra and singer at our convenience in our homes. But they are goods, not services. As Norris wrote in 1941: 'Goods are wanted because they can perform services'.

The support for Levitt's (1972) theory of industrialization of service seems to be incompatible if it can be said of the character-istics of the service that 'intangible, non-standardized and service consumption are closely intertwined with production' (Gum-messon, 1994). However, when Gummesson's (1993) theory of pure service being leftovers is put in context, this is valid and can be seen in the travel context. Many people now book airline tickets or buy books over the Internet and the use of this home-based technology means that they can bypass high-street service providers.

As an advocate of the customer-oriented approach, knowing what the customer wants and needs was paramount to Gummesson (1993); unlike other writers in the manufactur-ing sector, he questioned whether it is possible to measure service productivity numerically. The argument was that all quantitative methods have severe deficiencies and he went on to compare (Table 4.5) quantitative with non-quantitative assessment of service performance (Edvardsson, 1994).

The use of Gummesson's easier output performance indicators is readily found in

Table 4.5. Methods of measuring service quality. (Source: Gummesson, 1993.)

Service productivity (easy to measure)	Service quality (difficult to measure or not measured)
Number of patients a doctor can treat per hour	How many got better? How about burnout among doctors?
Number of students a teacher can handle in a classroom	How much did they learn? How about burnout among teachers?
Garbage collection: how many households can be handled per hour	How well was it done? Complaints? Injuries and other health hazards among the workers?
Short-term sales performance by an employee in a shop	The employee's ability to produce a sustained relationship with a customer

public sector leisure services monitoring, where measurement of effectiveness of services has been considered, but the methodology of how to do this is still evolving.

Gummesson (1985, 1989) questioned the relevance of market research using sampling techniques and suggested that personal con-tacts are far more important. This is similar to Grönroos's reliance on building relation-ships between staff and customers (moments of opportunities).

Gummesson (1989) gave service practi-tioners a series of nine lessons (Box 4.9) in applying his theory. Both Gummesson's 'Nine Lessons' and Grönroos's 'Principles of Service Management' have areas of similarity (e.g. empowering the front line). Grönroos concentrated on the employees and struc-turing the internal organization to support them. Although Gummesson did not neglect this, a much wider approach was taken, encompassing redesigning the process and changing the culture of the organization. Deming (1986) had previously advocated this type of strategy.

Gummesson also acknowledged the influence of manufacturing quality tools and techniques within the service sectors and the

Box 4.9.   Gummesson's nine lessons on service quality. (Source: Gummesson, 1989, pp. 83–87.)

1.   Pick out the relevant approaches and techniques from quality management in manufacturing but beware of the others.
2.   Service quality has to be approached at two different stages:
● Process quality
● Outcome quality
3.   Service design is required.
4.   Pursue a zero defect strategy and combine it with the junkyard strategy: when errors occur be prepared to solve them quickly and smoothly.
5.   Empower the front-line employees.
6.   When service organizations hide behind outdated values of authority and monopoly, quality never develops.
7.   Convert administrative routines into internal services known as process management.
8.   Quality of computer software is crucial for quality of services.
9.   Combine the management aspects of product quality, service quality and computer software with customer perceived quality into holistic quality.

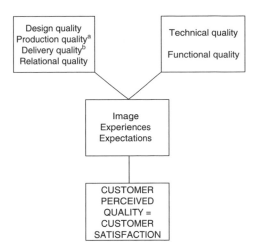

^{a}Invisible/visible
 Non-interactive/interactive
^{b}Own/subcontracted

Fig. 4.4.   The Grönroos–Gummesson integrated quality model. (Source: Gummesson and Grönroos, 1987, p. 15.)

problems this can cause. He also highlighted the reliance of all service organizations on information technology and its importance to the service delivery process (e.g. hotel and theatre booking systems). He did not give tourism and leisure practitioners clear answers on how to measure service delivery outcomes but went some way in explaining the limitations of a range of methods in existing practice.

As previously stated, both models were eventually integrated rather than developed individually.

INTEGRATION OF GRÖNROOS AND GUMMESSON MODELS.   A number of writers – Burca (1995), Edvardsson (1994) and Grönroos (1990a) – suggested that this integration of the two theories had taken place because they both have managerial implications.

As Gummesson's 4Q model had been devised for goods as well as services, two elements needed refining: production and delivery quality, to accommodate the service

characteristic of inseparability. It has been acknowledged by them (Gummesson and Grönroos, 1987) that in bringing together two different approaches (Fig. 4.4) Gummesson's design quality would have to set the foundations and produce benefits for Grönroos's technical quality.

A feature of the joint model in Fig. 4.4 is the interaction/non-interaction theory with visible and invisible parts of the service delivery process. The approach is that even the non-interactive parts of the process influence the total outcomes (and, therefore, customers' perceptions) and should be considered in the process design, as also seen in Chapter 8. The managerial implications of this to the tourism and leisure industry are that a customer-oriented interaction approach should be adopted by all areas of the organization (Burca, 1995). This concept is illustrated in Fig. 4.5.

Since this model evolved, both Grönroos and Gummesson have furthered their research into the importance of service encounters and this has led to the marketing paradigm shift into relationship marketing (Gummesson, 1995). This topic is outside the scope of this book.

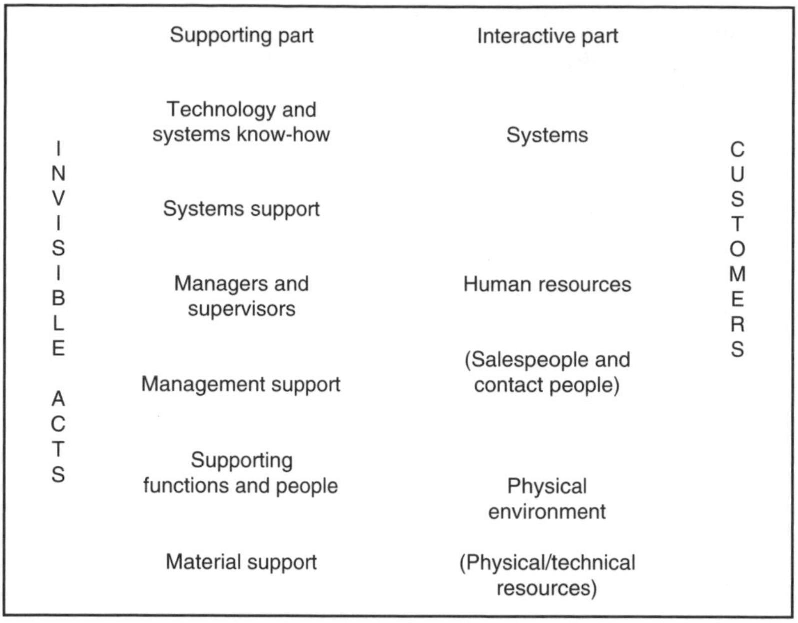

	Supporting part	Interactive part	
I N V I S I B L E A C T S	Technology and systems know-how	Systems	C U S T O M E R S
	Systems support		
	Managers and supervisors	Human resources	
	Management support	(Salespeople and contact people)	
	Supporting functions and people	Physical environment	
	Material support	(Physical/technical resources)	

Fig. 4.5.   A customer-oriented interaction approach. (Source: Grönroos and Gummesson, 1986, p. 23, cited in Burca, 1995, p. 411.)

In summary, the Scandinavian school of service quality considers personalized service to be an essential component of service delivery, and a relationship with a customer is required. The extent of this relationship is reflected in the quality of service offered. These notions would be rejected by some sections of the tourism and leisure industry, such as budget hotels that have no staff on duty, and fast-food outlets. The exchange of thoughts between academics and practitioners is one of the foundations on which this school was established and the writings of Grönroos (1988, 1990a) and Gummesson (1988, 1989) corroborate this.

US school of service quality

Commonality between the service quality schools of Scandinavia and the USA is generally in the area of basic concepts rather than practical application (e.g. a customer-oriented approach is common to both).

The US school's foundations came from the original American quality writers, which resulted in a narrow focus when transferring theories to the area of service. Juran's theory of fitness of use (Juran and Godfrey, 1999)

was interpreted by the service sector as still adequate service quality by offering similar or identical services. The global success of American fast-food and hotel chains was confirmation that this strategy is effective (Segal-Horn, 1994).

As early as 1972, Levitt wrote about service and service characteristics. Any notion of service being 'one individual administering to another under highly variable conditions' is dismissed. Levitt's main theory is the introduction of technology and industrial practices to eliminate discretion, 'the enemy of order, standardization and quality' (Levitt, 1972). Due to the number of people involved in services, Levitt admitted that mistakes can happen; the solution is the introduction of manufacturing techniques. Customers were not prominent in his approach to service quality management and therefore these theories have limited relevance to tourism and leisure practitioners (Levitt, 1976).

In the 1980s, a standardized service delivery took on a more customer-focused approach, especially in the US public sector (Osbourne and Gaebler, 1992). This was aided by the development of blueprinting and the introduction of information technology.

Blueprinting was introduced by G.L. Shostack (Grönroos, 1990a) to simplify the management of the service system (Kingman-Brundage, 1992). It is a method of producing flow charts to enable the service to be designed as a systematic process in a chronological order. It allows for the production and delivery processes to be placed within the context of the amount of participation required from staff and customers (Shostack, 1987). Due to the inseparability of service production from consumption, plus the concept of customers seeing and even participating in the delivery (e.g. a self-service café), this became known as the *Service Factory* (Chase and Garvin, 1989). Blueprinting is found in the commercial sectors of the tourism industry (e.g. hotels and food outlets) (see Chapter 8 for more details).

Both blueprinting and service mapping techniques allow for fail points to be itemized and service recovery steps to be designed into the service system (Edvardsson, 1994). The American school of service quality management theorists do not entirely agree with Crosby's zero defects concept, as fail points and service recovery initiatives can be found throughout the literature (Hart *et al.*, 1990; Berry, 1995; Zeithaml and Bitner, 1996).

Utilization of standardization techniques via technology and adaptation of manufacturing processes are available to all service organizations and have become recognized practice in the US tourism sector. Grönroos (1984) observed, therefore, that competitive edge is only possible where distinctions occur in staff/customer interactions. An alternative strategy to standardization adopted by some service organizations is to deliver the service to a level higher than the customer was promised or expected (Chase and Hayes, 1991; Scheuing, 1996).

American tourism practitioners are moving away from totally scripted encounters and standardized global services; together with the US school of service quality, theorists have become much more customer oriented. This has led to the development of instruments to measure customer satisfaction with the service offered (Parasuraman, 1995). These initiatives are still being influenced by

Deming, as the data outputs from these instruments are quantitative (Oliver, 1980; Knutson *et al.*, 1990; Cronin and Taylor, 1994).

The gap analysis model (Parasuraman *et al.*, 1985), known as SERVQUAL (Parasuraman *et al.*, 1988) (see Chapter 13) is dominant. It is not specific to service quality management: the theory of satisfaction gap had been used previously when considering factors that lead to social unrest (Davis, 1962).

SERVICE QUALITY THEORIES OF ZEITHAML, PARASURAMAN AND BERRY.   Service quality is simply defined by Zeithaml, Parasuraman and Berry as excellence, and this is determined by the extent of discrepancy between customer expectations and their perceptions (Zeithaml *et al.*, 1990). This coincides with the definitions given by Peters (1987) and Wyckoff (1992). Deming's (1986) and Crosby's (1979) conformance to specification is the basis of their definition, but it is adapted to include customer perspectives (Berry *et al.*, 1988). The pursuit of excellence is justified as a profit strategy (Berry and Parasuraman, 1994; Berry and Schneider, 1994) but it has to be achieved 'day after day and customer after customer' (Berry, 1995).

From later research, it was found that customers had a range of quality levels that were agreeable to them, known as the '*zone of tolerance*' (Parasuraman *et al.*, 1991b; Berry and Parasuraman, 1994). Their desired level of quality is formulated from what customers think it should be, and they also have a lower level of quality: the adequate or acceptable level. Although being lower, it is still within the range of tolerance. The latest version of the SERVQUAL model is said to be able to measure customer zones of tolerance (Parasuraman, 1995).

The ability to know the lower but satisfactory level of service delivery quality would enable tourism and leisure providers, especially the public and voluntary sectors, to reduce costs by saving on resources.

Zeithaml, Parasuraman and Berry have been consistent with other writers in agreeing the basic characteristics of service but believe that the inseparability characteristic is not constant, especially in organizations with low customer/staff interaction. When confronted by a problem, these organizations have to move to high levels of interaction as a personalized service will be required (Berry *et al.*, 1988).

Zeithaml, Parasuraman and Berry expanded the abstract characteristics of service by carrying out research into factors important to customers. The first phase of their research identified the ten determinants of service important to customers (Berry *et al.*, 1985). These were later refined to five.

Reliability, an outcome of service, was subsequently found to be the most important dimension to customers (Berry and Parasuraman, 1994). The four others are process dimensions of *tangibles, responsiveness, assurance and empathy* (Berry *et al.*, 1988; Berry and Schneider, 1994). Grönroos, as previously mentioned, added 'recovery' as a sixth dimension but this is extraneous, as it is a factor of the responsiveness dimension. These dimensions are seen as generic to all services and therefore applicable to those offered by operators of tourism and leisure facilities.

Zeithaml, Parasuraman and Berry subscribed to the 'service quality expectations equal perceptions' formula for customer satisfaction, with only customers able to judge service quality, and it is the basis of their SERVQUAL model (Berry *et al.*, 1990). These judgements should include the process as well as the outcomes of the service quality, though this is seen as difficult for the customers to do. They suggested that the use of their five dimensions of service should help (Zeithaml *et al.*, 1990; Berry, 1995). This view is not supported by others (Cronin and Taylor, 1994; Buttle, 1996) as research has shown that customers' judgements of a process can overlap from one dimension to another. For example, the poor state of the toilets was placed under two dimensions (tangibles and reliability) by some customers of an amusement park (Williams, 1997b).

One disagreement between the two schools of service quality is based on the validity of quantitative research methods to ascertain whether or not customers are satisfied with a service. Although the SERVQUAL model produces quantitative data, the use of qualitative data as well to obtain customer feedback is advocated (Berry, 1995). The generation of quantitative data is predominant in the tourism and leisure industry and tools that aid its collation are welcomed.

The SERVQUAL model has been applied for over 15 years in the US financial sector (Parasuraman *et al.*, 1985) and subsequently made available to the remainder of the service sector. There are many instances of SERVQUAL being adapted for use in tourism and leisure-related fields (see Chapter 13).

Zeithaml, Parasuraman and Berry took a holistic approach to improving service quality by changing the organizational culture, from the top managers to operational staff (Berry *et al.*, 1988). This echoes Crosby's (1979) and Feigenbaum's (1991) point of view.

To achieve this cultural change, they recommended the application of the SERVQUAL model, service mapping, staff training, etc. Reservations were expressed with regard to the overuse of service recovery systems, as Crosby's ethos of 'do it right first time' was advocated (Berry *et al.*, 1990; Zeithaml *et al.*, 1990; Berry and Parasuraman, 1994). They suggested that part of the service recovery initiatives should be to empower front-line staff to deal with customers' complaints. This is an area in which the two service quality schools have similar theories (Berry *et al.*, 1990; Berry and Parasuraman, 1992). Empowerment of front-line staff is not implemented in many tourism and leisure organizations; this is partly due to the use of low-paid temporary seasonal and casual staff in these positions. To empower staff, training is required and organizations are not prepared to invest in temporary personnel.

Berry and Parasuraman (1992) considered that there should be two levels of service quality strategies. The first level covers the strategies needed to raise customer aspirations of the service offered. This strategy goes beyond customers' expectations and is known as the 'service surprise' (Berry *et al.*, 1985, 1990).

The second level of quality strategies was devised so that organizations can attain excellence by continuous improvement.

These strategies include initiating service quality information systems to enable service performance to be reported, especially the impact on profit of poor service. The need for continuous improvement strategies is central to the original quality gurus' theories, whilst the costing of poor service is only advanced by Crosby (1979) and Feigenbaum (1991).

Berry and Parasuraman (1992) also discussed ways to improve the organization's image. This is the third dimension in Grönroos's model and is important when customers are formulating their expectations (Parasuraman et al., 1991c). They suggested that seeking an externally examined quality award not only promotes the organization's image but also improves its competitive edge (Berry and Parasuraman, 1994). This is a strategy that has been embraced by tourism and leisure organizations from all sectors.

Standardization is a feature of the American service industry but, unlike Levitt (1972), Zeithaml et al. (1990) did not consider that customer-oriented companies need to standardize their service completely. Strategies such as service mapping, previously advocated, bring about a degree of standardization, but these methods are regarded as primary means for improving service (see Chapter 8).

The main contribution of Zeithaml et al. (1990) to service quality has been the development of the gap analysis model SERVQUAL that gives insights into organizational shortfalls over five gaps and the possible causes. The model can be used for repeated quality audits with customer and employee assessments of a service (Parasuraman, 1995). Notwithstanding that the model has a number of critics, it has been applied to the service sector in the USA, UK and Australia by both practitioners and academics. It has also been adapted for specific facilities within the tourism and leisure industry. An in-depth study of the SERVQUAL instruments can be found in Chapter 13.

Differences between the Scandinavian and US schools

Table 4.6 gives a comparative analysis of the two schools of service management. The difference in measurement techniques indicates that two distinct approaches to customer interaction and relationships are present. The US school requires numerical data to be generated, which tends to be a management requirement of the tourism and leisure industry. The Scandinavian school rejects standardization of service and favours the need for a more personalized service.

Table 4.6. Comparative analysis between the Scandinavian and US schools of service quality.

	Scandinavian school	US school
Holistic approach to quality	✓	✓
Customer-oriented approach	✓	✓
Determinants of quality	4 or 6	5
Quantitative measurements of quality	×	✓
Measurement of customer perceptions – customer expectations = customer satisfaction (equals quality service)	✓	✓
Difficult for customers to judge service quality	✓	✓
Company image important in judgement	✓	✓
Process quality	✓	✓
Outcome quality	✓	✓
Teamwork important	✓	✓
Moments of truth important	✓	✓
Empowering front-line staff	✓	✓
Standardization of service	×	✓
Quality as a profit strategy	✓	✓
Service sector orientation only	×	✓
Relationship marketing	✓	✓

Although the service quality models from both schools are still being developed, a second strand of service management theory has evolved due to the prominence of customer feedback. This cooperation between customers and employees, plus the importance of building relationships, was developed into service marketing (Grönroos, 1989). Performance was added by Zeithaml, Parasuraman and Berry to the marketing mix to accommodate the service sector (Zeithaml et al., 1990; Berry, 1995; Zeithaml and Bitner, 1996). Brogowicz et al. (1990) suggested that a consensus has developed between the two schools.

Conclusion

As already stated, when trying to apply the theories and concepts discussed in this chapter to the leisure and tourism industry there is a need to be aware of their limitations. For example, Deming's service characteristics do not take into account the diverse nature of tourism and leisure experiences, as they focus on transaction analysis. These characteristics are especially irrelevant to those experiences provided free of charge by the not-for-profit sectors of the tourism and leisure industry.

SPC, advocated by both Deming and Juran, whilst having many advantages in monitoring quality in fast-food outlets, would be difficult to implement throughout the sector as few managers have the necessary statistical background.

The main lessons that can be learnt from both the original quality theorists and the two service quality management schools is that an organization must take a holistic approach to quality management (i.e. every functional area involved) and that the only appropriate target or goal is working towards continuous or continual improvement of the service.

The two service quality management schools see that it is imperative to know what the needs of the customers are and for this information to be included when organizational decisions are being made. The area of dispute between the two schools is whether or not to collect information on customer needs and satisfaction by quantitative means or qualitative. Most research is now pointing to the advantages of using a number of complementary methodologies which is leading to an eradication of any major differences between the US and Scandinavian schools' approach to managing service quality (Chapter 13 discusses the issue of data collection in detail).

Another issue of great importance to practitioners, as well as being the focus of academics, is how do customers judge quality? The next chapter discusses this in depth.

5

Customer Satisfaction

This chapter sets out to clarify how quality is judged by customers and monitored by an organization. If we can understand how this occurs, then it is easier to develop quality systems, tools and techniques to give accurate data to organizations searching for continuous improvement, customer retention, etc. Satisfied customers are more economical to an organization as they not only generate repeat business but they will also recommend the service to others.

On completion of this chapter it is expected that you will be able to:

- understand the difference between service quality and customer satisfaction;
- appreciate how judgements on service quality and customer satisfaction are formulated and what can influence them;
- understand how heterogeneity of individuals, both front-line staff and customers, impacts on customer satisfaction and its significance to global operators;
- explore customer dissatisfaction.

The lack of a definitive definition of quality (see Chapter 4) gives some indication of the difficulty of measuring customer satisfaction and therefore setting standards.

The definitions of quality and service quality that are considered relevant to the service industry all place the customers, both internal and external to the organization, centrally in the appraisal of the service or products being delivered (Crosby, 1979;

Parasuraman *et al.*, 1985; Peters, 1987; Garvin, 1988; Juran, 1988a; Feigenbaum, 1991; Wyckoff, 1992).

The notion of customer needs being important is a recent attitude in the public sector of the tourism and leisure industry. A range of other people may be interested in the service delivered, including council tax payers or donors to voluntary organizations, and they are known as 'stakeholders'. Their interaction with the organization is considered in Chapter 3, but this chapter concentrates on users of the services.

Service Quality and Customer Satisfaction

The customer could judge the quality of the service delivered as 'good' but they may not have had satisfaction from the experience (Randall and Senior, 1996). Crompton and MacKay (1989) submitted the premise that satisfaction and service quality are not the same thing, stating: 'Satisfaction is a psychological outcome emerging from an experience, whereas service quality is concerned with the attributes of the service itself.' Parasuraman *et al.* (1988) agreed but stated that customers use the same criteria to judge both, as the two are interrelated. Oliver (1997) alluded to the differences in how customers judge service quality and customer satisfaction (Table 5.1).

Table 5.1.   Customer judgement of service quality and customer satisfaction.

Service quality	Customer satisfaction
Evaluated using specific clues	Evaluation more holistic
Based on perceptions of 'excellence'	Based on needs
Cognitive	Emotional

Peters (1987), Normann (1991) and Anderson and Fornell (1994) considered that service quality is too subjective for customers to formulate their own judgements. Edvardsson (1994) also considered that the judgement of services has an element of subjectivity and that it is modified by customer socio-economic variables (e.g. income level).

Gummesson (1994) did not condemn customer judgements but suggested that the organization's interpretation of them may be faulty:

> Yet we know that asking the customer, particularly through structured questionnaires, only reveals a superficial layer of attitudes and behaviour, not the roots. We accept a customer's statement as a phenomenological fact, but the interpretation is loaded with uncertainties.

Customer Satisfaction

Most of the service quality management writers have considerable difficulty in understanding how customers judge services. This is important to the leisure and tourism practitioner, because until this is known it is not possible to develop methods to assess customer satisfaction.

One of the original service quality theories is that customers are satisfied when their judgement of the service they have received (perception) equals or exceeds what they expected:

Customer satisfaction (CS) =
Perceptions (P) = Expectations (E)

This is known as the *gap analysis theory* (Zeithaml *et al.*, 1990) or *Oliver's expectancy–disconfirmation* (Anderson and Fornell, 1994; Oliver, 1997).

Oliver's theory (Oliver and De Sarbo, 1988) has three potential satisfaction levels:

- **Negative disconfirmation** occurs when the service is worse than expected.
- **Positive disconfirmation** occurs when the service is better than expected.
- **Simple confirmation** occurs when the service is as was expected.

It has been questioned whether or not customers assess satisfaction in these terms (Crompton and MacKay, 1989; Buttle, 1996). Cronin and Taylor (1994) suggested that there is no research to support this premise. Although many writers are convinced that there is an interrelation between service quality and customer satisfaction, Berry (1995) pointed out that measuring the elements of service is not the same as measuring customer expectations and perceptions (Box 5.1).

Whilst the debate on whether or not service quality and customer satisfaction are interrelated is academic, these underlying theories have consequences for the validity of measuring tools that have been developed for practitioners to use. Two indicators of customer satisfaction are the Swedish Customer Satisfaction Barometer (SCSB) and the American Customer Satisfaction Index (ACSI). SCSB

Box 5.1.   Example of measuring service quality.

Monitoring elements of service delivery can be an internal event without involving the customers. An example most frequently encountered is the service standard of answering the telephone within a certain number of rings. Electronic telephone equipment can easily monitor the performance achieved. While the telephones may be answered 100% of the time to the set standard, it is frequently observed that customers are left standing at reception desks, box offices, etc. as they are not considered to be part of this process. Although a set of data would be produced by the telephone monitoring equipment, customer perception of the service cannot be accessed by this method.

measures overall satisfaction via customer expectations and perceptions of quality (Johnson, 1995); and ASQI measures the same plus value for money (Rosenberg, 1996). Visitors to free-entrance facilities (museums and art galleries) have been known to state that their experiences were not value for money, which is indicative of them including the costs incurred in travelling to the site.

Tourism and Leisure Satisfaction

Swarbrooke and Horner (1999) used the term 'tourism quality jigsaw'. They stated that the individual components of the tourism product are different in size but are of equal importance to the tourist (e.g. weather, in-flight services, bars and restaurants, shopping opportunities).

Customer satisfaction is impinged upon by all aspects of the service delivery processes (encounters with staff; tangible elements; time it takes the service to be delivered and whether or not it has been delivered correctly) as well as the outcomes of the experience.

Arousal Levels

One of the main satisfaction elements within the tourism product, in the opinion of Swarbrooke and Horner (1999), is arousal. This can be found on a continuum from too little to too much, together with its consequences (Fig. 5.1).

The initial selection of a holiday destination should form the basis for the correct arousal level. Others take a different point of view; they consider 'arousal' to be of a higher order than 'satisfaction' and that it can occur in many, if not all, service interactions. Their premise is that arousal is necessary to achieve 'delighted' consumers (i.e. exceeding customer satisfaction levels). Swarbrooke and

Horner's (1999) research is based on two leisure experiences: a zoo and a symphony concert. To leisure practitioners these are two areas where arousal would be considered as part of the basic service – the thrill of seeing the animals and the emotion of the music. To paraphrase Mosscrop and Stores (1991), 'Quality in Tourism and Leisure is the experience of knowing you've had a good time.'

The 'good time' experience of some customers could be a mediocre or bad time for others. The component of the tourism and leisure experience that has caused the overall feeling of a bad time may be external to the organization, such as transportation, other customers or members of the customer's own group, or even themselves. The interaction of all or some of these factors can create the perception of a bad experience. Swarbrooke and Horner (1999) noted that gamblers were dissatisfied with the resort of Las Vegas when they did not win.

Liljander and Strandvik (1997) commented that emotions play a part in being satisfied but those emotions need not be all positive. They cited Arnould and Price's (1993) work concerning high satisfaction caused by positive and negative emotions combined (e.g. watching horror films, or taking part in white-water rafting).

Customer Satisfaction in Multinational Organizations

The spread of service organizations throughout the world can be readily observed and tourism and hospitality companies are amongst the most prolific (e.g. theme parks, hotels, aquariums, fast-food outlets). The search for continuous improvement and customer satisfaction still has to be pursued in sometimes very different operational environments.

The transferability of a standardized service across the globe is reliant on the notion

Fig. 5.1.   Arousal level continuum.

of 'cultural homogenization', that is, the same market segments throughout the world require the same services. Segal-Horn (1994) suggested that there is some foundation to this debate, hence the success of companies like McDonald's.

It should be noted that in practice even standardized products and services are modified to meet the needs of the local community. In fast-food outlets, changes might be made to the amount of seasoning to suit local tastes, or items might even be removed from the menu if the main religion of the country forbids it. The ban on alcoholic drinks by Disney at its theme parks was lifted at Disneyland Paris to accommodate the French custom of drinking wine with meals.

In transnational hotel chains, customers select the same service provider to reduce risk by gaining a similar experience as they travel throughout the world. At the same time the organization will have to adapt some elements of the operations to accommodate the local culture (e.g. not serving alcohol or pork). A number of organizations import senior staff from their parent company particularly at the start of operations (e.g. Disneyland Paris) to try to ensure that service delivery systems are correctly adapted.

Another problem of transnational operations, highlighted by Varva (1998), is one of translating centrally produced questionnaires. The sense of the question can be totally lost if a direct translation is carried out. The word 'leisure' is almost unknown to the general public in The Netherlands, where this concept is called 'free time' or 'recreational recreation'.

A third element in the multinational dimension is the fact that tourist attractions and events attract many visitors from overseas. The Manchester Commonwealth Games in 2002 is but one example and the Football World Cup in 2006 will be another. Different nationalities will expect different service standards and if the service provider is not aware of these needs, satisfaction levels will be reduced. This applies to the participants as well as the spectators with these major multinational events.

The solutions to all three scenarios is for organizations to carry out research so that they know what their customers want and to be familiar with the general working environment, customs, practices and legislation for each country of operation and each cultural group using or working in the facility.

Zone of Tolerance Theory

Customers' subjective judgement as to whether or not they are satisfied with the service they have received is not as simple as a yes/no answer. Satisfaction can be to a lesser or greater degree, from 'adequate' through 'desired' to 'delight' (exceeding). Between 'desired' and 'adequate', Parasuraman (1995) suggested, is the customer's 'zone of tolerance'. Below 'adequate' the continuum represents totally unacceptable levels of service (Fig. 5.2).

Johnson (1995) gave instances of customer expectations having an effect on the width of the zone of tolerance. If customers perceive that the activity has a 'high risk' (e.g. whitewater rafting) their zone of tolerance will be very narrow; the same activity to someone who is very familiar with it may be perceived as a 'low risk' and therefore have a wider zone. It is suggested that service providers can manipulate these two extremes by giving information as well as assurance. With some spectator activities, even when no thought is given to customer service, manipulation is taking place (Box 5.2).

'Delighting' rather than just satisfying the customer is seen to be a positive surprise to the consumer. This strategy is increasingly implemented by practitioners. The implications for leisure and tourism practitioners of knowing the zone of tolerance of their customers is that they could reduce the level of service, reduce their costs and still satisfy them. Measuring these phenomena is difficult and many managers resort to trial and error especially in times of financial constraints.

The individual components that contribute to customer satisfaction, customer expectations of what a service should be and their perceptions of what they received, will be considered next.

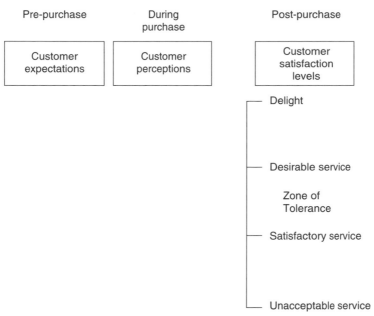

Fig. 5.2. Zone of Tolerance theory. (Adapted from Parasuraman, 1995.)

Box 5.2.   Football fans' expectations of service (pre-Taylor Report).

Fans of football and other team sports are in many ways different from customers of other service organizations. Sociologists refer to the 'tribalism' of team sports fans or suggest that they are part of a 'fandom' (Bale, 1989). It could be argued that football clubs prior to the Taylor Report (1989) manipulated 'their fans' into thinking that they were in low-risk situations – their zone of tolerance was so wide that anything was acceptable and nothing was unacceptable (e.g. poor toilets, poor catering facilities, inadequate safety standards). The only 'service standard' the spectators were interested in was whether or not their team won. Even after many British fans had experienced ultra modern overseas stadia, they did not include this in their expectations of a UK professional football ground.

Customer Expectations

Zeithaml *et al.* (1990) considered that the factors that influence customers' formulation of their expectations are *word of mouth, personal needs, external communications and past experience*. Gummesson and Grönroos (1987) also considered that the image of the organization plays a part in the formulation of this judgement.

Johnson and Mathews (1997) noted that the expectations of a frequent user of a facility would rely more on the influence of past experiences than on other sources of information (e.g. advertisements). Researchers have no way of knowing what a first-time user's expectations are based upon. Dale (1994a)

suggests that 'world class' experiences are used to formulate expectations, but Table 5.2 illustrates the problems of this for the tourism and leisure industry.

The examples in Table 5.2 are extreme, but customers' past experience could be via television programmes, especially for first-time visitors who have no previous experience. Museums and art galleries may be judged against a virtual reality site rather than an actual facility. Harrington and Lenehan (1998) pointed out that some holidaymakers have high expectations of the intangible aspects of a service, which are rarely achieved (i.e. a holiday becoming a 'dream experience').

Parasuraman *et al.* (1988) tried to set customer expectations in context by suggesting

Table 5.2. World-class tourism and leisure experiences. (Adapted from Williams, 1998.)

Location (judged against)	Best in the world
Leisure centre	Sydney 2000 Olympics facilities
Golf course	Open Golf Championship course
Amusement park	Disney World

that they are what an organization 'should' offer. Theoretically, this means that practitioners require customers to have expectations of what a three-star hotel should offer in order to be able to judge another three-star hotel. This may seem a reasonable request but it cannot be guaranteed (Teas, 1993).

Parasuraman *et al*. (1993) stated that expectations should be 'normative standards' and identified two norms for customer expectation service standards: desired and adequate service (Parasuraman *et al*., 1994). Having different types of expectation standards had been considered by Boulding *et al*. (1993) when they criticized Zeithaml *et al*.'s (1990) previous theory that customer expectations were 'one-dimensional'.

Miller (1977, cited in Randall and Senior, 1996) said that there are four levels of customer expectations: (i) ideal; (ii) predicted; (iii) deserved; and (iv) minimum tolerance. Most of the methods for measuring customer expectations and perceptions (e.g. SERVQUAL, see Chapter 13) concentrate on collecting data on customers' ideal expectations and the lower but acceptable levels are ignored. For public sector leisure and tourism organizations, knowing their customers' lower but satisfactory levels of expectations would aid them in devising service delivery specifications when the organization's resources are limited. Equally,

service providers have to be aware that customer expectations are constantly changing.

Changes in Expectations

Customers are more aware of alternative service providers than ever before, partly because of the increase in the number of organizations in the service sector. Also the public, via various consumer programmes on television, are not only aware of alternative services but are also given information regarding poor service providers. The ability to purchase services on-line (e.g. air tickets) means that the choice of service provider is now global.

This is affecting the tourism sector at present more than leisure. People still require local providers for regularly used facilities (swimming pools, aerobic or music classes). Increased competition means that service providers are not only escalating the standard of their core service but also augmenting their services (see Chapter 7). This leads to an upward movement of customers' minimum tolerance levels (Lewis, 1995). For example, tea-making facilities are now the norm in overnight accommodation, including inexpensive bed-and-breakfast establishments.

Factors such as changes in population demographics can affect the expectation of the service provider's clients. Demographic changes mean that the population has a higher proportion of older people in it. These people are more discerning about service standards than younger age groups; as well as having higher expectations they expect to get 'value for money'.

The case study in Box 5.3 shows that different levels of expectation can come about when an organization's image is included in customers' expectation judgement.

Box 5.3. Case study: Expectations of users of a public sector golf course.

Research carried out at a golf course suggested that its customers did not expect to receive an excellent service from a public sector organization. Comments were made such as, 'They do the best they can in the circumstances' and, 'Well, it isn't a private course.' They did not take into account the fact that the course was run by contractors but they still had lower expectations than if they were going to play on a site managed by the commercial sector.

Customer Perceptions

The final part of the customer satisfaction equation is their judgement of the service they have received: their perceptions. Oliver (cited in Taylor, 1997) defined customer perceptions as 'a comparison to excellence in service by the customer'. It has already been stated how difficult it is for practitioners to know what 'excellent' is in the minds of individual customers and whether or not it is appropriate to judge a particular facility at that standard.

It is often considered that customer perceptions of a service are made at the end of a service encounter. Zeithaml et al. (1990) disagreed. They believed that there is an endless potential for judgements to be made during the service delivery process (as customers generally have to be present) and then once more at the post-consumption stage. O'Neill et al. (1998) took the view that all of these judgements are interrelated and therefore a holistic approach to researching customer perceptions is required.

Berry and Parasuraman (1994) considered that some services are too technical for customers to judge whether they are being carried out correctly and stated that organizations need to be fair when offering them (e.g. passenger ferries). Berry (1995) and Grönroos (1990a) both discussed the notion of 'service fairness' and it would seem that an organizational philosophy of conducting business ethically must underpin the operational processes in these circumstances.

As previously stated, Peters (1987), Normann (1991) and Becker (1996) questioned the accuracy of customer perceptions. It is known that customer expectations are influenced by past experiences and that previous perceptions of the service contribute to this. It is also well known that people's memories are not reliable. O'Neill et al. (1998) suggested that exit surveys to ascertain customer perceptions will give little information as to how they will view the service some time later, when considering repeating the experience.

To add to the complexity of customer perceptions, Armistead (1994) outlined a range of influences on this judgement:

- **The purpose of the encounter.** Although tourism and leisure experiences could be seen as being secondary to other aspects of everyday life, they can be as significant and, for some people, more vital.
- **The importance the customer places on the encounter.** If someone has waited all year for a 2-week holiday, that service encounter is a major event to that customer. Gummesson (1995) expanded on Armistead's 'importance' factor by suggesting that customers buy 'offerings' rather than services. These offerings create value to them (e.g. the dream of the holidaymaker; the fitness gym providing a healthier lifestyle).
- **Perceived risk.** There is always an element of risk in purchasing an unseen tourism or leisure experience. The growth in multinational chains of hotels and fast-food restaurants enables customers to reduce that perceived risk.
- **Costs involved.** The effect that this will have is directly related to the availability of an individual's disposable income.

Research by Chebat et al. (1995) indicated that the mood of the customer could affect their perceptions of the service, in particular the interactive parts of the experience. It is quite possible therefore for two individuals to formulate totally different perceptions of an identical service experience; this is in part due to the subjective nature of their judgement (Johnson and Mathews, 1997).

Schneider et al. (1998) found that customer perceptions are directly related to employees' perceptions of the service and vice versa. They suggested that, as employees are internal customers of the organization, their needs must be met. Their level of effectiveness in delivering the service to external customers is a direct result of how they have perceived the service delivered to them.

Customer perceptions of a service are a complex series of judgements made during and at the end of the experience but are modified by a range of factors including their mood, importance of the encounter, etc. The tourism and leisure industry has to be aware of these elements, especially when designing methods of receiving feedback from customers.

Dissatisfaction

Dissatisfaction occurs when customer perceptions of a service do not meet their expectations. There are numerous possible causes but a few of these are: (i) research not being carried out as to what customer needs and wants are; (ii) external information (e.g. advertising literature) giving false expectations to the customer; (iii) staff not given adequate training to deliver the service as specified; and (iv) financial objectives taking priority, which, at the extreme, leads to unsafe custom and practices (e.g. not closing the bow doors on cross-channel ferries before leaving harbour).

Research has indicated that in many cases customer dissatisfaction came about as a result of an organization's failure to address a complaint, rather than the original service problem (Hocutt *et al.*, 1997). It is therefore imperative to design and instigate service recovery techniques (see Chapter 8) to safeguard customer satisfaction.

It is interesting to note that when a relationship has developed with an organization, a situation that would normally lead to dissatisfaction may not have that effect. Bolton (1998) suggested that this is due to the accumulative effect of previous encounters that satisfied the customer, which then reduces the impact of an unsatisfactory event.

Summary

Although customers of tourism and leisure organizations are making judgements all the time regarding their expectations and perceptions of a service (before purchase, during the delivery and after purchase), managers in the industry must not underestimate the difficulties in converting these judgements into actual operational strategies.

Customer satisfaction is a complex phenomenon to monitor, as it is a collection of events and emotions, many of which are outside the control of the service provider (this is summarized in Fig. 5.3). Not least, the heterogeneity of the customers has a major effect on their subjective judgement of the service provided. This is due to the fact that many customers do not regard the offerings of the leisure and tourism industry as just production and service, but consider it as an experience which has value and real benefits to themselves. Chapter 6 examines this in depth.

Customer satisfaction occurs when perceptions meet or exceed expectations

Expectations

Perceptions

Informed by

Informed by the total experience

Aspects that can be managed by the organization

Offerings or
'bundle of attributes'

Service delivery

Appropriate arousal level

Cost

Past experiences

Word of mouth

Customers' needs and wants

Risk perceived

Price

Aspects that can be influenced by the organization

Customers' needs met
by the organization

Importance of the
experience to the customer

The amount of risk the
customer perceives
is involved

Aspects that cannot be influenced

Pre-experience events
(i.e. transport)

Customer's mood

Companions
(e.g. argumentative)

Post-experience events
(i.e. meal in a restaurant
on the way home)

Fig. 5.3.   Factors influencing or attributing to customer satisfaction.

6

The Leisure and Tourism Experience

Introduction

Positive, enriching and rewarding leisure experiences are essential aspects of life and the role that leisure plays within health, the environment, culture, education, urban and rural generation and personal development is well established.

(ILAM, 1999, p. 3)

More and more, today's consumers want their goods and services to be packaged as part of a memorable experience.

(Ford and Heaton, 2000)

It has been argued that holidays represent important positive experiences for people.

(Ryan, 1997)

[Leisure activities] can help to increase the self-esteem of individuals; build community spirit; increase social interaction; improve health and fitness; create employment and give people a purposeful activity; reducing the temptation to anti-social behaviour.

(Coalter, 2002, p. 42)

Chapter 1 suggests that an important factor in the management of service quality in the leisure and tourism industry is the nature of the product and service. The product and service, as examined in Chapter 7, have a number of characteristics that impact on the management of quality. The management of quality becomes especially important given the significance of aspects of leisure participation suggested by the quotations at the beginning of this chapter. Chapters 1 and

7 highlight the mix of physical attributes of tangible elements of the product, especially the activity, and the process the customer goes through to engage with them. This book adopts the premise, highlighted in the ILAM (1999) declaration above, that there is an additional dimension to the leisure and tourism product, the consumer experience, and this is the focus of this chapter. We established that the product, seen as an activity and/or a setting, together with the way in which it is managed or delivered, creates and shapes the distinctive feature of leisure and tourism – the customer experience. The purpose of this chapter is to extend the analysis of the product into its experiential properties and to consider the implications for the management of service quality.

On completion of this chapter it is expected that you will be able to:

- appreciate the experiential properties of the leisure and tourism product;
- understand the importance and meaning of the leisure and tourism experience to the consumer;
- examine the relationship between the leisure and tourism experience and the management of service quality;
- consider how certain approaches to service quality can enhance the leisure and tourism experience.

The Growing Importance of the Leisure and Tourism Experience

The management of the leisure and tourism experience, with implications for service quality, is assuming greater significance as the industry is growing in size, sophistication and complexity. The industry is more global, more specialist, more competitive and more professional. The industry has a diverse range of organizations and contexts and its product development is becoming more commodified and based on a multifaceted experience. The relationship between the industry and an increasingly differentiated and demanding market is more significant. Greater importance is attached to consumer behaviour, customer expectations and perceptions, the product/service mix, technology multimedia and customer motives, satisfactions and benefits. Consumers are discerning and demanding and increasingly view leisure and tourism as more than a product or service. As the Henley Centre pointed out in two different reports: '. . . increasingly who you are matters less than how you feel at the point of consumption' (Henley Centre, 1996, p. 2) and: 'increasingly, we are buying experiences rather than goods' (Waterhouse, 2000).

A similar approach is evident in the mission statements of leisure and tourism organizations. For example:

> Together we will create even better experiences for our guests by offering authentic American food and drink with a memorable range of things to enjoy, wrapped up in A+ service, seasoned with fun.
>
> (TGI Fridays)

> Our mission is to deliver excellent value by achieving a unique breadth of hospitality, leisure, and drinks businesses, which bring increasing numbers of people together across the world to share great leisure moments.
>
> (Bass)

The challenge, therefore, for leisure and tourism professionals in the management of the quality of the leisure and tourism product would appear to lie in their understanding of its experiential properties and features. The overwhelming evidence from studies of the leisure and tourism experience is that its meaning in many managed contexts is shaped by a myriad of complex perceptual constructs and this explains why it is regarded as a multidimensional phenomenon (Tinsley and Tinsley, 1986; Gunter, 1987; Russell and Hultsman, 1987; Howe and Rancourt, 1990; Cooper et al., 1994; Lee et al., 1994; Hull et al., 1996; Ryan, 1997).

Yet the experiential aspects of leisure and tourism have not always been fully taken into account by the industry. It seemed that much of the leisure industry in the UK was product related; it thought in terms of activities, facilities, programmes and other tangibles (Haywood and Henry, 1986) and was, arguably, more concerned with recreation than with leisure. It was a characteristic of the public sector during the explosion of new facilities in the 1970s. The Wolfenden Report in 1960 (CCPR, 1960) concluded that much of the problem of the UK's low rates of participation in sport and recreation would be solved by the provision of additional facilities.

Developments in quality assurance also appeared to adopt a rather mechanistic approach. In 1987 we saw the adaptation of the standard for quality management systems, BS 5750 part 2 (now ISO 9002), for the service sector including leisure. Swindon Oasis was the first leisure facility to be registered in 1990 to a standard that was still written in manufacturing terminology. The accreditation body, British Standards Institute, found itself in new territory, and some difficulty, in applying the standard and the quality system to a consumer process with a diverse range of individual benefits and satisfactions, rather than to a conventional product with a clear specification. Chapter 11 demonstrates how the standard has been developed and implemented since then although it often appears to have been used in a mechanistic and essentially systems-based way. Likewise, the crown and stars system of classifying a range of hotels and leisure complexes by the tourist boards and other organizations is essentially concerned with tangibles – amenities, facilities and services. The 'mystery guest' methods employed by, for example, First Leisure and Whitbread are also more concerned with the physical and procedural dimensions of the consumer process. Even 'Best Value' in local government in the UK with its emphasis on consultation with stake-holders would seem to be encouraging the use of quantitative performance indicators and the neglect of tracking the perceptions of customers at the point of service delivery (Sanderson, 1998; Davies, 1999).

We would contend that an understanding of the nature of the leisure and tourism experience should be of importance to the leisure and tourism professional, whether in the public, voluntary or commercial sectors, and that this also includes its meaning to the individual customer. The leisure and tourism manager's skill lies in the ability to analyse and interpret the meaning attached by people to the events and phenomena taking place, for the study of leisure and tourism management involves complex perceptual constructs and relationships in many contexts. For example, the National Trust, in their National Strategic Plan 1998–2001, is committed to raising its standards of management and its ability to meet customer needs: 'By 2001 all properties will have produced Statements of Significance summarising their meaning for people and their relationship to the wider landscape' (National Trust, 1998).

The marketing of Gloucester Docks (Gloucester Docks Trading Company hand-book, 1999) also illustrates the point:

> Probably the most important part of market-ing is to make sure that when visitors come their experience is even better than they had imagined. Then they will tell family and friends and come back themselves. This experience includes how safe the visitors feel, how welcome they feel and the appearance of the site – not just the quality of the attractions and shop.

The example from Gloucester Docks illustrates the need to consider customer feelings and sentiments. As the Henley Centre (1997, p. 49) suggested, 'Going to the cinema has become more than just watching a movie – it is now an experience in itself.'

Therefore, the perceptions of consumers, their levels of satisfaction and the meanings they ascribe to leisure activities, and the impact of management processes upon their perceptions require description of leisure and tourism experiences, firstly, followed by explanation and interpretation of their meanings (Hultsman and Anderson, 1991). This can apply to the management of people in the least structured context (e.g. a national park) as well as more directly managed con-texts, such as leisure centres and theme parks. It can apply to superficial, commodified and passive activities or more creative, skilled and challenging activities.

An example is the 3 days of frantic race-going during the Cheltenham Gold Cup week every March when thousands of punters are squeezed together in very cramped condi-tions with very long queues, both inside and outside the course, at every stage of the pro-cess; they respond to market research that they are having a wonderful time although have difficulty explaining why (Oxford Part-nership, 1996). As shown in Chapter 7, a num-ber of elements contribute to the outcomes of many transactions, especially the service encounter, although the experiential nature of some transactions will be less apparent. For example, travel agents and tourism information services are more concerned with deferred outcomes and experiences, although the quality of the service is crucial to overall satisfaction, and in some instances the experi-ences of others may be a factor, as the Glouces-ter Docks Trading Company suggests in its office guidelines: 'A visit to the docks can be made or marred by the courtesy and help-fulness all staff show, whether the visitors experience it themselves or witness the way others are treated.'

Thus, the essence of managing service quality in most leisure and tourism organiza-tions would seem to lie in the relationship between the consumer and the managed con-texts or environments in which the consumer experience occurs and the patterns or themes of this relationship. All of these contexts, of course, contain a myriad of individual experi-ences, whether rich and fulfilling or superfi-cial and mere entertainment, and raise many questions about the managed processes and the interaction between the consumer and the leisure environment and leisure provider. The pivotal component is the product or experi-ence, and the way in which it is managed and delivered, and the recent developments in generic service quality literature underpin this. Increasingly, the customer is viewed as both consumer and co-producer (Normann, 1991) and often plays an interactive role in shaping the experience; the leisure and tourism experience can be perceived as a service process containing a service encounter or a series of sequential encounters, symbolized by the term 'moments of truth' (Carlzon, 1987).

The service encounter can be defined as the stage of the service process when the consumer engages or interacts with staff (the psychological service encounter) but also systems, procedures, information or even the organizational culture (see Chapter 14). The service encounter, as Fig. 6.1 demonstrates, can involve outcomes and therefore satisfaction or dissatisfaction supported by a post-transaction evaluation by the customer of the service performance. A central thrust of this chapter, and indeed this book, is that the level of satisfaction with a transaction represents more than the organization getting things right. As will be examined, the encounter and its evaluation are also affected by the experiential properties of the product or service.

The Experiential Properties of the Leisure and Tourism Product

Leisure theorists (Tinsley and Tinsley, 1986; Hull *et al.*, 1996) have suggested that experi-

ential qualities define what is and what is not leisure. Leisure and tourism managers, of course, are in the business of trying to provide diverse and high quality experiences. Others (Hultsman and Anderson, 1991) observed that leisure research tends to research not leisure *per se* but its manifestations, such as participation patterns, motivations and preferences. An example is provided by Nash's conceptualization of leisure (Fig. 6.2), which offers a hierarchical view of the use of leisure but regards emotional participation as a discrete element.

There is a need for a greater understanding of the leisure experience and its meaning and how it relates to the management of the contexts in which it takes place. Indeed, providers are beginning to build in such perceptions consciously, as the following example suggests:

> Our business is about delivering excitement to our customers. Every experience is built on organisation, anticipation, innovation and assurance. It is this combination that successfully delivers the Wembley experience.
>
> (Wembley plc *Annual report and accounts* 1998)

A second consideration is the timescale involved in certain activities, particularly holidays, and the impact it can sometimes have on how the experience is evaluated. Chapter 1 suggested that tourism was essentially concerned with certain leisure activities, albeit in a distinctive context. The

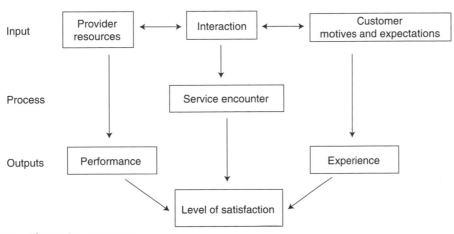

Fig. 6.1.   The service encounter.

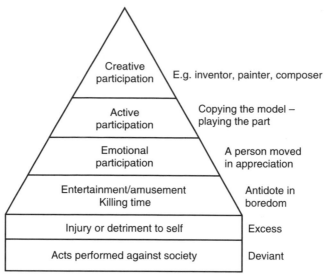

Fig. 6.2. Nash's conceptualization of human use of leisure time. (Source: Nash, 1960, cited in Torkildsen, 1986.)

task of this chapter is to examine the range of experiences and motivations for consumption in different contexts, including everyday activities in the home locality and foreign travel and cultures.

In order to do this it might be argued that there is one major significant feature of tourism, and that is the timescale involved. By definition, tourism occurs over a longer time span than conventional leisure activities; although a holiday is made up of a series of discrete leisure activities, it is also evaluated by the tourist as an overall experience or as one package. However, it could also be argued that many leisure experiences are made up of several elements or stages, which affect the final perception of the activity and its management. This begins to lead into the domain of not simply customer satisfaction management but also zones of tolerance and the nuances of satisfiers and dissatisfiers (see Chapter 13), which reveal that a customer's post-experience evaluation is not always as straightforward as it sometimes seems. There are a number of aspects in the study of the leisure and tourism experience to highlight, which can be synthesized with the theories and concepts of service management to enable more informed management of service quality in leisure and tourism.

Motives/preconditions

Figure 6.3 builds on the previous model and focuses on the nature of the leisure and tourism experience. It considers the conditions necessary for the attainment of leisure and the generic motives of consumers in engaging in leisure and tourism activities. Much evidence suggests that the prerequisites for achieving leisure are a sense of freedom of choice, freedom from evaluation and intrinsic motivation or the expectations of preferred experiences. It could be argued that all positive experiences will contain enjoyment and then will range from a level of relaxation to fun, entertainment, excitement and adventure or escapism, apart from the specific motives of, for example, health and fitness, education or personal development. Whichever applies to particular activities, the model points to the need for balance in the three key factors of time, flow and expression and emphasizes the dialectical nature of the leisure experience.

Time

Free time is integral to leisure and tourism but the requirement here is the balance

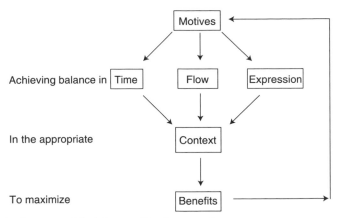

Fig. 6.3. The dialectic nature of the leisure and tourism experience.

between the purposeful use of time and a sense of timelessness. We have observed that it is important to distinguish between the characteristics of the leisure and tourism experience and the determinants or causal factors of that experience and to move beyond viewing leisure and tourism as merely residual time or an activity. Some leisure theorists (Lee *et al.*, 1994; Hull *et al.*, 1996) have demonstrated how the view of leisure changed from one of simply time away from work to perceived freedom, and then to a focus on the psychological attributes (motives and benefits) and the perceptual dimensions of leisure. Others (Ryan, 1997; Holloway, 1998), from a tourism perspective, also identified time or the sense of timelessness to be an essential ingredient to a holiday. Quality service delivery involves creating the appropriate conditions for the particular needs or motives of individual customers and perceiving time in a qualitative way. Ryan (1997) showed how holidays are a temporal experience in that they can include: (i) freedom from constraint by the perceived or actual lack of time; (ii) the passing of time (holidays have a chronological sequence); (iii) an experience of time in that, even for some intensive events or activities, time can appear to slow down; and (iv) possessing temporal boundaries beyond the holiday itself with all the stages including anticipation, recall and travel.

Therefore, the notion of time as a social construct in addition to a chronological sequence is relevant to the analysis of service quality and highlights the pivotal role of some professionals in enhancing the quality of the experience. The travel agent can help to shape the planning of time as well as the memories associated with its use; the airline, through its delayed flight, can have a deleterious effect; the tour operator, through schedules, mix of activities and the interaction with holiday-makers, can also contribute greatly to the temporal experience. In a different context, one of the authors was involved in some research in the 1980s with a leisure centre that was experiencing some dissatisfaction with its bowls users, most of whom were senior citizens with time-rich, cash-poor lifestyles. The centre was in the middle of the town and was built over a car park that was also used by many shoppers. Everybody paid the normal parking rates, which were in time bands and became quite expensive after a certain period of time. Unfortunately, at that time the centre's users did not have their parking fee refunded, which meant that the bowls players, in an activity and at a stage of life when time should not matter, were constantly looking at the clock. The sense of timelessness, which occurs with the best leisure and tourism activities, was not present and the overall experience was impaired. After the recommendation to refund the parking fee to users was accepted, usage, income and customer satisfaction were all improved.

Thus, it is possible to move beyond the uncomplicated notion of leisure as simply free time, which can often be regarded as what something is not, rather than what it represents. It will be shown that time is important but more in relation to its perceived absence. The sense of absorption, control or detachment is a key precondition for leisure and tourism activities, which can offer intrinsic benefits to the individual. Although much depends on the state of mind of the individual, the perception of timelessness experienced by the customer can be affected by the management of the activity and its space.

The flow

State of mind is also a factor in the next element of the model, which considers the relationship between the participant and the activity. There is a need to examine the distinction between serious, committed leisure and everyday activities, though perhaps this should be considered less in terms of a dichotomy and more as a continuum. There is a spectrum ranging from Maslow's peak experience theory and Csikszentmihalyi's concept of flow (Csikszentmihalyi and Kleiber, 1991), which describes more sporadic but intense moments of fulfilment and self-actualization particularly in physical outdoor activities, to activities of a more mundane and less memorable nature. It should be noted that the latter represents much managed leisure and tourism but, perhaps, poses as much of a challenge for the management of service quality as do the less common but distinctive and special moments in a range of contexts: the feeling of magic in a theme park; the feeling of wonder at viewing the Grand Canyon; the sheer exhilaration that some skiers can experience in the mountains; the sense of achievement and absorption that the individual learning a craft or a sporting skill can have; the feeling of utter relaxation quietly reading a book amongst the trees outside the villa at Center Parcs when the rest of the group are chasing from wind surfing to badminton; or the unique atmosphere and sensory stimuli as experienced by spectators at a sporting occasion, pop concert or opera. These and many other activities can be designed and managed by organizations with skill and sensitivity

and with Csikszentmihalyi's indicators of flow experience in mind: (i) the perception that personal skills and challenges posed by an activity are in balance (the grading of pistes in skiing is a clear example); (ii) the centring of attention where there is focus and the ability and opportunity to switch off; (iii) the loss of self-consciousness (or Samdahl's lack of self-awareness); (iv) clear feedback from a person's actions; (v) feelings of control over actions and environment; (vi) a momentary loss of anxiety and constraint; and (vii) feelings of pleasure and enjoyment.

The characteristics of flow or peak experience illustrate the attraction, and indeed function, of many activities in leisure and tourism, yet it must not be forgotten that the more regular activities (e.g. the visit to the health club or cinema or urban park) also involve feelings and sensations, as well as the benefits beyond the visit.

Expression

The third part of the dialectical process is closely related to the first in that the opportunities for personal identity and self-expression must be balanced against the lack of self-awareness that a sense of timeliness can evoke. For many people, the leisure and tourism experience provides the most natural means to expressing oneself and exploring one's identity. The lifestyle and the pattern of work and leisure for some people mean that leisure and tourism activities may be simply cathartic and an escape from the main activities of life. Stebbins (1996) described the essence of serious leisure in which, for some people, the activity becomes a central life interest. For them, leisure as a recreational activity is, perhaps, the greatest opportunity to explore, understand and express self (Howe and Rancourt, 1990). The provider's understanding of such motives and satisfactions and how individuals construct and perceive their social world is part of the skill in service design, programming and challenges posed. For example, the provision of allotments or the design of a package following the British Lions Rugby Team on an overseas tour or the management of Lake Windermere for various and possibly conflicting users will impact in a significant way on some people's lives. Skilful management will recognize the importance to the leisure experience of both the expression it provides and the need, in some cases, for little scrutiny of the process and the outcomes.

Context

Whereas the previous three elements can involve a delicate balance between contrasting demands, the impact of the fourth element depends on how it is perceived by the consumer. The context in which the activity takes place is particularly important to the quality of the consumer experience. Glancy (1993) referred to the significance of social settings for many consumer experiences and argued that people perceive and define leisure and tourism situationally. It is not enough to interpret the individual's thoughts and impressions as self-centred acts; the experience in which the leisure and tourism meaning is formed should also be studied. The nature of leisure as an experience demands it. Glancy is supported by others who pointed to the complexity of the natural social settings in which managed leisure and tourism take place (Glancy and Little, 1995; Hemingway, 1995).

Table 6.1. The most common positive holiday experiences: a categorization (Ryan, 1997).

Criterion	Domain
Relaxing/peaceful	Affective to self-actualization
A good climate	Physiological
Scenery	Self-actualization
Exploring/discovering new places	Self-actualization
Food	Physiological
Being with family/friends	Affective/social
A sense of freedom/ independence	Self-actualization
Friendly people	Affective/social
Good accommodation/good hotel	Physiological

Much leisure and tourism has a social element, where friendship or the desire to meet new friends is a strong underlying motive. Additionally, the nature and appropriateness of the physical context (the landscape and servicescape) are also key variables and explain the motive for some activities. It is known that walking is the most popular physical activity, with the quality and beauty of the environment as a part of the attraction. Ryan's (1997) research into tourists' motives and behaviour revealed the attraction of scenery to be one of the most important factors (Table 6.1).

Benefits and outcomes

Having examined the motives for consumption and the process and context involved, the benefits and psychological outcomes of the leisure or tourism experience also need to be considered. Manfredo *et al.* (1996) described their Recreation Experience Scales and suggested that recreational activities are behavioural pursuits that are instrumental in attaining psychological and physical goals. They argued that recreation emerges from a problem state – the need for participation in a recreational activity; leisure experience is the bundle of psychological outcomes desired from recreational activities, which influence the choice of activities and settings. In other words, the participant uses leisure time and money to participate in a chosen setting or context with certain outcomes (and long-term benefits) in mind. These preference scales link in with the idea of the recreation opportunity spectrum.

There is certainly a need to reconcile social and individual leisure choices based on a clearer understanding of the consequences of leisure activity for the individual, family, community or society. A conceptual difficulty for this book is that benefits tend to be judged on their value to society, especially in terms of social welfare or control, and also involve different stakeholder perspectives. The leisure experience and notion of service quality can only be based on the interpretation or perceptions of the individual. The way forward is to focus on identifying and measuring the psychological outcomes (or need satisfactions) of leisure participation as perceived by the individual. Yet the problems of measuring psychological benefits of leisure have been well documented (Tinsley and Tinsley, 1986; Driver et al., 1991). Until recently, Driver et al. (1991) relied on inferential definitions of benefits, linked to psychological need gratification, but the literature lacked understanding of human needs and the relative importance of each one.

For this reason, Driver et al. developed the PAL (Paragraphs About Leisure) model. They argued that leisure experiences result in the satisfaction of some of the psychological needs of the individual. This need gratification helps to maintain physical and mental well-being and life satisfaction, which then helps personal development. The needs being satisfied are regarded as intervening variables. PAL identified: 27 need-gratifying dimensions, including achievement, catharsis, creativity, play and social status, which could be achieved in varying degrees by different activities; and 17 common needs, such as autonomy, relaxation and recognition. Tinsley and Tinsley (1986) identified eight factors in recreational activity that represent the psychological benefits of a leisure experience: self-expression; companionship; power (control in social situations); compensation (especially in relation to work); security; service; intellectual aestheticism; and solitude. Gunter (1987), in his research into the properties of leisure, identified the following eight attributes as the most common in meaningful leisure experiences: separation from everyday life; timelessness; freedom of choice; fantasy (creative imagination); pleasure; sense of adventure; spontaneity; and self-realization.

Much leisure theory has been constructed upon the sociopsychological constraints of perceived freedom and intrinsic motivation. Manfredo et al. (1996) suggested that there are three interrelated approaches to the study of the psychological nature of leisure. One is definitional (leisure or non-leisure). The second is the immediate conscious experience approach; Manfredo et al. (1996) described it as a phenomenological topography of the leisure experience – its meaning, quality, duration, intensity and memorability. The third is post hoc satisfaction, related to the notion of expectations, though much service quality literature has emerged from the conceptual framework of 'disconfirmation theory'.

What our analysis does reveal is that many leisure and tourism experiences involve a dialectical process. There is a clear dichotomy between the desire for relaxation and tranquillity or for stimulus and action; between passivity and creativity; between the search for the new experience and the fear of the unknown; between the common requirement for social interaction and the need for space and solitude. People are different and the same person's moods and needs can vary according to circumstances. The attraction of a superficial, passive entertaining activity can be overwhelming and, indeed, necessary at certain times. At other times, especially for some people, the need for activity or exercise is paramount. Coalter (2002), writing in the context of the public sector but with a generic message, argued that there is much to be gained from encouraging people to be actively involved in the planning and delivery of their local leisure services. Similarly, the desire for knowledge and personal development (Aristotle's notion of eudaemonia embracing action and citizenship as well) drives some people's motives and, indeed, seems to be increasingly important, as Makinson-Sanders (1996) pointed out:

> We now live in a society where mere subsistence is not enough; self development through entertainment, mobility, social interaction, indulgence and altruism are all new idealistic necessities of modern life . . . the key challenge for leisure suppliers is how to adapt to social change and to integrate it into their products, as well as taking advantage of it.

Manfredo's three approaches are significant in the design and delivery of service and their understanding is important for the management of service quality. For the purposes of this book, we have established that leisure is not a unitary concept but a complex and multifaceted phenomenon that can also be multiphasic and transitory. Feelings of leisure can fluctuate according to the stage or circumstances of the activity and are linked to the benefits sought. It is suggested that the psychological benefits of the leisure and tourism experience can be seen in a number of ways, which incorporate the dichotomies described earlier but which also represent a hierarchy of needs and motives for leisure and tourism: (i) passive – relaxation, peace, tranquillity, solitude, space; (ii) stimulating – escape, fantasy, adventure, novelty; (iii) lively – fun, excitement, entertainment; (iv) competent – health, fitness, sport, crafts and hobbies (DIY); (v) social – family, friendship and esteem, social networks/groups; and (vi) personal development – cultural awareness, self-expression, personal identity.

As a final dimension it might also be possible to categorize the six groups of motives and Manfredo *et al.*'s three approaches into three levels of experiences and benefits (Table 6.2):

1.   The immediate experience, possibly incorporating Csikzentmihalyi's concept of flow, containing fun, relaxation, excitement, entertainment and other attributes, many of which are associated with commodified leisure and tourism.
2.   Experiential learning with an impact on skills and knowledge and physical and psychological health and a behaviourally observable condition.
3.   More of a concern with personal or self-development and life satisfaction, self-actualization and identity affirmation.

The Enhancement of the Leisure and Tourism Experience

If the definition of a benefit as an improved condition, a gain or an advantageous change

(Driver *et al.*, 1991) is accepted, there are some clear questions for the management of leisure and tourism activities:

- What do we mean by an improved condition or gain?
- How many managed activities would lead to such an improved condition?
- How are various need satisfactions linked to leisure and tourism activities, settings and experiences and how do they contribute to longer-term benefits?
- How far can we differentiate the market to meet and satisfy individual experiences?

From these questions, there are several implications for the management of service quality in leisure and tourism and they go to the core of what is distinctive and challenging about leisure and tourism management.

1.   Leisure and tourism managers must facilitate the consumer experience rather than simply provide the activity, facility or opportunity. Hollywood Bowl's mission statement is 'creating great leisure moments'.
2.   There is a need to view leisure as an interactive and socialization process and a multifaceted phenomenon with connotations of freedom, individual choice and personal autonomy (Kelly, 1980; Henderson, 1991; Stokowski, 1994; Burton, 1996).
3.   The ability to justify particular approaches and methodologies used in service quality is important to the development of firmer theoretical foundations for the study and practice of leisure and tourism management, particularly where the individual leisure and tourism experience within managed contexts and the application of service delivery principles are emphasized (Buswell, 1993a, Lentell, 1995). An example is provided by Center Parcs' marketing literature, which

Table 6.2.   The hierarchy of leisure and tourism experiences.

Level	Related preoccupations	Mode	Domain	Outcomes
Immediate	State of mind	Transient	Feelings/emotions	Enjoyment plus
Experiential learning	Activity and progress	Cumulative	Skills/knowledge	Achievement plus
Personal development	Progress and life satisfaction	Holistic	Lifestyle	Well-being

presents subliminal images of tranquil settings, traffic-free environments and activity breaks detached from the real world.

It will be seen in Chapter 8 that at a micro level the system of leisure and tourism becomes a system of service delivery and focuses on the human dimensions of individual consumption and participation. This chapter is concerned with the relationship between the system of delivery of the product and service and its experiential properties perceived by the customer. This approach embraces the contextual aspects of the setting, environment and activity and the social dimensions of the experience and interface. Leisure and tourism activities may be viewed not merely as self-centred acts but as experiences that have a particular meaning.

The meaning of the experience and its impact on personal identity, social relations and quality of life is significant and raises many questions and issues for the management of service quality in leisure and tourism; in turn, so does the way in which the leisure or tourism experience and its meaning and quality are affected by the other elements in the system. Secondly, the corollary suggests a similar relationship from the perspective of the leisure and tourism manager; the actions of the professional may seem to be deterministic but are also shaped by the actions and reactions of the consumer. The human dimension of such interactions provides the rationale for the approaches to managing service quality in leisure and tourism management examined in Part 3 and underlines the need for much research into the meaning of leisure and tourism and the features of leisure and tourism such as participation patterns, consumer behaviour and demand. As Glancy and Little (1995, p. 308) suggested: 'The fact that we know little about the interactive experience in which leisure meaning forms limit our capacity to understand leisure on a personal and empirical level.'

Furthermore, if it is argued that leisure and tourism are processes governed by human interactions (Henderson, 1991; Cooper et al., 1994) and that the basis of meaningful leisure and tourism is the human experience (Glasford, 1987; Glancy, 1993; Ryan, 1997),

perhaps the study of leisure and tourism service quality needs to focus on the process and the way in which the different elements of the process interact. As Bitner et al. (1997, p. 193) argued: 'Service experiences are the outcomes of interactions between organization related systems/processes, service employees and customers.'

Factors in the Relationship between Service Quality and the Leisure and Tourism Experience

It could be argued that the study of the relationship between service quality and the leisure and tourism experience is based on what might be described as 'interaction analysis'. The challenge is to break down the discrete elements of each topic and focus on particular issues, problems and contexts in a more integrated manner. The conceptual underpinnings to such an approach, as illustrated by Fig. 6.4, provide the basis for the model of the leisure service delivery system outlined in Chapter 8 and have two main domains: contextual and human.

Contextual

There are, perhaps, two subthemes here. Firstly, there exists an interaction between the customer and the physical setting of the leisure and tourism experience. The physical environment plays an important part in determining the outcomes of individual participation in leisure activities and is shaped in turn by the way it is used. Much work has been undertaken into the landscape of natural resources and the psychological and spiritual impact on individuals, particularly in North America. Management processes in this context are more concerned with environmental issues and with the stewardship of a sensitive resource. However, the design and management of built facilities and surroundings, such as tourist resorts, leisure complexes, theatres, visitor attraction sites, museums and sporting venues, are now

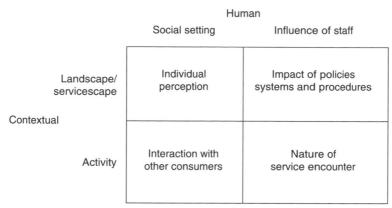

Fig. 6.4.   Human and physical dimensions of the leisure and tourism experience.

subject to critical enquiry where the term 'servicescape' depicts the relationship (Clarke and Schmidt, 1995; Wakefield and Blodgett, 1996). The notion of environmentalism in leisure does not simply relate to the physical context but also to sociocultural and attitudinal dimensions; Page (1997) refers to important features such as folklore, friendliness, language, loneliness and ambience of the place, local customs and costumes. The perceptions of a leisure consumer or tourist are clearly affected by such intangibles and it is important for leisure and tourism practitioners to appreciate the need to manage in a broader context.

Secondly, the interaction between the customer and the leisure opportunities provided by the activity must be acknowledged. This embraces many aspects of leisure and tourism management, including programming, the concept of substitutability, opportunity sets in which the two variables of consumer behaviour and product attributes interrelate (Stabler, 1989), the spectrum of recreational opportunities (Manfredo et al., 1996) and service design, which represents the creation and maintenance of the service package and the service process (Kingman-Brundage, 1991). There would appear to be scope for developing a typology of recreational opportunities to be planned and managed on the basis of combining chosen activities, preferred settings and desired experiences. Glancy and Little (1995, p. 306) suggested that:

It is interacting with rules, roles, re-enactments, realisations and rewards

created by recreation opportunities that the psychological individual meets society on a personal basis and becomes a social person.

The relationship between the goals and motives of the customer and the attributes of the product of the service package also helps to shape the outcomes of the transaction and the quality of the leisure or tourism experience. Gummesson (1995, p. 78) referred to the 'interactive productivity of services' which recognizes the value or benefits of the experience for the customer. Rosman (1994) demonstrated how activities, experience outcomes (such as fun or enjoyment) and long-term personal benefits are important dimensions for the professional to consider in designing programmes and services. Such a view provides a much more holistic theory of leisure satisfaction, motives and benefits, personal relations and social networks.

Human

The study of leisure and tourism management, through the different approaches observed, is founded on the belief that interaction occurs symbolically and that the interaction is dynamic and interdependent. An individual's reality is based on personal perceptions and interpretations of actions and events or social contexts, and individuals are neither free nor constrained. Typical interaction involves a network in which individuals are linked to others through perceived roles and expectations. They attempt to see themselves from the perspective of others in order to judge the appropriateness of behaviours and actions. There will always be some constraints in this self-awareness, though perhaps 'true leisure' has fewer constraints.

There are also two subthemes to this domain. Firstly, many managed leisure and tourism contexts create interaction between the customer and the social setting of the experience. Much leisure and tourism occurs in the presence of other people and, indeed, the need for socialization is one of the most significant motives behind leisure and tourism behaviour. The influence of other people and the meanings and identities ascribed to social settings have been studied through symbolic interaction theory, which provides a phenomenological framework for studying how people interpret activities, events and other people in their lives and act on the basis of that interpretation (Henderson, 1991). In other words, we behave as we think others expect us to and the role of the customer as a co-producer helps to create and shape the consumer experience in so many contexts. Others have focused on the specific meaning of leisure in social settings and on perceived freedom (Samdahl, 1988), lack of self-awareness (Samdahl and Kleiber, 1988) and personal identity (Kelly, 1983). In this way, such perspectives help to unlock the theoretical aspects of freedom and constraint, which are important concepts for leisure managers to understand.

Secondly, the nature of the leisure and tourism industry also involves considerable interaction between customer and staff. This draws on aspects of human resource management and service quality and, in particular, focuses on the psychological or service encounter that takes place between staff and customers. Communication processes and procedures and the meanings ascribed to such communication also provide the basis for much current enquiry into aspects such as service blueprinting (Kingman-Brundage, 1991), the customer as co-producer (Harris et al., 1995; Canziani, 1997) and information processing (Wathen and Anderson, 1996). They illustrate the need for a balance between management and leadership abilities. Leisure and tourism managers require the functions and skills of management such as human resource management, finance, law, information and communication technology, marketing, service operations and strategic planning but they need to combine them with an in-depth knowledge and understanding of the consumer and leisure behaviour. Leisure managers are required to operate in a conventional, bureaucratic, managerialist manner in certain respects but they also need the softer skills and vision of leaders. Many leisure and tourism contexts require the professional to facilitate, enable, motivate, guide, enthuse and animate customers and participants and to understand how they interact with the various referents in the service process. Rich qualitative data about the leisure and tourism experience should inform critical enquiry into how both the professional and the consumer view and engage in this interactive leisure process and how the experience can be enhanced.

Conclusions

In moving towards a more coherent approach to the study of service quality in leisure and tourism management, a number of points have been established.

1. It has been established that leisure and tourism involves more than a product or a service, and their benefits. The experience of the activity or its context is part of the motivation for the individual consumer and requires careful and sensitive management.
2. Consumers will experience the activity or context in different ways and a conundrum for operators is to decide how much the market can be differentiated. The greater the differentiation, the more difficult it is to achieve consistency of delivery.
3. Consumers help to create the very experience itself, whether through their encounter with staff, systems or procedures or in the atmosphere created at large events such as concerts or sports events. This also requires responsive and empathetic management.

The importance of giving managers and academics a grounded understanding of the differences between individuals and groups, rather than the average consumer based on aggregated results, has been highlighted but it also raises the issue of how far the market can be broken down.

The roles of the leisure and tourism professional require an understanding of how people define the world around them. Furthermore, they need to understand this reality in order to provide the most appropriate settings, activities and experiences. The approach of this book accepts that the leisure industry, at one level, is engaged in providing recreational activities and does this through managing facilities, amenities and programmes. There is a product and a process and they contain particular features or attributes, which are important to the customer. However, a premise of the book is that the leisure provider and the customer are engaged in more than a product transaction; there is the potential for the achievement of a leisure experience. Recreational participation and experience of the leisure and tourism product in the managed contexts that this book is addressing are affected by the individual consumer's self-awareness and personal motives, the system of service delivery and its understanding by the leisure or tourism provider. The move towards the use of systems models will help with the conceptualization of the study of leisure and tourism management and the understanding of the various interactions that provide the scope for the enhancement of service quality.

Part 2

Designing Quality

Introduction

As noted in Part 1, many leisure and tourism contexts contain a myriad of individual experiences, whether rich and fulfilling or superficial and merely entertaining, and have implications for understanding and designing the leisure and tourism product. The premise of giving the consumers what they want springs to mind when writing about design quality. Unfortunately it is not as easy as this suggests, because consumer needs and wants are constantly changing. What may have satisfied them at one time no longer does so. Leisure experiences, especially those catering for the youth market, can be in fashion one moment and out of favour the next (e.g. themed pubs, skateboarding, step aerobics).

Furthermore, the nature of services, particularly leisure and tourism services, is not straightforward. Specific service characteristics of perishability (services cannot be stored) and inseparability (generally customers need to be present when the service is performed) add to the operational management difficulty. These need to be addressed at the service concept and design stage.

The next three chapters will consider the writing of service delivery specifications, taking into account the characteristics of tourism and leisure services (tangibles and intangibles). The issues of service guarantees, queuing, customer complaints, service recovery techniques and capacity management are also included. To help with this complex design setting, a number of tools and techniques will be discussed, such as blueprinting.

7

Characteristics of Service

Introduction

Irrespective of the theories they believe in, most service quality academics consider the main difference between goods and services to be the extent of intangibility (elements that are illusive and therefore cannot be touched) in proportion to the physical product, the tangibles (Lovelock, 1992c; Schmenner, 1992; Buttle, 1993; Irons, 1994). Very few writers consider that intangibles and tangibles are the only two characteristics of service quality: Rust and Oliver (1994) added a third component, the service setting; predominantly the customer – staff interaction. Normann (2000) called these service encounters 'moments of truths' (MOTs).

On completion of this chapter it is expected that you will be able to:

- understand the difference between goods and services;
- be aware of a variety of service classification methods;
- identify the characteristics of services;
- gain an insight into the different approaches required to manage the tangibles (the physical environment) and the intangibles characteristic of services;
- appreciate the complexity of the heterogeneity of service encounters.

Goods versus Services

The general consensus is that services have a number of characteristics common to manufacturing: the tangibles. These are not only the physical features of the environment that the service is delivered in but anything that is taken away by the customers (e.g. advertising literature). Unlike manufacturing, at the end of the service encounter there can be an absence of exchange of tangible goods (Chandon *et al.*, 1997).

The main differences between goods and services are the *intangibles*. Leisure and tourism services are primarily intangible (Reisinger, 2001). The intangibles are: inseparability; perishability; and heterogeneity.

Inseparability

This is the requirement that customers to a greater or lesser extent need to be present when the service is being performed (e.g. sports coaching course), and sometimes they even have to carry out part of the service delivery process (e.g. self-service restaurant).

The phenomenon of inseparability can have an adverse effect on revenue if a customer does not show up for an appointment. To try to manage this, some restaurants (for example) require a non-returnable deposit to secure a table. Equally, the absence of specialist staff off on sick leave can lead to the very same effect on the organization and having additional staff to cope with these eventualities is not always cost-effective either.

Perishability

This means that services cannot be stored (e.g. a theatre ticket can only be sold for a particular seat on a specific day; if it is not, revenue is lost). Grönroos (1988) added the 'lack of transferable ownership' to this characteristic. Although the theatre ticket could be given to somebody else before the performance, afterwards the experience cannot be given away. Hotels use yield management techniques to try to minimize the effect of service perishability: they sell rooms at below the normal rate when they know they are not going to be at full occupancy, so at 8 or 9 o'clock in the evening unsold rooms for that night can be very cheap.

Heterogeneity

The individuality of both the customer and the front-line member of staff and the way they interact with one another is one of the most important aspects when managing the service delivery process. Some organizations standardize the service delivery to control heterogeneity of the workforce; this production-line approach is so that they neither do nor say anything that has not already been rehearsed (e.g. fast-food outlets). Unfortunately this strategy removes any initiative that the member of staff had, which could be detrimental to the organization (for example, they cannot build up a relationship with or acknowledge frequent customers because they are not able to deviate from the script) but it does inform them of the appropriate level of service that they should be delivering.

This strategy does not remove the heterogeneity characteristic from the customers.

One way in which this can be done is via the information that service organizations provide before someone experiences the service. For example, 'No jeans or trainers to be worn in the disco' should deter the younger age group for whom a manager feels that the service has not been designed. This is not a foolproof method: it is quite possible for someone to misinterpret this type of information, and even when dressed appropriately they may have an awful evening because the music or dancing was unsuitable and other customers were far older than them.

Typology of Service

Goods service continuum

To distinguish services, Voss et al. (1985) used the concept of a manufacturing-to-service continuum from pure manufacturing to pure service. They suggested that the position along the continuum depends on what degree of customer contact there is throughout the process, pure service having the maximum amount of customer–organization interaction (e.g. personal fitness trainer). Their continuum theory also acknowledged that manufacturing can have variations in customer–staff interactions.

The continuum was modified by Armistead (1994) by the addition of the intangible dimension. The proportion of this dimension in relation to the physical features (tangibles) dictates the position where a particular service lies. Armistead's continuum finished at quasi-manufacturing rather than pure manufacturing. Wright (1995) supported Armistead in that the percentage of intangibles is central to the typography of service and suggested that the notion of a continuum from pure manufacturing to pure service is more valid than the goods versus services dichotomy.

Although this seems to be an academic debate of no relevance to leisure and tourism practitioners, in Western society a manufacturing organization has more status than most service organizations.

Discrete services

Another school of thought is that service provision comes in discrete types, depending on the nature of the interaction between customers and employees and/or the delivery design. Oakland (1993) used this theory to group services under five types: (i) personal services (e.g. sports coach, hairdresser); (ii) service shop (e.g. leisure centre; cafeteria); (iii) professional services (e.g. accountant; solicitor); (iv) mass services (e.g. hotel; restaurant); and (v) service factory (e.g. equipment hire; cleaning firm). Table 7.1 illustrates Oakland's reasoning behind the groupings, showing that the attributes are at the same level for each individual service within a specific group.

Armistead (1994), whilst still embracing the service continuum theory, considered that there are only three types of service classification: (i) professional services; (ii) mass services; and (iii) service shops. Oakland's (1993) personal services can be found in Armistead's model in either professional services or the service shops categories. The service shop and factory have been merged.

The classification into either three or five types of service does not acknowledge that leisure and tourism operators, interpreting customer needs and wants, design a service. They would decide whether a service is designed to be standardized or personalized and that would affect the attribute levels in Oakland's classification. This could place some service providers separately from the rest of their industry.

For example, budget hotels, because of their use of technology, have no reception staff on duty and the lack of interaction would remove them from the main hotel classification. Oakland's classifier is not sophisticated enough to be of significance to tourism and leisure practitioners.

Lovelock's service classification

Lovelock (1992c) considered that the different types of service can be classified by the amounts (within the process of service) of three inputs – the customers, materials (quasi-manufacturing) and information – and that all or one can be involved at any one time. Lovelock's information classification is in terms of experts and their knowledge and he considered this to be the most intangible form of service. This perspective has the advantage for the tourism and leisure industries of allowing services to be movable throughout the process period, unlike the continuum or the fixed classification theories.

Other service classification systems have been referred to by Lovelock (1992b), as well as by Wright (1995), based on capital and labour input ratios, which have little to offer non-profit sectors of the tourism and leisure industry.

Table 7.1. Classification of selected services (adapted from Oakland, 1993, p. 62).

Service	Labour intensity	Contact	Interaction	Customization	Nature of act	Recipient of service
Beautician	High	High	High	Adapt	Tangible	People
Cafeteria	Low	High	High	Choice	Tangible	People
Cleaning firm	High	Low	Low	Fixed	Tangible	Things
Sports coaching	High	High	High	Adapt	Intangible	People
Equipment hire	Low	Low	Low	Choice	Tangible	Things
Hairdresser	High	High	High	Adapt	Tangible	People
Hotel	High	High	Low	Choice	Tangible	People
Leisure centre	Low	High	High	Choice	Tangible	People
Restaurant	High	High	Low	Choice	Tangible	People
Take away	High	Low	Low	Choice	Tangible	People

Core and Peripheral Services

The classification of service into types is an argument that has no consensus within service quality literature, but writers disagree with Crosby's (1979) theory that there are no differences between goods and services. The acknowledgement of different types of service does not help practitioners when they are considering service design, costs and operation constraints, as an individual leisure and tourism experience can also be made up of a number of services. In its simplest form, these are known as core and peripheral services.

Normann (2000) divided a service into two distinct components: core and peripheral or secondary services. In a leisure centre, the core service could be the swimming pool; the peripheral could be the availability of a café or the ease of car parking. It was suggested by Normann (2000) that it is the peripheral services that customers use to differentiate between similar service providers. The use of additional peripheral services was advocated by Wyckoff (1992), with two areas to gain competitive edge being giving customers security and promptness. This is contrary to Parasuraman *et al.*'s (1985) research findings, where security and promptness are so important that they are central to customer needs, not peripheral to customer expectations. In some leisure activities and situations (e.g. participating in dangerous sports: spectators at football stadia), safety is a major consideration.

Peters (1987) cited Levitt as advocating the total product concept as a way of differentiation between service providers. This comprises four components: generic, expected, augmented and potential. The **generic** equates to the tangibles of service (the fixtures and fittings); **expected** is the basic level of the core service; **augmented** is the extra services offered, generally entailing the organization spending more money on resources but is not necessarily noticeable to the customer; and **potential** is that which is offered over and above what is expected. Table 7.2 illustrates this in the context of a leisure centre's swimming pool and a theatre.

Peters (1987) suggested that to achieve competitive advantage, organizations must concentrate on, and stress to customers, the last two components – the augmented and potential services. He also emphasized the need for strategy planning to enable organizations to concentrate on the intangible elements of the whole service. As competition increases in many areas of the tourism and leisure industry, the strategy of augmented service has been adopted extensively.

Gummesson (cited by Barnes and Cumby, 1995) considered augmented services as the 'peanut syndrome', meaning that customers have to pay indirectly for the 'free' peanuts on the bar whether they require them or not. Budget airlines have taken the opposite approach and have capitalized on offering the core service only and thereby reducing fares.

Organizations that place customer needs central to their decision-making process, especially when considering the service design, will be able to make informed choices as to whether peripheral services should or should not be offered and what they should be.

Service Characteristics

Lovelock's (1992) theory demonstrated the mainstream thinking that service characteristics comprise the intangibles of *inseparability*, *heterogeneity* and *perishability* together with

Table 7.2. Examples of the total service concept.

Component	Leisure centre	Theatre
Generic	Modern swimming pool	Purpose-built theatre
Expected	Safe environment	Being able to see the stage and hear the performance
Augmented	Staff trained in excess of minimum standards	World-famous producer employed
Potential	Sports injuries clinic	Pre-performance lecture or dinner

the tangibles. This was confirmed by Buttle (1993), Oakland (1993) and Becker (1996) and suggests that the outcomes of service (i.e. the benefits gained by the customers) are also intangible and ephemeral; this is especially so when the services of the tourism and leisure industry are considered. It is why services are difficult to evaluate (Zeithaml and Bitner, 1996). *Labour intensity* was added to the list of service characteristics by Schmenner (1992), elaborating on both Normann's (2000) notion of MOTs and Lovelock's (1992) heterogeneity.

Tangibles

Normann's theory of core and peripheral service components is applicable to the tangible aspects (the physical clues) of a service. The tangible elements of the core service cannot be taken away (e.g. the outlet's fixtures and fittings; the appearance of the personnel). Tangible elements of peripheral services can be removed, such as the merchandise at pop concerts (Buttle, 1993); they also provide additional secondary spending opportunities on which tourism and leisure organizations can capitalize.

In a customer-oriented organization, customers are the main judges of the quality of service. Their presence in the production and delivery environment can lead to impressive levels of furnishing. When this occurs, customer evaluation will be influenced greatly by the tangible aspects rather than by the service as a whole. Becker (1996) was concerned that if customers' judgement is based on their evaluation of the tangibles this will encourage a service organization to take a manufacturer's perspective. This means that the importance of their customers' views and the interaction with the staff will not be considered.

Intangibles

According to Zeithaml and Bitner (1996), 'Intangible aspects of service cannot be displayed'. However, Berry (1995) and Becker (1996) instructed managers to 'tangiblize' the

intangibles if at all possible, in order to give clues to service quality. This helps customers to assess the quality of the experience prior to the visit and reduces risk (Buttle, 1993). This strategy is crucial for leisure and tourism organizations to follow, due to the ephemeral nature of many of their services. Taking the example of the quality of the tickets sent out from a theatre's box office to people making telephone bookings, elements such as the type and quality of the paper and printing of not only the tickets but also the envelopes need to be considered as part of the 'tangibilizing' the intangibles strategy. Such details can counteract any misgivings that customers may have about an organization's ability to provide an excellent service.

Inseparability

Inseparability entails the consumption and production of the service taking place simultaneously, an interaction that requires the service provider and customer to be present (Voss *et al.*, 1985; Buttle, 1993). This inseparability of customers from production has led to two concepts being established: firstly, the consideration that the service delivery takes the form of a performance (Buttle, 1993), or becomes a series of acts (Normann, 2000); and secondly, the notion of the *service factory* as most of the production processes of services occur in the presence of the customer (Chase and Garvin, 1989).

Service designers have used the integration of customers into the production as a feature of their experience. The kitchens of pizza restaurants are exposed to the customers and there the pizza bases are flamboyantly thrown about for the enjoyment of the clients. The performance of bar staff mixing cocktails in bars has also been using this strategy for many years.

Wright (1995) cited Ribble as defining inseparability of service as not being a constant (as the previous writers would lead us to believe), but as three distinct production processes determining this characteristic: pure service, quasi-manufacturing and self-service.

Pure service

This is the customer and provider working together, leading to a coproduction. This generally requires the decentralization of services to a number of geographical locations – a pattern frequently observed with health clubs (David Lloyd centres) and cinema chains (UCI and Warner Bros). Only if a particularly distinctive service is offered (e.g. pop star performing only in London) are people prepared to travel (Zeithaml and Bitner, 1996).

Quasi-manufacturing

Ribble's second type of process is the result of part of the experience being produced in isolation, without the customer present (e.g. a cinema film). This is classified as quasi-manufacturing and is undertaken to improve efficiency and eliminate variation. Bradley (1995) viewed the remoteness of the customer differently, suggesting that if communications are maintained throughout the service (e.g. an Open University course) this cannot be classed as quasi-manufacturing. His reasoning was that technology provides a constant communications link between the organization and the customer, therefore interaction is still possible throughout the service delivery.

Self-service

This occurs when customers use equipment with limited or no interaction with staff (e.g. self-service petrol stations or vending machines). The introduction of equipment is to improve efficiency, especially rate of throughput, with little variation but still meeting customers' needs. Zeithaml and Bitner (1996) disagreed, arguing that variations and inconsistencies can occur the higher the customer involvement in the production, as customers can interrupt the process through lack of training or skills.

Whilst Ribble's theory is not universally accepted, its concepts need to be considered by those in the leisure and tourism industry when they embark on designing the service processes. His theories are also relevant to the next characteristic of service: heterogeneity.

Heterogeneity

This service characteristic relates to the fact that many service delivery processes require a high level of labour input; therefore spontaneity from front-line employees is possible (Becker, 1996). Wright (1995) considered this as having potential for inconsistency of service production and that the introduction of technology is the only way to reduce this. This had been advocated by Levitt (1972) and is implemented in some budget hotels. There the systems have been designed, through the use of technology, so that there are no personnel on duty; bookings and payments (cashless) are all automatic, keys are computer generated and the bathrooms are self-cleaning (but beds are changed and bedrooms cleaned).

Although standardization is a concept of manufacturing, this has transferred to leisure and tourism service providers (particularly in the area of fast-food production) to try to remove the potential for staff inconsistencies.

Introduction to standardization or customization

Standardization is a way of designing service delivery to enable managers to control the heterogeneous elements of service. A product-line approach to service is designed using employee scripts, introduction of technology and Taylorism techniques (Berry et al., 1985; Zeithaml and Bitner, 1996). Berry (1995, p. 158) refuted this by saying that technology can reverse the 'standardized cornucopia'.

An example of Berry's premise can be seen in banks whereby 'hole-in-the-wall' bank teller machines relieve staff inside the bank to offer a customized service. If travel agents had introduced technology in a similar way, customers could have browsed the availability of holidays in the retail outlet, leaving the travel assistants free to answer more detailed questions. Unfortunately, travel agents have not installed this augmented service and customers are staying at home and using their home computers to access the World Wide Web and in doing so creating their own customized service.

Grönroos (1990b), like Zeithaml and Bitner (1996), was not in favour of a standardized service because the behaviour of customers cannot be predetermined. However, standardization strategies are said by many writers to have organizational advantages, such as giving an immediately identifiable image.

This external image is created partly due to the standardized tangibles (e.g. McDonald's golden arch) but also because the service design is aimed at a particular market segment and therefore maximizes customer satisfaction (Gilpin and Kalafatis, 1995). Dale (1994a) suggested that, for organizations with a large geographical spread, standardization allows for consistency in core services. Segal-Horn (1994) and Lyon et al. (1994) confirmed the benefits that standardization of a service offers, but rejected the idea that customer choice may be limited due to the targeting of one market segment. These writers accepted that choice is limited at one organization's outlets but suggested that its competitors, using the same processes of industrialization, will also offer a limited choice but different service (e.g. McDonald's and KFC).

Zeithaml and Bitner (1996) put forward the argument that standardization allows staff to work effectively and efficiently and therefore frees them for ingenuity in their jobs. Others, including Armistead and Clark (1994), have advocated either customization, which requires a flexible system with empowerment of the staff, or alternatively a standardized one based on procedures and systems of service, designed to determine the quality strategy with precise and inflexible service standards. Research by Collins and Payne (1994) into service standardization in relation to staffing costs and training deduced that a more customized service is more expensive. This is due to the need for a better-trained workforce to ensure consistency of service quality, as a customized service is more complex with flexible delivery systems.

Berry (1995) made the distinction between a customized and a personalized service. Customization, according to Berry, is offering only part of a standardized service, to meet an individual's known needs; whereas personalization involves designing a new service for each customer to very different concepts. Schmenner (1992) observed that some organizations only customize the peripheral services (e.g. garnishes on food) rather than the core service.

The heterogeneity characteristic of service, and its control, is a major issue for leisure and tourism practitioners. They need to decide whether or not to embark on the costs of providing a personalized or customized service or provide a potentially cheaper standardized service with advantages to the organization that can be passed on to the customer. The organizational objectives and understanding of customers' needs will drive this decision.

Zeithaml et al. (1990) and Zeithaml and Bitner (1996) highlighted the complexity of the heterogeneity dimension by stating that it is a characteristic of customers as well as service delivery process staff. They suggested that standardization of a service has limitations, as it can only address the employees' heterogeneity.

Perishability

The inability to store, resell, return, save or transport a service is one of the main differences between goods and services (Zeithaml and Bitner, 1996; Normann, 2000). Accurate assessment of the customer demand for a particular service is required (Voss et al., 1985). This can be a difficult aspect to manage when purpose-built facilities are involved. For example, at peak times squash courts are generally at full capacity but during office hours they lie vacant, with few bookings. After years of unsuccessfully trying to fill this spare capacity, the current solution seems to be a reduction in the number of courts. Some are being taken out of use and converted into two-storey fitness centres.

Summary

The significance of the characteristics of service to the customer is dependent on the type of tourism and leisure experience being provided and the sector supplying it. Tangible aspects are important to the customer, especially when services are provided by the commercial sector. Voluntary organizations have been known to provide facilities in less than desirable locations (e.g. village halls) and customers attend, as there are no alternatives. This confirms Parasuraman et al.'s (1991b); zone of tolerance theory (see Chapter 5).

Although the commercial sector utilizes standardization techniques (Lyon et al., 1994; Segal-Horn, 1994; Gilpin and Kalafatis, 1995), the public sector providers do not; instead they try, if possible, 'to serve all sections of the community' (Torkildsen, 1999). The voluntary sector as a whole provides a more personalized service, due to its diversity. The lack of standardization enables voluntary leisure organizations to remain flexible and meet changing customer needs rapidly (Torkildsen, 1992).

Other service characteristics of intangibles, perishability, heterogeneity and inseparability are as applicable to the UK tourism and leisure industry as to other service industries. Ribble's theory (cited by Wright, 1995) that inseparability characteristics are not constant is appropriate to tourism and leisure experiences. An example of this is home-based leisure, which requires very little involvement from the leisure manager (e.g. renting a video) and conforms to Ribble's concept of quasi-manufacturing. Similarly, Ribble's notion of pure service is relevant for many out-of-home leisure experiences (e.g. sports coaching).

8

Service Design

The development and use of service design methodology is a key, maybe even *the* key to the future of service management
(Gummesson 1994, p. 86)

The previous chapter examined the characteristics of services and highlighted the comprehensiveness of recent literature in its attempts to distinguish service management from product management. However, the area of service design has not been extensively researched or applied to services, particularly in leisure and tourism, and its links with the nature of services has not been fully explored. Service design and process management represent, perhaps, the first stage of service quality in leisure and tourism services but have received less attention in recent years than aspects such as measurement of customer satisfaction, and quality awards and programmes. Quality assurance and total quality management constitute familiar and substantial elements in the delivery of quality but represent systems-based or philosophical or cultural approaches and may not always acknowledge the need for customer requirements to be fully assimilated and built into the features of the product and service.

Many 'offerings' in leisure and tourism almost appear to have arisen through serendipitous circumstances and are managed in a similar way without a systematic approach to defining and understanding their relationship with the customers. They just happen! Where there has been a systematic approach, service design has often followed the principles of product design and has ignored the

significance of service encounters, their moments of truth and the experiential nature of the consumer process.

On completion of this chapter it is expected that you will be able to:

- appreciate the role and function of service design in the enhancement and delivery of quality in leisure and tourism;
- critically understand the nature of the service and consumer processes in leisure and tourism operations;
- understand the significance of the service encounter and customer involvement in designing leisure and tourism products;
- appreciate and plan for the involvement of the customer as a co-producer in many managed leisure and tourism contexts;
- apply the techniques of designing services such as flowcharting, service blueprinting and quality function deployment.

What is Service Design?

Chapter 6 showed how the leisure and tourism experience comprises a product and service, a mix of technical and functional quality and a process with particular outcomes. Chapter 7 showed how the characteristics of services provide a backcloth against which to examine service design. The features of intangibility, heterogeneity and inseparability of production and consumption exemplify the distinctiveness, if not the difficulties, of managing leisure and tourism services and highlight the lack of complete control over the activity by the provider (because of the nature of leisure and tourism activity, timing, the unpredictability of consumer behaviour or conditions such as the weather). When mistakes are made by the operator, in many instances it is impossible to rectify them because the customer consumes the product or service package as it is offered. Much of the typical leisure and tourism product, already noted, is a process with few tangible reference points and is potentially subject to considerable variation in the way it is delivered because of this factor as well as the difficulty of standardizing approaches by staff or volunteers. In fact, it is not just the variability of different staff that causes uncertainty but the approaches of the same staff (even the best may have an off-day). Furthermore, the customer is also viewed as a co-producer in many contexts and this is an additional factor to take into account.

Service design clearly links in with many other aspects of service quality, including market research, the identification and solving of problems and the development of clear service specifications. Maylor (2000) argued that a clear understanding of quality is necessary in order to design systems that deliver it. Service design involves the translation of ideas, solutions and intentions into a specific configuration or arrangement of equipment, space and other resources, as in a theme park with its complex circulation of people, or an airline with its movement of people.

According to Gummesson (1994, p. 85):

> . . . service design covers hands-on activities to describe and detail a service, the service system and service delivery process . . . it is the process of presenting needs in some physical form, initially as a solution, and then as a specific configuration or arrangement of materials, resources, equipment and people.

Gummesson went on to argue that poor service design will lead to problems with service delivery; indeed, the two aspects are inextricably linked and require a systematic process, which can also account for the experiential properties of leisure and tourism. Others highlight the cost of poor service planning and design in what Stebbins (1990)

described as inveterate waste – perhaps between 25 and 40% of total income.

There are a number of different contexts or levels, which the design process addresses in the leisure and tourism industry, in either new service development or service improvement, including: (i) sites such as theme parks, other visitor attractions, urban parks, country parks, retail and leisure sites, sports stadia and even town centres and their layout and management; (ii) buildings such as leisure complexes, theatres, museums, heritage centres and conference and exhibition centres; and (iii) services such as tourism information centres, travel agencies, airlines and sports development.

The skills and techniques of service design apply to both tangible and intangible features and have become increasingly significant in recent years. The next section examines why.

The Growing Importance of Service Design to Service Quality in Leisure and Tourism

There are several reasons why service design requires a knowledgeable and skilled approach:

1. **The classification of services** demonstrates the nature of the service act and the importance of the service encounter in the management of the service process. The service encounter or the interaction between customers and staff and systems is important in many services but particularly in leisure and tourism, where outcomes or benefits are inextricably linked to the process and the individual experience. Strategically, organizations also have to consider how the customization or standardization of a service shapes the way it is designed and delivered, or, indeed, is determined itself by the design process. The simultaneity of production and consumption means that the features of the process and product need to be planned carefully and managed systematically to avoid mistakes and variations in service quality. Examples include the management of

crowds at special events or the procedures for checking facilities and equipment so that problems such as cold showers or litter are prevented or kept to a minimum.

2.   **Operations are therefore now more complex** in many leisure and tourism settings and have more points of contact or stages where the 'moments of truth' will be present. The notion of a multifaceted leisure experience or product is more widespread; it represents both the multiplicity of activities or experiences available to the consumer in the same setting and the increasingly differentiated market for the same facilities. Flexible specialization, where the provider is constantly appraising the potential for adaptation of a facility or activity or the fine-tuning of a product or service, is part of the process of service design. This has been seen to occur recently in facilities such as squash courts that have been converted into fitness suites or soft play areas. Operations, of course, are also more challenging because consumers are more complex and sophisticated in their motives and requirements, as seen in Chapter 7.

3.   **The impact of technology is particularly significant**. It can have a bearing on the nature of a product in, for example, the rides in theme parks or the interactive activities in museums or science parks, or the equipment in a health and fitness club. Technology, in booking and membership systems and control of tickets and access as well as communications, also shapes the design of the service and the management of the service process. For example, TECHNIQUEST calls itself the 'Science Discovery Centre' and contains a science theatre, a planetarium, a discovery room on a variety of topics and, using latest technology in particular, a cyber library for access to the Internet and various CD-ROM packages. The Millennium Dome, despite its problems of finance, was a very technologically sophisticated facility and most customer satisfaction surveys showed the public to be attracted by it and happy with its use of technology.

In other words, the very product and the way it is delivered are not simply underpinned in many contexts by technology, but are manifestly based on the ability of the product to inform, animate, excite, stimulate and entertain. The potential of such technical

resources, in relation to other resources, adds to the complexity and the challenge to the design process as well as the scope for product development.

4.   **Service design is also necessary for the operations in the facility or service to meet their objectives and to function correctly**. Leisure and tourism organizations represent a very wide range of contexts, purposes and functions across the public, commercial and voluntary sectors. Comparisons, through the use of some performance indicators, are possible but many organizations should be judged on how effective they are in achieving the set objectives. Service design is an important element in implementing aims and objectives and identifying their implications for operations. As Kingman-Brundage (1991, p. 48) suggested: 'operationalising service quality dimensions is a crucial element of service design'.

5.   **The service design process enables the necessary systematic planning to take place**, particularly when it uses the tools and techniques examined at the end of this chapter, and an integrated and unified approach to its operations.

The challenge in all operations is to achieve a balance between maximizing customer satisfaction and the optimum use of resources, the two ostensibly conflicting objectives of service operations. Good service design ensures that resources are allocated as effectively as possible and that this occurs within a cross-functional and integrated approach, although Johnston (1999) urged organizations not to ignore the core disciplines in such a process.

Service Design as an Integrated Approach

Just as quality management should be an integration of service marketing, operations and human resources management, service design should be seen as a total process combining functions and adopting a certain approach. A number of observers have demonstrated how achieving service quality depends on the integrating and unifying function of the service design process

(Kingman-Brundage *et al.*, 1995; Stuart and Tax, 1996; Normann, 2000; Titz, 2001). The term 'total design' is often used to highlight the link between market research, design and development and the operational and marketing functions in the offering of the product or service (Stuart and Tax, 1996; Collier and Meyer, 1998).

Oakland (1993) demonstrated how many successful organizations adopt a market-led approach as opposed to a technology-led or marketing-led approach. In other words, it is customer requirements, and the organization's genuine understanding of them and responsiveness to them, that drive the design and delivery of the product or service, rather than the functions of the organization or an overemphasis on the tangible features of the product or service. Feigenbaum (1999) referred to the process as customer value enhancement and suggested that it would require a radical shift of approach by many organizations.

For example, many public sector leisure centres were preoccupied with the mere provision of facilities in the 1970s and the development of programmes in the 1980s, before the move to a customer-led approach recognizing a more differentiated market. Kingman-Brundage *et al.* (1995, p. 20) related such an approach to the service system:

> Service managers in particular are challenged to design service systems of the kind the customer desires: not mere assemblages of competing departments preoccupied with their own internal issues, but unified wholes focusing on the customer's needs.

They also demonstrated how a unified service system, in order to work, recognizes the complexity of customer needs (particularly the nature of the leisure and tourism experience) and incorporates a smooth, seamless service based on teamwork and collective understanding. Such an approach is described by the *service logic*, which embraces customer, technical and employee logic and needs to align with the service concept. *Customer logic* is the explanation for customer behaviour and its duality of customer needs and its role and performance as a co-producer. *Technical logic* describes how and why the service outcomes are produced; *employee logic* clarifies the employee's role and ability to perform. An illustration of this approach is provided by Key Travel, who implement cross-utilization at slack times when staff have the opportunity to swap roles with colleagues. It is the company's philosophy that everyone should know and understand what each member of staff's duties are in the day-to-day running of the company. It is their view that, if this were to be achieved, the pressures on each department would be better understood by other departments and there would be less bad feeling when a problem arises. It might depend on the cause of the problem and it could be argued that fewer problems should occur.

Kingman-Brundage *et al.* (1995) have thus shown how there is a need to move beyond the traditional organization with its specialist departments and its discrete functions in marketing, human resources management and service operations. In order to provide a smooth 'seamless' service, a systematic way of integrating the various dimensions of the customer experience has to be identified. This is achieved through designing and implementing a service system capable of creating outcomes that customers value and an ethos and culture that staff fully understand and share. Disney has demonstrably achieved such integration in five of its theme parks; the sixth, Disneyland Paris, has achieved more focus and integration recently than in its first 3 years of operations. A number of organizations, including TGI Fridays, Center Parcs and Esporta, also appear to have clear service concepts and outcomes for their customers and staff who understand this.

However, in order to understand and use the dynamics of the service experience, it is also necessary to consider not only the elements of service logic and service concept in the design of the service but also the service process and system of delivery (Edvarsson and Olsson, 1996; Ford and Heaton, 2000; Normann, 2000). The model in Fig. 8.1 demonstrates the relationship between the various elements in the service design process. It does not offer a technique or a method for service design but contributes to a understanding of

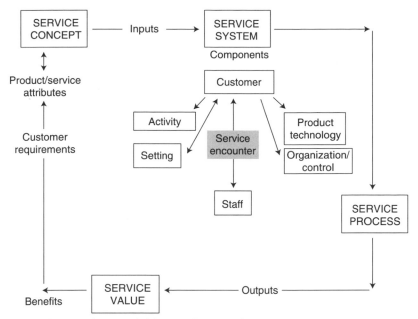

Fig. 8.1. Model of service design and delivery in leisure and tourism.

the complex process of designing systems and processes.

Model of Leisure and Tourism Service Delivery Management

As suggested earlier, service operations management and service design require managers to balance aspirations for service quality against the limitations of budgets and resources available. As Laws (1999, p. 282) suggested:

> The challenge for service managers is to design a service delivery system which combines maximising customers' judgements that the service experienced is satisfying, with technical efficiency in the use of resources used in delivering the service.

The model comprises several components and these are considered below.

Leisure and tourism service concept

The first component is the leisure service concept. This represents customer needs and

the features of the product or transaction. Customer utility and benefit – both the description of the customer needs to be satisfied and how they are to be satisfied through the design of service package – are important elements in the leisure and tourism experience. The leisure and tourism service concept contains the bundle of attributes or benefits that the consumer is seeking and relates to the core product or activity and the augmented product or additional services such as hospitality. It also defines what business the organization is in and how it should promote and organize itself. For example, Gloucester Docks Trading Company developed a three-point strategy for success from its service concept:

1. To create awareness, raising the profile and image of the docks and what they can offer.
2. To encourage visitors, especially first time, through events, special offers and other promotions.
3. To generate repeat visits and recommendations to others based on visitor enjoyment and satisfaction.

Gloucester Docks Trading Company has a long but relatively clear mission statement that helps to shape its marketing strategy and approach to service quality:

> Gloucester Docks Trading Company's mission is to maintain and improve our position as the number one free tourist attraction in the Heart of England Tourist Board Region through recognition of the variety, history and tradition of the Gloucester Docks, creating a quality location and service in a friendly environment of local, national and international visitors.

Its service concept encapsulates the heritage of the area and former functions and the image that most people now have of dockland areas. Its attributes include its location, variety of attractions and friendly environment, and it is committed to creating and delivering an enjoyable experience to its visitors (now estimated at 1.5 million a year).

Another example is provided by the David Lloyd Group, where there is a feeling that its approach to service quality is the distinctive feature of its service concept. The Group believes that its core product – the activities provided by its sports and leisure facilities – is important but is underpinned by highly trained staff, high standards of cleanliness and maintenance, friendly attentive service and a pleasant and relaxing environment. It is the company's aim to exceed its members' expectations by providing an enhanced service, delighting members and increasing their perceived value of their membership. The aim is also to give all members individual attention and to try to meet every service encounter with care and compassion. The David Lloyd core values are 'caring, passion and trust' and its philosophy on service quality is to offer every member the best combination of quality product, standard of service and value for money in the leisure industry.

The leisure and tourism service system

The production management model of adding value and converting inputs into outputs, adapted to apply to service industries, is further modified here to embrace leisure and tourism management. As Fig. 8.1 demonstrates, the leisure and tourism service system establishes what is needed in order to meet the customer requirements and the product features described by the service concept. It refers to the resources and inputs to the service process and how they are deployed, and helps to identify the service standards in all aspects of the operation. The leisure and tourism service system has several elements: (i) the customer; (ii) the activity; (iii) the setting; (iv) product technology; (v) staff; and (vi) organization and control.

The customer

The relationship between the goals and motives of the customer and the attributes of the product or service package also helps to shape the outcomes of the transaction and the quality of the leisure and tourism experience. Organizations increasingly differentiate their markets based on typologies and behavioural characteristics (Box 8.1).

The activity

The interaction between the customer and the leisure opportunities provided by the activity embraces many aspects of leisure and tourism management, including programming, the concept of substitutability, opportunity sets in which the two variables of consumer behaviour and product attributes interrelate (Stabler, 1991) and the spectrum of leisure and tourism opportunities. It more naturally represents the core element of the product such as a game of squash, an airline seat or a walk in a national park.

The setting

The setting refers to the physical and technical environments for the activity and also intangible features such as atmosphere and ambience. Indeed, the effect of the servicescape (Wakefield and Blodgett, 1996) on customer behavioural intentions in leisure and tourism settings is well documented. Their findings tend to suggest that customer satisfaction, particularly from a hedonistic perspective, is influenced by the nature and quality of the physical setting, though there can be a certain ambivalence in some settings;

Box 8.1.   Case study: Hollywood Bowl.

Moonlight Bowl Promotion

Primary objectives
To increase lineage during periods of low activity profitably

Secondary objectives
To reinforce awareness amongst existing markets
To increase brand awareness amongst new markets
To inform all markets of current unique selling points

Moonlight Bowl mission statement
Moonlight bowling will allow all customers to try the latest glow bowling experience within the Hollywood format. The 'Moonlight Bowling Experience' provides all customers with the opportunity to play ten-pin bowling in a new and innovative environment, with the added bonus of excellent value-for-money.

Market segmentation
Hollywood attracts a broad range of people from within the local community and, therefore, a number of different markets can be identified:

● Competitive	league/tournament bowlers
● Families	generally bowl on weekend during daytime
● Children	generally after school until 6–7 p.m.
● Youths (U18)	during evening
● 18–25s	evening (Wed–Sat)
● Couples	evening
● Over 50s	weekdays and early evening
● School groups	weekdays

Market targeting
Moonlight bowling is an innovative bowling experience that appeals to a younger audience. By combining the effects of ultra violet lighting, 'pumping music' and prize give-aways, the atmosphere is attractive to the following markets:

- Youths
- Couples

Promotional re-design
What type of promotion will appeal to these markets? We have seen that the previous package was very successful. Due to a seasonal fall off in demand this package has appeared to be unsuccessful. However, demand increases through the winter/spring months and the package will once again prove popular. It is my opinion that we need to change certain aspects of the evening and not the package itself.

An analysis of our competitors shows that similar glow bowling packages (e.g. cosmic bowling) involve prizes such as champagne. A successful Moonlight Bowling package will involve prize give-aways that are superior to previous Hollywood prizes and also the activities of our competitors.

Moonlight Bowling Experience
A typical Friday night shows a fall off in demand after 10 p.m. A suitable time to run the promotion would be from 10 p.m. until 1 a.m. Saturday night is normally busier during this period and would not be a feasible option. The moonlight package would be as follows:

- £6.85 per person
- 2 games
- 18–25s
- Burger munch box plus soft drink
- Additional games charged at £1.50 per person
- 10 p.m.–1 a.m. every Friday night

continued

Box 8.1.   *Continued.*

Event	Prizes
Pink Pin Strike	Bottle of Hollywood Bubbly
XXX	Bottle of Hollywood Bubbly + free game voucher for up to six people
Birthday	Bottle of Hollywood bubbly – free adult membership
Mystery Prize Voucher	T-shirt
Spot Prizes	Hit-the-Spot mug

Staffing levels
The direct staff to run a moonlight bowl:

- Receptionists (2)
- Security (2)
- Café servers (2)
- Lane servers (2)
- Technician (1)

---

for example, the access to remote mountain areas for skiing and other activities by lift systems has many social and economic benefits but causes concern in environmental terms, as demonstrated by the development of Albertville for the 1992 Winter Olympics or the long-running dispute over a chairlift extension in the Cairngorms. Clarke and Schmidt (1995) proposed that, in certain contexts, it is the aim of the service provider to link the service encounter in the consumer's mind with the environment encounter, thus creating repeat business and a long-term relationship.

Product technology

Product technology is concerned with tangibles such as facilities, equipment and technology in the activity itself. It includes buildings such as cinemas and leisure centres, the equipment within them and their use of technology as a feature of the product, such as screen and sound systems in cinemas or white-knuckle rides or simulators in visitor attractions.

Staff

Staff are also a key factor, because of the service encounter in many leisure and tourism contexts, and the interaction in such social settings defines the critical moments of truth. Receptionists, instructors, guides, attendants and waiters and waitresses are particular

front-line staff whose role is to animate, motivate and engage with customers.

Organization and control

This is the final element and, although regarded as bureaucratic, work procedures and other documentation and communication with customers are important aspects of service quality and also help with customer flow and circulation, as well as shaping attitudes. They can include ticket purchase, automatic entry, signage and sight lines, booking systems and the technology concerned with underpinning the delivery of the product (Box 8.2).

The leisure and tourism service process

The service process in leisure and tourism is the chain of activities and stages the customer goes through; it involves much interaction between the customer and the other inputs that make up the service system. It refers to functional quality (the how) as opposed to technical quality (the what) and, in many contexts, is more important in determining the overall quality of the consumer experience. Process management, design of the customer process and the service package are also assuming greater importance. The service process involves the variables of value, job task and the job environment as created

---

Box 8.2.   Case study: TGI Fridays.

TGI Fridays is one of the more innovative organizations in the leisure industry and sees itself as offering more than simply food and drink. It sets out to create a certain atmosphere in its restaurants and, with the provision for birthdays and other party groups and its high level of engagement with customers, its core product is more part of leisure provision than most food outlets. Product development involves managers in the marketing department at headquarters eating out several times a week to gain ideas, with other innovations coming from the USA. Feedback is also gained from mystery customer surveys, which are carried out every month, with results received by every restaurant every 4 months based on the overall percentage. Although the organization places great emphasis on the service encounter and the training of staff (see Chapter 14), technology is an important component in the delivery system. A computer system makes ordering quicker and more accurate and is also used to track the popularity of various offerings. A recent introduction is a computer-aided control system at the door to enhance the flow and seating arrangements of customers.

---

by the core logic and the three interfaces between service delivery by staff and customer perceptions of the service received. These three interfaces are described as: (i) the *encounter interface*, which links customer and employee logic through the values of the organization and the job environment, particularly with the significance of interpersonal relationships in high-contact services such as health and fitness and hospitality; (ii) the *technical interface*, which links customer and technical logic through value and work tasks and the customer's direct contact with technology and systems (important aspects are booking systems and the technology in visitor attraction sites); and (iii) the *support interface*, which links employee and technical logic through work tasks and the relationships between front-line and backstage staff.

Service value

The final component of the model returns to the needs and motives of the customer as identified or disseminated by the service concept. The model described provides a picture of the elements in the design of both the service and its system of production and delivery in leisure and tourism. It demonstrates the traditional view of production in which inputs are converted through a process into outputs or outcomes but also emphasizes the link, in the loop, between the organization's service concept and, eventually, the benefits that customers take away with them and

their satisfaction with how the benefits have been created.

Service value does not simply relate to the concept of value for money but also accounts for other variables such as cost, time (including travelling) and the general effort required for the activity (a problem faced by the Millennium Dome). These factors all have to be viewed within the context of increasing competing interests including not just other managed contexts for leisure and tourism but also the attractions of in-home entertainment.

The model provides a backcloth against which the service can be analysed and broken down to enhance its understanding by staff (and customers) and the way it is designed and managed. It facilitates the application of Juran's quality trilogy, highlighted in Chapter 4, which comprises the measurement and improvement of service delivery as well as its planning. However, the model does not necessarily highlight the interaction between the various components of the service system or some of the options open to management in their planning process. In order for managers to evaluate and to plan new developments, an understanding of the whole process is required.

Factors in Service Design

There are a number of key questions for the leisure or tourism operator to answer in determining the approach to service design in any particular context:

- What are the service concept and service package?
- Who are your customers?
- What standards do you wish to operate at?
- How can the package be delivered to the customers?

There are also supplementary questions:

- How standardized is the product and service?
- What is the level of psychological encounter?
- What are the customer's expectations?
- How technological is the operation?
- How complex is the process?
- What is the capacity of the operations?
- How productive is the delivery system and use of resources?

These questions underpin the entire process of planning and designing leisure and tourism services and represent a systematic approach. They also highlight a number of factors to be taken into account in designing the leisure and tourism product and service; they transcend the discreteness of the components in the model in Fig. 8.1 and indeed impact on them, but relate in particular to the service system.

Tangibles

An inevitable starting point is the tangibles of a product, since they are so often associated with the core element of the product and are integral to the first impressions created and the image presented. Tangibles also comprise several important elements:

Technology

So many contexts are influenced by the technology available and how it is utilized, from health and fitness facilities using sophisticated equipment to visitor attractions incorporating animatronics, simulators, virtual reality and white-knuckle rides. In the context of interpretation, Hines (1998) suggested that 'there is a growing realization that there is a synergetic relationship between the

visuals, the audio and the hardware which, if you get it right, creates a more transcendental experience'. Furthermore, the consumer experience is affected technologically not simply by the enhanced product *per se* but by the way it is delivered and administered. Booking systems, computerized access to facilities or ski lifts and improved information, signage and access all help to enhance the overall experience and the way it is managed.

Access

This ranges from the physical proximity of the facility to its market, transportation to it and parking (or provision of a train station in the case of Disneyland Paris), to provision for the disabled, and opening hours and programming policies.

Signage and sightlines

Circulation of people in large sites or buildings such as theme parks and airports can be greatly affected by the clarity and positioning of signs and notices (and the number – in some instances there are too many unnecessary notices). Sightlines for viewing in special events or museums or exhibitions are also critical in shaping consumer perceptions of the experience. Technology has helped, with sports stadia erecting large screens of the action, or providing more flexible configurations.

Health and safety

Many contexts in leisure and tourism contain a risk to safety, whether they are activities involving movement, or the congregation of people as spectators, or the provision of food and drink. There is the paradox in the case of, for example, theme parks or outdoor pursuits where the 'risk environment' or thrills from the activity are part of the attraction but where the consumer likes to feel that safety measure are still in place. In recent years, the design process has seen much attention to detail and procedures in white-knuckle rides, flumes and water slides, sun-beds, outdoor pursuits and football stadia.

Flexibility

It was noted earlier how the dynamism of leisure and tourism markets means that organizations must be able to respond quickly to market changes or, indeed, the competitive edge, which requires operators to innovate and experiment. Flexibility and adaptability built into facilities and systems and processes will enable the good operator to modify their product or service.

Aesthetic appeal

The concept of quality is a very subjective one but the leisure and tourism provider knows that the consumer experience is often affected by reaction to the decor, furnishings, colour scheme, architecture, landscaping or design of equipment and the challenge is to identify the features with the most widespread appeal. Public leisure centres no longer look like warehouses as they did in the 1970s. Free-form leisure pools transformed the physical impact of swimming pools into attractive, pleasant, relaxing environments. Center Parcs, with an 'all-the-year-round' holiday concept, have a large 'tropical dome' containing pools and other water features as the centrepiece of their operations. Futuroscope, in France, has combined the themes of leisure, education, technology and communications in a large, visually exciting site just outside Poitiers containing futuristic-looking buildings and a litter-free, landscaped site. Disney, in all its parks, has placed great importance on the quality of the environment with the visual impact of themed areas as well as the landscaping.

Atmosphere and ambience

The subjectivity of consumer perceptions is even more acute in the impact of the atmosphere of a facility and is perhaps the most difficult feature to design into a service package. Many of the factors cited earlier contribute to its overall impact. Customers will often point to the atmosphere of a restaurant or theatre, or even a leisure complex, as part of its attractiveness. Staffing as well as decor and lighting all play a part and, as

will be seen later, even the customer's own contribution is a factor. Fans at football stadia, racegoers at the Cheltenham Gold Cup Festival, visitors to the Edinburgh Fringe Festival and members of an aerobics group all shape the very atmosphere to which they are attracted. The design of Center Parcs' sports and swimming facilities provides an example of flexibility, attractiveness, relaxation and technology:

> Settle into our cosy villas, tucked away amongst the trees. Enjoy the Subtropical Swimming Paradise, the sports, leisure, Spa facilities and our own mini health and beauty retreat, Aqua Sana. Make your holiday simple or indulgent, busy or lazy. Share it with family or friends. It's a short break that thinks it's a long holiday – and with so many options, all you have to do is choose.

Social accountability

There is increasing pressure to take issues of sustainability, ethics and community relations into account in designing and redesigning services in leisure and tourism. Examples include energy consumption, ecotourism, climate change and conflict between recreational users and landowners. On the other hand, the social and economic benefits to an area or region are also promoted, and accounted, in examples such as Futuroscope and the Millennium Dome.

Focus

The extent to which organizations are focused is also part of the design process. The concept of focused strategies and operations has long applied to manufacturing industry and it was Johnston (1996, p. 12) who suggested that 'it was only a matter of time before the concept of focus was applied to service organizations'. He argued that service organizations can benefit from focus and that it can occur at different levels.

The **first level of focus** is the service concept and it can apply in one of four different ways, according to the number of markets and breadth of services offered:

1. *A market- and service-focused organization* provides a narrow product or service to a specific market segment. Many golf clubs fall into this category, as does Gulliver's Travels offering sports tours, or the Broadgate Health and Fitness Club in London providing a luxury, high-priced facility, or Leapfrog International offering expertise in special events organization and management.

2. *A market-focused organization* provides a range of services to a narrow market as in, for example, local authority youth services or Saga providing a range of service for the older consumer.

3. *A service-focused organization* provides a specific product or service to a wide market. Examples include cinemas, swimming pools, libraries, urban parks, museums and tourist information services. Alton Towers' service concept is 'to provide an inclusive package of magnificent surroundings, historic heritage, fun and fantasy to suit all ages and tastes'. The Young Vic Theatre in London has a service concept that attempts to make the theatre accessible to everyone; staff are encouraged to to be informal and friendly with black T-shirts and no uniform in reception.

4. *Unfocused organizations* provide a wide range of services to everybody. Some organizations are unfocused at the service concept level and choose to be focused at the business level – the **second level of focus**. This tends to be large conglomerates that specialize within divisions or on particular sites. For example, Whitbread caters for a number of different markets through several brands, including the David Lloyd Centres and the TGI Fridays chain. Thomas Cook sells the following range of products/services: holidays; flights; foreign exchange; travel vouchers; insurance; car hire; car parking; airport hotels; phone cards; stamps; guidebooks; maps; European rail timetables; Moneygram. The aim is to capitalize on the quality associated with the brand name of Thomas Cook (although the recent acquisition of JMC Holidays has not been an initial success, with poor levels of service quality and customer satisfaction).

The **third level of focus** occurs at the site level where a number of different facilities or resources cater for a wide range of activities and markets. Gloucester Hotel and Country Club is a reasonably small example, containing a mix of hotel, a 'Sebastian Coe Health Park', sports facilities including golf and squash and an additional market of activity breaks, and, as a separate venture, a regional dry ski slope. The Link Centre in Swindon contains a leisure centre, library and health clinic under the same roof.

The **fourth level of focus** is almost one of vertical integration on the one site and embraces focus on the service delivery system. There may be a little overlap with the site focus highlighted in the previous category but an example requiring thoughtful design and an understanding of its service logic would be a health farm such as Inglewood Hydro in Berkshire or Grayshott Hall in Surrey, where many guests will move between specialist functions such as fitness, beauty treatment, aromatherapy and nutrition.

Finally, some organizations may remain unfocused at the service concept, business, site and service delivery levels and be happy to offer a wide range of services to everybody. Perhaps some local authority leisure services are the most appropriate example in the leisure and tourism industry although some commercial organizations such as Whitbread have a wide portfolio of interests.

The service encounter

The level of psychological encounter between staff and customers varies greatly across the leisure and tourism industry but its importance in achieving customer satisfaction is well documented (Bitner, 1990; Walker, 1995; Normann, 2000; Lee-Ross 2001). Some operations (e.g. TGI Fridays or Disney) build customer contact into their service concept and package, and train and prepare key personnel for engaging in conversation with guests. The use of script theory provides further evidence for the opportunity in the design process to manage and manipulate exchange and rapport between staff and customers. Thomas Cook refers to its customer moments of truth and trains its staff to put themselves in their customers' 'shoes', as the case study in Box 8.3 shows.

As the model in Fig. 8.1 showed, a critical factor in many leisure and tourism contexts is the service encounter and how it is managed. Some observers regard the service encounter as the contact between staff and customers; it is interesting that many of the SERVQUAL dimensions of quality highlighted in Chapter 13 are concerned with human attributes. Yet others perceive it to be a wider concept that reflects any contact the customer has with the organization within the process of consumption. Danaher and Mattsson (1998, p. 48)

suggested that 'rather than just the one interaction, the summation of all the service encounters with the service provider are evaluated by the customer'.

Walker (1995) argued that service performance takes place within the service encounter, which includes facilities, procedures and systems as well as people. He suggested that, in addition to the influence of zones of tolerance, customer satisfaction is determined by the impact of three stages of the service encounter. The first and third are more concerned with peripheral aspects, linked to pre-performance and post-performance evaluations and may involve initial contact with the organization, perhaps in booking or initial enquiries, as well as the process of

---

Box 8.3.   Thomas Cook Moments of Truth Dos and Don'ts.

ENTERING THE STORE

DO THIS

I want to be acknowledged and greeted and want to see it happening to other customers as well.

I want you to come to me to start the conversation.

Ask me if I need help and take the time to find out what I really want.

Sometimes I just want brochures but I still want someone to talk to me and suggest holiday ideas.

It may be obvious but I want you to be friendly and smile.

I want to be dealt with courteously and see you doing the same for other customers.

If your shop is small and empty, think carefully about how you approach me. It can sometimes be intimidating.

DO NOT DO THIS

Don't leave me hovering in the doorway. It can be quite intimidating coming into a shop you do not know.

Don't be too pushy and persistently try to help me if I want to be left to my own devices.

COLLECTING BROCHURES

DO THIS

If I have a specialist request, then do get back up from other colleagues, and use the travel guides I know you've got.

Give me plenty of information on the resort and fact sheets if you have them.

I would like to be given brochures that tell me about the country I am visiting.

Talk me through the brochures and explain them to me.

Give me advice on which brochures to take, help me to narrow the choice down.

Lay out your brochures in a way that makes sense.

Respect my right to just look and browse if that is all I want to do.

Ask me about what I want from the holiday to ensure I get the right brochure.

DO NOT DO THIS

Don't pile me up with brochures when I need help.

Don't run out of brochures. This is very annoying.

departure or follow-up by the organization. There are contexts in leisure and tourism where there is a blurring between these stages and the second stage – the actual service delivery and performance, more concerned with the core product. Walker (1995) explained how customer satisfaction can change through the stages according to the manner with which complaints are dealt.

The service encounter and the role of the customer

The role of the customer is often more significant in services than in manufacturing industry and within services the involvement of the customer can also be more distinctive in the leisure, tourism and hospitality industry. It can be argued that the customer is inseparable from the service delivery system (Canziani, 1997) and Normann (2000) pointed out how the customer can appear twice in the service management system, both as consumer and as part of the service delivery system (as a co-producer). Furthermore, the customer's own contribution can help to enhance the overall experience and reinforce the view that the customer be regarded as a resource or input to be managed.

There are several ways in which the customer can participate in the service process:

1. The customer can *specify* some aspects of the service with different-priced tickets in theatres or airlines, different categories of membership in health and fitness facilities and golf clubs, or the design of a 'tailor-made' holiday.
2. The customer can be a *co-producer* in performing certain tasks, as in many facets of the voluntary sector such as sports clubs.
3. The customer can help to *maintain the ethos* of the organization in that the service encounter and the interaction can provide staff with great job satisfaction and fulfilment, particularly where there is some empowerment in place.
4. Customers can often be seen as *quality control* in that they observe and receive the work of employees and act as a check if things go wrong. The mystery guest method

employed by many organizations illustrates the possibilities of this.
5. Customers are also involved in *selling and promoting* facilities and establishments through word of mouth or the use of their happy smiling faces in publicity material, as seen in holiday brochures or advertisements.

For example, Holmes Place at Redwood Lodge in Bristol views all customer feedback positively and uses a 'moments of truth' book at reception to record comments. Whenever a member of staff receives a comment or suggestion, it is noted in the book and is discussed at a daily meeting, with responsive action agreed and implemented where appropriate. It also provides the basis for a response to the customer.

In designing the service package and service delivery system, the way in which the customer is involved raises several questions:

- How much customer participation is required?
- How much interaction with staff is encouraged?
- How is the interaction between customers/participants planned for?
- What are the implications for resource efficiency?
- What levels of customer competency are required?

The level of customer participation

We have seen how some contexts in leisure and tourism require, or allow, considerable participation in the service and its creation. Many instructional classes in a range of activities are highly participative; interactive experiences in museums and heritage centres, audiences in sports and entertainment venues or education as leisure all provide opportunities for active and creative participation.

The level of the service encounter with staff

It is also necessary to consider the impact that both customer and provider have on each other and how this is particularly significant in some contexts. There is a growing argument (Svensson, 2001) that the service encounter should be viewed as a dyadic or even triadic relationship in which the various actors (consumer, front-line employee and possibly manager) help to shape each other's perceptions, and that it should therefore be measured as such rather than in a 'uni-directional way'. For example, the aerobics class will certainly respond positively to an enthusiastic, competent and warm instructor and, likewise, the instructor's performance and attitude will be affected by the approach and response of the class. Thus, there is a shared experience between staff and customer and the contribution of one will impact on the levels of satisfaction of the other. Furthermore, the impact of the front-line employee can be significant if customizing the service for the customer, even within services that are ostensibly standardized (Bettencourt and Gwinner, 1996) in, for example, some of the health club chains.

The customer as part of the service concept and package

Not only can customers be regarded as partial employees but also their contribution to the features of the product and service can be an additional dimension, and in some cases an integral part, of the overall experience. The interaction between customers provides much satisfaction for many people and much participation in a range of activities incorporates the motive of socialization. Therefore, the very presence of other people is an important prerequisite to social events, many sporting activities, certain aspects of visitor attraction sites and other social contexts such as restaurants and bars. One of the attractions of the Cheltenham Gold Cup horse-racing festival every March, despite queues and crowded conditions, is the very atmosphere created by the 45,000 to 50,000 people squeezed into the racecourse. Similarly, thousands of spectators in sports such as football, rugby and ice hockey are attracted by the noise, singing and social bonding of which they are part. Furthermore, it can also be recognized that providers are also affected by the actions and behaviours of customers.

The customer as a productive resource

In viewing the interaction between customers and the organization, the implications for resource efficiency must also be considered. There is a continuum from reducing the impact of customer participation to a minimum, to avoid potential for mistakes or variation or demands on staff, to seeing the customer as a productive resource. As Bitner et al. (1997, p. 202) suggested: 'Services can be delivered most efficiently if customers truly are viewed as partial employees and their participative roles are designed to maximise their contributions to the service creation process.'

The implications for the skills of consumption

Where participation is encouraged and where service design accounts and plans for it, the skills or competences required of customers also raise an important question. How is the level of customer competence identified, to what extent is the provider involved in developing such competences and what is its potential for enhancing the quality of the experience and overall customer satisfaction? Canziani (1997) defined customer competency in terms of the fit between customer inputs (knowledge, skills and motivation) and the task roles required of customers (Table 8.1). The table also highlights the three categories of task roles: generic consumer competency; product core competency in health spas; and competencies in systems and procedures specific to a single organization.

The customer inputs of skills, knowledge and motives are also more significant because of the impact of technology and the competitive edge. Leisure and tourism operators are competing not simply with each other but with the increasing dominance of in-home entertainment. The consumption skills required to take part in sport, activity holidays or some visitor attractions can be seen as either a challenge or an opportunity for the industry. In some cases, the skills required become the service package, as in instructional classes. In other instances, especially with more demanding activities, the investment in time, effort and money by the consumer can help the provider to cement the relationship with the

Table 8.1.   Customer task roles and related customer inputs.

Customer tasks	Related customer inputs
Generic tasks	
Planning – assess personal needs for services	Literacy
Budgeting – assess available resources	Mathematics
Scheduling – bookings or appointments	Statistics
Communicating – tell service provider what needs are	Language fluency
Directing – tell service provider how to provide service	Interpersonal skills
Coordinating – the service system and its delivery	Problem solving/use of technology
Mediating – reduce gaps between process and employees	Cultural diversity
Evaluating – performance and customer satisfaction	Measurement techniques
Controlling – use of feedback	
Product core tasks for health spa	
Preparing a dietary plan	Nutritional guidelines
Planning weight-training circuit	Knowledge of anatomy and physiology
Timing heartbeat rates	Aerobics specifications
Sport	Knowledge of rules and equipment
Organization-specific tasks	
Signing up for an aerobics class	Scheduling and payment details
Turning on the sauna	Specific technical knowledge
Getting hand towels	Procedures knowledge
Organizing trim trail	Location knowledge

customer. From the perspective of the provider, there are also certain tools and measures that can enhance this relationship and the way the service is understood and designed.

Tools of Service Design

The model of service delivery in Fig. 8.1 demonstrates the interaction between various components and the translation of the service concept into a managed process with particular outcomes. It highlights the way the service delivery system is controlled and managed but there is a need to examine what Kingman-Brundage *et al.* (1995) described as 'pre-service management functions'. There are various methods or tools that describe the processes involved and the way in which an understanding of those processes can enhance the management of the leisure and tourist experience and help managers to cope with the challenges that service characteristics such as intangibility provide. They do this by depicting the service system and the planning, organizing, directing and controlling functions.

Service process flowcharts

The first of these tools is called *flowcharting* and is concerned with the consumer process and the sequence of actions, stages and activities that the consumer encounters and experiences. A service process flowchart follows the same principles as a manufacturing process and in engineering style will involve yes/no questions and responses. It incorporates an analysis of the duties and tasks of each front-line member of staff but also demonstrates how they are linked. A receptionist in a leisure centre deals with bookings, ticket sales, enquiries and queries but is not necessarily aware what happens when users encounter attendants, instructors or catering staff.

A health club provides a reasonably straightforward example of customer flow and its service encounters (Fig. 8.2). The stages and their moments of truth are depicted to demonstrate the contact or encounter with front-line staff or systems or procedures, which are evident to the customer as they go though the service process. From the initial decision (based on their knowledge of the facility and its marketing) to leaving the

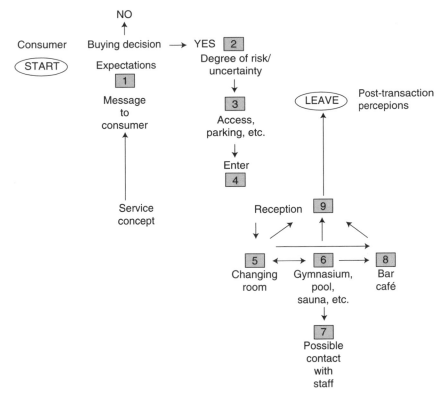

Fig. 8.2. Flowchart/moments of truth (health club).

premises, there are decisions or perceptual consequences of actions resulting in the final levels of satisfaction, and the decision whether to return (or eventually renew membership). What the flowchart fails to reveal is the actions and operations of the organization, which take place away from the service encounters but which impact on them. It is important to note how the operations interact not only with the external customer but with the internal customer and, particularly, how the front-line employee is supported behind the scenes. A method of demonstrating this is service blueprinting.

Service blueprints

A more complex approach matches the consumer process with the service system and demonstrates the interaction that takes place. It shows how a *service map* or *blueprint* depicts

a consumer process and its relationship with the service process. The map embraces the management function and intent at the bottom and how it relates to the requirements of customers who enter the map at the top. According to Laws (1999, p. 279), 'Service blueprinting is a diagram which shows all the elements that go to make up the service studied. It records and maps the events and processes which the customer experiences.'

Service blueprints demonstrate in a number of stages how management defines the service concept, allocates resources and coordinates the functions within the operation to implement the service concept:

1. Management defines or refines service concept. A clear example of the redefining of a service concept is the attempt in recent years of some Spanish resorts to upgrade their facilities and their image from their earlier development as concrete destinations for the mass package holiday market.

2. Management allocates resources – to what extent is the decision driven by a customer focus?

3. Management coordinates functions. Where everybody understands the service logic, this becomes a smooth, cohesive operation. The success and image of Disney can be partly attributed to such an approach.

4. Marketing develops advertising and sales promotion. An understanding of the service concept and how it can be communicated successfully to customers also depends on a fully integrated approach. Recent promotions by Center Parcs have successfully combined the sense of relaxation and tranquility associated with aspects of their product with the activity focus that also attracts people.

5. Response by customers. Much will depend on initial perceptions and the skill and understanding of staff in dealing with customers.

6. Front-line personnel greet customers. The service encounter, whether as a prelude to the core activity or as part of the core activity (with a fitness instructor, tour guide or waiter), defines many 'moments of truth'. Its effectiveness will often be determined by the fit between customer logic (the customer's needs and motives), technical logic (how the service outcomes are produced and why) and employee logic (what the employee is trying to do and why).

7. Shall I buy? The value the customer attaches to the expectations of the service is particularly important at this stage.

8. Special requests. The extent to which service systems have flexibility built into them will always be tested here. TGI Fridays allows customers to request individual requirements, within certain constraints.

9. The service is produced. The test of any operation is how seamlessly this process is carried out. Many have witnessed operations in restaurants, airports or holiday companies where the lack of cooperation and understanding between personnel in different functions was marked and resulted in a service breakdown.

10. Customer experiences the service outcome. This, of course, is often as the outcomes

are produced and is one of the biggest tests of the efficacy of the service design.

11. The remaining stages are concerned with evaluation and feedback and provide the link between service design and a total quality approach based on continuous improvement.

Posing and answering these questions provides many useful insights into the technical, and particularly functional, aspects of service quality. The performance of the organization, its interactive nature and outcomes achieved make up the service process but also require a wider view than this. In addition to process, service blueprinting also considers structure and how process and structure are inextricably linked in the best organizations. Service blueprints help to illustrate the model of service delivery and the interaction between its various components and enable the design and implementation of the service package and delivery system to be much more informed and appropriate. Fache (2000) argued that blueprinting enables attention to be focused on three key factors in achieving service quality: design; the role of staff; and the interactions between staff and customers.

To plot and read a service blueprint effectively requires systematic thinking, which embraces both the customer process and the service process or organizational structure. To examine the customer process and the service encounter with staff involves following the map in Fig. 8.3 horizontally from left to right and along the *line of interaction* and this highlights the potential moments of truth. Following the map from bottom to top through several lines of demarcation reveals the nature and clarity of the service logic and the structure of backstage and support functions in the organization. The *line of visibility* separates the front-line or on-stage operations from the backstage functions. On-stage duties are those that are visible to the public. Backstage duties are performed by contact staff but away from public gaze. It might be fitness instructors preparing their session, entertainers practising their routines, retail operators restocking or tour guides being trained for the substance and delivery of their material. Both on-stage and backstage

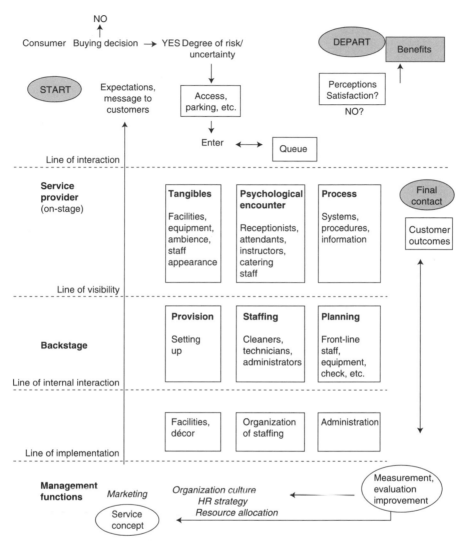

Fig. 8.3. Service blueprinting of a health club.

operations are supported by other functions and these are separated by the line of *internal interactions* and emphasize the importance of the quality chain and the concept of the internal customer. Disney theme parks are noted for their costumed characters and the friendliness and knowledge of other on-stage staff; yet they are dependent on thousands of support staff who supply the costumes (the largest theatrical wardrobes in the world) and uniforms, train staff in the 'Disney University', service the rides or supply the shops, restaurants and bars. This line, in particular, demonstrates the importance of

understanding the 'wider picture' incorporating the service concept and the service logic of the organization. Finally, the *line of implementation* separates the on-stage, backstage and support functions from the planning and organizing functions of management and the policy making and decision making this requires.

It follows that service blueprints can be used to design new services, to evaluate and modify existing ones and to control and manage service delivery. They help to communicate the values and nature of the service concept to everybody in the organization.

They connect employees with each other as well as with the external customer; they help different departments or functions to understand the notion of the internal customer. They represent, in particular, the unified or integrated approach so critical to the achievement of service quality and enhance the provision and management of service encounters and are an important stage in the process of operationalizing dimensions of quality in specific contexts. However, their ability to determine the dimensions or attributes of quality is less secure and, increasingly, organizations must formalize the way they identify customer requirements and incorporate them into the planning process.

Quality function deployment

A third tool for planning and designing a service package in leisure and tourism, which addresses customer requirements, is based on a method called quality function deployment (QFD). QFD has been applied successfully to manufacturing industry, particularly by the Japanese (it started in the Mitsubishi organization at the Kobe shipyards in 1972), but although its potential for services has been acknowledged in recent years (Lapidus and Schibrowski, 1994; Ghobadian and Terry, 1995; Stuart and Tax, 1996; Chin et al., 2001) little application, especially in leisure and tourism, has occurred to date. QFD has been variously described as a system, method, process or philosophy but its distinctiveness is the systematic way in which customer requirements are translated into the technical requirements of the product or service. Han et al. (2001) defined QFD as:

> a structured approach to seek out customers and understand their needs. It begins by matching customer requirements with the necessary corresponding design requirements, which in turn match with the necessary corresponding production requirements, and so on, to ensure that the needs of the customer are met . . .

QFD also reflects total quality management philosophy, as discussed in Chapter 4, as it emphasizes customer requirements,

continuous improvement and an integrated or holistic approach across the organization. It also embraces the constant need to listen to the customer, the VOC (voice of the customer), and all the methods considered in Chapter 13 for identifying customer requirements and measuring customer satisfaction levels.

Stuart and Tax (1996) argued that the features and assumptions of QFD are extremely relevant to services and can effectively meet the needs of service design. They highlighted several principles in presenting their case:

1. *QFD provides a common focus for the marketing, human resource management, service operations and ICT functions* in the organization and encourages the unified approach that is so important in service design and delivery. A clearer understanding of the service logic in the organization is likely, with everybody more conscious of the impact of their decisions and actions on attributes of the service.
2. *QFD recognizes that service design and process management must be customer led* and that the attributes of the service align with customer needs and wants. The causes of Gap 1 in the SERVQUAL model in Chapter 13 would be addressed by the QFD process and the service concept would be sensitive to market factors.
3. *QFD, therefore, highlights the importance of the service encounter and moments of truth* and the need to analyse each interaction in the service process.
4. *The overview provided by QFD enables the 'trade-offs' between features to be weighed up and evaluated*; for example, improving access to a site and enhancing its amenities but attracting visitors who may then impact on its perceptual capacity and quality; or adding to the features of an airline service (as Virgin Airlines does) with the risk of making more mistakes or standardizing or speeding up the delivery of a service but with the danger of making it less personal.

QFD in services is based on a three-part process that represents service planning (design requirements), element planning (service process elements and service delivery development) and operations planning

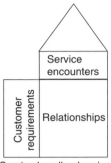
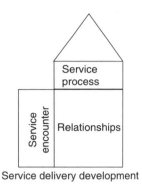
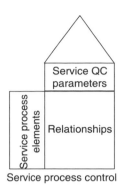

Service bundle planning   Service delivery development   Service process control

Fig. 8.4.   The houses of quality.

(process control) (Fig. 8.4). QFD, therefore, has three principal objectives: (i) to identify the customer; (ii) to identify what the customer needs or wants; and (iii) how to meet the customer's requirements.

Ghobadian and Terry (1995) explained the use of a form of QFD by the airline Alitalia, for designing a new Intercontinental Business Class service. They went through six phases in the process:

PHASE 1: IDENTIFICATION OF CUSTOMER REQUIRE-MENTS.   Alitalia, interestingly, used a team of managers to identify customer requirements in three categories: quality of flight attendants; quality of in-flight products; and quality of cabin environment. Ideally, customers would be involved, and the various techniques for measuring customers' views highlighted in Chapter 13 would be used.

PHASE 2: OBTAINING CUSTOMER IMPORTANCE RATINGS.   This phase also takes us back to customer satisfaction measurement and the benefits of establishing the importance that customers attach to different attributes of the service. Alitalia asked 3000 customers to rate the importance of service features and to compare Alitalia's performance with the 'ideal airline'. Cross-functional team meetings then determined the target quality level for each attribute as they were ranked by customers.

PHASE 3: IDENTIFICATION OF QUALITY ELEMENTS. This phase is related to functional quality and the team identified the measurable design features of the service together with the

methods and processes necessary for the service delivery.

PHASE 4: CONSTRUCTION OF CORRELATION MIX. This phase is important in order to achieve quality. Phases 1 and 3 enhanced understanding, but there is a need to demonstrate how the quality elements would meet customer requirements. Alitalia used a matrix with 47 customer requirements and 87 quality elements to establish the strength of the correlation between them (1 weak, 3 average and 9 strong).

PHASE 5: FEASIBILITY STUDY.   Pragmatism determines that the improvement to quality elements has to be planned over a number of cycles because of the technical, cost and reliability constraints. Alitalia attempted to quantify these by calculating the difficulty involved on a scale of 1 to 10 (10 being the most difficult) for each quality element and placing them in a matrix, which also presented the significance of each element by multiplying the correlations in phase 4 by the absolute weights of the customer requirements and adding them together.

PHASE 6: QUALITY PLANNING AND IMPLEMENTATION. This is what makes all the work in the first five phases worthwhile. The first four phases were concerned with identifying customer requirements, setting targets and determining how the service package could meet those requirements. Phase 5 acknowledged the constraints, which meant that the inevitable trade-offs would have to be managed by prioritizing planned improvements. Phase 6 represents the planning and implementation of the improvements: Alitalia achieved this by setting up four cross-functional teams, with each addressing a different facet. As a result, in 1993, a new business class service was introduced and improvements were made to seat pitch, seat comfort, seat design, interior design, food and duty-free range.

Application to a visitor attraction

A modern visitor attraction can be used to illustrate the application of the QFD to the analysis of the service's attributes and the needs of its customers. The process is progressive and begins with the identification of the attributes of the product or service which, of course, draw on the service concept. The service concept of the Olympic Museum in Lausanne might be an up-to-date, technologically sophisticated, informative and exciting presentation in delightful surroundings overlooking Lake Geneva. The technique translates the service concept into service bundle attributes and their relationship with service encounters in House 1 (Fig. 8.5). The attributes might be an extremely pleasant location, interesting/educational display, consumer participation and demeanour of staff, which

might be broken down further into more specific attributes. Service encounters, representing moments of truth (positive or negative), would occur at entry (reception), each major display, points of information and the restaurant.

House 2 (Fig. 8.6) then takes each service encounter and identifies the elements of the service process that represent customer needs. The encounters with the different displays or aspects of the museum would be concerned with the visual impact of the displays, their interest and excitement, their educational value, ease of circulation and the nature of the technology and overall environment. We shall address the service encounter at reception. The staff at the ticket desk have an important role in not simply admitting customers but also providing information about customer flow, timing, the technology (including tokens for viewing videos) and retail and catering opportunities – all done with a smile. The key characteristics are therefore the attentiveness, friendliness and helpfulness of staff, the speed of response, and the accuracy and clarity of information provided. It is necessary to bear in mind here the importance of service attributes and how they can be classified, and explained, as satisfiers, dissatisfiers and

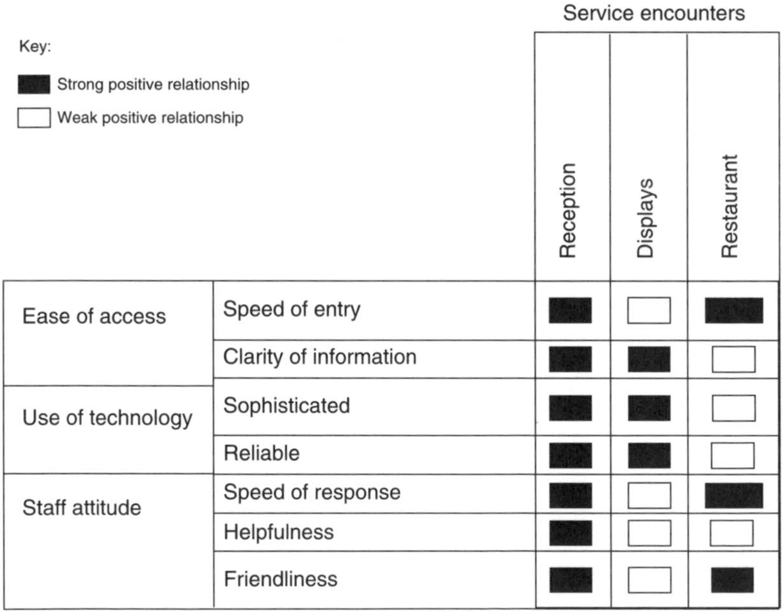

Fig. 8.5. House 1: service bundle planning, Olympic Museum, Lausanne.

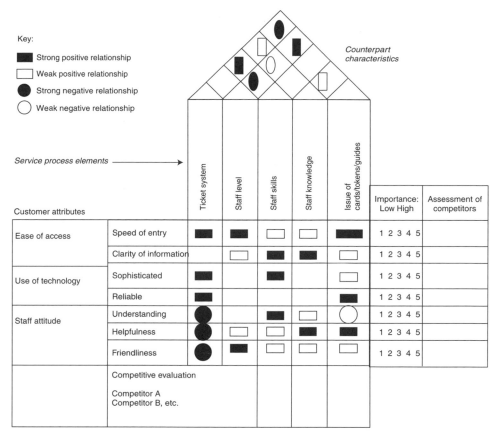

Fig. 8.6.   House 2: service delivery development in the reception service encounter.

delighters. Satisfiers tend to be associated with the core product (such as the film at a cinema or the game of squash at a leisure complex) and are constantly assessed by the customer – and have the potential to delight. Dissatisfiers tend not to be noticed until they go wrong because they are not the main attraction but enable the core product to be consumed – examples are parking or toilets or reception. The right-hand side of the house therefore denotes the relative importance of the customer attributes.

The next step is the development of counterpart characteristics. They represent the means of the organization to meet the attributes and requirements of the customer for each service encounter. For example, the scope for some involvement or participation is facilitated by the museum's use of state-of-the-art technology. However, the museum's use of technology also means that much of the usage or access to areas of provision is automatic, resulting in lack of contact with staff; this mitigates against the customer attribute of attentiveness and friendliness of staff and illustrates the benefits of QFD in identifying the trade-offs involved in planning and designing services. There will be positive and negative relationships between attributes and different counterpart characteristics. The house helps the organization to establish these relationships much more quickly and accurately. It is important to note that if a row in the house remains empty then the organization has failed to identify an element of provision to meet the specific customer requirement, requiring one of them to be reassessed.

The next stage in the house examines the interrelationships between counterpart characteristics and is shown in the roof of the house. It represents an effective way of making strategic decisions in the allocation of resources and the design of the delivery system and the consideration of further trade-offs. For example, the customer attributes of speed of response/access (no queues) is difficult to square with the desired attentiveness and helpfulness of staff who may have a number of questions to answer. The museum has to decide whether to provide more staff at reception, which may reduce its ability to direct resources into updating displays, or to have more staff around the different displays to provide the attentive and responsive service desired by customers.

The aspect to this stage provides the opportunity to measure the importance of each customer attribute and to gauge them against those of close competitors, thereby further refining QFD's ability to address the two objectives of maximizing customer satisfaction and optimizing the use of resources. A high importance rating for an attribute together with low rating for a competitor signifies considerable competitive advantage. A low rating for an attribute and a high rating for a competitor suggests a low priority for action. The museum, perhaps, can give slightly less attention to the range and attractiveness of its food and drink items because of the beautiful views over Lake Geneva from its rooftop terrace. A health club may find that its customers tend to regard the competence and attitude of staff more highly than the nature and extent of equipment – the feature of a rival facility.

House 3 finally links the service process elements with key aspects of operations that control the process and its outputs to ensure customer satisfaction for each service encounter and builds on the format of House 1. At reception, for example, staff's speed at admitting people could be enhanced by training in the use of technology and their knowledge of the whole process in order to answer any specific questions. Their attitude will be affected by their dress, what they say to customers

(script theory) and their manner (courtesy, friendliness and helpfulness). An additional advantage of QFD is its ability to identify the existence, and strength, of any relationships between different elements.

QFD, therefore, is a reasonably complex and quantitative approach to planning and designing services (still being adapted from its manufacturing origins) which encapsulates many of the facets of service quality, and particularly total quality management, which this book has examined. For QFD to work in a leisure or tourism organization, the following features should be present: (i) a market driven approach; (ii) clearly identified customer requirements based on both internal and external customers; (iii) commitment to continuous improvement; (iv) systematic use of tools and techniques for achieving this; (v) clear culture and vision; (vi) teamwork and cross-functional teams; and (vii) a unified and integrated approach.

Conclusions

This chapter has considered the processes and methods involved in designing quality into the leisure and tourism product or service and the way it is consumed. In highlighting the factors that are significant in designing service systems and processes, it has examined the elements and components of service design and presented an integrated approach to their management to meet customer requirements as fully as possible. Methods and tools such as blueprinting and quality function deployment help to achieve integration as well as reflecting customer-driven approaches. Such approaches also highlight the need to achieve productive potential, as well as to maximize customer satisfaction, and the next chapter considers the management of capacity across leisure and tourism operations and its relationship with the achievement of service quality.

9

Capacity Management and Organizational Performance

Introduction

This chapter addresses a number of operational issues that are particularly significant in the management of service quality in leisure and tourism. They link with other aspects of the book and especially the principles of service design and delivery in Chapter 8. The management of capacity draws on the core elements of service operations management, and in particular, the aim of reconciling the maximization of customer satisfaction with the optimum use of resources and the pragmatism of budgetary control. In the context of visitor attractions there is now a national code of practice to encourage high standards of customer care, maintenance and safety, and, of course, similar codes of practice in adventure leisure and tourism.

The purpose of this chapter is to examine the nature of leisure and tourism services and products and to highlight the problems, or challenges, of variable demand and yield management and their implications for the delivery of service quality.

On completion of the chapter it is expected that you will be able to:

- understand the relationship between capacity management, service standards and service quality;
- apply the knowledge and skills of controlling supply and manipulating demand;
- understand the process and psychology of queuing and the means for reducing customer dissatisfaction with waiting;

- appreciate the principles of yield management and their implications for the management of capacity;
- critically understand the relationship between the management of capacity, service standards and organizational performance;
- recognize the need for service specifications, customer charters and service guarantees;
- recognize the importance that performance indicators have to the success of quality management systems.

Service Quality and Operations Management

There is a key relationship between the management of resources and the management of service quality. Johnston and Clark (2001) suggested that service operations are the configuration of resources and processes to create and deliver the service offering to customers. Many of the facets of capacity management are linked with the control and regulation of demand. They can be viewed as problems or as natural elements of the consumption experience and even, perhaps, an opportunity to be exploited. Good capacity management means that the organization can cope with any level of demand without its affecting levels of customer satisfaction; it can meet its targets and its customers' requirements whilst its systems, procedures and resources are stretched. Most contexts in leisure and tourism experience pressures of this nature. Visitor attractions, especially theme parks, are affected by seasonality and can experience long queues. Airlines have queues at their check-in desks and often have to manage the problem of delays or over-booking; national parks and other popular areas can experience real overcrowding and use various methods to control the problem. There can be problems of erosion and over-demand, with some facilities also suffering from slack usage or demand and using other methods to even out demand.

Capacity management is concerned with achieving a balance between extreme posi-tions and clearly reflects the objectives of service operations management, which are to reconcile the maximization of customer satis-faction with the optimum usage of resources. The problems of overloading, especially at peak times when there are queues or per-ceived overcrowding, can affect customer satisfaction and service quality and, indeed, lose custom through people going elsewhere either at the time or subsequently after a poor experience. Pressure on resources, especially staff, can lead to mistakes or rushed imper-sonal service, leading to customer dissatisfac-tion and a drop in service standards.

However, problems of overcapacity or underwhelmed customers can also affect the quality of the consumption experience. Some contexts that are too quiet detract from the atmosphere and experience that customers are anticipating, or present images of failure or unpopularity in the minds of suspicious customers. For example, a restaurant or cin-ema that is empty lacks some of the attributes one expects from such a context, and poorly attended sporting venues do not develop the atmosphere that attracts people in the first instance. Staff in such environments do not always enjoy the lack of involvement and atmosphere and also begin to build up a negative image of the organization.

Capacity Management and 'Real Time' Service Delivery

Capacity, therefore, is not necessarily a straightforward concept to examine. It can certainly be viewed in terms of its resources and their impact on numbers of customers at any given time, as with a cinema, fitness club, airport or theme park. Yet time is also a key variable and much depends on the speed with which customers are processed, whether there is a fixed time (as with some sports, a special event or a guided tour) or the duration of the visit or experience is highly variable (as with tourists on a beach, or visi-tors to a museum or art gallery). In catering, the service concept incorporates this approach as in 'fast-food' outlets encourag-ing a rapid throughput and turnover (even through the use of bright colours in their décor – which stimulates people to eat more quickly) or the 'gourmet' restaurant, which offers the table for the evening. The Jorvik Centre in York, in contrast, received com-plaints when it attempted to speed up its ride to reduce the length of queues.

The concept of capacity is also compli-cated by the characteristics of service delivery considered in Chapter 8. The issue of intangi-bility means that output cannot be stored and lost capacity in the guise of theatre seats or swimmers or holidaymakers cannot be recovered. The corollary means that uneven demand cannot be smoothed out since consumption takes place as the service is produced (inseparability). Furthermore, the uncertainty of demand and delivery in many contexts is compounded by the uncertainty over the time it takes to process some custom-ers highlighted in the previous paragraph – a 'stochastic' pattern, which results in queuing and is one of the main features and problems of capacity management in leisure and tourism operations (as will be considered in more detail a little later). It is easier to predict demand and patterns of usage where there is a single product, such as a cinema film or a gym, but where the product is mixed and complex, as in multi-activity sports and leisure facilities or theme parks, the notion of heterogeneity means that it is very difficult to predict with any accuracy the decision making of consumers as they move around.

The real-time nature of leisure and tourism services means that the likelihood of consistently matching actual output to poten-tial output is very uncertain and is dependent on three main factors: (i) the management of demand through the range of services, pricing policies and marketing; (ii) the management of usage through programming, scheduling, queuing theory and coping strategies; and (iii) the extent of capacity leakages when staff are late or absent or when facilities or equipment are out of commission.

Output, sales and usage in leisure and tourism operations are determined by productive capacity, which also affects customers' perceptions and their overall satisfaction with the experience. Perceptual capacity is a difficult facet of provision for organizations to plan for because of variations in consumer behaviour and helps to explain the fine line that providers have to tread between customer satisfaction and maximizing participation (which is considered a little later in this chapter). Whatever the nature of perceptual capacity and the context being managed, organizations need to plan their operations strategically.

Operational Strategies

There are two broad strategies that organizations adopt to manage their capacity and their productive potential: (i) control of the supply, which can be fixed or variable; and (ii) manipulation of demand.

Control of supply

Fixed supply

The first challenge is to manage capacity or supply but there are limited opportunities for this in the leisure and tourism industry, where there are fixed capacities or limits that cannot be exceeded once they have been planned. Some operations require a fairly elastic capacity (e.g. special events with pressures on their catering facilities and toilets) but many contexts have a relatively inelastic or fixed capacity as determined by factors such as the car parking spaces or rules (e.g. fire regulations or the number involved in particular sports). There may be upper limits

but there are also fixed resources, which means that the operational goal is to maintain demand as far as possible.

Service quality can suffer with this approach. Airlines, for example, are notorious for overbooking scheduled flights so that they will always hit their fixed capacity, as normally 6% of passengers do not show up for their flights. When they do show up, it means that the airline has to refuse seats to passengers or to ask for volunteers to receive compensation and accept the next available flight. In some cases *bona fide* booking systems, as with some sports or the theatre, can help to match supply with demand. In other cases, the resulting problem for service quality is the queue. Euro Disney (now Disneyland Paris) provides such an example. In its first few years it experienced a number of problems with capacity because of both demand and supply factors. Income was affected by poor take-up in winter months (no real surprise) and also the lower-than-expected secondary spend in shops and restaurants (compared with the American parks). There were also problems with queues at the busiest times in the summer because of limited provision of rides – 29 rides in total, with a capacity of 50,000 people per day (1724 per ride), compared with Disney World's 72 rides with a capacity of 90,000 guests (1250 per ride).

Variable supply

In some contexts there is a need for as much flexibility as possible, with the attempt to match supply to demand referred to as the '*chase*' strategy. This requires either more resources being made available (such as staff or equipment) or a quicker response time (in a busy travel agency). Flexible staffing levels and skills are the most important factor in the chase strategy but, in some operations, facilities can be closed off or opened, depending on demand, as in catering outlets at sports stadia or in special events. There is the need for flexible staff; for example, leisure centres often employ leisure attendants or assistants who can also coach sports. Special events in leisure and conference facilities are often staffed by a high proportion of casual employees, who therefore represent a variable cost. There is also the need for elasticity in other areas, for example, there is no use increasing capacity of a facility if its car parking is limited or it does not have the catering facilities to cope. Examples of such problems are provided by the British Grand Prix when it returned to Silverstone in 2000, and some people never made it because of the traffic queues; or the Millennium stadium in Cardiff when it staged the Worthington Cup Final in 2001: the number of cars was grossly underestimated and the approaches to the city centre were gridlocked.

There are, therefore, circumstances in which there is insufficient capacity to cope with demand and the provider literally has to adopt a 'coping' strategy and effectively maintain a 'level capacity' in which demand is constant or customers are forced to wait. In these cases, there are implications for service standards; there may be no control of any elements of the service offering, or there is an attempt to maintain standards in the core product and some aspects of the augmented product will suffer. An example of the former occurred some years ago when the Channel Tunnel advertised extensively that motorists could just turn up and go straight on to the train; they were met with many hours of queues and extremely disgruntled holiday-makers. Examples of the latter are stately homes unable to offer guided tours at their busiest times or health and fitness facilities offering more personal guidance and help at slacker times. The corollary of this would be when the core product is unavailable and consumers have to make do with additional provision (e.g. actions of local authorities in promoting limited countryside resources and amenities in the worst of the foot-and-mouth disease crisis in the UK in 2001). There are, therefore, a number of options in day-to-day capacity management for adjusting capacity to meet variable demand and they can be viewed as long-term or short-term options (Table 9.1).

Many of the options in Table 9.1 are used right across the leisure and tourism industry – an industry known for its use of part-time and casual staff and its scheduling of customers. The Cheltenham Racing Festival again provides many examples. It takes on hundreds of casual staff and provides additional viewing and catering space through renting marquees and temporary stands, and it does require a 'superhuman' effort from the staff employed. They use a number of the options listed, as do most organizations, and it is important to note that rarely are they independent of each other. For example, cross-training of staff, or increased flexibilization, probably means fewer staff employed. Several of the options, such as changing location and hours or providing

Table 9.1. Capacity management options (CMOs). (Adapted from Klaasen and Rohleder, 2000.)

	Longer-term CMOs	Shorter-term CMOs
Base CMOs (must do)	Hiring full-time employees Lay off full-time employees Yearly scheduling (e.g. annual leave)	Hourly/daily scheduling Weekly shift scheduling
Optional CMOs	Part-time employees Rent capacity Share capacity Cross-train Provide more information to servers Simplify the service process Reorganize servers to specialize Redesign service Build excess capacity Change hours of operation Change location Automation (e.g. entry) Change level of customer participation	Temporary employees Overtime Idle time Schedule extra staff Periods of super-human effort Customers wait Non-urgent work falls behind Do non-urgent work when quiet Turn away custom Allow customers to reserve/book Subcontract out Change allocation of resources

automated entry, overlap with the control of demand.

Management of demand

The other strategy is to manage the pattern of customer demand and much of this is achieved through encouraging customers to change their behaviour in relation to timing and frequency. This is where service quality has close links with services marketing and consumer behaviour, and an understanding of the market and its segments is particularly important. There are predictable patterns of demand associated with work and other commitments, the weather and seasonality, which affect all aspects of provision, and the challenge is to move some peak-time demand to off-peak times. An example of this is the use of price reductions to encourage participants in health and fitness facilities to attend at off-peak times, such as early morning sessions before work. The willingness of tourists to travel out of season is another example. The scheduling of major events and festivals (such as the Munich Beer Festival) requires an understanding of the motives and requirements of various target groups and the resources and processes needed to meet them. Alton Towers undertakes a considerable amount of systematic research and planning in order to adapt its operations through knowledge of demand and customer requirements. This is achieved by having trained staff ask visitors to complete questionnaires to establish levels of customer demand for different services. This is called 'real-time research' and through it Alton Towers has been able to identify the greatest demands on its resources and to adjust accordingly.

The approaches to manipulating demand include the following:

- **Price incentives**. In fact such pricing strategies are almost used as a disincentive in that they are deployed to shift some demand and usage from the most popular times. Their rationale is also based on the concept of marginal costing, in which the price is linked to just the direct costs of the additional usage, and the public sector traditionally has been slow to use this practice. It is limited by the speed of local government decision making and less dynamic practices. Examples from the commercial sector include nightclubs that are cheaper during the week, pubs that offer 'happy hours' during early evening and golf clubs that offer reduced rates for play at certain times.

- **Promotional activities**. In some cases aggressive marketing and advertising, linked to pricing policies, is sufficient. In other cases, programming and scheduling methods and skills can pay off in promoting demand and take-up at less popular times. Leisure centres use their programming policies to schedule more popular activities such as five-a-side at less popular times to increase usage (if they can get away with it). Ski resorts have promoted their facilities, including lifts, for summer usage. Theme parks have targeted schools through their educational features in order to fill off-peak times.

- **Product development**. Another approach is to alter the product, especially in order to fill unused times or capacity. The development of racket ball as an alternative to squash was seen a number of years ago, as was the conversion of squash courts to soft play areas when the demand for squash began to decline.

- **Booking systems**. Where organizations can 'reserve' capacity there are fewer problems with demand, as exemplified by airlines, restaurants, hotels and some sporting events. Booking systems are in place in facilities such as golf clubs, leisure centres and health and fitness clubs to help to even out demand and prevent queues from a customer perspective, and under-use from the organization's perspective. Other contexts such as bars, cinemas and travel agencies cannot always accurately predict demand and require contingency plans to manage the extra numbers and the problem of the queue.

The study of the manipulation of demand to manage capacity also contains some variables that affect overall approaches. Whether the demand for a particular product or activity is independent or is dependent on other products and services is a key factor. The number of participants or customers at many facilities or events will be directly related to the demand for food and beverage operations, although, interestingly, Euro Disney in its early years overestimated the secondary spend by visitors in the restaurants and shops.

Queuing or Waiting

Despite the application of these methods, a significant feature of many leisure and tourism contexts (though not always a source of dissatisfaction) is the queue. However, in many cases there are constraints on the extent to which supply or demand can be manipulated and some problems of undercapacity, from the customer perspective, will always be apparent, as in the queues that feature in particular establishments. This is the problem of fluctuating service demand, which managers in some contexts regard as the most difficult aspect of demand and capacity management. Queuing is a major problem in certain contexts but an established feature in others. Theme parks expect queues with their more popular rides, especially their recently introduced ones, and even argue that, in some cases, their customers perceive an attraction or ride to be suspect if it does not have a regular queue. They are often managed to enhance the overall experience by adding information or displays to entertain, or are controlled with precision and care to pleasantly surprise customers eventually (a good technique is slightly to overestimate the time it takes from a certain point so that expectations are exceeded). Communications are especially important when delays are not expected or are not part of the experience (as with airlines and train companies) and, when sensitively and promptly effected, can greatly dissipate feelings of unrest.

Queuing is particularly acute in visitor attractions such as theme parks and museums and with airlines, but can also be present in operations such as travel agencies, ski lifts, special events and sports stadia. Alton Towers has always had problems with queuing at the various rides and many leisure and tourism operations face waits or delays in the receiving or processing of customers as well as the actual activity or experience. In this examination of service quality, customer satisfaction and the management of operations, the queue can be the one factor that impairs the overall experience for the consumer, especially since the wait often occurs at the first service encounter and also provides ample opportunity for the individual to dwell on the experience. The contexts and consumer motives or requirements may be different but there are some aspects of commonality. The delivery system and its design (examined in Chapter 8) interact or engage with customers and the customer process at the point of queues.

There are several consumer characteristics that help to influence the consumer's perception, and tolerance, of the wait: (i) the pressures of time on the individual (e.g. holidaymakers might be more tolerant of a wait); (ii) where there are children (especially young ones), the wait can be a test of the most patient; (iii) waits in groups can be less noticeable than when people are on their own; and (iv) prior experience and therefore expectations.

The conclusions of the research on the psychology of waiting times demonstrate that it has an overall negative effect on customer perceptions of service quality, although Alton Towers argues that its customers do expect to queue for certain rides and place an additional value on the ride if there are long queues. Alton Towers, over a period of time, developed its system of virtual queuing, in which people can reserve their places on the most popular rides via a computerized ticketing system and simply return to the ride at the allotted time. A similar system is used by the 'London Eye' to regulate demand over a period of months.

There are several methods that providers can use to improve customer satisfaction with waiting and its impact on the overall experience:

- Provide details of the time it takes from certain points in the queue.
- More importantly, overestimate the time left so that the only surprise is a pleasant one.
- Keep people occupied as they queue (which has the effect of reducing the perceived time). Some attractions such as Futuroscope in Poitiers entertain with people on stilts or dressed as James Bond and other characters; others provide promotional videos: and Disney designs features, related to the themed area, into their queuing space to relieve the boredom or uses sound as a means of distracting or stimulating. A hotel with queues at certain times for its lifts installed mirrors by each one and this immediately reduced the number of complaints.
- Physically organize the queue so that parts of it are out of sight for a time or it is at least broken up by barriers.
- Convince customers that the wait was worth it even for a 45-second white-knuckle ride. In other words, the perceived quality of the activity or experience is high enough to justify the wait and word of mouth will help to establish the expectations of others.

It's Not Just Queuing!

There are several other factors that shape the approach to capacity management in the leisure and tourism industry.

Firstly, there is the problem of *perishability*, which elaborated on in Chapter 7. The 'real-time' delivery of the leisure and tourism experience means that capacity cannot be stored and sold at a later time. An empty squash court or vacant seats in a cinema or theatre cannot be sold again for that particular session and represent lost income.

Secondly, the problem can be alleviated and exacerbated by the features of *seasonality and peak usage times*. For example, most theme parks receive the majority of their customers in 4 months or so, with weekends especially busy. Many facilities, such as leisure centres, tend to be underused during the day and parts

of the weekend but with over-demand, perhaps, in the early evening.

Thirdly, the challenges of capacity management also highlight the *need for balance* between emphasis on organizational performance and customer satisfaction and the importance of identifying and communicating the standards of the service as they represent the management of capacity. On the one hand, capacity management is concerned with maximizing productivity through yield management and embraces the use of performance indicators in aspects such as sales, throughput and usage and especially in relation to space and resources, as will be seen later in this chapter. Yet, as already established, there can be a very fine equilibrium involved in the management of such indicators of organizational performance where an overemphasis on achieving greater throughput or usage can run the risk of affecting customer perceptions and satisfaction and, subsequently, the equilibrium.

An important aspect of service quality that permeates both service design and capacity management is therefore the *setting of service standards and their impact on customer expectations*. These aspects will be considered together with their relevance to the development of strategies for managing capacity, but first the growing significance of performance indicators in capacity management and the setting of standards will be examined.

The impact of performance indicators on capacity management

Performance indicators are used mainly to monitor performance of financial elements of an organization but are inextricably linked to capacity and yield management as well as service standards. The Audit Commission and the National Audit Office have devised other uses for them and have developed model performance indicators to set standards and monitor the efficiency, effectiveness and economy of public sector organizations, including local government leisure services and national museums and art galleries. Because of the ease of collating and displaying numerical data, their model performance indicators are quantitative in nature rather than qualitative. Examples of quantitative performance indicators are the number of admissions to a cinema and the percentage of late-arriving aircraft. Examples of qualitative performance indicators are analyses of customer comments, including complaints, to indicate customer satisfaction levels.

Gummesson (1993) questioned whether or not it is possible to monitor service standards numerically. The number of visitors to a location, although it is inexpensive to collect because of computerized tills and quick to analyse, gives managers very little in-depth information on which to base decisions. It is easy to measure service productivity quantitatively (number of meals served; number of transactions) but it is hard to calculate the quality of those service encounters. It can be difficult for practitioners to write service standards for effectiveness of the service, as many of the benefits attributed to the leisure and tourism experience (e.g. improving quality of life, improving health and fitness or mental well-being) do not readily lend themselves to quantitative evaluation. Sanderson (1998, p. 10) suggested that areas of service that are difficult to measure will be neglected.

Crosby (1984) stated that a problem organization is one without clear performance measures set by the managers. In these instances each individual employee can develop their own standards. The monitoring

of performance is not enough; the actual causes of varying standards need to be identified (Lovelock, 1992).

Writing appropriate indicators that have the ability to monitor every objective of an organization is difficult. This is especially so where public sector organizations are concerned, as they have to consider social as well as financial objectives. The Audit Commission (1998) stated that 'good indicators of the quality of outcomes remain elusive because of the nature of the service provided'. In its consultative document the Audit Commission (1998) considered that it was difficult to write performance indicators (PIs) for the arts but has still published them for leisure centres. The complexity of the multi-service provision of leisure centres was commented upon by Williams (1997), as opposed to the single service nature of leisure facilities such as golf courses.

The DETR and Audit Commission's (1999) model PIs for leisure and cultural services (Table 9.2) are indicative of setting standards and monitoring how economic and efficient the service is.

The standards and monitoring of the effectiveness of a service to the community is limited (the social objectives) and there is only one PI: 'Percentage of residents by target group satisfied with the local authority's cultural and recreational activities'. Some recent changes have been made to the cultural service PIs but again they continue in the same vein (see Table 9.2).

Table 9.2.   Leisure and cultural services performance indicators. (Source: DETR and Audit Commission, 1999.)

Source	Performance indicators
Swimming pools and sports centres	Number of swims and other visits per 1000 population Net cost per swim/visit
Playgrounds	Number of playgrounds and play areas provided by council per 1000 children under 12
Museum services	Number of pupils visiting museums and galleries in organized trips Number of visits to or usage of museums per 1000 population (can include e-mail or phone enquiry) Number of visits in person per 1000 population Number of museums operated by the local authority
Service delivery outcome for cultural and related services	Percentage of residents who have participated in a local sporting activity or event or have attended a local sporting facility in the last 3 months or in the last year Percentage of residents who have participated in a local arts activity, or attended a local arts facility in the last 3 months or last year

The inclusion of two service delivery outcome indicators (DETR and Audit Commission, 1999) does not redress this imbalance, as knowing only the percentages of the population using a service cannot give insight into its effectiveness (see Table 9.2). Only the PIs 'Fair Access', as outlined previously, 'Quality' and 'Percentage of library users who found the books/information they wanted, or reserved it and were satisfied with the outcome,' achieve this.

PIs are the foundation stones that organizations need to devise before the setting of standards and the monitoring of their services can begin. This is irrespective of whether or not the quality management system, tools and techniques have been devised in-house or accredited externally. The success or failure of a quality initiative can depend on PIs being appropriate to monitoring standards that meet the organizational objectives.

Yet it is not always the case that customers, both internal and external, are consulted about service standards. Beale and Pollitt (1994) and Stewart and Walsh (1994) were concerned that managers will meet PI standards rather than what their customers want. The needs of the customers have to influence the service standards and their monitoring by PIs and service guarantees or customer charters provide the means for achieving this.

Service guarantees and customer charters

Customer charters and service guarantees set down what an organization or a group is going to provide in terms of general service standards and have become important in not only communicating standards to customers but also reducing the element of risk perception in customers. The nature of leisure and tourism services, as has been established, involves some uncertainty and unpredictability, and service guarantees or customer charters can go some way towards convincing customers of the reliability of the service. Many leisure experiences can be viewed as a complex extended service encounter in which there is high involvement and a high risk for the customer. As Johnston and Bryan (1993) suggested, 'in customer processing operations, management has to deal with inherent variability and uncertainty caused by the physical, mental and emotional existence of the customer inside the operation'.

Much of the typical leisure product is, therefore, a process with few tangible reference points and is potentially subject to considerable variation in the way it is delivered because of this factor, as well as the difficulty of standardizing approaches by staff. Furthermore, the combination of uncertainty and intangibility can make it much harder to evaluate the quality of the service. Clear service standards will help both customer and provider to arrive at informed judgements about the quality of the service. Indeed, Hart and Tzokos (2000) and Wirtz and Kum (2001) argued that the importance of service guarantees is in direct proportion to the magnitude of the purchase risk. Not only do they make clear what customers can expect but also they help to provide feedback on errors and the appropriateness of published standards (Box 9.1). Kandampully (2001) highlighted the following benefits to organizations:

- They are able to learn from complaints.
- They are forced to respond to customer feedback.
- They are able to measure quality failures as they happen.
- They can critically analyse the data in a meaningful way.

The setting of service standards underpins all of the quality management systems, tools and techniques discussed in this book. The standards determine how they should be delivered and enable them to be monitored. They should be directly related to the objectives of the organization and the service they wish to supply. Wise (1995) saw the interpretation of an organization's broad objectives and key themes into service standards as 'an essential step to planning and controlling actions'.

Two types of service standards have been identified by Martin (1990): procedural and personal.

Box 9.1.   Case study: Premier League Fans Charter.

The Premier League Fans Charter has been specifically developed to ensure that the fans get value for money from individual football clubs in the Premier League. The main clauses in the Fans Charter are as follows:

- At least 5% of tickets should be available for non-season ticket holders.
- Visiting supporters should be offered 3000 tickets, or 10% of the seats if the stadium holds fewer than 30,000.
- More concessionary tickets should be available at each football match.
- The price of tickets to away supporters will be the same as for home fans.
- A new playing strip should not be introduced within 2 years.
- There should be improved training for stewards.

A Premier League football club that does not adhere to this charter, once it is a signatory to it, will be fined.

This has come about after a number of football seasons that have seen admission prices rising at an alarming rate and the number of times a team brings out a new playing strip has escalated beyond that which is affordable for their fans.

- **Procedural standards** appertain to the timing of service specification procedures (e.g. how long it should take for someone to answer a telephone; how long a customer should wait before being attended to). McDonald's has clear timescales for dealing with customers. Procedural standards also indicate the flexibility of procedures and systems in tackling problems, the clarity of communication and information given.

- **Personal standards** set standards for an employee's performance, including appearance, courtesy and, if appropriate, keeping to the predetermined script (fast-food outlets and tele-sales). Standards may also be linked to different aspects of service quality. Technical quality applies to tangibles such as staff appearance, decor and impact of buildings; standards of equipment and common standards will relate to areas such as water temperature and cleanliness, as do a number of the Cambridge City standards in Box 9.2. Functional or interactive quality is concerned with the process and permeates both of Martin's categories. Cambridge City's standards include reference to answering the telephone and responding to complaints or enquiries within a certain time.

As Martin (1990, cited in Buswell, 1993b) stated, standards have to be written so that they are clear, concise and observable but most important is that they must be thought to be achievable by the staff. It is equally important that standards are developed and met, as it is no good delivering a consistently bad or incorrect service that does not meet customer requirements.

Many public sector leisure and tourism services are aware of this and have devised customer charters under the Service First and Charter Mark Quality Award Scheme administered by the Cabinet Office (see Chapter 11). These charters are generally displayed in a prominent position in a facility or published in the organization's marketing literature. The results are threefold: the customer has the reassurance that the organization will deliver a particular service as stated to the standard laid down (e.g. the swimming pool will be kept at a temperature of 84°F) and most reduce the risk of poor service by stating what a customer should do if they have a problem. In some cases the charter outlines what will be done to solve a customer's problem.

These outline what an organization will do if a customer has a problem. This is an alien concept to some of the original quality theorists, such as Crosby, whose main goal was to eliminate non-conformity. Service quality academics and practitioners are slightly more realistic and understand the complexity of

Box 9.2.   Cambridge City Council: sports development service guarantee.

Our Commitment to You

We will . . .

- oversee all our courses from start to finish;
- only use qualified coaches, always checking police records where they are working with children;
- adhere to guidelines set by governing bodies and other agencies concerning the coaching and care of young children;
- provide all the basic equipment required which will be in a satisfactory and usable condition;
- ensure that all venues are suitable for the course activity, including adequate changing and toilet facilities;
- respond to your written enquiries within 7 working days;
- aim to answer our telephones within 12 hours;
- provide full details of your chosen course including clothing requirements and catering requirements as part of the booking confirmation process;
- do our best to accommodate the special needs of any disabled people participating on our courses;
- give you the opportunity to feedback your comments to us and voice your opinion about our events and activities to help improve them in future years.

You will . . .

- be treated with the highest standards of courtesy and helpfulness by our staff;
- receive a high quality standard of service at our courses and activities;
- find all our courses and activities to be excellent value for money;
- if you do experience problems with our standards of our service we will . . .
  - help you to use our complaints system 'How to make a complaint'
  - acknowledge your complaint within 5 working days and respond to your complaints within 10 days in the first instance.

customers judging the service delivered. Non-conformance can occur purely because customer expectations were very different from anyone else's.

Organizations can view customer complaints in a number of ways. The two extremes are 'the customer is always right' and the organization uses any complaints as a learning exercise (this will be discussed later), or 'the customer is out to "get" the organizations' and therefore their word cannot be trusted.

The intermediate stage between these two strategies is that an organization sees customer complaints as a way of disciplining employees. Management spends time (and money) investigating and searching out the offenders rather than using the event as a learning or training opportunity and seeing that processes are reviewed, if appropriate. A culture of blame is in operation and no one takes responsibility for even minor mistakes, as the consequences are too great. Customer

Box 9.3.   Case study: 'Customer is out to "get" the organization'.

One leisure organization took the latter stance and instigated methods to 'catch the customers out'. When receiving a complaint, employees had to call a supervisor, who then walked the complainant to a very unwelcoming room at the back of beyond. The room was spartan, poorly decorated and partly used for storage. The supervisor took a 'statement' and passed it on to a manager. The manager then investigated the complaint with the customer and any associated employees. The customer was expected to wait throughout the process and some customers left before any conclusion was delivered.

Some managers were quite elated when they found in favour of the organization and not the customer. Whilst the authors are sure that some customers will make unfounded complaints, the genuine complainant is not being treated fairly and their perceptions of the organization will be even lower than before.

complaints are kept away from managers as much as possible and clients can become frustrated, as staff at low levels are not empowered to give compensation or redress in any form. This again leads to even lower perceptions of the organization.

The first strategy for dealing with customer complaints is one in which the organization thinks that 'the customer is king (or queen)'. The organization is prepared to listen to every comment or complaint from a customer and use it in a constructive way. Whilst evaluation and review of complaints is part of the process, this is an open-minded activity looking at all aspects, not just which employee to blame. These types of organization have come to be known as 'learning organizations'.

One of the main difficulties is in getting customers to comment or complain in the first place and one strategy that has been used is service guarantees. These notify the customer in advance what will happen if something goes wrong and generates feedback even if it is mostly negative in nature. Guarantees also reduce customers' perceived risk, especially if they are purchasing an expensive service (e.g. a holiday; membership of a private health club). These service guarantees are in excess of a customer's legal rights.

For example, if a pizza is not delivered within 15 min then the customer does not have to pay for it. Hotels in the USA will not charge a customer if there is something not to their satisfaction about their stay. This is an automatic refund with no questions asked or investigation carried out in the presence of the customer.

In the latter case it was felt that some customers would take advantage of the guarantee, but the organizations considered the information they received from genuine complainants to be of great value – more than the costs of a night's stay.

Hart (1988, cited in Tucci and Talaga, 1997) suggested that service guarantees are effective when: (i) the price of a service is high; (ii) repeat business is critical; (iii) word of mouth is a critical marketing tool; and (iv) when trying to reposition a poor organizational image. These effects will only be seen if an organization adheres to its service

guarantees at all times and empowers all staff to administer them. To minimize any disadvantages, a good organizational communication system needs to be in place. A number of hotel chains in the USA have allegedly paid a 'customer' in excess of US$140,000 over a period of 2 years for 'dry cleaning' a jacket that had had wine spilt on it. The dry cleaning bills were paid without question under the service guarantee strategies. It was later found that the person had not even been a customer of the hotel in question at the time of the alleged event and had made multiple claims over a number of years. Criminal proceedings were instigated.

However, there are several good examples of organizations communicating their dimensions of quality and empowering their staff to deliver clear standards. One of these is Disney, whose philosophy, for years, has encapsulated the same message and includes a 10-point code followed by all employees (see Box 9.4), which is aimed at identifying and maintaining standards. As the organization points out: 'Walt Disney left a legacy of creating happiness through imagination, attention to detail, and an appreciation of people's needs and desires.'

Similarly, organizations such as Techni-Quest highlight important attributes as well as their philosophy in their statements about their standards. The Hyatt (Hotel Chain) philosophy points out that:

> service doesn't only refer to how we serve our guests, but also how we look and present

---

Box 9.4.   The Disney 10-point code. (Source: Disney University Information Sheet, Walt Disney, 1998.)

1. We're committed to quality.
2. We're friendly, helpful and courteous.
3. We smile.
4. We are a team.
5. We're positive.
6. We never say 'no'.
7. We're impeccable.
8. We're on stage and we know our role in the show.
9. We're professional and efficient.
10. We strive to be the best.

ourselves to them. To give a professional image, it is our responsibility to take care and pride in our personal appearance, cleanliness and grooming.

TechniQuest refers to aspects such as access, courtesy, safety, cleanliness, education and entertainment in their communications to staff and customers (Box 9.5).

Summary

Managers in the tourism and leisure industry must not underestimate the need to review and revise their service design and specification. Customer needs are ephemeral and frequently changing and the dynamics of the marketplace also require constant attention to the innovations of competitors. The use of charters and service guarantees can inform the customer of what they should expect from a particular leisure and tourism experience and minimizes the risk of poor service. It is important that when a leisure or tourism organization places its service standards in the public domain, it has the resources to deliver those standards at all times. That, in turn, requires skilled and careful management of capacity in order to achieve the necessary balance between meeting customer needs and using resources as cost-effectively as possible.

The planning and design of services and the management of capacity are very much operational issues, which require systematic methods and techniques. However, they also reflect and, indeed, shape the organization's wider approach to quality management. Part 3 examines the organizational, behavioural and philosophical aspects of managing service quality.

Box 9.5.   Techniquest.

TECHNIQUEST IS:

- the UK's leading science centre, a company limited by guarantee and a registered educational charity;
- a friendly place to become intrigued by and involved in science, engineering and technology;
- an exciting resource for teachers and pupils at all levels of the formal education system;
- an internationally recognized centre of excellence for creativity and innovation in non-formal science education.

Through the activities and events in its building, together with its outreach programme, TECHNIQUEST aims to:

- establish the place of science as part of popular culture;
- enhance the public's understanding and appreciation of its individual visitors;
- make science accessible to everyone, regardless of their previous background;
- motivate, encourage and inform school pupils of all ages;
- provide every visitor with attentive, courteous, informative and entertaining service in a clean and safe setting.

TECHNIQUEST provides:

- a range of opportunities for interactive participation in the exploration and enjoyment of science, at the visitor's own pace and under their direct control;
- expertise and enthusiasm in the communication of science;
- a lively and colourful environment which welcomes visitors of all ages;
- the excitement and fun of science in a safe environment;
- a relevant and stimulating programme for school and college students and their teachers.

Part 3

Achieving or Delivering Quality

Introduction

Parts 1 and 2 have been more concerned with the concepts and processes of service quality in leisure and tourism than with the underlying philosophy of quality management and the tools and techniques for achieving service quality. The business of designing the service package, identifying the service standards and implementing a quality approach through certain methods and techniques is important and the earlier chapters highlighted these aspects. They also suggested that the nature of the service encounter and the interaction between staff and customers were key determinants in the achievement of quality service. Effective management of the service encounter requires a systematic approach and the deployment of a number of quality techniques and measures, some of which have implications for management of the human resource.

The assumption of the authors is not that organizations are failing to achieve customer satisfaction in anything but that most are only achieving it in some areas or only at certain times. Monitoring and measurement of the quality of service delivery is fragmented throughout all sectors of the tourism and leisure industry, with a diverse range of tools and techniques being used.

Organizations that regularly give poor service tend to go out of business or appear as an item on a consumer programme on the television. It must be remembered that some organizations can have a historical reputation for giving excellent service quality but have still gone out of business as they have not taken into account that their customers' needs have changed (e.g. Westerly Yachts, the UK's premier sailing-boat builder). The counting of admission numbers at a range of leisure and tourist venues was found to be a major element in the monitoring of service delivery (Williams, 1997a). Organizations take the view that, if admissions are high, then 'we must be doing it right'. Unfortunately, this does not provide in-depth data for use in the organization's decision-making processes.

At one leisure centre a small number of women attended aerobics classes five times a week; a similar level of usage was found at a municipal golf course. The majority of players were retired and had purchased a weekday session ticket and therefore, weather permitting, played golf every day. As the golf course ran at full capacity with no spare booking times, customer feedback was not formally researched; the main monitoring tool was unsolicited thank you letters, together with financial information. The actual customer base in each example was relatively low and this could make the facilities vulnerable; fortunately, golf and aerobics are very popular. The golf course had the additional advantage that the number of courses in the immediate vicinity was low and they were very expensive.

In the service quality management literature, the meeting of customer needs and expectations central to recognizing whether or not the right quality has been delivered or achieved. Lehtinen and Lehtinen (1982), when referring to services, pointed out that there are two moments when customers judge whether or not they are satisfied: during the service production process and again at the end (the outcome). Organizations need to be able to monitor to see whether they have been successful at both junctures.

The next five chapters will explore a range of concepts related to what quality goals an organization should aim for, and how to achieve and deliver quality to meet the needs of their customers. Part 3 will also examine the advantages and disadvantages of implementing an array of quality systems tools and techniques, including ways of measuring and monitoring customer needs and satisfaction. The importance of employees, their roles and responsibilities will be determined within a quality culture, as will the need for evolving that culture. Chapter 4 examined the thinking of gurus such as Deming and Juran and demonstrated that systems and procedures may be important but are controlled by people; the human and cultural processes in place will lead to more appropriate and effective systems and procedures. The task of Part 3 is to examine the behavioural and cultural aspects of service quality and what is required for leisure and tourism organizations to move beyond efficiency and systematic thinking and into the domain of total quality management.

al text *In Search of Excellence* in 1982
om Peters and Bob Waterman, who
ded Disney and McDonald's within
survey of the American organizations
ated with high quality. They identified
rtant features such as 'management
alking about' and the 'smell of the cus-
r'. Unfortunately, within 5 years, two-
s of the companies in that survey were
ouble, giving testament to those critics
anagement gurus and theoreticians who
se them of peddling fads and fashionable
s. Interestingly, their approach was to
light the features of services or products
the characteristics of individuals, partic-
ly the bosses, rather than to consider
ity from the external customer's point
ew.

Both sides probably have some validity in
r approaches. The style and commitment
he boss is known to be a significant factor;
the theorists do a useful job in investigat-
organizations and developing new theo-
and ideas, and support for the principles
TQM in that nothing must stand still. Yet
re is often a flaw in that the new ideas do
necessarily represent progress on the part
the gurus but rather new theorists who
he along with new ideas (and would not
heard unless they did). The critics, on the
er hand, will point to the need for pragma-
n, realism and practical applications rather
n simply theories. As with so many issues,
argument is not clear-cut; the complexity
service quality and TQM is a significant
tor.

However, analysis of quality manage-
ent and the pursuit of excellence underlines
e need for constant reappraisal and rethink-
g about approaches and methods. If there
one message from the service quality
erature, it is that there is no single method
at will work every time with every organi-
tion. Much will always depend on the
cumstances and the context in which the
ganization operates and, invariably, the
libre, enthusiasm, vision and commitment
the person at the very top. This point
ghlights the ethereal nature of much busi-
ss and the problems of 'fade-out' and inertia
at can confront any organization that is a
tle complacent, as demonstrated by recent

examples such as Marks and Spencer and
Sainsbury's.

Failure to Change

Many organizations fail to achieve total
quality, despite having a number of sound
procedures in place. As Atkinson (1990, p. 10)
suggested: 'The great fear is that we can be
exposed to the secrets of TQM, have the
answer to improving performance, but still
find 10 reasons why we should not do it.'

Dale *et al.* (2001) found that many organizations, and their senior managers, simply do
not understand the fundamentals of quality
management. A recent *Economist* Intelligence
Report also suggested that quality improvement programmes had, at best, delivered
incremental improvements in quality and,
at worst, made it more difficult to increase
organizational competitiveness in recent
years. The western world, including the UK,
cannot be accused of eschewing programmes
and strategies for achieving service quality
but the efficacy of those programmes in a
number of organizations does not appear to
have matched that of many Japanese organizations in the last 30 years. There are several
reasons for the apparent lack of progress.

1. *There has been a tendency to regard quality
approaches as a quick fix.* 'Short-termism' is a
feature of the thinking of many British organizations, encouraged to some extent by the
political economy of the UK for a number of
decades. Planning and actions by successive
UK governments, like those of many organizations, have lacked vision, continuity and
overall strategy. Some Japanese companies
plan up to 50 years ahead and all successful
organizations have a clear idea of the direction
in which they are heading and the overall
strategy for achieving that progress.

2. *A concomitant point concerns the lack of clear
objectives and targets shaping the operations of
certain organizations.* Public sector leisure
provision through the 1970s and 1980s was
accused of lacking clarity and precision in
defining what its business was and what
exactly it was attempting to achieve. Interestingly, compulsory competitive tendering,

10

Quality and Culture Chang

Introduction

This chapter considers how cultural and behavioural factors are essential prerequisites for the achievement of service quality and, often, are dependent on the organization changing its philosophy and practices. Indeed, a feature of an organization committed to total quality is the need for constant change, for continual reappraisal of the ways things are done and what customers expect and desire. The chapter focuses on the pursuit of excellence and the principles of total quality management (TQM), especially those relating to people, and in so doing re-examines the theories and beliefs of 'quality gurus' such as Deming and Juran, outlined in Chapter 4. It was seen how TQM can be regarded as a management philosophy and involves the whole organization in the pursuit of continuous improvement. It also embraces the organizational culture that is in place and how all stakeholders, but particularly customers and staff, react to it and help to shape it. This chapter will consider specific examples and will demonstrate how TQM, through cultural change in leisure and tourism organizations, is differentiated from the use of specific quality tools and programmes. They might have a specific purpose and are really symptomatic of quality assurance and with 'doing things right'. TQM is also concerned with 'doing the right thing' and 'doing it better'. This chapter will consider the role of cultural change in facilitating such an approach and how achieving this in the

leisure and tourism indu: tive challenge.

> On completion of the chapt
> you will be able to:
>
> - define and understa culture in the context tourism industry;
> - appreciate the impor change in achieving ser
> - identify and understand achieving such change;
> - recognize and apply the lent leisure and tourism (

A Cautionary Word ab(

Although it is important t(organizations that have ach in their own way and have (characteristics that can be quality, the analysis is not a one. It may be prudent at tl sider the dangers of simpli: that offer a blueprint for si tinued success. There are al whenever excellence and e: best organizations are cons: and theories are digested evidence is sifted to identif; characteristics of organizati excellence and then it is sugg can be applicable to any c(and Prabhu, 2001). That was t which was introduced to overcome these shortcomings as well as to inject some competition into the process of running these services, did little to improve matters. It is its successor, 'best value', that is encouraging public sector organizations to question the very rationale for the service before setting clear and agreed goals for the service. Discussion of the public sector also raises the issue of customer focus and, indeed, who the customers are. Commercial organizations interact with internal and external customers and are directed by shareholders' interests and, perhaps, some notions of social and community responsibility. The issue of sustainability is causing some organizations, for example, to look at their environmental policies and their wider image in the community, not just with their customers; yet, in essence, commercial organizations are driven by the needs and wants of their external customers. The public sector is not so straightforward and Robinson (1997) showed how the needs of multi-stakeholders can be another constraint in the pursuit of TQM. She identified the following 'customer groups' for local authority leisure and tourism services:

- the direct user of the facility or service;
- the internal customer, including other departments and council members;
- council tax payers;
- the person who benefits directly from the service without using it.

These groupings highlight the difficulties in achieving focus and customer-led strategies when there are different interests to acknowledge. The concept of public good has always applied to local authority services in that the whole community can benefit if there is less crime or juvenile delinquency, and a sense of well-being, as a result of rational recreation based on the impact of positive, wholesome activities. This point helps to explain the element of paternalism, historically, in the approach of leisure professionals in the public sector and the legitimacy for decisions made on the basis of wider benefits. McNamee et al. (2000, 2001) examined this issue and distinguished between those professionals in more strategic roles and those involved in direct service delivery, although Best Value is beginning to obfuscate such distinctions.

3.   *The desire to achieve quality can be undermined by the setting up of dedicated and discrete quality departments* or units, which can begin to build an empire. It could be argued that service quality is not an exclusive programme or resource but should permeate the whole organization and be the responsibility of everybody working at all levels. Whether there should be a separate unit with responsibility for quality is a moot point although some awards (e.g. ISO 9002) require a 'quality manager or officer' and some coordination is always required. However, frequently no more than lip service can be claimed by organizations who proudly point to the size of the quality department.

4.   *Quality approaches are sometimes seen in terms of tools and techniques and have ignored or neglected the importance of people.* Systems and processes are important to the achievement of quality, as shown in Chapters 11 and 12, but they are determined by people; many products or services in leisure and tourism depend on the nature and effectiveness of the service encounter, which involves the interaction between staff and customers. Alton Towers' creation of magic requires more than the technology of rides and the efficacy of its procedures; Thomas Cook's approach to its 'exceptional service' is through what it refers to as its 'exceptional people'.

5.   *Poor communication and a lack of internal marketing* can reinforce the dominance of systems and structures over the 'people' factor. Good internal marketing can only work if there is clear thinking in respect of mission, vision and objectives, and sound communications in the first place. The approach to internal marketing of Amelia Island Plantation in Florida is based on its 'Great Wisdom' as illustrated later in Box 10.1.

6.   *Lack of management commitment at the very top* is another factor identified as a significant constraint (Lovelock, 1991; Leonard and McAdam, 2002). The leisure and tourism industry in the UK has been no different from other sectors in that its leaders and senior managers have, perhaps, not always given the very firm lead and commitment displayed

---

Box 10.1.   Case study: Amelia Island Plantation, Florida.

Amelia Island Plantation Resort in Florida places great emphasis on its culture and the transmission of that culture to its staff. The establishment has a very clear focus and sense of direction that is communicated to the staff in a systematic way. The process begins with the vision and the beliefs that it represents and includes the mission statement and the guiding principles that underpin it. The final aspect is the identification of service standards and behaviours expected of staff shown in its 'Service Plus Commitments' called 'Great Wisdom'. The language used underpins its values and strategy and refers to, for example, its 'highest quality props and decor' or 'the best in service'. The guiding principles draw attention to empowerment (own), the need for teamwork (team), the importance of atmosphere (wear, greet, respond) and the goal of customer satisfaction (exceed). The company also uses what it calls 'Critical Few Objectives', which identify the particular goals that have been set in that year. Some will refer to growth and shareholder expectations but others focus on customers and employees. For customers, it might be to set accurate expectations, improve responsiveness and increase price/value perception; for employees it might be to increase employee satisfaction, educate employees to deliver consistently high levels of service and promote teamwork through better communication.

Vision

To be a premier total resort committed to making people happy by providing a consistently high quality experience that emphasizes the unique beauty of and natural environment of Amelia Island Plantation.

Its 'new Employee Orientation Workbook' is very comprehensive and highlights a full training schedule and specifies in great detail, like Disney, the requirements of all employees, including aspects of dress and grooming.

Mission

The Amelia Island Company provides a consistently high quality total resort experience at Amelia Island Plantation by fulfilling the expectations of all who share in the experience.

Guiding Principles

- We are committed to making people happy.
- All who share Amelia Island Plantation – property owners, club members, resort guests and employees – are customers who demand the utmost respect and a high return on their investment and commitment.
- We respect, protect and preserve the unique beauty and natural environment of Amelia Island Plantation.
- We practise honest and open communication within the company and with our customers.
- We are dedicated to having well trained and motivated team members who share the Vision while living the Mission. We understand that the strength of our team is greater than the sum of our individual strengths.
- We stress innovation and creativity in marketing Amelia Island Plantation as a true destination resort.
- We understand the need for, and are committed to enhancing and preserving, the company's financial health.
- We are a community of people who respect, trust and care about each other. We work together to ensure that our quality of life is equal to the beauty of the natural environment.
- We recognize the significance of the local community, especially Fernandina Beach, in being able to deliver the total resort experience.
- We subscribe to the highest standards of business and professional ethics by being fair and practising honesty, directness and sincerity in everything we do.

Greet	Wear
Respond	Improve
Exceed	Secure
Act	Decide
Team	Maintain

---

by Japanese leaders in the last 30 years. Many observers, including Garvin (1988) and Wilkinson and Wilmott (1995), believe that this factor has helped Japanese organizations to achieve their success of recent years.

The consistent theme behind Japan's rise to industrial pre-eminence has not until recently been due to particularly advanced technology. Instead the key has been the efficient, reliable improvement and manufacture

10

Quality and Culture Change

Introduction

This chapter considers how cultural and behavioural factors are essential prerequisites for the achievement of service quality and, often, are dependent on the organization changing its philosophy and practices. Indeed, a feature of an organization committed to total quality is the need for constant change, for continual reappraisal of the ways things are done and what customers expect and desire. The chapter focuses on the pursuit of excellence and the principles of total quality management (TQM), especially those relating to people, and in so doing re-examines the theories and beliefs of 'quality gurus' such as Deming and Juran, outlined in Chapter 4. It was seen how TQM can be regarded as a management philosophy and involves the whole organization in the pursuit of continuous improvement. It also embraces the organizational culture that is in place and how all stakeholders, but particularly customers and staff, react to it and help to shape it. This chapter will consider specific examples and will demonstrate how TQM, through cultural change in leisure and tourism organizations, is differentiated from the use of specific quality tools and programmes. They might have a specific purpose and are really symptomatic of quality assurance and with 'doing things right'. TQM is also concerned with 'doing the right thing' and 'doing it better'. This chapter will consider the role of cultural change in facilitating such an approach and how achieving this in the leisure and tourism industry poses a distinctive challenge.

On completion of the chapter it is expected that you will be able to:

- define and understand organizational culture in the context of the leisure and tourism industry;
- appreciate the importance of cultural change in achieving service quality;
- identify and understand the key factors in achieving such change;
- recognize and apply the features of excellent leisure and tourism organizations.

A Cautionary Word about Excellence

Although it is important to consider those organizations that have achieved excellence in their own way and have displayed certain characteristics that can be associated with quality, the analysis is not a straightforward one. It may be prudent at this stage to consider the dangers of simplistic assessments that offer a blueprint for success and continued success. There are always problems whenever excellence and examples of the best organizations are considered. Figures and theories are digested and anecdotal evidence is sifted to identify the common characteristics of organizations achieving excellence and then it is suggested that they can be applicable to any context (Robson and Prabhu, 2001). That was the basis of the seminal text *In Search of Excellence* in 1982 by Tom Peters and Bob Waterman, who included Disney and McDonald's within their survey of the American organizations associated with high quality. They identified important features such as 'management by walking about' and the 'smell of the customer'. Unfortunately, within 5 years, two-thirds of the companies in that survey were in trouble, giving testament to those critics of management gurus and theoreticians who accuse them of peddling fads and fashionable ideas. Interestingly, their approach was to highlight the features of services or products and the characteristics of individuals, particularly the bosses, rather than to consider quality from the external customer's point of view.

Both sides probably have some validity in their approaches. The style and commitment of the boss is known to be a significant factor; and the theorists do a useful job in investigating organizations and developing new theories and ideas, and support for the principles of TQM in that nothing must stand still. Yet there is often a flaw in that the new ideas do not necessarily represent progress on the part of the gurus but rather new theorists who come along with new ideas (and would not be heard unless they did). The critics, on the other hand, will point to the need for pragmatism, realism and practical applications rather than simply theories. As with so many issues, the argument is not clear-cut; the complexity of service quality and TQM is a significant factor.

However, analysis of quality management and the pursuit of excellence underlines the need for constant reappraisal and rethinking about approaches and methods. If there is one message from the service quality literature, it is that there is no single method that will work every time with every organization. Much will always depend on the circumstances and the context in which the organization operates and, invariably, the calibre, enthusiasm, vision and commitment of the person at the very top. This point highlights the ethereal nature of much business and the problems of 'fade-out' and inertia that can confront any organization that is a little complacent, as demonstrated by recent examples such as Marks and Spencer and Sainsbury's.

Failure to Change

Many organizations fail to achieve total quality, despite having a number of sound procedures in place. As Atkinson (1990, p. 10) suggested: 'The great fear is that we can be exposed to the secrets of TQM, have the answer to improving performance, but still find 10 reasons why we should not do it.'

Dale *et al.* (2001) found that many organizations, and their senior managers, simply do not understand the fundamentals of quality management. A recent *Economist* Intelligence Report also suggested that quality improvement programmes had, at best, delivered incremental improvements in quality and, at worst, made it more difficult to increase organizational competitiveness in recent years. The western world, including the UK, cannot be accused of eschewing programmes and strategies for achieving service quality but the efficacy of those programmes in a number of organizations does not appear to have matched that of many Japanese organizations in the last 30 years. There are several reasons for the apparent lack of progress.

1.   *There has been a tendency to regard quality approaches as a quick fix.* 'Short-termism' is a feature of the thinking of many British organizations, encouraged to some extent by the political economy of the UK for a number of decades. Planning and actions by successive UK governments, like those of many organizations, have lacked vision, continuity and overall strategy. Some Japanese companies plan up to 50 years ahead and all successful organizations have a clear idea of the direction in which they are heading and the overall strategy for achieving that progress.

2.   *A concomitant point concerns the lack of clear objectives and targets shaping the operations of certain organizations.* Public sector leisure provision through the 1970s and 1980s was accused of lacking clarity and precision in defining what its business was and what exactly it was attempting to achieve. Interestingly, compulsory competitive tendering,

of relatively standard designs. Central to that approach has been a universal commitment to quality within the country's leading companies from the very top to the bottom of the enterprise (Garvin, 1988; Cao *et al.*, 2000; Largrosen, 2001).

Laszlo (1999) argued that commitment from the top must be followed by commitment of resources and of time. The commitment of organizational resources provides a message but also involves training and staff development, including the key managers whose task it will be to facilitate change across the organization. Their role is important in terms of identifying the training needs of other staff as the process cascades and of undertaking monitoring of the changes in place. Laszlo (1999) suggested that many quality management programmes falter because of the lack of close monitoring and, with it, loss of focus and commitment. The third manifestation of commitment he pointed to is management time and requires senior managers to be visible and active (Peters and Waterman's 'walking about'). Allen (1994) explained his approach as Chief Executive of Granada Television in developing a positive organizational culture – through a focus on 'how' rather than 'can't'. The Granada plan was called 'Fit for the Future' and was based on a 3-year programme for the company, with targets and clear implications for the structure of the company and its training programme. He stressed the importance of clarity of purpose and communication and simplicity. The key points in the plan were: (i) keep it simple; (ii) create clear objectives; (iii) communicate the objectives; (iv) create clear management information; (v) promote responsibility with control; (vi) make training real; (vii) give quality feedback; and (viii) recognize and communicate success.

He also stressed the importance of management by walking about and of internal marketing, with communication seen by everybody as a two-way process. His example reinforces the view that one of the critical factors in the success of Japanese companies that have achieved considerable change in the last 30 years was the visible leadership and commitment from the very top (although the seeds were sown by Deming in the early 1950s). Indeed, some resonance between the rhetoric and reality would seem to be essential; flatter hierarchies and closeness between management and employees would seem to encourage it and factors such as trust, integrity, honesty and openness are also important.

7.   The final factor identified is *the need for a change of internal culture*, which is related to all the earlier points. According to Wilkinson (1995, p. 273).

> There is growing evidence that TQM has not achieved its objectives. Major problems identified are an overemphasis on quality and not enough on total, too much emphasis on processes and not enough on results and a failure to achieve changed attitudes and culture.

A culture of quality will be based on sound communication and teamwork with an ethos of cooperation and interdependence. That culture will help to create good practices although it always needs certain principles and practices in place to start with in order to facilitate change. It is often argued that an organization, in order to achieve service quality, must have a 'quality culture'. In fact, it could be argued that all organizations, but particularly excellent ones, have a certain quality or, even, *are* a culture.

What is Organizational Culture?

The culture of an organization is created by a number of factors and can be very difficult to change, although clearly once an organization is led by a service quality culture then the very process of change becomes an intrinsic part of that culture. However, with increasing pressure on organizations in leisure and tourism to deliver quality service, change management, through cultural and behavioural change, becomes an essential prerequisite for success. Before examining change to organizational culture, it might be useful to establish briefly what is meant by organizational culture.

Organizational culture can be described as 'a system of shared values, beliefs, norms, expectations, and experiences that shape a firm and the people in it' (Lengnick-Hall and Hartman 1995, p. 88) although there is no precise blueprint for all organizations to work to. Much will depend on the nature of the business of the organization, its mission and service concept and the customers it attracts and serves. O'Hanlon (1999) described the characteristics of organizational culture as: *taboos* that nobody talks about, such as being seen to leave on time; *rituals*, i.e. the ways things are done, such as staff development reviews or dealing with customers; *totems*, in which symbols of success are highlighted and ignore many of those who are really behind the achievement – perhaps employee of the month awards; and *values* of the organization, i.e. who or what does the organization really value – people, safety, profit? Although there is no one culture that will apply to all organizations, there are some common elements and the most important prerequisite is that, whatever the culture, it is clear and coherent and communicated with clarity and purpose to staff.

An example of an organization's philosophy is provided by the Broadgate Health and Fitness Club in London. The Broadgate Club believes that business is achieved by all staff having shared responsibility to deliver an uncompromising level of service. This can only happen if every member of the team operates within a creative and progressive culture in which high value is placed on personal development, complete professional competence and integrity and fun. This culture will encourage and sustain openness, confidence, pride and quality.

We are not in a position to comment on whether the reality does match the rhetoric but the words in the club's philosophy present a clear message and emphasize some important concepts. Key words feature, such as shared, values, culture and team, and do suggest a certain style and organizational culture; other words such as pride, integrity, quality and professional competence represent the standards of the club and management's expectations of staff.

The implications of the analysis of the Broadgate Club have some affinity with the views of Jeffries *et al.* (1992), who suggested that the culture of an organization includes: management style; who makes decisions and how; communications (one-way or two-way);

who participates in decision making; status; perceived power or powerlessness; whether people feel listened to; how people react to new ideas; opportunities for individual development and growth; the degree of support, openness and trust; the amount of feedback people give each other; how conflict is handled; whether people compete with each other or work cooperatively; how problems about race, gender and disability are handled; the way feelings are handled; involvement, commitment and motivation.

Another important factor is the language used, which can be an expression of the organizational culture in place. The way jobs are titled and described is one example; customers being called 'guests' in Disney and other establishments is another.

Woods (1996) proposed a 'levels of meaning' approach to understanding the nature of organizational culture, where each level has a certain purpose and impact on staff and customers. The first level is the *manifest level*, which is most obvious to external observers and customers. It includes tangibles such as buildings and other technology, staff uniform, procedures, ways of doing things such as booking systems, the way customers are addressed and other conventions. It involves depicting the organization and its product and service as the organization would wish its customers to see it. Disney has seven guidelines for guest service, which it emphasizes through training (all cast members attend 'Traditions 1' as part of their induction) and everything else it does: (i) make eye contact and smile; (ii) greet and welcome each and every guest; (iii) seek out guest contact; (iv) provide immediate service recovery (when needed); (v) display appropriate body language at all times; (vi) preserve the 'magical' guest experience; and (vii) thank each and every guest.

The second level is the *strategic level*, which is less obvious to external customers but is derived from the distinctiveness of an organization's service concept and service package. Its areas of competence are closely matched to its available resources and embrace the strategic beliefs that staff have about the establishment and their own roles within it. For example, Jarvis Hotels has a clear vision, which states: 'Customers shall receive our total obsession to meet their needs through a structured service approach to making those small, noticeable improvements which improve the customer's experience with us.' The chain was established in 1990 by John Jarvis and David Thomas with a philosophy of 'first time, every time' and a culture that involves all staff in ensuring total customer satisfaction. John Jarvis would argue that their approach is not one of TQM because it is an ideal that can never be achieved. There are four categories in this second level: *strategic vision*, which provides the long-term view of the organization's future and the direction it needs to take; *capital-market expectations*, which represent all stakeholders and are an important feature of 'best value' in public sector services; *product-market expectations*, which represent the rationale for the belief in the product or service; and *internal approaches to management*, which include marketing, human resource management, strategic planning and finance. Disney's 'Traditions 1' training includes learning about Disney's history and origins; its vision, mission and brand essence; and sharing the 'pixie dust' (learning how to preserve the magical moment, and not just as a 'character').

The third level is the *level of deep meaning*, which encapsulates, perhaps, the essence of TQM that lies in the values and ethos of an organization and how they are internalized by all staff. Disney's 'Traditions 1' outlines the philosophy behind the Disney organization and works on the premise that all staff should understand the very nature and purpose of the organization and where their role fits in. Woods (1996) suggested that this level contains shared beliefs and is necessary for the construction of the other two levels. The National Exhibition Centre (NEC) in Birmingham has developed five core values, which are explained to new employees on their first day with the company: *friendliness* towards both customers and colleagues helps to create a relaxed and comfortable atmosphere: *teamwork* helps to solve problems for customers as well as each other (e.g. the provision of a crèche for staff with small children); *honesty* encourages staff to admit it when they do not have an answer but can refer to someone who

does; *openness* means being provided with maps that describe and explain how the NEC functions and where everybody fits in; and finally, *trust* is important for the other values to succeed.

Conrad *et al.* (1997) studied the mix of four different types of organizational culture in creating organizational change. The four types are: the *market culture*, where organizations stress the competitive edge, market superiority and goal achievement; *adhocracy culture*, which encourages innovation, growth and development and a spirit of enterprise; *clan culture*, which emphasizes teamwork, commitment and the general morale of everybody; and *hierarchy culture*, which is concerned with stability, predictability and efficiency, with importance attached to rules, order and uniformity. Conrad *et al.* (1997) confirmed that many organizations contain a mix of all four cultures and, although their study was concerned with the optimum mix for an organization's tracking of the link between relationship marketing and customer satisfaction, it is useful to apply a similar approach to achieving cultural change and total quality.

O'Hanlon (1999) suggested that it is not necessarily the culture, or resistance to change to a new culture, that is to blame but failure by the advocates of change to recognize and accommodate the culture. He maintained that many of them do not really know how to manage change, and perpetuate the mistakes that made change necessary in the first place. It should be accepted that there will always be resistance to change, even from those who are likely to benefit from it, as Atkinson (1990, p. 48) pointed out. He suggested that the following factors cause people to resist change:

- *Fear*. It is a natural response and requires a clear and consistent message to overcome it, especially as rumours can grow and become exaggerated very quickly.
- *Personal uncertainty*. Individuals will experience some insecurity about their abilities to cope with changes; the identification of training needs and the gradualness of change are important factors.
- *It may mean more work*. Atkinson argued that it does, but it is certainly an aspect that has to handled very carefully,

particularly where staff already perceive themselves to be stretched.

- *Past resentments.* This point reinforces the need for trust and honesty in the ways in which individuals and departments deal with each other; there can be no baggage from previous conflicts and the harbouring of grudges. The Japanese example of cooperation and interdependence in the style of so many organizations is a salutary comparison with the perception of colleagues as rivals and competitors seen in a number of western organizations.

- *Flavour of the month.* Short-termism has already been identified as one of the major factors in undermining quality approaches and the conviction that any quality measures are not a fad or a whim of management or consultants.

- *It may go away if I ignore it.* Atkinson suggested that leadership by example is the only effective way of overcoming such inertia, especially where the commitment from the top is evident.

- *Unwilling to take ownership and be committed.* Although Atkinson drew attention to the reluctance of supervisors and first-line managers to accept responsibility and commitment, especially when change creates the pressure of conflicting goals for them (cost savings but increased quality), the point, as shall be seen later, applies to everyone.

- *It's your responsibility.* This is where the understanding of TQM focuses on the second word. Quality has to be managed by management but its responsibility, just like marketing, is everyone's. Organizations such as Disney and Jarvis Hotels are good examples of this approach.

- *First you change, and then I will.* In some ways this is like the issue of whether culture change and quality initiative should be a top-down' or 'bottom-up' process when neither is entirely appropriate. It reinforces the need for mutual trust and an ethos and spirit of cooperation and interdependence.

For these reasons change cannot be pushed through especially quickly. O'Hanlon (1999, p. 33) argued for a strategy that slowly unmasks the unstated reasons for resisting change and involves everybody in explaining the rationale for change, its substance and the consequences for people and the organization:

> When changing a company culture employees must be listened to and attitude and/or cultural perception surveys conducted. It is not just management who creates the culture – the people are the culture. Understanding people is about understanding their needs, values and beliefs and expectations. A company which understands the culture and how to integrate change will suffer less pain and have greater success.

He suggested that time and timing are both important and that the timescale will vary according to the circumstances. We have, therefore, established that, in spite of the resistance and reluctance to change and the dangers of rapid change, the need to address the process of continuous improvement and to build it into organizational culture is crucial to the future success of leisure and tourism organizations. It is more likely that a quality culture will emerge in this context, and this can be seen as the way quality is received, handled, interpreted and audited – and the appropriate attitudes, values and behaviour are created. A distinctive example is provided by Disney, which does much to ensure that cast members are happy in order that the guests will also be happy, including the following aspects:

- Everyone is on first name terms and has to wear a name badge. It gives cast members more confidence in approaching management and puts guests at ease in approaching cast members.

- There is an annual Cast Excellence Measurement Survey, where cast members can confidentially air their views.

- Disney believes that Cast Excellence Measurement plus guest satisfaction measurement equals operational and financial success.

- Disney always encourages new ideas and change. Management is encouraged to move locations within the company every couple of years. They can take their experience and fresh ideas with them and will probably be less resistant to change.

- Ninety per cent of cast members are in temporary positions and are more likely to be enthusiastic, fresh and more easily trained.

Culture Change

There are lessons to be learnt from many other organizations in the leisure and tourism industry, whether from good practice or bad practice. What becomes clear from such case studies is that the desire to change needs to be built into the very culture of the organization and that the view that TQM is a change agent rather than a journey or a result is not quite accurate. It is easier to think in terms of Juran's message of continual improvement – improvement in every facet, which contributes to overall performance. The quotation from Popham in Box 10.2 also demonstrates the simplicity of any messages about total quality; attention to detail, getting things right and putting the customer first are the building blocks for any quality approach. Furthermore, the success of Japanese companies in Europe, staffed mainly by Europeans, exposes the myth that the internal culture of Japanese organizations would clash with the wider culture of European countries. Indeed, as noted in Chapter 4, the principles of TQM have emerged from critiques of Japanese organizations in the last 30 years and their approach to management.

It is worth reminding ourselves that, despite the impact of Deming in 1950 (he spoke to the Japanese Union of Scientists and Engineers in June of that year), it did not constitute a revolution in the thinking of the Japanese towards the management of organizations. They had already begun the process of reappraisal (hence the invitation to Deming) and demonstrated the point just made about the need to change organizational culture very gradually.

A number of authors, including Hutchins (1990), Pike and Barnes (1996) and Fache (2000) have shown how organizational performance and the management of total quality are multidimensional in composition and execution. Hellsten and Kleffsjo (2000) suggested that TQM should be seen as a management system made up of values and ideas but also tools and techniques. Hutchins (1990) identified four components in TQM comprising systems, processes, management and style; Athos and Pascale (1981) had earlier constructed their 7S model of management, from their study of Japanese organizations such as Matsushita, which distinguished between the 'hard S's' of strategy, structure and systems and the increasingly important 'soft S's' of staff, style, skills and what they termed superordinate goals. Their analysis bracketed western organizations more naturally with the hard S's, highlighting their traditional, bureaucratic approach to management, whereas the Japanese approach that encouraged and fostered cooperation, collaboration and interdependence as well as development of the human resource fully utilized the soft

---

Box 10.2.   Things can be done right!

The best way to understand how a Japanese reacts to the UK is not to ask (he will be too polite to let on) but to spend time in Japan. Famously, everything works. Trains run meticulously to the timetable. The Shinkansen 'bullet' trains have been careering through Japan for over 25 years and have yet to be involved in a single fatal accident (compare with the UK record including the tragedies of Southall in 1997 and Ladbroke Grove in 1999 which accounted for a combined total of 37 deaths). Mugging is a crime that is practically unknown . . . Litter is equally uncommon except in famous beauty spots and on the peak of Mt Fuji where the Japanese unaccountably forget themselves and turn into barbarians.

In the UK the 'customer as peasant' philosophy prevails. In Japan the customer is still king: the proverb to that effect is taken very seriously. Visit a Tokyo department store at opening time and that's exactly how you will feel: the immaculate troops of assistants lined up like a guard of honour bow profoundly as you pass. Tokyo was once notorious for its pollution: that cliché is as dated as the notion of the Japanese as a producer of things that fall to bits . . . The inventory of perfection is tedious and endless. The Japanese like to do things right.

(Popham, 1991, p.106)

S's. This latter element embraced the shared values and vision for the organization that are now seen to be so important in culture change. Athos and Pascale (1981) felt that the two sets of elements, although dichotomous in some respects, should also be seen as an integrating whole. Pike and Barnes (1996) suggested that the management of quality is made up of both individual and organizational elements. The individual or intrinsic factors include attitudes, aptitudes, knowledge, skills and behaviour, whilst organizational or extrinsic factors include policies, procedures, systems, structures, processes, leadership style and the internal culture of the organization. This has been identified by many observers to be, perhaps, the most important factor in the creation and sustainability of service quality; the example of David Lloyd Leisure in Box 10.3 illustrates an organization's attempt to achieve this. Indeed, there must also be continual improvement of the organizational culture, the very trigger that can nurture and encourage the concept of continual improvement. Jeffries *et al.* (1992, p. 145) suggested that 'cultural change is a very complex business which requires a lot of commitment, a lot of patience and a desire to succeed'.

According to Dale *et al.* (1994a), organizational culture can only be changed if there are changes in attitudes, behaviour and ways of working. They highlighted several ways in which this can be achieved:

- Everyone in the organization must be involved and take personal responsibility for their own quality assurance.
- This involves the inspection of one's own work; therefore errors or defects should not be passed on.
- Customers should be seen as external and internal.
- All customers and suppliers should be built into the improvement process.
- Mistakes should be part of the improvement process.

Further analysis suggests that even before attitudes and behaviour can be changed the wider philosophy of the organization needs to be reappraised. The Industrial Society (1998) suggested that it is the commonly held attitudes, beliefs and values that

underpin the organization's systems and procedures and shape the actions and behaviours of staff. The report went on to argue that many change programmes attempt to change attitudes and behaviour when really it is the underlying values and beliefs that need to be changed in the first place before behaviour and ways of working can be genuinely improved. The Industrial Society carried out a survey of 341 human resource professionals in 1998, of whom 94% said their organization had been involved in culture change at some point. One third were undergoing culture change at the time of the survey, but one third did not have any formal programme in place. Most of the formal programmes in place appeared to be using either an evolutionary approach or one based on performance management and appraisal processes, although both approaches can be problematic; a gradual approach can be confusing, and a sudden change can be off-putting and demotivating, particularly for the longer-serving employees. The Industrial Society recommended a certain approach, as Box 10.4 illustrates.

Jarvis Hotels provides an example of such an approach. The Jarvis Hotel Group has been acknowledged for some time to have a reasonably distinctive approach to quality, with visible and committed management style by the managing director, John Jarvis. The mission statement is simply 'First time, every time' and presents a clear message to staff and customers. The philosophy of the organization is also lucid and open:

> Fundamental to their success are the core values they believe in and practise which are based on three caveats:
>
> - *Employees* shall be given early responsibility in roles where initiative, self-motivation, ability and enthusiasm are quickly recognized and rewarded.
> - *Customers* shall receive our total obsession to meet their needs through structured service approach to making those small, noticeable improvements which create the customers' experience with us.
> - *Our products* are something we feel passionate about and through exciting new concepts for customers and staff alike we aim to offer service, efficiency and

---

Box 10.3.   Case study: David Lloyd Leisure.

David Lloyd centres, perhaps, do not have a strong internal culture at present, partly because of high staff turnover, but their commitment to quality is evident in their continued success and the methods employed to train and develop staff and maintain morale. The group offers a package of benefits to its employees but also receives employee feedback through its scheme. In reporting back, the group highlighted the critical aspects that had been raised: pay, benefits and supervisory practices and the lack of regular performance reviews, which 59% of the survey (754 respondents) raised. Communications also attracted some criticism from 34% of respondents, who felt that communications, both up and down the organization, needed improving in addition to information about general matters. Almost half felt that working conditions were affecting work organization and efficiency and a number suggested that their training could also be improved. On a positive note, 65% said they would recommend the organization as a place to work and many identified management style (86%), team spirit (95%) and morale (58%) to be good. Also emphasized were the organization's excellent image (86%) and the company's customer focus.

An important factor would appear to be the company's willingness to listen to its staff, as well as customers, and its recently published 'agenda for change':

> We are taking your comments and criticisms on the chin. And neither will we let your praise go to our heads. This research has given us an agenda for greater corporate fitness. That is why we did it. We wanted to know. You told us and now we are doing something about it.

The company is following the survey with some focus groups to extend examination of the issues raised and a number of initiatives were under way:

- The setting up of an internal communications group with members from Human Resources, Training, Service Quality, Operations and Information Technology.
- A review of pay and benefits.
- Plans to improve service quality in every club and Head Office underpinned by local plans to tackle communications, team building, the working environment and training and the wider plan published on the company's intranet.

Particular attention was paid to appraisals, with over 200 people trained to undertake them and training with several features: a company induction programme taking place every 7 weeks in different clubs; an intensive 2-day programme for managers on 'managing the future'; IT training for at least one person from each club; courses on member focus and sales and marketing; and other training on first aid, membership rules and regulations and membership communications. Communication with staff is also important:

> At David Lloyd Leisure we are listening to our employees. It is part of our commitment to continuous improvement; we believe that if we improve things for our employees this will lead to improvements for our members.

In its communication with staff the company refers to 'the three rings of perceived value', in which the first and second rings are owned and influenced by management and the third, which is the largest, signifies the domain of front-line performers. It is argued that their ability to delight and surprise members will help to widen the gap between David Lloyd Leisure and its rivals.

Its mission, as it enters the new millennium, is to increase membership to 135,000 by implementing: (i) a programme of training and staff development; (ii) a structured and focused mechanism for evaluating competition; (iii) researching what members feel and think about the company; (iv) developing and acquiring sites that are able to provide 'state of the art' facilities; and (v) maintaining or increasing profit levels.

The plan is based on the service quality plan embracing passion, caring and trust and represents a significant attempt, on paper at least, to develop a strategy and organizational culture driven by customer needs.

---

reliability to ensure each facet of our business 'works', **right first time, every time**.

The philosophy is communicated through training, including a CD-ROM system, where employees can work under their own direction and learn about health and safety, and also dress code and other aspects of brand awareness. The approach also involves the organization's 'quality signatures' and training in Jarvis's team building. There are a number of 'quality signatures', in different facets of work, with a minimum standard in

---

Box 10.4. Industrial Society dos and don'ts for managing a culture change process. (Source: Industrial Society, 1998.)

Dos

- Communicate the concept in ways which do not put off employees who have not yet participated. Graduates of the process have a tendency to overdramatize.
- View it as a process, not an initiative.
- Make sure the time is right.
- Ensure line management is sufficiently motivated to be able to 'walk the walk, talk the talk' and demonstrate personal commitment, action and change.
- Make it easier to do things the new way than not to.
- Talk about best practice rather than culture change.

Don'ts

- Promise what you cannot deliver.
- Ignore conflicts.
- Rush the issue.
- Expect people to change for the same reasons that you do. It must be in their interests.
- Seek to identify and announce an end product. Culture change is a continuous process, a normality.

---

each for staff to reach. Each one contains five categories: (i) quality smile and genuine welcome; (ii) feels fresh, sounds and looks good; (iii) magical merchandising; (iv) super selling; and (v) service delivery.

A core belief of the company requires that 'employees will be given early responsibility in roles where initiative, motivation, ability and enthusiasm are quickly recognized and rewarded'. To enable this to succeed, the organization has a quality service manager, solely responsible for continuing improvement and for ensuring that the 'quality signatures' programme operates effectively. This manager liaises with the human resources department and is supported by weekly quality meetings to audit service and brainstorm ideas for improvement.

Counsell (1999) also referred to the need to change the traditional culture in which managers are seen to think, supervisors to talk and employees to do. Irons (1997) emphasized the importance of a 'strategically cohesive culture', which has a clear focus and vision and embraces the passion and enthusiasm for both the service and the customer by all staff. Holmes Place Leisure Management is a successful chain of health and fitness clubs and, through its vision and goals, places great emphasis on a friendly and relaxed atmosphere in order to achieve guest appreciation

and loyalty. Its whole approach is based on this philosophy and it begins the process with induction and the use of appropriate training packs. The examples of Andover Leisure Centre (Box 10.5) and Amelia Plantation Island (see Box 10.1) present a similar message.

It has been seen from the analysis of both Jarvis Hotels and the Industrial Society that the vision of the organization is important to the process of culture change but, of course, there is still the need to communicate the vision, as Irons (1997) and Hodgkinson (2002) suggested. Thomas Cook provides an example of another organization that communicates clearly with both staff and customers, as the case study (Box 10.6) demonstrates.

It is also important to communicate to all the stakeholders involved and an example of an organization committed to an open approach is the National Trust. It is committed to ensuring that the Trust is as concerned with people as it is with places and it sees this as its most significant role into the new millennium. The Trust recognizes the importance of first impressions and how they are created and managed (National Trust, 1998): 'We intend to devote more resources to ensuring that every visitor is received with warmth and sensitivity through training programmes designed to enhance visitors' enjoyment and understanding of our properties.'

Box 10.5.   Case study: Andover Leisure Centre.

Andover Leisure Centre's mission is 'Working for excellence in leisure' and its values and principles are reasonably clear:

- The customer will always be the focus of our attention.
- We will treat every customer as an individual and recognize their needs.
- We will aspire to exceed customer expectations.
- Working in partnership with Test Valley Borough Council and the community to provide customers with the finest facilities backed by top quality service.
- Committed to continuous improvement.
- Provide the opportunities for staff to realize their true potential.
- Encourage staff that individual performance does matter.
- All are responsible for the financial strength and growth of the company.
- Provision of leisure opportunities for all.
- Provide environments which are welcoming, friendly, fun, safe and clean.

The values of Andover Leisure Centre acknowledge the importance of both customers and staff and its mission represents a constant goal.

Box 10.6.   Case study: Thomas Cook.

Thomas Cook employs over 12,000 staff worldwide who serve some 20 million customers each year. Thomas Cook is acknowledged as being one of the best travel agents in the world and has a reputation for delivering excellent customer service. The company's mission statement was re-launched in December, 1995 and is a very clear focused one:

Exceptional Service from Exceptional People.

It presents a clear message to both customers and staff.

Its previous mission was to 'create the best and most profitable travel-driven service business in the world'. This represented a clear business goal but said less about the company and its values than the present one does. As Chapter 8 shows, the concept of 'moments of truth' underpins much of the approach to service delivery, and training in the company is shaped by the nature of the service encounter.

Staff are encouraged to deal with customers in a number of ways:

- Make every customer feel valued and important.
- Be helpful and offer advice.
- Listen to the customer's needs.
- Create a positive image for the company.
- Share in the excitement of the holiday.

The mission statement is pivotal because it draws attention to the staff as the most important resource and the final guideline in dealing with customers is underpinned by the staff's own experiences of destinations and packages. Thomas Cook serves a number of market segments, including mainstream charter operations, scheduled flights, short breaks, cheap packages, exotic holidays and tailor-made holidays. Staff are trained in selling skills with four stages – lead, find out, match and close – and are therefore hard-nosed and commercial in their approach but are still conscious of the company's commitment to service quality and, particularly, their 'exceptional service'.

TGI Fridays is another example of an organization communicating a shared vision. It is a destination restaurant chain but offers more than the core product of food and drink, as the mission statement referring to the experience in Chapter 8 illustrates. Its approach is a distinctive one and merits highlighting because of its approach to the customer through a shared vision and passion and its systematic training and staff development. The standard objective is 'delivering consistent standards tailored to guest expectations'. This point builds on the earlier reference, in Chapter 8 to the importance of focus in service organizations (Johnston, 1996). The degree of focus, at the levels of service concept, business, site, delivery system and encounter, will have a bearing on the overall culture and the way in which it is described and shared.

The examples highlighted in this chapter such as Andover Leisure Centre (Box 10.5), David Lloyd and Amelia Island Plantation (see Box 10.1) also support the view that 'culture change must come from the bottom but be led by the top' (Schneider and Bowen, 1995). The Broadgate Health and Fitness Club, whose philosophy was described earlier in this chapter, also has a 'bottom-up' approach in that it consults all staff members and changes are implemented by the staff involved at that point of the operations. A prerequisite for developing such a culture is the degree of customer focus in the organization and Cranfield School of Management has developed a diagnostic tool for assessing it (Macaulay and Clark, 1998). It is called the *Culture Web* and is designed to reflect how the organization views the world and its customers. It achieves this through asking three questions:

1.   Is the real focus on meeting customer needs or simply delivering the service, or in the case of some leisure facilities, particularly in the public sector in the 1970s and 1980s, providing them on the basis of political whim, paternalism and standards approaches?
2.   Is short-term profit or return the overriding goal or does long-term survival depend on the customer focus?
3.   What are the central preoccupations of the organization?

In addition to the broad diagnostic approach of the 'Culture Web', there is also a need to use more specific ways of measuring the impact of cultural change:

1.   Qualitative data from staff and customers through before and after surveys, interviews, focus groups.
2.   Quantitative data through:
●   sickness and absenteeism;
●   turnover of staff;
●   staff development reviews;
●   positive attitudes to training opportunities;
●   number of suggestions for improvement.

Conclusions

Many of the examples and case studies illustrated in the book demonstrate establishments and organizations that know and understand their customers and their needs. Disney has led the way for over 40 years and is, literally, close to its customers because of the use and training of its 'cast members'. One feature of a genuine culture of total quality is that of constant change as continual improvement is built into the ethos and processes of the organization. Irons's (1997) process for creating cultural change also supports such an approach:

1.   Find out exactly what customers want and what really matters to them. Working on zones of tolerance and satisfiers and dissatisfiers (see Chapter 13) helps to clarify this point.
2.   What resources, including the capabilities of staff, are needed to meet customer requirements? This means personal qualities as well as technical and interpersonal skills.
3.   Develop a clear vision of what this means. This follows the strategy and the values of the culture referred to earlier.
4.   Communicate the vision.
5.   Learn from experience to innovate constantly.
6.   There has to be leadership as well as management.
7.   The service encounter is the moment of value creation to the customer.
8.   This point of interaction is integral to the planned delivery.

For this to succeed, it is important that there is harmony between the organizational culture and the human resource strategy in place. For example, where a philosophy based on TQM emphasizes the importance of teamwork and cooperation, it will be undermined if performance-related pay is still in place, including, perhaps, incentives such as employee of the month. Zeithaml *et al.* (1990, p. 2) contended that:

People in service work need a vision in which they can believe, an achievement culture that challenges them to be the best they can be, a sense of team that nurtures and supports them, and role models that show them the way.

The case study of Amelia Island Plantation (Box 10.1) illustrates such a culture where much is done to harness the energy and commitment of staff and to develop a clear human resource strategy. The other case studies and examples highlighted also emphasized the importance of organizational culture and values but the contribution that systems and quality tools make towards the culture should not be forgotten and the next chapter addresses these aspects. Chapter 14 examines the important components of human resource strategy in relation to achieving and delivering service quality in leisure and tourism and contextualizes these elements within a wider approach to quality management.

11

Quality Management Systems

A quality culture is difficult to achieve without a context or framework. A quality management system will give that framework, which can act as a catalyst for quality to become embedded throughout the organization. This can be seen in the BS EN ISO 9000 2000 definition of a quality management system: 'a system to establish quality policy and quality objectives and to achieve those objectives'. The system will comprise a few or many of the quality management tools and techniques explored in Chapter 12 and should provide the framework for their integration to meet the quality policies and objectives of the organization. Dale (1994b) stated that 'a quality management system is good management practice'.

Quality management systems should not be confused with total quality management (TQM), which is a philosophy by which the entire organization is managed; it affects the culture as well as the processes and procedures (see Chapter 10).

As the quality management system encompasses all aspects of an organization's quality approach, it is necessary for every member of staff to understand that quality is part of their role and responsibility and not just the domain of the 'quality department'. However, members of staff need to be delegated with the responsibility for overseeing the management of the quality management system, either from a dedicated department or decentralized throughout the organization.

On completion of this chapter it is expected that you will:

- have an understanding of what a quality management system is;
- be able to explain the difference between an accredited quality management system and a non-accredited system;
- have an insight into the advantages and limitations of a range of quality management systems;
- be aware of the extent of their application within the tourism and leisure industry.

Non-accredited and Accredited Quality Management Systems

There are two distinct categories of quality management systems: non-accredited and accredited. It is important to understand the differences between these two types of system and the advantages and disadvantages of both.

Non-accredited quality management systems

These are systems that have been devised purely by the organization and are monitored solely by them (*self-assessment*). They are also known as *in-house* systems. The most famous companies using in-house systems in the tourism and leisure industry are Disney and McDonald's.

Advantages of a non-accredited quality management system

THE SYSTEM CAN BE TAILOR-MADE TO MEET THE ORGANIZATION'S OWN REQUIREMENTS.   When Disney and McDonald's were devising their own quality systems it must be remembered that quality management was dominated by manufacturing. The accredited systems being developed were to meet those needs and not those of the service sector. These companies had no alternative but to devise an in-house system.

LOWER COSTS.   Once the in-house system has been developed there are few direct costs involved in implementation.

FREQUENTLY CARRIED OUT.   Due to the cost advantages of self-assessment it can be carried out on a regular basis. Some commercial leisure and tourism organizations do this on a weekly basis, over a limited number of criteria (e.g. admissions, receipts, secondary spend levels).

Disadvantages of a non-accredited quality management system

NOT RECOGNIZED BY EXTERNAL ORGANIZATIONS. When tendering for a contract or applying for a grant, an internally validated and monitored quality management system may not be recognized; it can be seen as not being as rigorous as an externally accredited one.

CUSTOMS AND PRACTICES PROLIFERATE.   The industry's existing customs and practices are not challenged, and a loss of competitive edge can result.

ORGANIZATIONAL CULTURE PERSISTS.   This is interlinked with proliferating existing customs and practices: the existing organizational culture can remain unchallenged.

MONITORING.   Two different scenarios can occur when internal monitoring of a service takes place. Both are equally unhelpful to the organization as neither situation allows the

organization to get a true representation of service quality:

1.   The staff do not want to criticize or find fault with the work of colleagues, resulting in a higher score being given than is warranted.
2.   Staff do not want another department to be seen to be better than them and so a lower score is awarded.

Self-assessment is seen by many as a way of enhancing overall business performance and it involves assessing the quality policy and goals set by senior managers. It was suggested by Zink and Schmidt (1998) that it needs to be carried out on a regular basis if continuous improvement is going to be achieved. Being an internally validated system, there is no way for customers or other organizations to know how rigorously the assessment is being executed and there is no external 'seal of approval' to be displayed.

Accredited quality management systems

These are systems that have third-party certification. The original system is not prescriptive as to how the individual organization's procedures and processes should be designed but it stipulates how they should be documented to prove that implementation is in accordance with the clauses laid down. The ISO 9000 series is an internationally recognized quality management system that requires certification to be renewed every year. The Business Excellence Model, which is the basis for many of the quality awards, can be used in two ways: either as a non-accredited self-assessment system, or to enter the 'competition' for the quality award and be assessed externally.

Advantages of an accredited quality management system

RECOGNIZED EXTERNALLY.   This accredited quality management system is acknowledged throughout the industry sector, or in the case of ISO 9000 series, the global business environment. This can have a major benefit when an organization is tendering for a contract or applying for grant aid. The gaining of an external accreditation can be said to enhance the company's image within the industry sector as well as to the customers (Williams, 1997b). This can have the accumulative effect of the organization gaining competitive edge over its rivals.

CAN ACT AS AN AGENT FOR CHANGE.   The case study that follows (see Box 11.1) illustrates that an external assessment can highlight problems within an organization and act as a catalyst for change.

INTEGRATION OF QUALITY TOOLS AND TECHNIQUES CAN BE UNDERTAKEN.   A range of quality management tools and techniques can be integrated into the formalized structure within an accredited system.

CONSULTATION WITH CUSTOMERS.   Both informal and formal consultation with customers and other stakeholders is a requirement of accredited quality management systems.

CONTINUOUS IMPROVEMENT.   The need to demonstrate continuous improvement is another requirement.

ORGANIZATIONAL APPRAISAL.   The design of procedures and processes required by an accredited quality management system enables an in-depth review of how the organization works. All managers and staff should be involved in reappraising what is being done, how it is being achieved and why.

IMPROVEMENT TO SERVICE DELIVERY.   The constructive management of all aspects of the service delivery process highlights areas of *non-conformance* (mistakes). Any reduction in this element reduces costs to the organization. The organization will in turn gain a reputation for reliability – a major consideration for customers (Zeithaml *et al.*, 1990) – and will retain them, engendering their loyalty.

Disadvantages of an accredited quality management system

IMPOSED.   Criticisms of accredited systems from the voluntary sector and small

commercial businesses have been that they were not compatible with their organization's structures. A number of accredited systems are addressing this problem.

COSTS.   Costs of designing and subsequently maintaining the systems are prohibitive for many smaller organizations. This is because the preparation for accreditation generally requires a major input from consultants, as organizations do not have surplus staff to carry out these tasks or the experience to do so. The re-registering is an additional operational cost that can be prohibitive.

SELECTIVE CERTIFICATION.   Organizations generally only put forward for certification those sections that are the easiest to manage, with few problems. Quality management systems should cover the whole of the organization, as the service that a customer (either internal or external) receives is an accumulation of all the acts within the organization.

LIMITATIONS.   Many organizations do not understand that the implementation of a quality management system is only 'an element of TQM; it is not an alternative' (Dale *et al.*, 1994a). The elements that are omitted from a quality management system but can be found in TQM are those dealing with innovation and creativity.

BS EN ISO 9000 Series Quality Management System

Historical perspective

The predecessor to the BS EN ISO 9000 series in the UK was the BS 5750 quality management system, devised by the British Standards Institute (BSI) in the late 1970s. It was developed and driven by the needs of the defence industry and had the potential for third-party assessment (Mills, 1992). The philosophy was to improve quality throughout the management processes by the introduction of a formal documented system of standards and procedures. Prior to this, British industry had relied on self-certification on

---

Box 11.1.   Case study: theatre – accredited vs. non-accredited quality management systems.

A theatre in the voluntary sector was trying unsuccessfully to develop a total quality management (TQM) culture throughout the organization. Unfortunately quality management was not perceived to be the role of the whole of the organization; the creative side of the organization was left to continue in its old style of ethos, giving very little thought to the needs of its internal customers.

This was reinforced by senior management concentrating on how to improve the front-of-house services (e.g. ticket sales, secondary spend). The needs of the front-of-house staff as internal customers of the creative side of the organization were never addressed. For example, casting of the lead part was regularly done after the date when the publicity materials had to be at the printers. The marketing staff could not capitalize on the 'star' to optimize ticket sales – a standard technique used in theatre management. Senior managers felt that they could not address this issue with the Creative Director.

The senior managers instead addressed the issue of reducing ticket sales by regularly introducing a variety of quality management tools and techniques and even went so far as to engage consultants to set performance standards for the business elements of the theatre. A considerable amount of time and effort was put into implementing these by the front-of-house staff but, as Juran (1988a) pointed out, 20% of quality problems are due to the staff but 80% are caused by the managers.

All the initiatives were self-assessed (e.g. monitoring by performance indicators, staff appraisals and quality circles) with the goal of trying to achieve a TQM culture in future. The introduction of an outside accredited quality management system rather than always looking towards self-assessment would act as a catalyst for change. Curry and Monaghan (1994) suggested that ISO 9002 (as it then was) could be used as a change agent, stating: 'Change does not come about of its own accord, but has to be both driven and led.'

Dale's (1994b) research findings supported this strategy. He suggested that 'it is not easy to get every function and person involved in taking responsibility for their own quality assurance and to make quality improvements . . . The ISO 9000 series . . . can assist in making it happen'.

Whilst all the theatre's quality initiatives are not within a quality system framework and are internally validated, the fundamental problems will remain. The inherent problem with the ISO 9000 series accredited system (see below for more details) is that the business side of the organization may go for accreditation but the creative side may not and the problems will still be there, especially if the quality manual is written without reference to procedures that integrate the two. A quality award (see below for details) may overcome this problem. As Zeithaml and Bitner (1996) observed: 'Breaking down the walls between functions is difficult and time consuming, but high quality service cannot be addressed without it.'

The theatre is heading for stagnation, with a strong possibility it will wither away. Unless the concepts of quality management are embraced completely by all of the senior management team and the necessary resources are provided (e.g. full-time quality manager with the power to address the fundamental issues), success in any terms will not be achieved (Crosby, 1979).

---

an industry-by-industry basis, each of which had a set of voluntary standards (Warner, 1977).

From the 1980s, the Department of Trade and Industry was actively encouraging British industry to consider the introduction of quality initiatives, especially BS 5750, to enable organizations to compete with the rest of the world (Department of Trade, 1982).

To aid international trading, in 1987 the International Standards Organization (ISO) launched the ISO 9000 series. This was in addition to the European standard EN 29000 and the modified BS 5750 1987. The three standards were the same but multiple registrations were necessary. Whilst these standards were originally driven by the certification

needs of the manufacturing sector, the service sector was registering as well. The public sector was preparing to undergo operational changes with the passing of the Local Government Act, 1988, which instigated the compulsory contracting out of leisure facilities management, with the requirement that local authority direct service organizations should bid alongside the commercial sector. A contractual requirement was for contractors to be BS 5750 registered or working towards registration (Freeman-Bell and Grover, 1994). The need for registration for all sectors for contractual purposes has been well documented by, amongst others, Gaskin (1991), Juran (1993), Dale (1994b), Griffin (1995) and McLachlan (1996).

In 1994, the three standards were amal-gamated into one: the BS EN ISO 9000 series, but referred to as the ISO 9000 series. The use of the term *series* is important, as ISO 9000 has multiple parts, some of which are not applicable to each and every industry. The 1994 series has been reviewed as part of the 5-year mandatory process and the details below follow the new 2000 series. It needs to be remembered that the transition period will be approximately 3 years: the two series will run in parallel until 2003.

Implementation by the leisure and tourism industry

Most of the commercial leisure and tourism sector has not thought ISO 9000 worthwhile, because of the ratio of costs to perceived benefits (Rowe, 1992). The catering elements of the industry have developed their own in-house systems, with ISO 9000 clauses as the foundation (East, 1993). This is due to the ease of being able to integrate the procedures required by the Food Safety Act 1990 and Hazard Analysis Critical Control Point analysis. Hotels are different; certification to ISO 9000 series is often a requirement of their contracts, especially if they are a supplier to the manufacturing sector.

In the public sector, although very little research has been carried out into areas other than leisure centres, Walsh (1998) estimated that over 200 (10%) leisure centres had certificated to ISO 9002. One of the main factors for this is the contracting out of services due to the Local Government Act, 1988. Robinson (1996a) stated that central government's policy of introducing compulsory competitive tendering into leisure services 'had the dual aim of trying to improve the quality of services and to cut costs of service provision'. Monitoring of services became inevitable with this new management regime and ISO 9002 was specified in some of the contract documentation.

Whilst the voluntary sector is a major provider of leisure opportunities, the implementation of any quality management system is limited. This is said to be due to the extensive costs of designing and registration for ISO 9000 series. As the majority of voluntary organizations have fewer than 20 paid staff and are governed by volunteers, this point may be valid (Astbury, 1993).

The main reason for the leisure and tourism industry adopting ISO 9000 series is to give organizations a competitive edge when tendering for contracts, especially those from the public sector (e.g. leisure centre management, institutional catering services). The gaining of ISO 9000 can go some way to improving the organizational image but this tends to be within the industry rather than in the eyes of consumers of the services.

Research by Robinson (1996a) into public sector leisure facilities suggested that financial efficiency is one of the major benefits of implementing this system. As local authorities are reducing subsidies to leisure provision, this is a consideration (CIPFA, 1994).

ISO 9000 2000

The latest revision of the series comprises four parts (Vine and Hele, 1998):

- ISO 9000: Concepts and terminology (this is the revised ISO 8402:1995).
- ISO 9001: Requirements for quality management (to provide confidence as a result of demonstration in product/ service conformance to established requirements).
- ISO 9004: Guidance for quality management of organizations (to achieve benefits for all stakeholders through sustained customer satisfaction).
- ISO 19011: Guidelines for auditing quality management systems (formerly ISO 10011).

ISO 9001 2000

For leisure organizations, ISO 9002 from the 1994 series of standards has been superseded by ISO 9001 2000. The main change is said to be an emphasis on a process-driven approach based on the 'Plan Do Check Act' (PDCA) scenario of Deming (1986), demonstrated in Fig. 11.1. The PDCA model allows for continuous improvement to be central but still enables more flexibility when organizations wish to revise their systems and is compatible with the environmental management system standard, ISO 14000. The model is said to be able to control the interface between activities and processes by providing vertical as well as horizontal process integration, both in its entirety (major loops) and in small loops from one area to another (BSI, 1998).

There is less paperwork with the new ISO 9000, (*Qualityworld*, Aug., pp. 32–33).

ISO 9001 clauses are divided into five parts as displayed in the model in Fig. 11.1:

- **Quality Management System** – the purpose and requirements of the system need to be stated.
- **Management Responsibility** – covers policy formulation, procedures and control of documentation, as well as customer needs. Planning for improvement is a task set for senior management in this revision.
- **Resource Management** – the majority of this section is assigned to human resource management and training but the working environment and its infrastructure are included.
- **Product Realization** – this is to ensure that there is a pathway from customer requirements to customer satisfaction.

The need to design, operate and control the processes to meet customer requirements is emphasized. Most of the clauses from the existing standard have gone into this section.

- **Measurement, Analysis and Improvement** – this is arranged into a number of monitoring areas: customer satisfaction, internal audit of the system, processes and the product/service provided. The analysis of the data is stressed, as is the need for feedback mechanisms to achieve continuous improvement.

Under ISO 9001 2000 senior management is tasked to establish the organization's quality policy and to undertake a review of the whole of the system at predetermined intervals. The quality objectives for the organization have to be stated and how to achieve them has to be planned.

As ISO 9001 is based on principles of quality management (BSI, 1998) these will provide a framework for integration. The eight principles are: (i) customer focus; (ii) leadership; (iii) involvement with people; (iv) process approach; (v) system approach to management; (vi) continual improvement; (vii) factual approach to decision making; and (viii) mutually beneficial supplier relationship. These eight principles reflect the teachings of the early quality theorists (e.g. Juran's triology, Fiegenbaum's holistic approach) and, focusing on people (staff, suppliers and

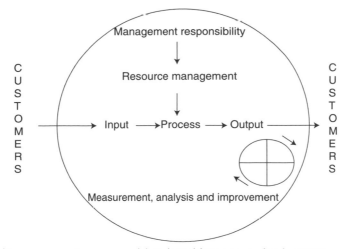

Fig. 11.1.   Quality management process model. (Adapted from Vine and Hele, 1998.)

customers), good practice in service quality management is followed.

The previous version of the standard was criticized by Dale (1994b) as it did not have a clause to demonstrate that standards had improved. He considered that this led to a 'steady state' rather than continuous improvement and Juran (1993) confirmed this view. Goult (1995) disagreed and suggested that this stable state is an advantage in that it enables an organization to move forward from this platform of stability to drive improvement.

An ISO 9001 requirement is that it is audited by a third-party certification body and that the quality system has documented procedures and work instructions collated into a hardcopy or electronic quality manual (Johnson, 1993).

ISO 9004 2000

As the leisure and tourism industry's use of quality management tools and techniques has matured, it is familiar with their concepts and implementation and more sophisticated holistic approaches are required.

The clauses of ISO 9004 are itemized under the following headings:

- **Management Responsibility** – this includes being aware of the needs of all interested parties (i.e. suppliers and investors as well as staff and customers). Other responsibilities include quality policy formulation and planning as well as compliance with legal requirements. The control of the actual quality system and its documentation is also specified.
- **Resource Management** – the majority of this section is assigned to human resource management and training but the working environment and its infrastructure are included. This is the same as ISO 9001 2000.
- **Product and/or Service Realization** – this has five parts to it. Some of these are similar to ISO 9001 2000 (i.e. the need to design, operate and control the processes) but it requires the needs of all

stakeholders of the organization to be taken into account rather than only those of the customers. Under this section there are clauses dealing with the production and delivery of goods and services. This complies with the public sector Best Value management regime (see Chapter 13).

- **Measurement, Analysis and Improvement** – the clauses in this portion require monitoring to take place at all stages of the process and include all non-conformances. As well as internal audit of the system, and the monitoring of stakeholder satisfaction with the performance of the organization processes and the product/service provided, information must be gathered to allow for continuous improvement to be monitored. It needs to be demonstrated that a coordinated communications system is in place.

According to Griffin (1995) when debating the ISO series, 'The prime objective has always been to provide a model of good management practice for the mutual benefit of both the customer and supplier.' It was explained that 'it was never intended as a rigid specification'.

It was said by Clements (1998) that the emphasis is on satisfying customer requirements by continuous improvement and also enables consideration of other stakeholder needs.

ISO 9004 2000 has the ability for self-assessment to take place, which has some of the advantages of a non-accredited system (listed earlier in this chapter) and reflects a major advantage of the Excellence Model (discussed below). The new version allows for 'opting out' of clauses if they are not applicable to a specific organization. This should have some benefit to the voluntary sector of the industry and small commercial businesses but ongoing costs will still have a major negative impact for them.

ISO 9000 series had many critics, including Seddon (1997), who saw it as a means of quality inspection and the instigator of 'sub-optimization of performance' rather than a quality assurance system. Unfortunately the previous ISO 9000 series of standards was used by some organizations as a mechanistic quality system, whereby the gaining and registering of the award were the most important elements. Continuous improvement and customer orientations were not the focuses for these types of organizations. The previous versions of the standard allowed organizations to ignore these factors; this is no longer the case.

ISO 9000 2000 is not as popular with the leisure industry as it once was, especially in those organizations that manage public sector facilities. Due to the introduction of the Best Value management regime into that sector, the QUEST quality system is gaining popularity. It is said that QUEST enables local authorities to comply with Best Value regulations (see Chapter 12).

E-Quality Manuals and E-Audits

A requirement of ISO 9000 2000, as with all other quality initiatives audited by a third-party certification body, is that the quality system has documented procedures and work instructions that can be produced as a quality manual on paper or electronically (e-quality manual).

Many software houses and quality management consultants have developed packages that can process and manage all the data that a quality management system involves. The next development is for electronic audits (e-audits) to be carried out. These can be regular in-house audits or where all documentation is sent on-line to the third-party certification bodies. The authors know of few tourism and leisure organizations that have yet embraced this concept.

Quality Awards and the Excellence Model

A number of accredited quality awards are based on the Excellence Model, which is a generic model that allows a holistic approach to be taken to the management of the quality system. An individual organization has the flexibility to insert numerous quality tools and techniques within the model's framework.

Excellence is the focus of the quality awards and many writers, including Galloway (1996), would have difficulty in defining quality this way, considering it 'transcendent' and something to be 'recognized rather than identified or measured'.

Search for excellence and dissemination of 'best practice' form the underlying philosophy and are a major function of the quality award organizers. The following are UK quality awards available based on the Excellence Model (Oldfield, 1999): Quality Scotland; Northern Ireland Quality Award; Excellence North East; Midland Excellence; British Quality Foundation; Wales Quality Centre; Excellence North West; Excellence South West; Meridian Business Excellence; Sheffield Excellence; Business in the Community.

There are also industry-specific awards such as QUEST (see Chapter 12), which is a quality management system for sports development and leisure centre management and is said to be based on the Excellence Model.

Whilst there seem to be many different quality awards, their use of the Excellence Model as their foundation makes it easier for organizations to benchmark (see Chapter 12) against each other.

The model allows organizations to develop either an accredited or a non-accredited quality system by way of its two stages: the first is to monitor the organization by using the self-assessment criteria of the model; and the second phase is to apply for a specific quality award, which requires an external assessment. For every organization that enters an award, over 1000 others have asked for the model's assessment criteria so that self-assessment can be undertaken (Smith, 1999).

The process of self-assessment is a means for continuous improvement, as advocated by Berry (1995) and Coulambidou and Dale

(1995). The self-assessment vehicle is not without its critics. Research by Davis *et al.* (1996) showed that the scores can be higher than when externally assessed but that overall benefits were still gained.

Berry (1995), writing about organizations applying for a quality award but not winning one, said that they

> report significant benefits none the less. Not only does the application process offer a framework for thinking about quality and a mechanism for identifying weaknesses, but the process itself requires broad participation and leadership.

Davis *et al.* (1996) stated that the Excellence Model is

> based on the premise that customer satisfaction, people satisfaction and impact on society are achieved through leadership driving policy and strategy, people (employee) empowerment, resources and processes and this leads ultimately to business results.

This is illustrated in Box 11.2, which uses the European Quality Award Scheme (EQA) as well as the Excellence Model framework. As the model has an all-embracing framework, this allows for the incorporation of the principles of many of the quality tools and techniques discussed in the next chapter.

Jones (1995) expressed the opinion that the EQA gives 'meaningful scores', which have weightings that reflect the importance of the dimensions. Unfortunately, Jones did not state to whom they are important – the customer or the organization?

These quality awards based on the Excellence Model enable all aspects of the business to be managed. Zink and Schmidt (1998) suggested that the model is a 'multi-dimensional target system'. Dale and Lascelles (1997) saw organizations that have reached this stage of their quality evolution as being at 'a point at which continuous improvement has become total in nature'.

Box 11.2.   Case study: European Quality Award (EQA).

This annual award has been administered, since its inception in 1991, by the European Foundation for Quality Management (EFQM). EFQM was formed in 1988 and its purpose is 'to enhance the competitive position of European organizations and the effectiveness and efficiency . . . by reinforcing the importance of quality in all aspects of the organization's activities' and 'assisting the development of quality improvement' (EFQM, 1996).

The award is given to the most successful organizations that 'show a high level of commitment to quality' (EFQM, 1996), whilst the lesser European Quality Prize is given to a number of organizations that display excellence in quality processes towards continuous improvement.

The awards objectives are to:

● Focus attention on total quality management activity in a dramatic way.
● Provide encouragement to individuals and companies to develop quality improvement activities.
● Demonstrate the results achievable in all aspects of the organization's business.

The means for achieving these objectives are by:

● Obtaining recognition of the European Quality Award around the world.
● Recounting top quality performance of people and organizations in Western Europe.
● Spreading information on quality programmes and creating role models of excellence (Peacock, 1994).

The model shown in Box 11.3 is based on the **RADAR** logic (EFQM, 1999):

Results	Determine results required
Approach	Plan and develop
Deployment	Deploy approaches
Assessment and **Review**	Approaches and their deployment

Box 11.3. Model based on RADAR logic (EFQM, 1999).

Summary criteria for enablers:

1. Leadership
How leaders develop and facilitate the achievement of the mission and vision, develop values required for long-term success and implement these via appropriate actions and behaviours, and are personally involved in ensuring that the organization's management system is developed and implemented.
2. Policy and strategy
How the organization implements its mission and vision via a clear stakeholder-focused strategy, supported by relevant policies, plans, objectives, targets and processes.
3. People
How the organization manages, develops and releases the knowledge and full potential of its people at an individual, team-based and organization-wide level, and plans these activities in order to support its policy and strategy and the effective operation of its processes.
4. Partnership and resources
How the organization plans and manages its external partnerships and internal resources in order to support its policy and strategy and the effective operation of its processes.
5. Process
How the organization designs, manages and improves its processes in order to support its policy and strategy and fully satisfy, and generate increasing value for, its customers and other stakeholders.

Criteria for results:

6. Customer results
What the organization is achieving in relation to its external customers.
7. People results
What the organization is achieving in relation to its people.
8. Society results
What the organization is achieving in relation to local, national and international society as appropriate.
9. Key performance results
What the organization is achieving in relation to its planned performance.

Evaluation Systems:
Two monitoring or evaluation systems have been devised:

1. Pathfinder Card
This is for use in the self-assessment exercise to facilitate improvement. There are no scores to be calculated, but a series of searching questions; for example:
● Is the approach focused on stakeholder needs?
● Is the approach sustainable?
2. Radar Scoring Matrix
This is the system used by the European Quality Award assessment and the weighting of each criterion is shown in Box 11.2. The percentage scores are combined to give an overall score out of 1000 points.

   This scoring system can be used as a benchmarking tool (see Chapter 12) with organizations that are using this matrix. Spider diagrams can be constructed for a comparative analysis to be made (Chapman, 2000).

Other Significant International Awards

Deming Prize

The Union of Japanese Scientists and Engineers award this prize to individuals, organizations or industries that have contributed to statistical process control. Whilst once restricted to Japanese organizations, it is now open to all.

Malcolm Baldridge Award

This is as a result of American legislation that established an annual national award

to promote quality awareness and to disseminate good practice. This is only open to
US organizations in three categories: manufacturing, service and small businesses. The
seven categories of assessment are very similar to the Excellence Model, but the points
allocation is somewhat different.

From the tourism industry, the Ritz-
Carlton Hotel Company was a service
category winner in 1992.

Summary

Dale and Lascelles (1997) saw the introduction of quality management systems into
an organization as the stage below TQM in
their four levels in the evolution of quality
management and quality assurance. The
fundamental difference between this stage
and the two previous ones is that quality
permeates the whole of the organization,
rather than control or inspection. Quality
leads the decision-making process and the
results are that the meeting of customer
needs and the quest for continuous improvement are tireless.

The choice of which system and or
whether or not it is accredited is actually
immaterial as long as those last two factors,
driven by senior management, are adopted
into the culture of the organization. External
factors will determine if an accredited system
is required (e.g. local authority contract
specifications).

12

Quality Management Tools and Techniques

Quality management tools and techniques should be used not on an individual basis but as a route to total quality management, each one having a cumulative effect to improve quality (Dale, 1999).

Most tools and techniques require a foundation of service standards known as performance indicators (PIs) to be set and this will be discussed in this chapter. The majority of the tools and techniques are certified by outside bodies and therefore rigorous documentary evidence is required to demonstrate that the organization is implementing them against the set PIs and assessment criteria. One of the most common components of certificated systems is the need to have a formalized complaints procedure.

On completion of this chapter it is expected that you will have acquired:

- an understanding of how to implement a range of generic quality tools and techniques;
- an overview of a range of specialist quality monitoring systems for the tourism and leisure industry;
- an insight into the limitations of each quality tool or technique;
- an ability to outline the philosophical backgrounds to the development of these quality initiatives.

Investors in People

Investors in People (IIP) is a central government initiative from the UK Department of Employment devised by the National Training Task Force. It is externally assessed by either the Learning and Skills Councils. It was launched in October 1991 (Employment Department, 1990).

The task force has developed a national standard to enable organizations to become more effective, especially in developing their human resource. This is reflected in their definition of quality: 'A commitment to quality in an organization must be backed by a commitment to involve and develop everyone to play their part' (Employment Department, 1992). This is achieved by the underpinning philosophy of IIP, 'that there is the need for employers to link business strategy plans coherently with the staff training and development cycle' (Institute of Personnel Management, undated).

This system concentrates on assessing training needs via staff appraisals on an annual basis. Zeithaml *et al.* (1990) stressed the need to acknowledge that staff are a major resource, whose contribution is vital to delivering services. The training and development of staff is a major contributor in reducing the heterogeneity that is characteristic of service delivery.

In the UK, training budgets are only 2–3% of the labour costs; the service sector tends to be slightly lower than this (1.8%). This is low in comparison with other European countries. Also training, especially in the tourism and leisure industry, tends to be of a low level, driven by statutory requirements of Health and Safety legislation or the Food Hygiene Act rather than a long-term commitment to continuous professional development.

Implementation of IIP

Investors in People is about action and excellence. It helps you to raise the performance of your organization through the effective development of people.
(Employment Department, 1990)

To facilitate this the organization is judged over the four principles outlined in Box 12.1. Documentary evidence needs to be available to show that these are being adhered to before the IIP award is granted.

The benefits to an organization are said to be higher productivity, greater competitiveness, higher customer satisfaction, more motivated staff, better company image, improved internal communications and more focused and productive training (*Building Capability for the 21st Century*, 1999, cited in Investors in People, 2001b).

Robinson (1996a), researching the effects of quality programmes in leisure centres, found that 29% of the organizations using such programmes found an improvement in staff motivation and customer satisfaction. She also found that implementation of IIP was 'time consuming and does not necessarily include part-time staff' – the use of part-time and seasonal staff is a major facet of the tourism and leisure workforce. Walsh (1998),

working in a similar area of the industry, suggested that the popularity of IIP was due to there being fewer direct costs, as it required 'little or no consultancy input'.

Maynard (1995) pointed out that IIP can play a role in developing an organization's overall quality philosophy, as it can be a contributor when complying with other quality initiatives such as ISO 9002 and the European Quality Award (see Chapter 11) under the 'people management' criteria.

Reasons for adopting IIP

The author's own research into quality initiatives in the UK leisure industry revealed that the reasons why leisure organizations adopted IIP were that it enhances the organization's image to customers and other organizations in the sector, provides marketing opportunities and highlights skills shortages within the organization (Williams, 1997a). None of these are detrimental to an organization, yet there are some concerns. This technique does not embrace the whole of the organization but concentrates on the human resource function only. It is also an internally focused initiative with no customer input, and only if it is integrated into a holistic quality management system can its benefits be fully gained.

Service First and Charter Mark Award

This initiative and its associated award are only available to public sector tourism and leisure organizations. It is based on the Citizen's Charter, which was launched in 1991 with the publication of the White Paper,

Box 12.1.	Investors In People principles. (Source: Investors in People, 2001a.)
Commitment	An IIP is fully committed to developing its people in order to achieve its aims and objectives.
Planning	An IIP is clear about its aims and its objectives and what its people need to do to achieve them.
Action	An IIP develops its people effectively in order to improve its performance.
Evaluation	An IIP understands the impact of its investment in people on its performance.

The Citizen's Charter: Raising the Standard (Cabinet Office, 1991). The UK government has expressed continuing support for Citizen's Charter principles with the 'Service First' initiative, stating: 'Our aim is to help public services deliver a better society for our citizens' (Cabinet Office, 1998).

Implementation of Service First

Following the ten principles (Box 12.2), local authority leisure services can develop customer charters, stating the type and promised level of service, the redress that is available if the organization fails to deliver to the set standards of service and how to complain or contact the organization. The Service First Unit has the right to veto central government departments and state-owned organizations' charters but not those from local authority service providers.

The Service First criteria allow for redress, including compensation, if service delivery falls short of the standard that was promised. This contradicts Crosby's (1979) zero defects concept whereby total elimination of mistakes is the only valid strategy. The Service First criteria reflected the service mapping theories of Shostack (1987) and Gummesson (cited by Armistead, 1994). They stated that it is not possible to get it right every time and so it is necessary to have pre-planned service recovery mechanisms.

Another criterion requires 'Planned Improvements and Innovations' at no additional cost, which is likely to put pressure on the delivery systems, including the staff, and result in declining service quality. Bone (1991, cited in Buswell, 1993b) stated that the setting of standards is not enough; there must be the resources to deliver them.

Who are the customers?

Service First requires that customers be consulted about service targets and standards. When referring to the Citizen's Charter implementation, practitioners such as Richards and Le Grove (1992) suggested that

> **Box 12.2.**   Service First Principles. (Source: Cabinet Office, 1998.)
>
> 1. Set standards of service.
> 2. Be open and provide full information.
> 3. Consult and involve.
> 4. Encourage access and promotion of choice.
> 5. Treat all fairly.
> 6. Put things right when they go wrong.
> 7. Use resources effectively.
> 8. Innovate and improve.
> 9. Work with other providers.
> 10. Provide user satisfaction.

some adjustment had to be made to local government culture before the notion of customers could be assimilated.

Pollitt (1994) considered that customer and citizen are not the same. Unlike a customer, a citizen may not necessarily interact with the service provider. Prior *et al.* (1993) had previously written of the Citizen's Charter that 'the consumerist approach assumes certain common characteristics and behaviours on the part of service users, which do not reflect reality'. They classified users of local government services into two different types: voluntary and compulsory. Leisure service participants are typical of their first classification where they have made 'a decision to acquire desired services'. Robinson (1996b) would agree that local authorities have had to become customer oriented and this is reflected by the change of terminology from 'users' of leisure facilities to 'customers'.

Gaster (1992) was an advocate of an open, multi-stakeholder consultation process. He saw it as a way of defining the organizational objectives and setting of the performance standards. Davies and Girdler (1998) itemized seven possible stakeholders of local authority parks and open spaces. Although the 'dedicated users' will be easy to consult, 'the whole of the electorate' will not be. Wide-scale consultation will not only be costly, diverting resources away from services, but also time consuming.

One category of stakeholders that Davies and Girdler (1998) omitted is organizations that grant-aid the facility, such as the National

Lottery Heritage Fund, which offers grants to restore historic parks and gardens.

The government is committed to the public sector having a customer focus and this is demonstrated in the setting up of a 'People's Panel' of a maximum of 5000 people specifically for customer research (Cabinet Office, 1998).

Although the Service First initiative can be used for self-assessment, the associated quality award Charter Mark is a third-party assessment, which is free to apply for. The main advantage is that it is externally recognized by other public sector organizations, and it provides a free consultant's report on the service provision of the organization.

To facilitate the writing of customer charters, the Audit Commission (a government agency tasked with monitoring local government spending) publishes model standards. These are based on a range of PIs discussed in depth in Chapter 9.

Most of the model service standards are indicative of monitoring economy and efficiency only. Monitoring the effectiveness of the services to the community, a stated aim of the Service First quality initiative (Cabinet Office, 1998), is missing.

Reasons for adopting Service First

One of the authors (Williams, 1997a) found that the reasons why organizations applied for the Charter Mark award were not to do with improving services to their customers but depended on other factors: (i) pressure from central government (i.e. cutting of grant-aid if an organization did not conform); (ii) political ideology of the ruling party of the local authority (i.e. when the Conservative party was in power at central government level, Labour ruled that local councils did not apply for the Charter Mark award); and (iii) the desire to improve the council's image to its citizens and other public sector organizations. Unfortunately, improvement of services is not mentioned in this list, but the writing of a customer charter and the associated self-assessment monitoring that this entails seem to be synonymous with

improvement to service delivery. The gaining of the associate award was a secondary aspiration for many councils.

Quality Circles

Dale and Boaden's (1994) definition of a quality circle is 'a voluntary group of between six and eight employees from the same work area'. The function of a quality circle is to allow employees to meet, in the organization's time, to solve problems for functional areas for which they are responsible. Whilst they seem to operate in isolation, quality circles should be networked via a coordinator so that information can be passed throughout the organization.

This is an internal system with no external customer involvement and, depending on how the quality circle is constituted, can allow vertical and horizontal communications throughout the organization. The authors would disagree with Dale and Boaden that staff should come from the same area, as this would facilitate only vertical communications.

Although vertical communications are important, allowing front-line staff to disseminate customers' comments to others in different areas of the organization may be of equal importance. Quality circles comprising staff from across the organization comply with Deming's (1986) idea that institutional barriers need to be broken down for a holistic quality culture to develop. (Quality circles will be explained in more detail in Chapter 14.)

Benchmarking

The Institute of Quality Assurance Workshop defined benchmarking as 'a continuous systematic process of evaluating companies against recognized industry leaders. It determines business processes that represent "Best Practice" and establishes performance levels.'

Benchmarking is seen as a way of reducing operating costs, improving service delivery efficiency and quality and thereby increasing customer satisfaction. Benchmark comparisons need to be carried out in an in-depth and systematic way to achieve most benefits. According to Bogan and English (1994) benchmarking can have a more radical effect on an organization as it can act as a catalyst for learning and can accelerate change. The underlying philosophy is that the sharing of ideals enables all organizations to improve and is therefore beneficial for the community as a whole. For example, improving service delivery could enable an organization to win more contracts; this could then lead to the creation of jobs and improve the economic wealth locally and nationally. This approach does not suppress healthy competition but acknowledges that service providers have wider responsibilities and have to operate in a complex, ever-changing operational environment.

Benchmarking partners

In the past, organizations have informally and unofficially sent their employees to experience their competitors' services. In recent years this has been formalized into benchmarking, a quality management tool. Three classifications are used for benchmarking, based on the organization that is chosen as the partner (Love and Dale, 1999).

Internal benchmarking

This indicates that one part of an organization is being compared with another. This is useful if there is a geographical spread (a number of branches) or a decentralized organizational structure (whereby each outlet carries out a number of similar tasks, such

as finance or personnel functions). It is considered that internal benchmarking overcomes the 'not invented here' syndrome that can be used as a criticism against another organization's customs and practices.

Two problems that can occur with internal benchmarking are: (i) that the people assessing may know or have worked in the section they are benchmarking, which can result in high scores being given that may distort the actual situation; and (ii) that the opposite of (i) can happen: a section gives low scores as they do not wish anybody to be better than them. Either scenario renders the information useless and a waste of resources.

Competitive benchmarking

This is benchmarking against an organization's own competitors. The difficulty of obtaining partners that are able to share business-sensitive information should not be underestimated. Although the public and voluntary sectors of the leisure industry will be more predisposed to this mutual help, the commercial sectors of the tourism industry have developed benchmarking clubs (see Box 12.3). In the tourism sector, airlines and hotels have formal competitive benchmarking programmes.

Drew (1997) has highlighted that breakthroughs are very rarely achieved by competitive benchmarking, as the industry's customs and practices may dominate. Keehley and MacBride (1997) cited Juran, who said that military generals in the early 19th century watched a circus to ascertain the best way to erect, dismantle and move equipment, people and animals frequently and in short time

---

Box 12.3.   Case study: competitive benchmarking of tourist attractions in New South Wales, Australia. (Source: Thatcher, 1998.)

Competitive benchmarking is being facilitated by the introduction of an on-line web site for the tourist attractions industry. Deloitte Touche Tohmatsu has developed key performance indicators in consultation with the industry and tourism organizations. Twenty key generic industry-specific indicators are supplemented by two additional sets: one for large operators and the other for smaller ones.

From information supplied by the subscribers, Deloitte Touche Tohmatsu updates generic performance indicator data monthly and the use of a secure password enables subscribers to download 'flash' reports. A more in-depth report can follow later.

Commercially sensitive data, such as revenue or expenditure, are not included.

periods. This logistics exercise may not have been as instructive if observations had been confined to other military organizations.

Functional/generic benchmarking

This compares a particular process or function of an organization with the same process in another. The industrial base or sector will be different; therefore sharing of in-depth information can be less threatening. Good relationships with suppliers can result in this type of benchmarking partnerships.

What to benchmark?

Selecting the right type of benchmarking partner is only one element in achieving success. Drew (1997) categorized the activities that can be benchmarked into three types:

1. **Process benchmarking** is the easiest. A comparison is made between specific work practices or operations (e.g. reception desk operations).
2. **Service benchmarking** is the comparison of a whole service (see example in Box 12.4) and is far more complex and time consuming (e.g. sports development unit).
3. **Strategic benchmarking** is a far riskier activity when the partners are competitors, as the plans of the organization are involved. To make this a worthwhile exercise, commercially sensitive information needs to be divulged.

Managing the benchmarking process

Karlof and Ostblom (1993) stated that the 'pitfalls' of benchmarking are as follows:

*   Time allowed is too short. Time is needed to negotiate access into an organization before the task even begins. This can be underestimated.
*   Preparation has not been carried out prior to undertaking the task. This includes objectives not identified and in-depth understanding of the partner organization not undertaken.

*   Too many processes are benchmarked at once.
*   Staff have not been allocated specifically to the benchmarking task, therefore do not devote enough time to it.
*   There are too many inter-organizational problems, and trust is not forthcoming. Time needed to build a relationship is not allocated.
*   Benchmarking is without depth, due to a small number of key indicators being developed.
*   Data analysis is incorrect.
*   Customers are not included in the comparative analysis.

As tourism and leisure organizations try to meet the constantly changing needs of the customers, continuous improvement becomes the quality 'target or goal' for which they are striving. Even with all its problems and limitations, the use of benchmarking can help to create a learning organization. Benchmarking is not accredited by an external organization but has been incorporated into the monitoring criteria of a number of management systems

---

Box 12.4.   Case study: benchmarking the arts in Australia. (Source: Radbourne, 1997.)

Traditional performance measures for identifying best practice in the arts are:

*   getting a government grant;
*   good reviews;
*   increased audience or visitor size;
*   number of subscription tickets sold;
*   number of standing ovations;
*   status of the people opening the exhibitions;
*   number of pictures sold;
*   length of queues.

It is traditionally considered that an artist is being measured against best practice every time they or their work is exposed to an audience. Benchmarking criteria for the arts have now moved to embrace managerial aspects and these now include:

*   assets and profit made by state-owned museums and galleries;
*   effectiveness of marketing to sponsors;
*   level of public awareness;
*   plus the traditional monitoring of the role of the arts to the local community.

(e.g. the Best Value management ethos of the public sector) and the Business Excellence Model also encompasses this type of self-assessment tool into its framework.

Business Process Re-engineering

Hammer and Champy (1993, cited in Leach, 1996) defined business process re-engineering (BPR) as:

> The fundamental rethink and radical redesign of business processes to achieve dramatic improvements in critical, and contemporary measures of performance, such as cost, quality, service and speed.

It is therefore necessary to consider BPR after benchmarking processes against other service providers. Unlike the other quality tools discussed in this chapter so far, BPR is not a stage in working towards a change in organizational culture. Deming (cited by Leach, 1996) expressed concern that the goal of BPR is continuous improvement, which he saw as disruptive, as the changes are never-ending. He was in favour of continual improvement, where change takes place at specific times after a period of planning, training, etc. Although BPR is revolutionary rather than evolutionary, it can easily comply with Deming's need for continual improvement even though it can identify far-reaching solutions (Hammer and Champy, 1993, cited in Leach, 1996).

Radical changes (e.g. going from waitress service to buffet service in a hotel) that BPR could bring about were considered by Burke (1997) as being of moderate to high-risk organizational strategies. Clemons (1995) stated that there are intermediate BPR strategies that do not carry the same risk to the organization. These are as follows.

Business process redesign

The least radical strategy includes the redesign of the procedures for booking of sports facilities in a leisure centre or theatre seats. The main aim is to save on operation costs and may result in the introduction of a computerized booking system. Kawalek (1994) was concerned that, whilst staff are spending time concentrating on benchmarking simplistic processes, they have no time for radical innovative thinking.

Process innovation

Trying to redesign processes to add value to the business or organization entails medium risk. This is based on offering an 'adequate' rather than 'ideal' service (Clemons, 1995).

An example of this is a national tourist office cutting down the level of information given to clients at any one telephone enquiry. This increases the number of enquiries that the call centre can handle but still allows a personalized service to be delivered. The introduction of premium telephone numbers increases the income to the organization from the telephone company.

Business revision

This is the highest risk and Clemons (1995) saw it as coming from two sources: functional and political.

- Functional risk is when the wrong changes are made that have major consequence to the business.
- Political risk comes from internal resistance and the task is never completed, wasting the organization's time and money.

The more radical the change, the more resistance employees will have to it. One way to try to overcome this is to engage consultants to drive through to implementation any difficult changes in working practices (e.g. weekend work to be paid at standard hourly rates and not attract premiums).

An example of a business revision was brought about by the introduction of compulsory competitive tendering into local authorities. This required the creation of direct service organizations so that they could compete against commercial contractors for management contracts for local government leisure centres.

Advantages of BPR

The management of (and changes to) business processes is important as it allows service providers to: (i) be responsive to changing customer needs; (ii) be flexible, enabling them to meet other external changes (e.g. legislation); (iii) review the service specification and its delivery; and (iv) be in a position to reduce costs.

Disadvantages of BPR

Burke (1997) stated that the radical improvement of a few processes may have benefits to that small area of operations but suggested that those who are involved in this process must not lose sight of the total service. The question needs to be asked as to what are the effects of these changes on the rest of the organization and its customers.

BPR embraces change that many employees find threatening and attempt to resist. Part of this perception is due to the fact that BPR has been linked with cost reduction (i.e. downsizing of the workforce). Cooper and Markus (1995) stated that staff will not offer the best ideas when redundancy may result.

Champy (1995) dramatically stated that a second managerial revolution is taking place. He suggested that this is due to the rapidly changing business and political environment in which organizations are operating. To survive, he advocated that radical and innovative thinking is needed and that BPR is the most appropriate tool for managers to implement to achieve this.

Specialist Quality Tools and Techniques for the Tourism and Leisure Industry

Unlike hotels, where the level if not the quality of the service is indicated by a range of schemes (e.g. crowns and stars, see Chapter 8), the diverse nature of the leisure and tourism industry means it does not have any industry-wide systems. The next section gives an overview of a range of specialist quality monitoring tools and techniques for specific subsets or sectors of the industry.

UK Quality Scheme for Sport and Leisure (QUEST)

QUEST is an industry-specific quality award based on the Excellence Model (see Chapter 11). Its development was commissioned by the four UK Sports Councils for monitoring of the quality of delivery of leisure centre facilities management, but adaptations for other leisure-related facilities are envisaged in the future (e.g. fitness and health clubs) (Sports Council, 1999).

The programme enables self-assessment and is said to be able to facilitate the change in public sector management philosophy from compulsory competitive tendering to the needs of Best Value monitoring (see Chapter 9). Self-assessment is achieved by answering a range of statements covering four areas: facilities operations; customer relations; staffing; and service development and review (QUEST News, 1998).

For example, the statements could include: 'a customer care policy exists and is implemented' and 'staff are generally helpful and pleasant'. These are answered by giving a score from 1 to 4, in which a score of 1 indicates that performance is poor or has not been considered; 2 indicates reasonable performance, but with room for significant improvement; 3 indicates good performance with a few minor problems; and 4 indicates excellent performance in all aspects (Sport Council, 1999). The scores can be added together, with a maximum of 632 being possible, but the individual scores give a better indication of a facility's performance.

This is a very inexpensive self-assessment system, which can integrate other certified quality tools into it (e.g. IIP). Due to its relatively recent introduction, the transfer rate from self-assessment to gaining the award is low and take-up in the first place was somewhat lower than the Sports Council's targets.

The validity of the model is questioned because of its inability to monitor effectiveness of service delivery. An overemphasis has been placed on users, who are an easier group to collect data from than trying to monitor non-users and other stakeholders in the community – a requirement of Best Value monitoring system. However, QUEST is evolving and it will be interesting to observe whether or not effectiveness monitoring is adequately addressed in the future.

Centre for Environmental and Recreational Management

This is a research project of the Centre for Environmental and Recreational Management (CERM) of the University of South Australia. The centre has developed an industry-specific monitoring system for public sector sport and leisure facility providers. Whilst this system was developed and piloted in the Australian leisure industry, it is being applied in other areas of the world, including New Zealand and the UK.

The system is said to measure efficiency and effectiveness over 18 customer service quality attributes, two key efficiency indicators and other working indicators (Crilley et al., 1997). The attributes measured are based on a four-dimensional model of core services, staff quality, general facility and secondary services (Howat et al., 1996) that incorporates the five dimensions of service identified by Zeithaml et al. (1990): tangibles, responsiveness, reliability, assurance and empathy.

The model has the ability to compare customer expectations with the actual performance of the centre (customer perceptions). This is known as the gap analysis model, the most famous and in widest use being SERVQUAL (Zeithaml et al., 1990) (see Chapter 13).

Examples of the PI measures include:

- Attributes, e.g. value for money, attitude of the staff, and cleanliness of the facilities.
- Key efficiency indicators – visits per square metre and expense recovery.
- Working indicators, e.g. marketing financial ratios, training costs.

A key element in effectiveness monitoring is consultation via focus groups with managers, staff and users. The industry-specific PIs allow for benchmarking to be facilitated.

Unlike most of the tools and techniques mentioned so far, this is one of the few to have been devised by academics working in conjunction with practitioners. Together they are trying to develop an industry-specific model to enable public sector leisure facilities to monitor effectiveness as well as efficiency of their service, effectiveness being the most difficult element to evaluate (Audit Commission, 1998).

Hospitality Assured mark

This is the quality initiative of the Hotel and Catering International Management Association (HCIMA) and the British Hospitality Association, to improve the level of service offered by their industry. It comprises self- and external assessment over 12 areas, see Box 12.5.

Organizations have to achieve scores of 50% in all areas to gain the award. The assessment is designed to show organizations what standards are acceptable but without describing how to carry out an activity.

It is said that the Hospitality Assured mark, as well as enabling organizations to gain competitive edge, motivates staff and enhances their training (Howard, 1999). Organizations that have achieved the award are DeVere Hotels, Center Parcs and Directors Table.

Box 12.5. Hospitality assured mark assessment areas.

- Customer improvement
- Process improvement
- Service performance assessment
- Service delivery
- Training
- Resources
- Process and procedures
- Service planning
- Service standards
- Business goals
- The service concept
- Customer research

Training courses

Training is a fundamental concept of quality management. The following training courses are concerned with improving customer care and service delivery within the service industry and especially with meeting the needs of tourism organizations.

Welcome Family

According to the English Tourist Board (now known as the English Tourism Council), this is a series of 'result-orientated courses for staff and management that develop skills, service and revenue'. They are specifically developed for the UK tourism industry but are now available to organizations involved with transport, sport and recreation, retail and the arts. The Welcome Family courses are based on a Canadian concept and were originally introduced by the Wales Tourist Board in 1991 (English Tourist Board, undated).

The costs are kept to a minimum, as grant-aid is available from the European Social Fund via the Learning and Skills Councils. These are accredited training courses and delivery is via a regional tourist board accredited trainer, which in large organizations can be a member of staff.

The main benefit of the series of courses is said to be the gaining of competitive edge via a well-trained staff. This is due to a range of factors, which have been identified by the English Tourist Board as: (i) potential to achieve a higher level of repeat business; (ii) potential to gain new business by word-of-mouth recommendations; (iii) potential to improve staff recruitment and retention; and (iv) help to create a more productive working environment. These are very high ideals for a range of short courses, and only if they are part of a more extensive programme can they be achieved.

The scheme comprises the following courses.

WELCOME HOST.   This is a tourism industry customer-care course lasting for 1 day. It gives a basic introduction to the tourism industry and customer care. The handling of complaints and enquiries features in this course, as does the importance of communications.

The course gives a good overview of the industry and the basic skills required. It is suitable for employees who have not worked in the industry before, particularly as part of their induction programme. For example, Haven Holidays has instigated this course on an organizational-wide basis, but this is unusual, as the norm is for only front-of-house staff to attend (e.g. receptionists).

WELCOME ALL.   This was introduced as a way of informing the leisure and tourism industry of its need to comply with the Disability Discrimination Act 1996. The 1-day course enables staff to be aware of the legal requirements of the Act and to be predisposed to the various requirements of people with a range of special needs. Again it is a good course for inclusion in an induction programme and may also be necessary for existing staff. It allows for a basic introduction to this area but no more.

WELCOME LINE.   This 1-day course covers not only basic telephone answering techniques but also aspects of relationship marketing (e.g. every encounter with a customer or potential customer is a marketing opportunity). Whilst ideally every employee needs to be trained in these elements, cost can be a limiting factor. The tourism and leisure industry tends to employ many part-time and seasonal members of staff to facilitate peaks and troughs in the service delivery. Many are students on their long vacation from university or college and they have little (or no) loyalty to their employer; they will leave a seasonal job if more money is available elsewhere. A UK amusement park employs over 300 workers every summer, and even though the fee for this course is only £35 at present, that amounts to direct costs of £10,500 plus travel and indirect costs of one day's pay. This is a large investment if staff are not going to stay for the whole season or return in future years.

WELCOME MANAGEMENT.   It is stated by Cumbria Tourist Board that the aim of the programme is 'to look in detail at some of the management implications of providing excellent customer service'. Unfortunately the list of who should attend includes only those managers who have responsibility for developing customer service. This is seen as a major limiting factor by the authors, if a more holistic approach to quality is taken, as customer needs and service delivery are the responsibility of all managers (Deming, 1986; Feigenbaum, 1991; Oakland, 1993). The content of this course is extensive, covering most of the important issues in service delivery and monitoring techniques (e.g. benchmarking, staff empowerment, recruitment) but these concepts and issues can only be sketchily addressed in one day.

WELCOME HOST INTERNATIONAL. The English Tourist Board has forecast that the number of overseas visitors to the UK will grow by 78% by the year 2003. This 1-day course is designed to increase awareness of the expectations of overseas tourists. It is suggested that a basic introduction to the language of up to six countries is possible, which is followed up with distance learning materials (e.g. an audio tape). Whilst the awareness element of the programme is excellent, tailor-made to a particular region and its visitor, the attempt to speak other languages is superficial. If an organization needs staff with a second language ability, they should recruit or train them properly.

Other courses in the series

Individual tourist boards have developed a range of specific Welcome Family courses to meet the needs of the local industry (e.g. Welcome Retail and Welcome Host for the Arts). The Welcome Family package of courses is a quality tool that can be integrated with a range of quality systems, tools and techniques, especially IIP. The underlying philosophies are the same in that staff are the most important resource to the service industry and trained staff will know how to communicate with customers and deliver a service with a minimum of mistakes. This leads to

a lowering of operational costs but a gain in competitive edge through offering an appropriate service.

Components of the Welcome Family of courses have been successfully used in induction training for major events such as the Welsh Garden Festival and Euro 1996 football championship. For Euro 1996, more than 2000 seasonal staff plus permanent staff (e.g. grounds staff, stewards) were inducted using the Welcome Host programme. It is said that retailers close to the match grounds were offered the opportunity to attend as well.

As pointed out when discussing IIP previously, most of these training packages are only appropriate for new employees or as an introduction to a subject (e.g. Welcome Management), and ongoing continual professional development is left to others.

Summary

The introduction of a quality tool or technique may be done in isolation, particularly at the start of an organization's quest for quality improvements. Each tool or technique should be implemented after careful planning as to how it fits into the organization's quality strategy.

However, Dale and Shaw (1999) were critical of an isolationist approach, suggesting that only short-term benefits will be achieved. To gain longer-term improvements, they stated that the organization's culture towards quality must be changed. As examined in more detail in Chapter 10, we agree with Dale that one tool or technique must not be singled out as more important than another, as they can all contribute to the quality improvement system. Practitioners must understand the benefits of each one and be aware of their limitations. Continuous or continual improvement and a customer focus must be the targets to aim for irrespective of how they are achieved and, as the next chapter demonstrates, based on knowing what customers think.

13

Measurement of Quality

No matter what quality management system, and the associated quality tools and techniques embedded within it, is implemented by an organization, there comes a point when the service delivered needs to be monitored and customers' opinions sought. A variety of qualitative and quantitative methods can be used to carry out these two tasks.

This chapter will concentrate on specific service quality survey methods and will not repeat material readily available in market research and other texts.

On completion of this chapter it is expected that you will be able to:

- understand the difference between qualitative and quantitative survey methods in the context of monitoring service delivery;
- appreciate the limitation of specific audits (e.g. mystery shopper);
- appraise whether or not to engage consultants to monitor service delivery.

Feedback methods need to be able to access a range of people's opinions including not only internal and external customers but also other stakeholders of the organization (shareholders, council tax payers, grant-aid bodies, etc.). The same information-gathering method will not necessarily be used with each and every segment, partly because the type of data to be collected changes from group to group and also from survey to survey. For example, existing customers can be asked questions in investigating at least four

different scenarios: (i) the service they have just received; (ii) the service they expected to receive; (iii) the services they would like to have in the future; and (iv) the service they receive from the organization's competitors.

The data can be gathered in three distinct ways: (i) *unsolicited* (e.g. letters of thanks or complaint, informal comments to staff); (ii) *passively solicited* (e.g. comment cards left in every hotel bedroom); or (iii) *actively solicited* (e.g. asking people to fill in questionnaires, attend a focus group or give an interview). Both solicited methods of gaining feedback require thought as to what are the objectives of the survey, which research methods are best to achieve them, and in what format the data should be collected (qualitative and/or quantitative).

Qualitative and Quantitative Research Methods

Osborne and Gaebler (1992) stated that 'there are dozens of different ways to listen to the voice of the customer'. The main difference is the kind of data that are able to be generated from the information collected. This initially depends on how the questions are formatted but some methodologies can produce both qualitative and quantitative.

Qualitative research methods are those that result in the collection of data that are in the respondent's own words (e.g. interviews). This tends to take longer to collect and analyse, though there are a few computer software packages that can analyse qualitative data (e.g. NVIVO). It is also more difficult to display the research findings as they do not readily fit into graphs, etc.

This is unlike quantitative research methods, which generate numerical data. A variety of computer packages (e.g. SPSS, EXCEL) can be used to analyse this data quickly and readily and display the results in graphic form.

Depending how the questions are formatted, some surveys (e.g. electronic mail, customer surveys) can be either qualitative or quantitative. It is also not unusual to have a mix of qualitative and quantitative questions in the same questionnaire.

The list in Table 13.1 is divided between methods that produce qualitative and quantitative data.

It is also not unusual, and is actively encouraged, to use a variety of research methods to gain as full an evaluation of a service as possible; in this way the limitations of each individual research method can be overcome. Monitoring needs to be carried out on a regular basis as customer needs and expectations are constantly changing. Berry (1995) called this *systematic listening*.

Qualitative Methods

In-depth customer interviews

Although a very valuable way to solicit customer views, interviews sometimes gain information about the organization that was not anticipated. It is very time consuming and thus expensive, and so only a limited number can be carried out. Whilst some of the problems of administering a questionnaire are removed (e.g. misinterpreting the questions), the preparation of the data collected for analysis is also very time consuming. It takes approximately 3 h to transcribe a tape recording of a 1-h interview. Berry (1995) advocated structured interviews with predetermined questions as a method for extensive service reviews. The set questions enabled comparisons to be made from one interviewee to another and from one review to another.

Customers participating in leisure and tourism experiences are very reluctant to give up their free time to answer questions.

Focus groups

A particular theme or topic is discussed by a small group of people with a moderator selected for the purpose. Various writers have suggested what the role of the moderator should be. Seay *et al.* (1996) thought that they should direct the proceedings, whereas others see the role as only a note taker. Williams and Parang (1997) considered whether or not there would be any advantage in using a trained moderator external to the organization. An external person would not be a stakeholder in the organization but would not be able to ask supplementary questions or

Table 13.1.   Service quality research approaches.

Type of survey method	Qualitative methods	Quantitative methods	Either qualitative and quantitative
Customers	Customer interviews Focus groups Customer advisory panels Complaint monitoring Ombudsmen Critical incident technique	SERVQUAL	Transactional surveys Total market surveys Customer surveys Internet and e-mail surveys Conjoint analyses
External organizations	Inspectors		Mystery shopper
Internal	Suggestion schemes Quality circles Quality improvement teams Employer reporting	SERVQUAL	

extend areas of debate, due to their lack of knowledge regarding the organization.

The reason that focus groups are used in the service sector is said to be because they are easy and cheap to administer (Berry, 1995). Seay *et al.* (1996) disagreed with this, as moderators (and sometimes participants) are paid. Unfortunately focus groups can be as ineffectual as quality circles if the aims and objectives are not considered and the composition is not appropriate.

Zeithaml *et al.* (1990) considered eight to 12 people to be a suitable number but from the same gender and age, and reflecting the same geographical spread as the organization. The composition of Zeithaml *et al.*'s individual groups means that more than two will have to be convened to get the opinions of the whole customer base. Berry (1995) is not as specific, suggesting only that each topic should be brainstormed by at least three groups of between eight to 12 people.

Even when they are functioning well, focus groups will not represent the full customer base. Young (1993, cited in Seay *et al.*, 1996) reminded us that trying to find a convenient time for a representative sample to be present is very difficult. Williams and Parang (1997) suggested inviting 15–25 people, as a number of them will not turn up. However, if they do all turn up, the debate can be difficult to manage.

The advantage of focus groups is that they can be arranged in a short period of time, and so new ideas, or changes to service delivery etc., can be discussed and feedback disseminated quickly. The tourism and leisure industry frequently uses this method, as many of its customers (e.g. school teachers, social and sports club secretaries) are not the consumers of the service (e.g. pupils, social and sports club members).

Customer Advisory Panel

While customer advisory panels seem to duplicate the focus group methodology, the difference is that, whereas a focus group generally only meets once, panel members serve for a period of time and a relationship builds up. An example of this can be seen in connection with the management of Lake Windermere in the Lake District National Park. The Windermere Users Committee meets with South Lakeland District Council and the Lake District National Park Authority representatives to discuss issues to do with the management of the lake. The committee's membership includes representatives from the commercial users of Lake Windermere and the various clubs (sailing, water-skiing, motor boats, etc.).

Complaints monitoring

Reip (1988, cited in Sampson, 1996) suggested that the monitoring of complaints is the most frequently used method to 'bring quality problems to management's attention'.

Complaints tracking systems

This can be as simplistic as keeping a record of the number of complaints and categorizing them into specific areas of service delivery, or as sophisticated as reviewing how each individual complaint was dealt with. Organizations should be aware of the limitations of this method, as research has shown that only 4% of customers complain. Five factors have been identified to account for this reluctance: (i) fear of hassle or too much trouble to complain; (ii) no one available to complain to; (iii) customers feel that it will do no good; (iv) they do not know where to complain; and (v) they attribute the problem or part of it to themselves, as they participate in the service delivery process (Horovitz and Cudennec-Poon, 1990).

Organizations will have to implement procedures to ensure that these barriers are not in place before carrying out in-depth complaints monitoring. Analysis of data needs to be fed back to appropriate areas of the organization to be used as a learning opportunity.

Whilst this seems to be an internal, informal monitoring system, a number of accredited quality systems (e.g. ISO 9000 2000) require a formalized complaints monitoring system before certification can be given. They require all complaints to be logged and investigated, service recovery actions monitored and, most importantly, information provided so that managers can re-evaluate the service.

Most tourism and leisure organizations actively solicit comments from their external customers by placing comment cards in rooms or on tables. Hotels and restaurants then forget the comments of their internal customers.

The advantage of instigating a formal complaints tracking system is the potential for learning, and this therefore is a strategy in which organizations should be actively engaged. Graham (1990, cited in Sampson, 1996) found that there can be a disadvantage in this method as it can make customers think negatively about the organization. Unfortunately, research has not been carried out to see if soliciting positive comments had the opposite effect.

Critical incident technique

As early as 1954, Flanagan wrote that this technique comprises 'a set of procedures for collecting direct observations of human behavior in such a way as to facilitate their potential usefulness in solving practical problems'. Interestingly, Flanagan reported that one of the first studies to use this technique was by Gallon in the 1880s; observing recreational activities, but its application to an industrial setting did not occur until the late 1940s.

Edvardsson (1998a) first saw critical incidents in a simplistic way, citing the monitoring of customer complaints and the ability to identify when a customer is not satisfied with the service received as examples. He suggested that putting service recovery techniques in place is the solution to these incidents. In his later study of public transport, an area of major importance to the tourism and leisure industry, Edvardsson (1998b) stated that customer dissatisfaction is caused by an event and suggested that the study of these occurrences will aid continuous improvement. Not all events were classified in his study as critical incidents, only those that recur.

By identifying and concentrating on managing critical incidents, organizations can begin the process of achieving continuous improvement. These solutions may involve additional staff training, redesign of the service delivery or, as the case study in Box 13.1 shows, generating a customer profile, which can then be managed.

Flanagan (1954) and Grove and Fisk (1997) described this technique as applied to the industrial setting in great detail, and the following is a summary:

1. Data collection can be carried out in a number of ways.
● Focus groups
● Interviews
● Questionnaires with open and closed questions.
2. Classification of data:
● One of the most difficult and time-consuming tasks is to devise the incident classifications into which the data can be placed. Grove and Fisk (1997) classified the data by repeating the task three times, each time using a different person. This increases the validity of the methodology.

Box 13.1.   Case study: an example of critical incident technique in practice.

This example is from the study of the effect of other customers on service delivery (Grove and Fisk, 1997) using tourists in Florida for critical incident research. The study set out to find out if, and how, critical incidents occurred and whether they were a collective (all customers) or an individual phenomenon. Whilst the majority of the literature on critical incidents concentrates on negative effects, this study also classified positive ones. Indeed, monitoring of critical success factors is seen as equally important to an organization (Wise, 1995).

A series of 486 interviews was conducted, using open and closed questions. Of the 330 critical incidents recorded, 161 were positive (e.g. sociability of other customers; nobody trying to jump the queue). The negative ones included people using bad language, smoking, and too many older people.

- Large categories can be divided into subgroups. A simple example is the category 'Sociability', which is divided by Grove and Fisk into 'friendly' and 'unfriendly' incidents.

Lovelock (1996, cited in Grove and Fisk, 1997) suggested that managing the customer portfolio is important in the reduction of negative effects. An example is applying dress codes – a facet of some restaurants, which require men to wear jackets and ties, or discos that do not allow in people wearing jeans and trainers.

In the research in Florida (Box 13.1) by Grove and Fisk (1997), many negative incidents were attributed to the length of time customers had to wait in theme park queues. A redesign of the service was required and they suggested that entertaining the people while they waited would reduce these encounters – a strategy already implemented by Disney.

The service characteristic of heterogeneity can be observed in customers. Gummesson (1993, cited in Grove and Fisk, 1997) advocated that recruiting the right customers is as important for customer satisfaction as recruiting the right staff.

Limitations

When applying this technique to six different industries, Wels-Lips et al. (1998) found a number of limitations.

CUSTOMERS NEED TO RELY ON THEIR MEMORY. As any police investigation illustrates, people interpret the same event in different ways.

MULTINATIONAL ORGANIZATIONS AND OVERSEAS VISITORS.   Wels-Lips et al. found that the 'determinants of critical incidents are also at least partly culture or country specific'. The tourism industry comprises not only multinational organizations (e.g. hotel chains) but also major tourist attractions and events (e.g. Buckingham Palace, London; Beatles Experience, Liverpool) that welcome visitors from all over the world. Organizations cannot use one set of data to identify critical incidents and apply them to every country or culture.

IMPLEMENTATION.   As with other qualitative methods, it is very time consuming and therefore expensive. Wels-Lips et al.'s interviews (80 people at each of six sites) took 'several weeks'. Meyer and Westerbarkey (1996) suggested that a way to overcome this is by comment cards, with two columns (one for positive statements and the other for negative ones) but as with all passive unsolicited methods the reply rates will be low.

Advantages

Critical incident technique can be applied to the total customer experience, including external factors (e.g. transportation to the facility, or accommodation available in the immediate area of the site) or internal (e.g. to ascertain what the customers' positive and negative experiences have been). Internal monitoring need not be confined to customer/staff interactions but can include fellow customers, as the case study (Box 13.1) illustrates. Critical incident technique is a very versatile research method.

Inspectors

All of the externally accredited quality management systems (e.g. ISO 9000 2000) require that an 'inspection' is carried out for the initial certification and then further inspections on an cyclical basis. The various quality awards carry out one inspection to see if the organization can 'win' the award; in the case of Service First, the public sector award, this is kept for 3 years before the organization needs to reapply.

The Best Value regime within local government services requires inspection on an annual basis. This does not include a site visit, unlike the other examples above, but an appraisal of the documentation.

Examples of inspection regularly encountered in the tourism and leisure industry are given below:

Restaurants

A number of organizations send out inspectors to ascertain whether the service is up to their very specific standards. Two of the most famous are Michelin and Egon Ronay, which allocate various levels of awards to restaurants. The best restaurants in the world are said to be those with the Michelin award but, apart from the inspectors, it is not known by what criteria they are judged. Whilst in both instances the inspectors act as paying customers and are not known to the establishment, the views of other customers are not included in the appraisal.

Hotels and guesthouses in England and Wales

The criteria for judging hotels and guesthouses are known. The three organizations that used to give stars and crowns to rate service delivery (English Tourist Board, Automobile Association and the Royal Automobile Club) have joined together to standardize the system. Hotels are now judged on a one to five-starrating scheme and guesthouses on one to five diamonds by the Tourist Board Quality Assurance Advisors.

Most of the criteria relate to the tangible elements of the service. For example, the quick reference of the minimum requirements for an hotel to achieve one star lists the following: (i) meet the quality requirements in all areas of operation; (ii) normally a minimum of six letting bedrooms; (iii) all bedrooms with *en suite* facilities; (iv) guest-controllable heating in bedrooms; (v) restaurant or similar eating area; (vi) dinner for residents and their guests; (vii) lounge or sitting area; and (viii) residential liquor licence (English Tourist Board, 1998a).

Some criteria venture into the intangible areas of service provision, especially those dealing with welcoming guests. As Table 13.2 shows, 'all guests greeted and acknowledged in a friendly, efficient and courteous manner' is a requirement that has to be achieved at all levels of the quality standards.

It has been established that the 'quality rating' of an establishment will take precedence over the facilities rating; therefore in the case of a hotel having a three-star facilities specification but only achieving a two-star rating on service quality, two stars will be awarded (English Tourist Board, 1998b).

Hotels and guesthouses in Scotland

The Scottish Tourist Board has a different philosophy in ranking establishments. It does not concentrate on the tangible elements at all and any hotel or guesthouse can be awarded the highest grade irrespective of what specific service specification it delivers, as long as the organization is customer oriented.

'Trade' inspectors have a valuable role to play in making sure that industry standards are adhered to or, in the case of Michelin, exceeded, but inspections have their limitations. By their very nature they are perpetuating industry customs and practices. Existing customers do not have a voice within the restaurant and hotel inspectorates.

Organizations need to embrace quality improvement strategies and gain feedback from as many sources as possible. Inspection, whether sought or not, is just another element that aids their ability to improve their service continuously.

Mystery shoppers

This is a participant observation method used by many tourism and leisure organizations, where people pose as customers so that they can experience the service delivered by an organization.

After experiencing the tourism or leisure facility, the mystery shopper uses a ratings form 'to systematically and comprehensively record their evaluation' (Berry, 1995). Wilson (1998) considered that the most important facet of this method is that it rates the process rather than just the outcomes. Some breweries use this to ascertain whether the methods taught on their training schemes are being put into practice; this includes greeting the customer within a specific time and serving the drinks correctly.

As well as identifying poor service, this system should be used to reward good service. Berry (1995) suggested that it is necessary to instruct employees as to why this type of exercise is being used, and subsequently rewarding good service removes some of the feeling of being 'spied' upon. Unsatisfactory

Table 13.2.   Quality standards for hotels: guest care, general quality. (Adapted from English Tourist Board, 1998a.)

One star (basic entry requirements)	Two star (requirements in addition to one star)	Three star (requirements in addition to one and two star)	Four star (requirements in addition to one, two and three star)	Five star (requirements in addition to one, two, three and four star)
All guests greeted and acknowledged in a friendly, efficient and courteous manner. All enquiries, requests, reservations, correspondence and complaints from visitors dealt with promptly. Management and staff well informed about their hotel, local attractions and events.				
Style of service may be very informal, with few staff, or perhaps run exclusively by owners. Whilst always presentable, dress may be accordingly informal. Although service should be competent, technical skills may be limited.	Style of service may be quite informal, with few staff, or run exclusively by owners. Management and staff smartly and professionally presented. Service skills more evident.	More formal style of service, with higher staffing levels. Management and staff smartly and professionally presented, and staff usually uniformed.	Formal and structured team of staff, with a management and supervisory hierarchy and with uniformed staff smartly presented.	Formal and structured team of impeccably presented staff, with a management and supervisory hierarchy. Doubling up of duties would indicate that a hotel is not operating at this level.
		Technical and social skills of a good standard in responding to guest needs and requests.	Technical and social skills of a very good standard, anticipating and responding to guest needs and requests.	Regardless of the style of service, technical and social skills will be of the highest order.
Incoming telephone calls to residents should be handled in a professional and discreet manner.				

service encounters generally result in staff being sent for further training but service design problems can also be highlighted, requiring a redesign of the service procedures. Erstad (1998) considered that the latter should be the main function of the exercise.

To increase the reliability of this method, organizations should set performance standards by which staff can be judged. The utilization of as many objective measures as possible is preferred (e.g. did the member of staff have the correct uniform on?) rather than subjective ones (e.g. was the member of staff helpful?). Whilst the use of subjective questions cannot be avoided due to the intangibility of services, the use of rating scales tries to minimize this problem (see example in Box 13.2).

The most successful mystery shopper exercises are those that use trained people external to the organization. Wilson (1998) stated that in 1996 over £20 million was spent on this technique. It is not unknown for the families of Head Office staff to carry out this task. Apart from the fact that these people tend not to be specifically trained to be mystery shoppers, they soon start to become recognized.

External mystery shopping

By completing a series of mystery shopper observations in a number of competitor facilities as well as the organization's own outlets, a benchmarking exercise can be carried out. This enables direct comparisons to be made.

Seay *et al.* (1996) considered that the data collected by using mystery shoppers in either

---

Box 13.2. Mystery shopper at a reception desk in a hotel.

---

1. Were you acknowledged within 30 seconds of arriving at the check-in desk?
Yes No Length of time: . . . minutes . . . seconds
2. Were you spoken to in a courteous manner at all times?
Yes No
3. Did you receive all the information you needed?
Yes No
4. Were you shown the way to the lift or stairs?

---

situation had a major limitation brought on by its 'keyhole or snapshot approach'. They did not like the fact that organizational decisions are being made from a one-off observation of the service. This gives validity to the authors' original statement that a variety of survey methods need to be used to gain an in-depth evaluation of the service provided.

Employee research

Whilst all the above techniques deal with soliciting customer feedback, internal customers should not be forgotten. It must be remembered that they are the only ones who can appraise internal procedures and internal service delivery, which will eventually impinge on the external customers. Berry (1995) suggested that employees, unlike external customers, will not only point out problems but can also come up with solutions to rectify them.

Many organizations have instigated suggestion schemes that reward employees if an idea is implemented. Very few of these schemes are still running after a few years, generally because there were no properly constituted systems to appraise the suggestions. Employees became disillusioned and stopped participating. Another reason for lack of participation was the lack of an appropriate reward. If employees see the organization benefiting from their ideas, especially in the area of cost saving, and they were given a 'paltry' sum as a reward, this results in them being dissatisfied.

Alternative ways of actively soliciting comments from internal customers can be by quality circles or quality improvement teams (see Chapter 14). Whilst similar, they are not as permanent as quality circles being constituted to consider a specific aspect.

Employee reporting

Carlzon (1987) referred to the event of front-line staff delivering services to customers as *Moments of Truth*. At this point the operations staff are privy to a whole range of comments from their customers and systems need to be in place to enable formal feedback of this information vertically and horizontally throughout the organization. Some organizations require that their senior management act as front-line staff from time to time, especially if their own position keeps them away from external customers. This also gives them insight into what it is like to work in front-line positions as well as having the opportunity to have contact with the customers.

Grönroos (1990a) calls these front-line encounters with customers *Moments of Opportunity* due to the potential value of the information gained from this source. Customers will be unaware that these data are being passively collected from them. As Sampson (1998) pointed out, there is no control over the sample size, etc., because the respondents select themselves.

Quantitative Methods

SERVQUAL gap analysis model

This measurement tool is based on the underpinning theory that customers judge service delivery via the formula that customer perceptions should equal or exceed customer expectations for them to be satisfied with the service provided. Customer perceptions are based on the actual service delivered, whilst customer expectations are based on past experiences, word of mouth and personal needs.

Zeithaml *et al.* (1990) devised the SERVQUAL model in the mid-1980s to measure gaps in service delivery numerically. It was originally used in the US financial sector (Parasuraman *et al.*, 1985) and subsequently made available to the remainder of the service sector.

In the fields of tourism and leisure, SERVQUAL or an adapted version of the instrument has been used as a measuring tool by a number of academic writers (Table 13.3).

Whilst the model has been applied extensively in the commercial sector of the tourism and leisure industry, not-for-profit examples are in the minority. Williams's (1997b) UK research sites included two local government sports facilities (a golf course and a leisure centre), two sites funded by central government (a museum and an art gallery) and a theatre run by a charitable trust.

Implementation of the SERVQUAL instrument

Measuring the service gaps 1 to 5 (Fig. 13.1) is by three questionnaires, each one to survey a different response group: customers; managers; and operations staff.

Table 13.3.   Adapted version of SERVQUAL instrument.

Application	References	Alternative name for the model
Travel and tourism, at variety of sites	Fick and Brent Ritchie (1991)	
Hotels	Knutson *et al.* (1990)	LODGSERV
	Saleh and Ryan (1991, 1992)	
	Richard and Sundaram (1994)	
	Akan (1995)	
	Gabbie and O'Neill (1997)	
	Ekinici *et al.* (1998)	
Resort – Varadero, Cuba	Tribe and Snaith (1998)	HOLSAT
Fast-food industry	Johns and Tyas (1996)	
Restaurants	O'Neill (2001)	DINESERV
US recreational services	Crompton and Mackay (1989)	
	Hamilton *et al.* (1991)	
	Taylor *et al.* (1993)	
Private clubs and estates, Hong Kong	Lam *et al.* (1997)	
Heritage sites	Frochot (1996)	HISTOQUAL
Leisure and tourism facilities in the UK	Williams (1997b)	

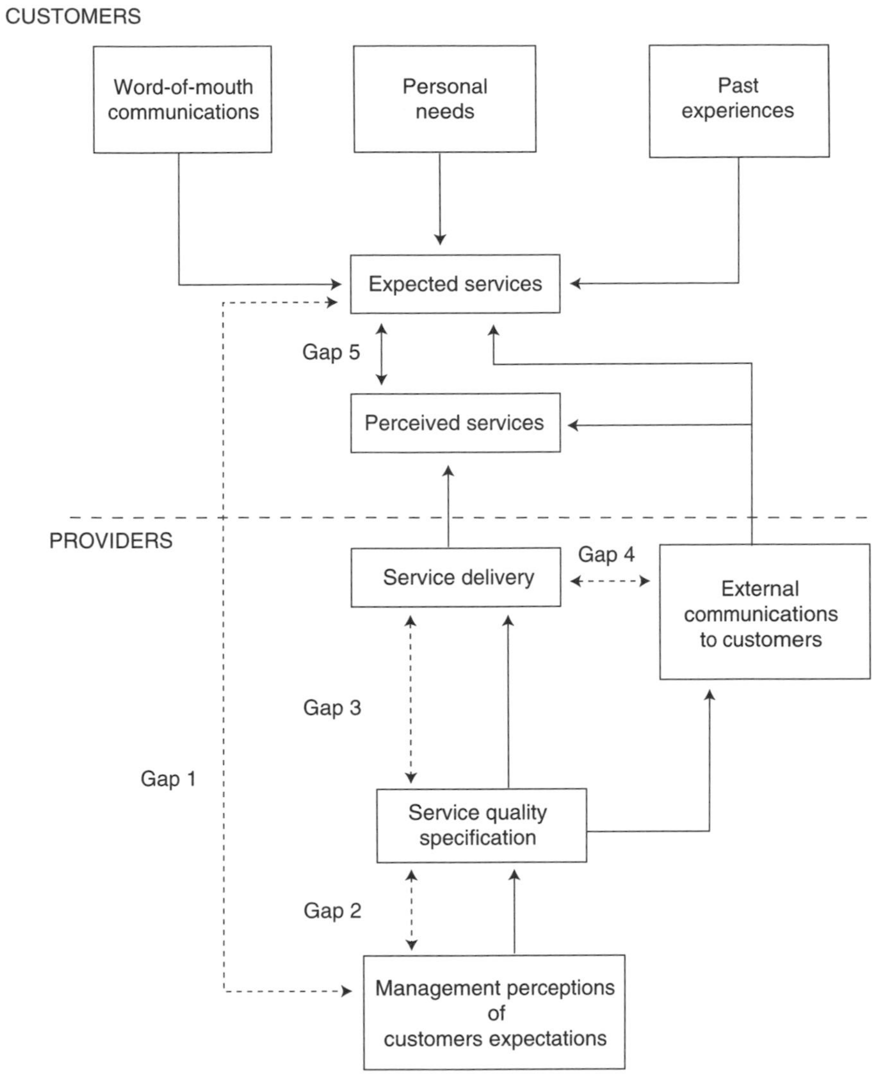

CUSTOMERS

Fig. 13.1. SERVQUAL gap analysis model. (Source: Zeithaml *et al.*, 1990.)

GAP 5: CUSTOMER EXPECTATIONS VERSUS CUSTOMER PERCEPTIONS.   The service quality gaps can be generated both internally and externally to the organization. Gap 5 is external: customer expectations of the service judged against perceptions of the service received. Expectations of a service are affected by word-of-mouth opinions, customers' personal needs and their past experiences of their current and previous service providers (Zeithaml *et al.*, 1990).

The SERVQUAL customer questionnaire to measure gap 5 comprises two sets of 22 statements on a seven-point Likert scale (see examples in Fig. 13.2) and has the ability to give gap scores in the range −6 to +6.

The 22 statements are categorized into five dimensions of service: tangibles, reliability, responsiveness, assurance and empathy (see Table 13.4). By analysing the scores for individual dimensions, specific elements of the customer service experience can be monitored.

SERVQUAL's gap analysis theory is that the closure of gaps 1 to 4 can rectify any discrepancies at gap 5.

Perception statements	Strongly disagree						Strongly agree
At .... insert generic name for the site 6. When a customer has a problem, excellent .... will show a sincere interest in solving it.	1	2	3	4	5	6	7
11. Employees in excellent .... will give prompt service to customers.	1	2	3	4	5	6	7
19. Excellent .... will have operating hours convenient to all their customers.	1	2	3	4	5	6	7

Expectation statements	Strongly disagree						Strongly agree
*At *** insert name for the organization site* 6. When a customer has a problem, *** will show a sincere interest in solving it.	1	2	3	4	5	6	7
11. Employees in *** give you prompt service.	1	2	3	4	5	6	7
19. *** has operating hours convenient to all its customers.	1	2	3	4	5	6	7

Fig. 13.2. Examples of SERVQUAL customer questions. (Source: Zeithaml *et al.*, 1990.)

Table 13.4. SERVQUAL dimensions. (Adapted from Buttle, 1996.)

Dimension	Definition	Questionnaire statements
Tangibles	Appearance of physical facilities, equipment, personnel and communications materials	1 to 4
Reliability	Ability to perform the promised service dependably and accurately	5 to 9
Responsiveness	Willingness to help customers and to provide prompt service	10 to 13
Assurance	Knowledge and courtesy of employees and their ability to convey trust and confidence	14 to 17
Empathy	Provision of caring individualized attention to customers	18 to 22

GAP 1 AND 2 SCORE GENERATION.   Gap 1 occurs when managers do not know or understand their customers' needs and expectations. The managers cannot design or specify the service that is required, creating gap 2. The first section of the questionnaire has been designed so that a direct comparison can be made between customers' gap 5 score and the managers' score for gap 1. The second part enables managers' opinions to be sought on service operations.

GAP 3 AND 4 SCORE GENERATION.   The managers' questionnaire continues by measuring gaps 3 and 4. Gap 3 is when the service specification has been designed incorrectly, thus causing the operational staff to deliver an inappropriate service. Gap 4 is when inaccurate or incomplete information is given to customers and expectations are too high.

The third and final questionnaire is distributed to operational staff. This only generates scores for gaps 3 and 4.

CONSTRUCTS.   Zeithaml *et al.* (1990) considered that the causes of each of these four gaps are distinct, and produced by internal influences, referred to as 'constructs'. Once gaps have been detected, the checklist of 'constructs' (see Box 13.3) enables organizations to make specific changes to their internal procedures and therefore reduce the gaps.

Box 13.3.   Constructs hypothesized to influence service quality gaps within the providers' organizations. (Source: Zeithaml *et al.*, 1990.)

Constructs Influencing Gap 1
Market Research Orientation (MRO) Extent to which managers make an effort to understand customers' needs and expectations through formal and informal information-gathering activities.
Upward Communication (UC) Extent to which top management seeks, stimulates, and facilitates the flow of information from employees at lower levels.
Level of Management (LOM) Number of managerial levels between the top most and bottom most levels.

Constructs Influencing Gap 2
Management Commitment to Service Quality (MCSQ) Extent to which management views service quality as a key strategic goal and allocates adequate resources to it.
Goal-Setting (GS) Existence of a formal process for setting quality of service goals.
Task Standardization (TS) Extent to which technology and training programs are used to standardize service tasks.
Perception of Feasibility (POF) Extent to which managers believe that customers' expectations can be met.

Constructs Influencing Gap 3
Teamwork (TEAM) Extent to which all employees pull together for a common goal.
Employee-Job Fit (EFIT) Match between the skills of employees and their job.
Technology-Job Fit (TFIT) The appropriateness of the tools and technology that employees use to perform their jobs.
Perceived Control (PC) Extent to which employees perceive that they are in control of their jobs and that they can act flexibly.
Supervisory Control System (SCS) The extent to which employees are evaluated/compensated on what they do (behaviour) rather than solely on output quality.
Role Conflict (RC) Extent to which employees perceive that they cannot satisfy all the demands of all the individuals (internal and external customers) they must serve.
Role Ambiguity (RA) Extent to which employees are uncertain about what managers and supervisors expect from them and how to satisfy those expectations.

Constructs Influencing Gap 4
Horizontal Communication (HC) Extent to which communication and co-ordination occur between different departments that have contact with and / or serve customers.
Propensity to Overpromise (PTO) Extent to which the firm feels pressure to promise more to customers than can be achieved.

DATA PROCESSING.   The vehicle of three questionnaires generates a large amount of numerical data but the SERVQUAL scores can be easily calculated if a statistical software package (i.e. SPSS) or a spreadsheet (i.e. EXCEL) is used.

Criticism of the SERVQUAL model

Although both academics and practitioners have used the SERVQUAL model extensively in the service sector since its inception in the mid-1980s, both in the USA and elsewhere, it is not without its critics. Criticism is largely concerned with the design and reliability of the instrument rather than its implementation.

The application of the model in different countries or cultures is very rarely commented upon. Only Kettinger *et al.* (1995) suggested that specific cultural 'factors' should be taken into account when applying the model.

HOW CUSTOMERS JUDGE SERVICE..   The underpinning theory of SERVQUAL (i.e. that customers are satisfied when they judge that the service they receive meets or exceeds their expectations) was questioned by Cronin and Taylor (1992, 1994) and Buttle (1996). Crompton and MacKay (1989) offered the premise that satisfaction (a psychological out-come) and service quality (an attribute of the service) are not the same thing. Parasuraman *et al.* (1988) stated that their original premise is valid, indicating that the same 'evaluation judgement' occurs in each case.

CUSTOMER EXPECTATIONS AND EXCELLENCE. Zeithaml *et al.* (1990) considered the factors that influence the formulation of the custom-ers' expectation judgement to be: word of mouth; personal needs; external communi-cations; and past experience. The wording of the customer expectation questionnaire asks them to judge the service provided by an *excellent* facility of the same generic type (see Fig. 13.2) but the organization has no way of knowing what their concept of excellence is. This was discussed at length in Chapter 2.

SUBJECTIVE JUDGEMENTS BY STAFF.   The SERVQUAL model is based on subjective judgements. According to Williams (1997b), staff judge the services provided quite severely; they can be more critical than their customers.

Two examples of this can be seen at a museum and a leisure centre. At the museum, staff commented on artefacts being out on loan, but as this site had a high number of first-time visitors, customers had no know-ledge of a 'worsening or reduced' service. The consequence was that staff were inaccurate in judging their customers' expectations.

At the leisure centre, all the staff surveyed mentioned the problems of the centre's location within the boundary of a secondary school (e.g. bad behaviour of the pupils). Only one customer commented on the location as being a negative factor and the pupils' behaviour was not referred to at all.

In these instances, if the customers' gap scores do not take priority over those of the managers and operational staff, facilities may incur additional running costs by providing a level of service in excess of customer needs. Whilst this is a strategy sometimes implemented in the commercial sector of the industry, the public sector would find it difficult to sustain, necessitating reduction or even cuts in some other services.

QUESTIONNAIRE DESIGN.   To facilitate cus-tomer judgement via expectations and perceptions, the customer questionnaire asks two sets of similar questions (see Fig. 13.2). Williams (1997b) observed that customers not only find this tedious but the respondents also get embarrassed at frequently choosing the number 7 when judging an excellent facility. Research by Brown *et al.* (1993) confirmed this, but when Parasuraman *et al.* (1993) were responding to this criticism, they defended the two-part instrument as giving more accurate diagnostic information. They went on to suggest that rating expectations and perceptions on scales in adjacent columns could reduce the length of the questionnaire.

The customer questionnaire also takes a considerable time to fill in. When Williams (1997b) used it as an exit survey at tourism and leisure facilities, respondents became anxious about keeping the rest of their party waiting and 'wasting' their leisure time. Putting the expectation and perception scores on adjacent columns may reduce the time but the pro-posed expansion of the instrument to three columns to allow transaction-specific data to be collected will exacerbate this problem (Parasuraman, 1995).

SCORING.   An irregularity commented upon by both Teas (1993) and Brown *et al.* (1993) concerns the meaning of the gaps, as different numerical scores can give the same gap scores (e.g. $3 - 7 = -4$; $2 - 6 = -4$). Buttle (1996) questioned whether or not identical scores calculated from different values indicate the same perceived quality. Saleh and Ryan (1992), Taylor *et al.* (1993) and Mels *et al.* (1997) advanced the need for 'care' to be taken when using the numerical data, suggesting that follow-up research should be of a qualitative nature.

DIMENSIONS.   The 22 statements are group-ed into Zeithaml *et al.*'s (1990) five service dimensions: tangibles, reliability, responsive-ness, assurance and empathy. Babakus and Boller (1992), Cronin and Taylor (1992) and Taylor *et al.* (1993) have questioned the number and stability of them.

Overlapping dimensions was experi-enced when SERVQUAL was implemented at an amusement park, (Williams, 1997b). Customer comments indicated that the scores for the 'tangible' and 'reliability' service dimensions were both being affected by the physical environment of the site, especially the condition of the toilets. The managers did not have any confusion. To them the 'reliability' dimension was purely to do with the safety of the rides.

Crompton and MacKay (1989) considered that the dimensions change with the type of service. Scott and Shieff (1993) agreed, maintaining that the five dimensions are only applicable to homogeneous services. This is rare to find in the tourism and leisure industry.

This leads to the question of whether or not SERVQUAL is a generic model capable of being applied to all of the service industry or if each typology of service requires an adapted instrument.

INDUSTRY-SPECIFIC ADAPTATIONS.   A number of authors have produced not only industry-specific adaptations of the model but also actual site-specific ones, such as Frochot's (1996) HISTOQUAL.

When Carman (1990), Babakus and Boller (1992) and Brown et al. (1993) could not replicate Zeithaml et al.'s research findings, Parasuraman et al. (1991a) blamed this on the changes they made to the instrument. They later contradicted themselves by reasserting this issue, saying that the SERVQUAL instrument was 'the basic skeleton. . .that can be supplemented with context-specific items when necessary' (Parasuraman et al., 1993).

The reliability of the instrument may be brought into question if tourism and leisure practitioners deviate too much from the SERVQUAL model, as they may not have the statistical expertise. An alternative could be to employ consultants to carry out this task.

Implementation in the tourism and leisure industry

Williams's (1997b) application of the model to a number of leisure and tourism attractions highlighted a number of implementation problems, as follows.

SAMPLING FRAME.   The original research of Zeithaml et al. (1990) was carried out in financial institutions that have a large number of managers and operational staff. This is not the case in tourism or leisure facilities.

NON-PARTICIPATION IN THE SERVICE.   Williams (1998) found that comments from most visitors were very complimentary when responding to open-ended questions about a museum, but that negative SERVQUAL gap scores had been achieved for the service dimensions of 'reliability' and 'responsiveness'. The negative gap was even more pronounced if first-time visitor scores were calculated separately.

A further analysis of the quantitative data showed that negative scores could be generated when excellent service was delivered. This is due to the customers not testing the organization's service recovery systems. As previously commented upon, tourists who are first-time visitors to a facility may not be aware of changes to service delivery that regular users may perceive as problems.

These customers would therefore mark '7' against customer expectations questions and '4' on the perceptions, as instructed, if they did not know or did not have an opinion. The '4' does not act as a neutral point but influences the gap scores: $4 - 7 = -3$.

Parasuraman et al. (1988) stated that participation in the service is a requirement for the SERVQUAL model but in this case it would seem the visitors have in effect become partial non-participants. To try to overcome the effect of partial non-participation, Williams (1997b) filtered out cases in which the respondents had chosen the number '4' for either the 'reliability' or the 'responsiveness' dimension, and positive scores were obtained but the sample size was very much reduced.

One way to overcome this is to sample only customers who have had a problem, (McDougall and Levesque, 1992) but an excellent service delivery organization may have very few respondents. These organizations need to be aware of partial non-participation, as inappropriate changes to operational procedures could be undertaken.

Whilst some debates arising out of these criticisms are purely in the academic domain, they have consequences for the validity of the model to practitioners.

Both Qualitative and Quantitative

Transactional or exit surveys

These are carried out immediately after the customer has received the service (e.g. package holiday companies giving out questionnaires on the flight home). In the UK a traditional questionnaire paper is given out; in the USA new technology is taking over and electronic mail surveys have been conducted. Most of these surveys are devised in-house, with the majority of the questions soliciting numerical (quantitative) data so that large survey numbers can be accommodated, but qualitative data can also be generated by this method if open-ended questions are asked.

Total market surveys

These are rarely carried out as they are very costly to implement, requiring that users and non-users are included in the sample. In the public sector of the tourism and leisure industry, under the government's Best Value management regime for local government services, total market surveys are required (DETR, 1988).

Davies and Girdler (1998) indicated that the total number of consultative groups for urban parks and open spaces was nine (see Table 13.5). Wide-scale consultation will be not only costly, diverting resources away from services, but also time consuming. Both quantitative and qualitative data sets can be generated but, due to the size of the samples, quantitative methods are usually used.

Customer or user surveys

These are considered to be the easiest questionnaires to distribute, cheapest to

Table 13.5. Parks and open spaces consultative groups. (Source: Davies and Girdler, 1998.)

Dedicated users	Those who use the facilities (e.g. footbal pitches)
Direct users	Those with a direct interest (e.g. residents of the estate)
Indirect users	Again benefit but do not use the service (e.g. gardeners)
Marginal users	Informal users (e.g. dog walkers who use the sports fields)
General public	Anyone who passes through the neighbourhood
Council tax payers	Residential and businesses, financial stakeholders
The whole of the electorate	Councillors have to answer to

administer and allow for a large sample to be accessed. Either qualitative or quantitative data can be generated but usually they are a mix of both.

Seay *et al.* (1996) outlined a number of problems with this method, previously highlighted by a number of authors: (i) respondents misinterpreting questions; (ii) failure to reach non-users (Schlichter and Pemberton, 1992); (iii) respondents do not like filling in questionnaires, so either do not or do so carelessly (Baker and Lancaster, 1991); (iv) inadequate sampling frame; (v) administered at the wrong time; (vi) inaccurate data analysis (Summer, 1985); and (vii) resistance to lengthy questionnaires. Fieldwork by Williams' (1997b) at six leisure-related organizations demonstrated that people do not like giving up their 'valuable' free time to be involved in a customer survey.

General implementation

Vavra (1998) advocated that four different customer groups should be surveyed.

1. **Current customers**. Ongoing monitoring of their needs and expectations as well as their perceptions of the existing service. Berry (1995) segmented current customers into two distinct categories, new and declining.
- **New customers**. The reasons for their attraction to the services provided by the

organization are worth knowing, as are the reasons for leaving their previous service provider. Attracting new customers can be a very expensive undertaking, especially if the marketplace is saturated already (e.g. health and fitness clubs).

- **Declining customers**. Berry (1995) suggested that surveying these customers can give an indication as to the level of loyalty that customers have towards the organization as well as the reasons why they are not using the services to the same extent.

2. **Past customers**. To gain information as to the reasons they have stopped using the service and which organization they are using instead.

3. **Potential customers**. One of the most difficult groups to access but potentially worthwhile if developing new services for a different customer base. Amending existing services to fit the needs of these potential customer has a high level of risk, as it could alienate existing ones.

4. **Competitors' customers**. It is always useful to access information regarding major competitors but this should be done in an ethical way.

Most theorists recommend that customer surveys should be carried out on a regular basis but Vavra (1998) pointed out that the current trend is a decline in survey response rates. To increase response rates, he suggested that a pre-recruitment strategy should be implemented before administering the questionnaires (e.g. a letter or a telephone call). An alternative is to offer a reward for participating (e.g. names going into a prize draw or money-off vouchers). These strategies would increase the cost of the research, which can be ill afforded in the voluntary and public sectors of the tourism and leisure industry.

Follow-up activities should include acknowledgement of customer participation, either individually (if not anonymous) or collectively via reports, by giving feedback on how customers' ideas or suggestions have been incorporated into the organization.

Internet and e-mail surveys

Sampson (1998) recommended a structured form of passive feedback via the Internet. The web page of an organization could include an area for customer feedback (e.g. 'How might we improve our service?'). In his comparative study he found that in a 4-week period the web resulted in 32,000 returns (sample not known), whereas a telephone survey over the same period gave 4200 returns from a sample of 280,000 calls.

The disadvantages of web feedback are obvious. Only customers with access to the Internet can respond and this has been found to give biased responses, as at present the majority of the users have been found to be 25–44-year-old male college graduates. In the travel trade, companies such as Easyjet (the budget airline) are offering more services via this technology and therefore this will become a valid tool for their e-commerce customer feedback.

Conjoint analysis

This was first developed by Luce and Tukey (1964, cited in Claxton, 1994) and applied to mathematical psychology. Its use in consumer research was a little later, in 1971, when Green and Rao applied it to transportation issues.

According to Green and Wind (1975), this technique is the breaking down of customers' complex holistic judgement on a service into its component parts. It is based on the premise that each customer evaluates various aspects (known as attributes) of the service, judging that some attributes are more valuable or important to them than others. It can be useful for practitioners to know how their potential and existing customers have ranked service attributes in a number of different scenarios, as follows.

1. When making a decision on whether or not to purchase an existing service

Customers make compromises between meeting their needs and expectations and what services are available. The different services available when wanting to travel from A to B by an airline or attend an aerobic session can illustrate this phenomenon (Table 13.6).

According to Claxton (1994), customers will give up one element that is not as important in order to gain from another attribute (e.g. price). As all of these services have customers, not every person 'trades off' the same attribute.

Whilst Claxton used multi-attributes in the appraisal of services, this is too simplistic. He cited the example of 'trade off' decisions using the journey from an airport to downtown, with one of the three services available being a quick but expensive helicopter transfer. However, if someone were unable to travel by this method because they were, say, frightened of heights, carrying out the correlations given would not have exposed this 'trade off' reason. Green and Wind (1975) identified this limitation. Factors external to the service provided would need to be investigated to get a reliable set of data; open-ended questions would achieve this.

2. Evaluation of new or amended services

Unlike other techniques (e.g. SERVQUAL) that ask customers to appraise the service just delivered, conjoint analysis enables organizations to explore the importance of the attributes of hypothetical services (e.g. introduction of a slide into a swimming pool) or possible changes to the existing service (e.g. changing from waiter service in a hotel dining room to buffet service).

As conjoint analysis 'decomposes' customer judgements, it is possible to reconstruct those values and apply them to 'what if?' scenarios without carrying out further data collection. Green and Wind (1975) suggested that this is a major advantage of using this method, especially if an organization has a diverse customer base. They also pointed out that some managerial decisions may not be solved by this method as they cannot be accommodated within a reductionist approach (e.g. what the next blockbuster film will be).

3. Multiple objectives

Danaher (1997) used conjoint analysis to ascertain three sets of customer responses (Box 13.4). Customers were asked to rank each service attribute, and to state which one they would like and which one they had received. The basis of this analysis is the level of satisfaction the customer has from the

Table 13.6.   Availability of services: airlines and aerobics.

Airline	Ticket	Aerobic	Session
Charter airline	Cheapest Inconvenient departures in time and location May have to purchase accommodation as well Delays more frequent Entertainment and refreshments included	Local authority leisure centre	Reasonable price Concessions prices May not be at a convenient time or day of the week
Schedule airline	More expensive Frequent to destinations allocated to it Different seat types Entertainment and refreshments included Flying first or business class can have status and element of exclusivity	Private fitness club	Generally more expensive and have to pay monthly fee whether you use it or not Joining fee to pay as well Can have status and element of exclusivity
Private plane hire	Most expensive Most convenient in time and available from nearest airport No other passengers May not be large enough to have entertainment or refreshments Has status	Personal trainer	Most expensive Most convenient One to one in your own home Facilities available may not be as good as the two above Has status

Box 13.4.   Breakdown of attributes: examples for three groups.

1. Hotel

Main attribute	Attribute breakdown
Reception desk	24-hour service Polite and attentive staff Bookings recorded accurately Correct information given Give wake-up calls Knowledge of the area Able to book tours

2. Children's holiday play scheme at a leisure centre

Main attribute	Attribute breakdown
Creative art class	Adequate numbers of qualified staff Vetted staff Attentive staff Good quality materials Sufficient materials Appropriate and safe room Interesting and challenging tasks

3. Performing arts series (Currim et al., 1981)

Main attribute	Attribute breakdown
Demand for subscription	Price and discounts Seating benefits Nature of the individual events that comprise the series Number of events Timing

various attributes of the service. The 'main attributes' (or features) of the service are evaluated by customers on a numerical scale to rank how important each attribute is to them. The 'attribute breakdown' list appertains to a number of features that each main attribute has been broken into. As a number of scenarios can be investigated by this method, the ranking scales can vary (e.g. 'very dissatisfied' to 'very satisfied', or, when introducing a new element, 'completely unacceptable' to 'very acceptable' and 'I am willing to pay for it'). Numerical values can be analysed by the SPSS computer program, especially when a collation between two or more attributes is required. Claxton (1994) called this approach a 'trade-off matrix'.

Collection of data can also take other formats, from complicated self-completion questions to the use of pictures as stimulants (Johnson, 1975, cited in Claxton, 1994). The various methods of collection should enable most market segments to be targeted. When applying this to an aircraft flight, Claxton (1994) found four major groups: ground services; in-flight services; airline decor; and 'other', with 27 attributes in total. Most writers agree that the most critical element is correctly identifying the attributes. One way is to hold a focus group or carry out interviews in preparation for the conjoint analysis exercise; this will ascertain what attributes are important to the customers.

Other limitations

For complex services (e.g. package holidays) or a multiple service provider (e.g. a leisure centre) the various main components of the service need to be surveyed separately. Customers could suffer from 'survey fatigue', and the technique would also be very expensive to administer.

Conjoint analysis can be difficult to implement, as well as to design and analyse. Practitioners without extensive research experience may find this task too daunting. If accurately executed, conjoint analysis enables in-depth insight into what customers think of the attributes of the services provided or proposed.

In-house Research or Engage Consultants?

The advantages and disadvantages of an organization carrying out its own research or commissioning the work from a specialist organization are shown in Table 13.7. The questions that organizations need to ask to formulate a decision include the following:

1. Have we the expertise within the organization?

2. Have these staff within their existing workload time to devote to the task within the time frame available?

3. Is there money to pay for outside help?

4. What level of importance does the organization place on having reliable data about its customers', employees' and other stakeholders' views of the service provided?

By answering these questions in the context of the complexity of the task to be carried out (from the simplistic task of devising, collecting and collating data, i.e. market research, to the more sophisticated consultancy project where devising market research methods are the start of a major business review), the decision whether or not to engage consultants should be partly made.

Summary

The monitoring of service delivery and collection of feedback on customer and other stakeholders' satisfaction is important and needs to be known by the organization. With the management regime of Best Value, central government is forcing local authority tourism and leisure service providers into widespread consultation. The introduction of various accredited quality management

Table 13.7.   The advantages and disadvantages of in-house research versus engaging consultants.

Methods	Advantages	Disadvantages
In-house research	Indirect costs, therefore can seem cheaper Experience within the organization's area of operations	May interfere with other roles and responsibilities of the staff assigned to the task May not have the expertise to carry out complex research methodologies, etc.
Engaging consultants	Additional staff for a short period of time Have the expertise to carry out the task accurately Different approach, not related to the existing traditions and culture of the organization Catalyst for change 'Blaming' changes on the recommendations of a third party is one way that managers can overcome resistance to them	Direct costs, therefore can seem expensive Not experienced with the organization's area of operations Not responsible for implementation of recommendations nor subsequent success or failure Member of staff needs to be assigned to liaise with the consultants and be responsible for the project A large project may need an in-house team assigned Conflict and disagreement may result; whilst a certain amount is healthy, time must be set aside for their resolution Can be difficult to find a consultancy that is right for the organization

systems and quality awards into the voluntary and commercial sectors of the industry require proof that customers have been consulted.

This chapter has been designed to give an overview of a variety of methods that can be used, especially those that have specific application to the service sector (e.g. SERVQUAL). This examination has included both quantitative and qualitative techniques.

The conclusion must be that a variety of research methods needs to be used at any one time to facilitate different information-gathering objectives. These investigations must have no end if they are to facilitate the quality management 'goal' of continuous improvement.

14

Quality and Human Resource Management

Introduction

The previous three chapters highlighted the importance of systems and quality initiatives that promote not merely quality assurance but the notion of continuous improvement. 'Keeping close to the customer' is inextricably linked to these processes; together, they are part of the organization's overall approach to service quality. Indeed, Chapter 10 demonstrated the overwhelming significance of organizational culture in the performance of leisure and tourism organizations in delivering service quality. Organizational culture is associated in particular with the values and ethos of the organization and the way in which it operates and interacts with the external customer. Our analysis identified the mix of hard and soft factors or combination of systems, procedures, style and people that represent the culture in all organizations and help to shape the service process and service delivery, with the clarity of the organization's vision central to its efficiency and effectiveness. We have already established what an important input staff are to the service process in leisure and tourism. The way staff interact with customers is crucial to the quality of the experience. However, the philosophy of total quality management requires the appropriate attitude and response from all staff in any industry, simply to create the culture in the organization to encourage change. As Lovelock (1992, p. 225) pointed out:

Defining the service role is an important step, but it won't get a company very far unless the company has personnel with the attitude, ability and flexibility to fulfill the role.

The purpose of this chapter is to examine the distinctive role and function of the human resource in service quality in leisure and tourism organizations and the key elements in its management. The relationship between quality management approaches and human resource management is the focus and the issue of this chapter. As will be seen, education and training and the development of staff are central to the delivery of appropriate products and services, but this process is also dependent on, and linked to, the communication of values, beliefs and vision and how they are created in the first instance. The other two broad elements, therefore, are concerned with internal marketing and with the way in which staff are able to operate, interpret and create the vision and values of the organization.

On completion of the chapter, it is expected that you will be able to:

- understand and analyse the relationship between the ethos and philosophy of a leisure or tourism organization and the management of its human resource in the achievement of service quality;
- appreciate and evaluate the role of internal marketing in developing necessary values, attitudes and behaviours for culture change;
- assess and explain the role of education, training and professional development in

> the provision and management of the service encounter;
>
> • understand and apply methods for enabling and encouraging front-line staff to exercise independent judgement and contribute to organizational development.

The Importance of Staff in the Leisure and Tourism Service Encounter

All employees are responsible for service quality. This applies to all organizations but particularly to those in the leisure and tourism industry, with its emphasis on the service encounter and the interaction between people. The significance of the psychological encounter between staff and customers suggests that much of the marketing that takes place is of an interactive nature; there is the opportunity to influence customers at each point of contact and to encourage and receive feedback and opinion, which constitute valuable market research. Additionally, as Randall and Senior (1996, p. 173) observed 'every service encounter must be seen as yet another opportunity to please a customer, to encourage them to return and pass around the good message'. How staff support and respond to each other is also important: Chapter 8 showed how appropriate service design is based on knowledge and understanding of all staff about each other's roles and the notion of the quality chain. However, certain staff, who deal directly with the public and are perceived by customers as the public face of the organization, have a particular responsibility for service quality. Attitudes, behaviour and tangibles such as dress and what is said are important and represent the culture and values of the organization.

Yet there is an *interactive process* in that although the values and ethos of an organization will shape the pattern of work and way staff operate and deal with customers, they should also be created by all employees in the first instance. Deming (1986), in his critique of approaches to quality, argued that the people factor is the most important. He was a scientist and was instrumental in the development of statistical process control but he recognized

that the way in which staff were managed and motivated was central to any approach to quality. He observed that management often blamed their employees for faults when over 90% were caused by system and procedural problems; the latter, of course, were designed and controlled by management. Deming felt that employees should be encouraged to become involved in problem solving and decision making as well as developing a sense of ownership for the product or service. It is not insignificant that Deming and Juran were both employed in the Hawthorne Plant of the Western Electric Company in Chicago, where the 'Human Relations' school of management thinking emerged in the 1930s.

According to Dale (1994a), 'the real key to the success of TQM is people'. He suggested that, in many services, customers value more highly the human dimensions of quality than the tangibles, but this remains one of the intriguing questions for any analysis of leisure and tourism organizations. Much will depend on the nature of the product and the characteristics of the market group, but the need for a competitive edge points to the impact of customer care and service. Kerfoot and Knights (1995) also suggested that there are no longer such clear market forces, with price fixing and homogenized products, and that service encounter and service delivery are the means to achieve a competitive edge. For example, Mintel (1997), in a report into the health club market, forecast that in the next 5 years health club operators would spend more time and resources focusing on customer service and how they can use it as a means of achieving competitive advantage. Virgin Atlantic has established a reputation in recent years for service quality and for continual improvement. Richard Branson's Virgin organization is driven to a large extent by the competitive edge and how it can differentiate itself from its rivals but also keep ahead of them as they attempt to catch up. Virgin calls this approach the 'Eternal Escalator'. Barney suggested that there are four empirical indicators of competitive edge – value, rareness, imitability and substitutability – and that, increasingly, it is the human resource that is capable of meeting them through its competencies, capabilities and creativity.

Creating a competitive edge is not straightforward and is dependent on several factors in addition to the facets of TQM already examined. As Fig. 14.1 demonstrates, there are three main strands to a strategy for service quality in leisure and tourism organizations, which focus on the management and contribution of staff, once clear structures and processes are in place. Internal marketing provides the link between the organization, its vision and values, and its most important resource, people, and is a means of communicating and creating its organizational culture. Appropriate and effective internal marketing will encourage and facilitate employee autonomy in decision making and problem solving and the proactive approach to handling the service encounter, which can enhance the consumer experience in so many contexts. Both aspects, and particularly the ability and aptitude of staff, also require selective and sensitive education, training and staff development. The government, in its recent report *Tomorrow's Tourism*

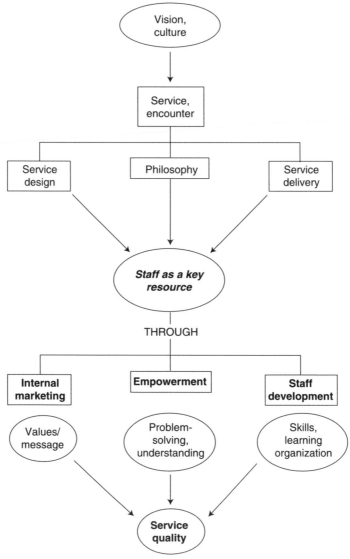

Fig. 14.1. Quality and the human resource.

(DCMS, 1999), also recognizes the importance of appropriate, well-trained staff:

> People are vital to the delivery of quality tourism products . . . Forward-looking tourism businesses recognize that investing in their staff makes good business sense. They know that well-trained and motivated staff raise product quality, improve customer satisfaction and lead to higher profits.

The DCMS is making an important point that applies across the whole of the leisure and tourism industry and underpins the message of this book. Staff, and the way they are managed, in turn play a major part in how the product is delivered and consumed and how quality is perceived by the consumer. A key question for employee empowerment and quality management concerns the responsibilities and processes of human resource management (HRM). Swain (1999) argued that HRM is too valuable a function to leave to human resource specialists and points to an increasing number of organizations in which the HRM function is being assumed by line managers; like marketing, it permeates the organization and its structures and relates to every role and function. It is also linked with the understanding of the organization's values and philosophy. Similarly, empowerment has clear implications for marketing and its involvement of everyone rather than simply as 'top-down' strategy.

Internal Marketing

The first of the three broad issues in the management of people and the achievement of culture change and service quality concerns the notion of the internal customer and the nature and clarity of internal marketing. The superimposing of a supplier–customer chain on internal organizational relations is one of the fundamental principles of TQM. The perception of a colleague as a customer and the identification of a quality chain has particular implications for leisure and tourism, where there may be a number of stages of service encounters involved, when staff may be working different hours to each other and,

in the case of the public sector, where there is often a complex set of internal relations between different functions, departments or suppliers and customers. Clearly, the efficacy of internal marketing will be considerably influenced by the overall approach to marketing (Seaton, 1996, pp. 19–20):

> Marketing requires an organizational structure which identifies everyone with its philosophy and goals. It is not enough for marketing executives to understand marketing programmes – marketing can only be effective when everyone in the organization is identified with its goals and their roles in implementing the marketing programme.

It has already been seen in Chapter 10 how the staff of Amelia Island Plantation are all trained to the same guiding principles and shared values. The organization's internal marketing is designed not only to create an environment that supports customer consciousness and sales mindedness amongst all staff but also to focus on staff care. Its internal marketing provides benefits such as increased motivation, reduced employee turnover, teamwork and improved communications. It uses several methods, including its weekly newsletter, which communicates the vision as well as publishing details of incentive scheme awards achieved and general information about the resort.

Alton Towers is the UK's leading theme park and comes closest, perhaps, to emulating Disney's approach to managing, training and developing its staff. Alton Towers' mission to create 'magic' is promoted through a systematic approach to internal marketing in which staff inculcate the organization's philosophy and values and feel that they are contributing to the magic. A training scheme with its focus on customers enables staff to identify the contribution they are making and Alton Towers refers to its staff as service providers. Its internal marketing has been found to improve levels of intrinsic motivation and, ultimately, service quality.

The case study later in the chapter (see Box 14.1) also shows how Viva! Health Club encourages staff to get to know internal customers as well as external ones and to share

Box 14.1.   Case study: Viva! Health Club, Bristol.

The Viva! Health Club was opened in Bristol in 1993 to address a gap in the market for up-market health and fitness facilities. Since then it has achieved a good reputation and is the most expensive health club in the Bristol area. The Viva! organization presents some brief and straightforward core values.

To ensure that the Viva! product lives and breathes quality by:

- maintaining five star housekeeping standards;
- unique, functional and inspiring club designs;
- developing programmes and service standards of the highest quality.

To ensure members and staff have fun at Viva! by:

- recruiting, training and developing all staff to their full potential;
- communicating effectively internally and externally;
- encouraging member and staff feedback in order that we can continue to improve the product and services in line with the members' needs.

To be profitable by:

- developing new clubs to cover our fixed cost base;
- controlling costs relative to budget;
- maximizing revenue opportunities through membership sales, retention and selling Club services.

The reference to quality is clear and underpins all aspects. It provides a message for both customers and staff and suggests that customer care is a vital ingredient in this and is directly linked with staff care and their sense of enjoyment and satisfaction with work. Customer care training for staff permeates all aspects of work because of the central focus on the needs of the customer and the benefits that accrue to both staff and customers. The philosophy of the company recognizes that staff who enjoy their work will have a positive impact on productivity and members' satisfaction levels. It is felt that the key lies in the quarterly goal-setting for every employee with each line manager. This is based on the club's business objectives for the year, the direction in which it is going and the identification of goals and targets that link the individual and the company.

There are two methods for recording the development of staff. The first is qualitative, in which observations made during the review are recorded and areas for development are highlighted and agreed. The second method is an attempt to make the review more objective and quantifies progress with a rating out of ten for each objective set for the individual. The staff handbook states that where areas of weakness are identified, staff can expect support, encouragement and training to assist in the improvement process. The company manual highlights the 'seven steps to success' that comprise the in-house training package.

BE A VIVA! PERSON
A Viva! person:

Shares the vision
Understand the company core values, your team's goals and constantly review your own goals with your manager.

Has a sense of ownership
Rather than trying to single out somebody for upgrading your job performance, your productivity, response time, quality, cost control and customer service should show standard gains and your skills should be in a state of constant renewal.

Sees himself or herself as a centre for service
Get to know your internal and external customers. Stay in regular contact with them and build a strong working relationship. Deliver the highest quality service possible, anticipate their needs, and develop a reputation for responsiveness.

Continually strives to add value
Prove your worth to the company. Make a difference. Add enough value so everyone can see that something very important would be missing if you left.

Box 14.1. *Continued.*

Makes himself/herself accountable
Consider the big picture. Look beyond your own immediate behaviour – beyond the specifics of your job description – to see if you're really doing all you should to bring about the right results. Learn to work across departmental boundaries. Combine your efforts seamlessly with others who, though very different from you, are contributing to the same end results.

Is business-like
Consider how you – personally – can help cut costs, serve the customer better, improve productivity, and innovate. Constantly think in terms of commercial success.

---

the vision and the core values of the company. The Young Vic Theatre's philosophy to customer care is that 'the customer is worth more to us than an individual ticket'. The theatre stresses the importance of loyalty and branding and trusts its staff to deliver a good theatre experience and communicates this message clearly to both staff and customers.

An important aspect of internal marketing and culture change is the way communication takes place within the organization. It is known that any move to change organizational culture and quality measures has to be communicated very carefully and fully within the two-way process demonstrated in Fig. 14.1. However, a quality culture requires the process of communicating to be seen as more than a technique but a part of the values and ways of working pointed to in the previous chapter. The Broadgate Health Club, for example, communicates with its internal market through meetings, memoranda, posters and newsletters. The club offers its staff weekly reports on what is happening within the club and developments in wider aspects that impact on the club such as legislation and possible mergers or takeovers.

Tourish and Tourish (1997, p. 97) identified several key factors for effective communication and internal marketing of a quality culture:

1. *Widespread informal and face-to-face communication* appears to generate more trust and cooperation. This will later be seen to be an important factor in the success of employee empowerment.
2. *A management philosophy that encourages the maximum flow of information* also promotes the positive attitudes and behaviour referred

to at the beginning of this chapter. Tourish and Tourish argued that this helps to reduce feelings of uncertainty and unease; staff are more contented and relaxed and have more 'cognitive space' to focus on the demands of the job and the organization's wider goals.

3. *The use of communications audits* can provide managers with more objective feedback about the effectiveness of communication systems and processes. In one example, a manager's 'managing by walking about' style was perceived by employees as snooping even though his intentions were honest. Communications audits guide organizations in:

- with whom they should be communicating;
- with whom they actually do communicate;
- what they should be communicating;
- how they should communicate with them; and
- how they actually do communicate with them.

Tourish and Tourish (1997) also showed how leisure organizations have gained from the use of communications audits in terms of reduced absenteeism and staff turnover. Many organizations in the leisure and tourism industry face this problem and Alton Towers is no exception. It has been affected by staff turnover and the seasonality of its operations. In fact, during its peak season of May to August, between 330 and 400 temporary staff are employed in addition to the 80 to 150 permanent staff. Training and motivating them is a major challenge. Alton Towers is using its customer-oriented training scheme to reduce staff turnover but a rigorous communications audit may help them in this process.

Employee Autonomy and Involvement

An important issue in service quality in leisure and tourism organizations is the decentralization of decision making and problem solving, with empowerment and quality circles as particular methods or approaches. These two facets of employee participation are inextricably linked and are both concerned with the definition, correction and anticipation of problems. Indeed, they are at the heart of the principle of continuous improvement or kaizen as Juran and Ishikawa, in particular, advocated. It is argued (Sparks *et al.*, 1997) that as service standards and consumer expectations increase, so the need for empowerment and employee involvement in decision making especially is strengthened with discretion and autonomy on the part of all staff. In particular, empowerment is concerned with those staff who are involved in creating value at the service encounter.

Empowerment

Empowerment has been a significant development during the 1990s, not least as an important principle of TQM, if not as a feature of modern HRM practices. An important issue that this section will attempt to address is the relationship between quality management and HRM, especially from the strategic perspective; it will also tackle the question of whether initiatives such as empowerment are more rhetorical than substantive. Analysis of the approach of leisure and tourism organizations towards empowerment demonstrates a concomitant point to the question of whether a leisure or tourism service is standardized or customized. Empowerment involves a similar dichotomy in that an autonomous approach on the part of employees in their dealings with customers may occur in both highly standardized operations, such as some

cinema chains, and individualized operations where the nature of the interaction between staff and customers is a unique selling point. Fitness instructors and others involved in teaching and coaching need to assess the capabilities of customers. Tour guides often need to respond to questions and the level of knowledge of particular groups. Empowerment features strongly in the Broadgate Health Club's mission statement in Chapter 10, which states that all staff should have a shared responsibility to deliver an uncompromising level of service quality. The approach is to delegate responsibilities to all staff rather than to a selected few. This means that duty managers do not need to attend every problem that arises and receptionists have powers to deal with complaints as they occur and to resolve problems where possible.

What is empowerment in leisure and tourism?

It may be useful at this stage to consider further what is meant by empowerment in the context of leisure and tourism organizations. It includes the control of one's work (to a fuller or lesser extent) employee autonomy, teamwork and the sense of ownership of the service encounter and its organizational context. Its essence is the flexibility and self-judgement required of many front-line staff in leisure and tourism organizations and, indeed, the opportunities for decision making encouraged by organizations; it involves decentralization of authority and decision making and the more immediate service recovery to which organizations such as Disney are so committed, and is necessary because of the characteristics of service delivery examined in Chapter 8. In particular, the role of the customer as a co-producer and the nature of the service encounter raise the significance of the critical moments and the need for staff to 'think on their feet'. Hjalager (2001) showed how the empowerment of both staff and customers is symbiotically linked in achieving higher levels of service quality, as Fig. 14.2 demonstrates. The Boots approach of educating staff to vary their manner according to the mood and demeanour of customers is seen in organizations

Organized industry pull
> ➤ Certification
> ➤ Staff empowerment
> ➤ Information, training of proprietors
> ➤ Investment support

Empowered tourists push
> ➤ Push via purchasing power of tour operators
> ➤ Independent consumer organizations
> ➤ Legislation/regulations
> ➤ Anarchic sharing of experience
> in press, guidebooks and Internet

Fig. 14.2. Two modes of quality improvement (Hjalager, 2001).

such as TGI Fridays, where staff are encouraged to take the initiative and engage with customers in a flexible, autonomous way. Holmes Place Health and Fitness Clubs uses empowerment as a tool for achieving service quality; it believes that all staff should be able to listen and learn from customers as well as act proactively to respond to customer wants.

It has been established that the service encounter is at the very core of the leisure and tourism experience and yet is subject to failure in every instance because of its nature. Consequently, service providers, and particularly front-line staff, are there not simply to provide the service and enhance the experience but also to solve problems as they arise. When this occurs quickly and effectively, it can greatly increase levels of customer satisfaction. Walker's (1995) conceptualization of customer satisfaction breaks the service encounter into three stages (pre-service, core service and post-service) and demonstrates how customer dissatisfaction with aspects of the first two stages can be overturned by prompt and responsive service recovery in the third stage.

The nature of the empowerment can also affect customer responses. Sparks *et al.* (1997) examined the effects of three different levels of empowerment and their relationship with the communication style in use: (i) full and

flexible empowerment, in which the decision-making process stays close to the customer; (ii) limited empowerment, with more standardization and control; and (iii) detached empowerment, where often there would be a delay in response, although with some consistency and a feeling by customers that their concerns are being taken seriously. Sparks *et al.* (1997) suggested that the full and flexible approach should normally lead to the highest levels of customer satisfaction, but only when the communication style used was accommodating, informal and personal. They found that there was no difference in levels of customer satisfaction between full and detached empowerment approaches when the communication style was under-accommodating, formal and impersonal.

Disney has 'home run meetings' where all cast members are divided into groups with a member of management and discuss problems as well as information passed down to them. Communications appear to be of the accommodating, informal and personal type and are effective and well received.

In other words, empowerment clearly suggests that the major implications are for the role of employees and, to a certain extent, this is true. However, it is simplistic to think of it as simply a transference of power and authority and a delegation of tasks and responsibility. In many ways the task of management becomes more complex and challenging but in a positive and enlightened way. As Macdonald (1998) suggested:

> Empowerment quite simply means granting supervisors or workers permission to give the customer priority over other issues in the operation. In practical terms, it relates to the resources, skill, time and support to become leaders rather than controllers or mindless robots. The concept lies at the heart of managing with common sense.

Requirements of successful empowerment

As with TQM, it is not simply a matter of using empowerment as part of a wider strategy for changing the culture. The culture, to some extent, must be receptive to the requirements of successful empowerment. According to Cook and Macaulay (1996), empowered organizations display the following characteristics: (i) shared vision and values; (ii) customer-focused strategy; (iii) leadership; (iv) structure; (v) teamwork; and (vi) learning. These are all common factors that appear in so many analyses of service quality and business excellence and replicate the features of organizational cultures receptive to quality approaches. Nevertheless, the key question, which is not always an easy one to answer, is which came first? Empowerment and, certainly, quality circles as has been seen in Japanese examples, have undoubtedly helped to create dramatic changes in culture, organizational performance and customer satisfaction. Yet it is also known that such initiatives are doomed to fail unless there are certain predisposing factors in place. An organization cannot take the step towards 'total quality' unless it has some of the features in Cook and Macaulay's list already in place and, as Naylor (2000) argued, does not blindly follow Japanese practices but is selective and geared to the cultural characteristics of its staff.

Of all the features listed by Cook and Macaulay, the last – learning – is perhaps the most significant. The harnessing of individual desire for improvement and personal development and the processes in place that allow the organization to evaluate critically its performance, structures, procedures and operations create a healthy and proactive environment. The learning organization has the values and vision considered earlier and is sufficiently innovative and enterprising to create opportunities for action that can be evaluated and learned from. Its ability to conduct self-assessments and apply, perhaps, the Excellence Model examined in Chapter 12 is an added dimension.

Clearly, other features such as teamwork, a supportive and caring environment and a structure that has few layers between management and staff and customers is more likely to succeed. The understanding of service logic, active participation by all employees, openness, mutual support and help, and confidence in the competence of colleagues are all important elements in empowerment. Furthermore, empowerment is most likely to succeed when there are

high levels of self-motivation amongst staff (Coleman, 1996; Hales and Klidas, 1998). At Disney World, there is an award called 'Partners in Excellence'; other cast members nominate someone who has tried to exceed guests' expectations, has been a great team member and has always given of their best. It is a highly recognized award and carries some status. Everyday awards include the 'Guest fanatic' cards where the cast member has been noticed for having done something special such as creating a magical moment or dealing with a difficult situation or problem. All cast members are trained not to say 'no' to any question or problem but to deal with it or to seek someone who can. Guests who make comments or complain are viewed positively and are used to improve matters or put things right. Managers are encouraged to be visible and to interact with guests but staff are empowered to deal with complaints as they occur and to do so without being defensive.

TGI Fridays encourages its staff to be proactive and animated with customers but also to assess the character and mood of the guests in order to achieve the appropriate level of interaction. Everton Foootball Club has a comprehensive training programme for all its support staff and has developed a programme called 'The Customer Service Formula' in which staff are encouraged not to 'pass the buck'; instead they should own the problem and should not make false promises. Jarvis Hotels has encouraged empowerment through giving staff early responsibilities and autonomy; it has developed its 'Quality Champion Awards' given to staff who display consistently high levels of initiative and quality service.

Such examples are testament to the positive features of empowerment and the benefits that they bring to organizational performance. However, there are also some misgivings and negative experiences with empowerment in leisure and tourism organizations. Unless an appropriate culture is in place, employee empowerment will fail; too often, empowerment has been used as a means of changing the organizational culture rather than being part of a wider strategy. Honold (1997) in her critique of empowerment, identified four main perspectives to recent literature, which represent a balanced commentary on the implementation of empowerment schemes and initiatives.

The first factor is *leadership* and the extent to which empowerment is imposed or facilitated. Intervention by management can be viewed as positive or negative, depending on the style and methods of management. An important variable is whether management perceives empowerment in terms of devolved power of delegated tasks. Appropriate and enlightened leadership will encourage employees to opt to become involved and to perceive a supportive and open environment around them. Scarnati and Scarnati (2002) identified the important attributes of leadership necessary to develop the teamwork and quality processes for empowerment to succeed.

A second facet is the *collaborative nature* of empowerment and its role in countering the problem that can arise from the heterogeneous nature of leisure and tourism contexts. The link with quality circles and improvement teams is clear here and will be addressed in more detail later. The implication is that teamwork extends into the concept of the internal customer.

Thirdly, the *resonance* between the achievement of empowerment and the culture and internal processes of an organization is also significant. Maxwell (1997) showed how empowerment became more important in some UK hospitality organizations through the changing nature of markets and the desire for organizational legitimacy by human resource departments. Empowerment is more likely to fail in such environments.

Fourthly, the *links* between job enrichment, multi-skilling, cross-training and creative and open professional development encourage the personal responsibility and reflective thinking that are integral to successful empowerment.

The flexibility that exists in many aspects of the industry, including the public sector after the introduction of compulsive competitive tendering and the reduced influence of trades unions, has been linked to empowerment. Suspicion by middle management has also been a component of the general resistance to change outlined earlier in the chapter, with managers anxious about handing over their powers to subordinates. Kerfoot and Knights (1995) highlighted the paradox of empowerment in that employees have to accept its introduction and be submissive, yet to succeed it requires employees to be interpretive and enterprising. The corollary of their point is that the successful introduction of full empowerment also needs strong leadership, which may be incompatible with full empowerment and its devolved powers. Other critics (e.g. Dale *et al.*, 2001) have shown how resistance to initiatives such as empowerment can develop when management appears to be acting firmly on behalf of shareholder interests and is seeking cost cuts and an increased competitive edge. Performance-related pay (so abhorrent to Deming) simply for managers may also accentuate such perceptions. The consensus of critics of empowerment is that it fails, not because of inherent flaws in its principles but because of half-hearted efforts by management, the perception that it represents manipulation and coercion and the lack of an appropriate organizational culture (Honold, 1997). A similar view can be held against the use of quality circles for problem identifying and solving. Kerfoot and Knights (1995) suggested that an inappropriate culture is linked with the retention of traditional hierarchies and their associated divisions, which mitigate against the acceptance of shared values.

Quality circles

Another initiative based on employee autonomy, but which can falter like empowerment, is the quality circle. The concept of the quality circle was devised and developed by Kauru Ishikawa in the early 1960s and is arguably the most significant factor in the success of many Japanese organizations since then. Quality circles are concerned with problem solving by the employees closest to where the problems occur and, if not allowing full empowerment, can be construed as encouraging employee involvement and the process of continuous improvement. The

National Society for Quality Circles (1992) defined a quality circle as:

> A small group of between three and twelve people, who do the same or similar work, voluntarily meeting together regularly for about an hour a week in paid time, usually under the leadership of their own supervisor, and trained to identify, analyze and solve some of the problems in their work, presenting solutions to management and, where possible, implementing the solutions themselves.

Service recovery may not be as immediate with quality circles as with examples of employee empowerment illustrated earlier but there are some similar principles. They encourage employees to become more active and engaged in improving the service they are delivering. They may not devolve authority quite to the extent that full empowerment does, but on occasions the solution or improvement is introduced by members of the team and the sense of ownership of the service delivery can be strong.

In order for a quality circle to be an effective tool in improving service quality and leading the way towards total quality, it must be introduced with care and sensitivity. Mullins (1996, p. 543) suggested a number of criteria for successful implementation: (i) commitment and support of top management; (ii) full consultation with staff; (iii) a participative approach by management and an appropriate style of managerial behaviour; (iv) delegation of decision making; (v) trust and goodwill on both sides; (vi) an effective support structure of consultation and negotiation; (vii) support of trades unions and/or staff representatives; and (viii) continuous monitoring and review of results.

The success of quality circles depends on members being assured that they do belong to them and that they have a genuine contribution to make to enhancing service quality.

There are several problems associated with quality circles. They can be dismissed as another management gimmick, especially at a time of rapid culture change. If they are used too early in the process they can be seen as management abdicating responsibility. If they

are enforced they immediately lose much of their value based on the intrinsic motivation of members. The third reason for failure stems from the lack of proper training and preparation of members. The high staff turnover in some leisure and tourism organization exacerbates this problem.

However, quality circles can offer a number of benefits for both the organization and its staff. They can offer solutions to problems that may not even have been identified in the first place. There is staff development in that group members receive additional training in communications and problem-solving skills; indeed, the literal translation of the Japanese term for quality circles is 'the gathering of the wisdom'. There may be other spin-offs in terms of increased staff morale, better teamwork and improved communication throughout the organization, as well as the main outcome in greater customer satisfaction. At the Broadgate Club, there are weekly departmental meetings that identify current problems and their possible solutions. The minutes of the meetings are sent to top management, who liaise with staff to implement changes. This process is complemented by fortnightly focus groups with customers where at least two members of staff are involved in informal discussions with guests, and their findings are fed into the weekly meetings highlighted earlier.

Education and Training

Clear communication and empowerment of staff can take an organization so far but the ability of staff to respond and to perform appropriately is also critical. Education and training are key factors in service quality and achieving culture change. Armstrong (1996, p. 529) argued that: 'Training means investing people to enable them to perform better and empower them to make the best use of their natural abilities.'

The learning process applies to both TQM methods and the values and philosophy of the organization. There is a symbiotic relationship between an organization's training programme and its quality culture. It could be argued that any training programme needs a quality culture and that this is built into the training programme but the programme itself, if appropriate, can help in the development of a quality culture. TGI Fridays has a book of WOWs ('Walk on Water') for staff, which lists extras that staff can offer customers, such as lighting their cigarette, and which is almost a game entered into by all staff. Before each shift staff are involved in role play through a board game (based on the service encounter), which promotes a light-hearted approach and, again, shared experiences and values. The training programme is based on the culture and philosophy of the organization and the objective of training is to inculcate each employee with the values of the organization. The organization has identified five star values (Fig. 14.3) to represent its philosophy and culture; each value is depicted as a triangle and each side of the triangle must be balanced in order to deliver service quality the TGI Fridays way.

In addition to these star values, the three rings of perceived guest value are also taught to all staff. Ring one represents the *core offering* of authentic American food and drink plus unfailing standards of service. Ring two represents *additional features* that guests have come to expect on every visit. Ring three represents the real '*WOW*' *moments* to guests, which surprise and delight them.

Cook and Macaulay (1996) referred to surveys which, worryingly, suggest that 80% of service training is inadequate and ineffective. Peters (1998) argued that the move from quality assurance to TQM as a focus for management thinking has not always been matched by appropriate developments in HRM and education and training. He suggested that quality assurance can be supported by straightforward training based on individual skill development. TQM is more complex and requires both organization design and skill development as a human resource strategy to support its philosophy and practice.

Peters (1998) also pointed out how TQM needs to be underpinned by a three-level approach to education and training based on action learning.

1. *Learning how to do things correctly* regulates behaviour and is more task oriented.
2. *Learning how to do the right thing* is more concerned with processes and wider understanding of the organization's values and goals; change is proactive and aimed at innovation.
3. *Learning how to learn* highlights the dynamics of a TQM approach based on continuous improvement in all facets of the organization, in addition to the growing acknowledgment of the benefits of the individual having responsibility for their own learning and personal development.

The view that the organization is a learning establishment is also pertinent to the development of a quality culture. As seen earlier, the competitive edge is encapsulated in the knowledge, skills potential and commitment of its people. The challenge then becomes not simply creating a learning organization but allowing staff to unlearn outmoded or inappropriate ways and attitudes and to create a climate of trust. It has also been argued that the term 'human resource management' should be replaced by the term 'human potential management' (Kalra, 1997)

Fig. 14.3.   TGI Fridays five star values.

to imply an environment in which the individual employee is encouraged, and assisted, to achieve their full potential as well as helping the organization to achieve its goals. An example of an organization that professes to do this is Viva! Health Club (Box 14.1).

Education and training are also important in the development of employee autonomy and collective problem solving. Empowerment will not work unless employees are provided with the necessary training and development. Cook and Macaulay (1996b) suggested that the most important aspects are: (i) technical skills; (ii) interpersonal and influencing skills; (iii) customer handling skills; and (iv) problem solving. Our analysis of the leisure and tourism industry would support their view, with particular emphasis on interpersonal and customer handling skills. Some research carried out by one of the authors into customer satisfaction levels of a leisure centre run by a commercial contractor showed that most users were largely satisfied with the tangibles and with the operation and delivery of the core activities. There were some complaints about sudden changes made to programmes and the availability of facilities, and the occasional problem with equipment such as lockers or showers, but the main source of dissatisfaction concerned the rather diffident attitude of some front-line staff and their overt lack of responsiveness to problems and customer complaints.

Disney has always emphasized the importance of training, particularly in customer service skills. It provides endless opportunities for training and staff development, including job shadowing, general courses on ICT, languages and customer care. The 'discovery day' provided early in training is based on the seven guidelines noted in Chapter 10 and the following procedural and processual aspects: (i) familiarity with the park; (ii) fire and safety issues and regulations; (iii) park language; (iv) costuming; (v) guest service recovery procedures; (vi) guest satisfaction (listen and learn; measure; take action; re-measure; recognize and celebrate); and (vii) learn the key drivers (why customers keep coming back).

The focus on the customer must be reinforced with assurance of moments of truth.

Reliability and meeting expectations are the essence of quality assurance and can be achieved through training needs analyses, which identify the skills to be developed for each stage of the service process. The terms 'competence' and 'competency' are significant and need distinguishing at this point. ISO 9001 2000 uses the term 'competence' and marks a radical development for the standard with its previous emphasis on quality assurance and procedures and processes. A competency is a collection of skills, standards and qualities required for a job or a task. Competence is simply the ability to demonstrate the competency. The use of the terms is a recent development and they are often used interchangeably. They reflect the view, by human resource specialists, that the way a person carries out their job is just as important as the outcomes, especially if the organization is keen to reduce variation in the delivery of its service package – a high priority for many leisure and tourism organizations. Competencies can be used, first, to build standards into job descriptions or person specifications, especially if they link in with NVQs/SVQs, and, second, to help to shape recruitment, selection, training and staff development practices.

Scottish & Newcastle (S & N) is now one of the largest operators in the hospitality and leisure sector and recognizes that staff and the way they are trained is essential for success. It feels that training helps to communicate the essence of each brand and has even appointed specialist brand trainers for the purpose. S & N delivers over 50,000 training days to its staff across all operations and awarded 16,000 NVQs and 500 modern apprenticeships in 1999. S & N's emphasis on training and career progression has resulted in reduced levels of staff turnover and increased levels of staff motivation and profit. Jarvis Hotels, likewise, has over 12% of its workforce following NVQs that build on the induction for all staff, which includes customer care skills and information about the organization.

Thomas Cook regards its staff as the company's most important asset and substantial sums of money are invested in comprehensive training programmes to ensure that their experience and expertise is retained within the company. Having the best staff is a crucial factor in delivering a demonstrably better service to customers than a rival's customers. The group's philosophy is that the customers come first, that all company policies are formulated with customer service in mind and that training is geared to this requirement.

These developments also dovetail with the government's plans and intentions for developing the human resource in tourism and hospitality. Action is needed (DCMS, 1999) to: (i) provide the skilled employees the tourism industry needs; (ii) challenge negative perceptions about careers in hospitality; (iii) encourage best employment and management practice; (iv) encourage investment in training; and (v) enhance industry coordination on training.

Finally, a competency statement will have a title, a description of the occupational standards required to demonstrate the competency and a statement of outcomes. It should link individual competencies with organizational development and performance. It should also be capable of measurement and one method that is gaining credibility is the concept of *360-degree feedback*, where there is systematic collection and feedback of performance data on an individual or group, derived from the stakeholders involved. This would include staff, external customers, suppliers and councillors in local authorities. It has been argued (Barker and Ward, 1999) that the use of competency statements and 360-degree feedback can help to overcome the most difficult aspect – that of changing attitudes and behaviours. Such an approach has two main advantages: (i) the ability to identify precise standards and to measure them helps to promote the concept of continuous improvement; and (ii) the concept of the internal customer or quality chain is also supported by feedback from everybody involved.

As already observed, service quality requires the integration of quality management methods with approaches to customer service. The training and deployment of staff provides the means to achieving the integration but also needs an appropriate system. Canziani (1995) proposed a diagnostic

training system to prepare staff for the demands of quality customer service. His system contained two phases, which represent organizational development. Phase 1 begins with the statement of quality formulated and disseminated throughout the organization and is designed to raise awareness about the importance of meeting customer needs and of striving for continuous improvement. It can be seen that Canziani's system also engages staff in the blueprinting activities examined in Chapter 8 and that it involves feedback and reward. Phase 2 comprises a developmental process where colleagues are invited to be members of a team that is trained to monitor data from all sources of customer feedback and to measure each other's performance and improve it through the use of role-play and other aspects of co-training. Canziani advised organizations to begin with departments or individuals who are the most supportive or receptive and then move through the whole organization. One of the authors had an unfortunate recent experience on a skiing holiday in the French Alps where there were problems across the whole of the operations: staff were diffident and uninformed and communications were very poor; talking to staff did not suggest that there was a positive organizational culture, as examined in Chapter 10, and there was manifestly little attempt to engage and involve staff in the mission and purpose of the organization.

Conclusions

This chapter has attempted to examine the pivotal role that people and staff have in the process of delivering service quality in leisure and tourism contexts. The service encounter and the contact between staff and customers can so often determine the overall perception of a transaction. The model in Box 14.2 contains the important principles of TQM and demonstrates how they begin and end with the organization's closeness to the customer – but through their closeness to staff. The caveat *'good customer care through good staff care'* underpins all the examples of service excellence in the book and is integral to the implementation of culture change and the achievement of a quality culture. The model is designed to highlight the key points that have been examined throughout the text as, indeed, the concluding chapter reiterates.

Box 14.2.   Service quality through people.

1. Total quality management starts with the customer – internal and external
   CLOSENESS TO THE CUSTOMER

2. The desire to identify and meet customer expectations is seen as a strategic issue
   STRATEGY

3. Keeping close to the customer implies constant change and innovation
   CONTINUOUS IMPROVEMENT

4. The improvement process both creates and depends on cultural change
   CULTURE

5. Cultural change requires leadership and commitment from the very top
   LEADERSHIP

6. Leadership of quality can only work if there is a spirit and ethos of cooperation and teamwork
   INTERDEPENDENCE

7. Teamwork must be based on an open, two-way flow of information
   COMMUNICATION

8. Good communication will facilitate 'upstream preventive management'
   PROACTIVE PROBLEM SOLVING

9. Problem solving should move away from judgemental management
   STATISTICAL PROCESS CONTROL

10. The focus, therefore, is on the process and not just the product or service
    PROCESS FLOW ANALYSIS

11. The process involves the service encounter and the need for decentralized decision making and authority where possible
    EMPOWERMENT

12. Empowerment and handling the public have real implications for education and training
    STAFF DEVELOPMENT

THEREFORE CLOSENESS TO CUSTOMERS THROUGH CLOSENESS TO STAFF.

Conclusions

We have attempted in the previous 14 chapters to explore the phenomena of leisure and tourism experiences in managed contexts and the relationship between the way they are managed and the quality of the experiences. The book has examined the fundamental principles and methods of quality management and service quality and applied them to leisure and tourism operations. We have adopted a perspective that attempts to draw out the distinctiveness of the subject and relate many generic aspects of service quality to the consumption experience and the characteristics of leisure and tourism services.

Our examination of the nature of leisure and tourism services has emphasized its intangibility and the difficulty both consumers and providers have in evaluating the quality of the experience. The interaction between customers and the organization, and particularly staff, has been highlighted as a key factor in the delivery of service quality, and the distinction between technical and functional quality is more blurred as a result. The way an aerobics session is delivered, and the charisma and style of the instructor, may be almost as much of the core product, and its technical quality, as the activity itself. The courier or holiday representative, through the way they interact with tourists, can also be a key component in the core product. In the same way, the involvement of the customer as co-producer in some contexts, especially, is another significant feature that we have incorporated into our analysis and overview of quality approaches in leisure and tourism.

Since we have argued that the impact of people, as customers and employees, is considerable, another important theme in the book has been the management of people and the development of organizational culture, where often the values and philosophy of the organization reflect the needs and wants of customers and the benefits offered through the product and service.

Nevertheless, we have not eschewed the roles and applications of tools and techniques and the harnessing of mechanistic approaches with the softer human and experiential aspects of leisure and tourism consumption. The identification of clear service standards or specifications is especially important where the desired consumer motives and achieved outcomes are less easy to identify. Progress has been made since the Oasis Leisure Centre in Swindon became the first leisure facility to be registered to BS 5750 (ISO 9002) and the British Standards Institute adapted to the lack of precision in identifying customer satisfaction and goals. The growing application of the Investors in People Award illustrates the point about people in the previous paragraph and suggests that the industry sees the training and development of staff in relation to the features and attributes of the service offering as critical to their success in meeting customer expectations.

The ability to identify customer expectations and to know when they are met is also highlighted as the prerequisite for organizational effectiveness and the book has addressed the needs of managers in monitoring and tracking organizational performance as well as measuring customer satisfaction and service quality. SERVQUAL has been considered, as have other methods, and the philosophical challenge of providing for a phenomenon considered to be based on individual freedom and personal identity raises questions for the extent to which services can be customized and categorized.

The book, in highlighting the importance of service quality in leisure and tourism management, has raised, and attempted to answer, several questions:

- What do organizations and managers need to know and understand about quality?
- What is particularly distinctive about service quality in the leisure and tourism industry?
- How is the industry responding to the challenges posed by the competitive edge and increasing customer expectations?
- How important are creativity and design in relation to the tools and techniques of quality assurance quality management?
- What is their relationship with the philosophy and ethos of the organization?
- What specific skills are required for the achievement and maintenance of service quality in leisure and tourism?

The answers suggested a number of key points, which establish the integrity of service quality as a management perspective or discipline but also identify its relationship with other management functions in leisure and tourism management:

1. Quality is a strategic issue and many aspects of quality management involve the operationalizing of strategic thinking within organizations about their customers and their requirements. The characteristics of service delivery in leisure and tourism, and the nature of the leisure and tourism experience, illustrate the potential in this industry for achieving a competitive edge through management of the process and the customer experience.

2. The management of service quality is an issue and a facet of management that has emerged in recent years from other management functions and is continuing to establish its integrity and parameters. As service quality continues to establish its frameworks and concepts and its literature and body of knowledge and skills, its relationships with other management functions will also become clearer and help to shape the intellectual development of service management and quality management. Marketing, and particularly interactive marketing (where customers meet the organization), provided the theoretical underpinnings to many of the early developments. Service operations management embraces particular challenges facing leisure and tourism managers, such as the peaks and troughs in customer attendances and the problems of managing queues, and is particularly concerned with management of the service encounters, which are at the heart of many service offerings. Human resource management is the third function of management; it connects closely with service quality and frequently demonstrates the strategic advantage associated with delivering quality through the best use of staff and their qualities and competencies.

3. Developments in the leisure and tourism industry and its external environment are also adding to the increased importance of service quality and formal approaches to its management. The contribution of formal awards and initiatives, such as Quest, Charter Mark and Investors in People, is one aspect. The pronouncements by the Tourism Minister, Kim Howells, in June 2001, about the need to raise standards in UK hotels, is another.

4. Managing service quality in leisure and tourism requires a distinctive approach because of the nature of the leisure and tourism product. It is no different from service quality in any other service industry in that the tools and techniques of quality management apply. It is no different in that its ability to identify, and to consistently meet, its customers' requirements will determine the level of service quality and the very success and long-term survival of the organization. It is no different in that the ethos, philosophy and culture of the organization will have a direct bearing on the attitudes, willingness and capability of its staff to deliver service quality. Where leisure and tourism management are different in the challenges that face them in

their management of service quality is in the nature of the service (and product) and way it is managed. It is a service in which its core is based on an experience and the success of the service is determined by the enhancement of that experience and the emotional responses of the individual to the attributes of the service offering. The service offering is a complex mix of attributes and quality dimensions, including contextual, human, social, environmental and physical factors, with the interaction between customers and staff and the frequent role of the customer in the service encounter providing distinctive characteristics.

5.   The service encounter, and how it is managed and perceived, is at the core of the management of service quality. The service encounter helps to define the outcomes and the benefits of the leisure and tourism experience, which are concerned with the well-being (physical, mental and spiritual) of the individual as well as the intrinsic enjoyment and satisfaction with the experience itself.

6.   Formal methods and approaches provide organizations with the opportunity to progress beyond the serendipitous circumstances that have sometimes determined industry and product developments in the past. The final part of the book is particularly concerned with these aspects and is a contribution to the more systematic and rigorous approach required by the dynamics of the contemporary leisure and tourism industry.

7.   Yet, finally, the essence of the book is the attempt to marry the use of tools and techniques, and systems-based approaches, with the more philosophical aspects of quality management and, in particular, the knowledge and understanding of the experiential properties of the leisure and tourism product.

The first part of the book examined the background to the service encounter and the conceptual framework for developing an understanding of the consumer perspective to service quality in a leisure and tourism context. This was necessary in order to contextualize the application of quality methods and approaches, including the stages of design, assurance and total quality and continuous improvement in the service concept, the service standards and their delivery. The

second part related this conceptual framework to the formulation of the product and the service and, in particular, demonstrated how an important aspect of service quality is the way in which both the process and the tangible product are designed and improved organizationally. The final part incorporated the more established aspects of service quality and quality management but also showed how their application to leisure and tourism management is shaped and enhanced by knowledge and understanding of the components of Parts 1 and 2. Achieving service quality included the methods of evaluating customer satisfaction in what is essentially a very subjective consumer experience as well as applying the more mechanistic elements of systems, quality tools and awards to such uncertainties. Finally, the contribution of organizational culture and the management of the human resource to the service encounter and the consumption experience are particularly significant and return us to the opening chapters of the book on the integrity of the leisure and tourism product and service and its evolving nature.

In our treatment of this relatively new topic, we have attempted to synthesize the concepts, theories and principles of consumer and management-based studies with the consumer process and the experiential properties of the leisure and tourism product as the central thrust. Through this synthesis, some key issues and questions are raised:

- How will organizations continue to achieve a competitive edge in what is a very dynamic and competitive industry?
- To what extent will the tourism sector be able to produce new concepts and destinations and the leisure sector continue to redesign and tweak existing concepts and products?
- Will the integrated approach to developing and designing products and services become more evident?
- Will techniques such as service blueprinting and quality function deployment be more commonly applied to the appraisal of existing systems and processes?

- Will the industry develop and implement more specific and tailor-made awards and methods, like Quest, which embrace the distinctive nature of the industry and its products encapsulated in its consumption experience and involvement of the consumer in so many contexts?
- How symbiotic will the relationship be between service quality and progress in sustainability and environmentalism?
- Will the present emphasis on facilities and sites be more widely applied to town and city environs with greater use made of the term 'servicescape'?
- Will advances in technology create more standardized and impersonal experiences and processes or will the interaction between staff and customers continue to be pivotal to many organizations?

The topic of service quality in leisure and tourism is continuing to develop and this book is an attempt to contribute to this emergent subject.

References

Akan, P. (1995) Dimensions of service quality: a study in Istanbul. *Managing Service Quality* 6, 39–43.

Allen, C. (1994) Managing strategic and organisational change: the role of the chief executive and the board. In: Taylor, B. (ed.) *Successful Change Strategies*. Director Books, Hemel Hempstead.

Anderson, E.W. and Fornell, C. (1994) A customer satisfaction research prospectus. In: Rust, R.T. and Oliver, R.L. (eds) *Service Quality: New Directions in Theory and Practice*. Sage, London, pp. 289–312.

Armistead, C. (1994) The journey to date: lessons from past services management research. In: Armistead, C. (ed.) *The Future of Services Management*. Kogan Page, Cranfield, pp. 27–40.

Armistead, C. and Clark, G. (1994) service quality and service recovery: the role of capacity management. In: Armistead, C. (ed.) *The Future of Services Management*. Kogan Page, Cranfield, pp. 81–97.

Armstrong, M. (1996) *Personnel Management Practice*. Kogan Page, London.

Astbury, M. (1998) Long term relationships are far better than one night stands. *Qualityworld* July, 8–10.

Astbury, R. (1993) Voluntary sector transitions. *Managing Service Quality* 3, 11–13.

Athos, R.T. and Pascale, A.G. (1981) *The Art of Japanese Management*. Penguin Books, London.

Atkinson, P.E. (1990) *Creating Culture Change: the Key to Successful Total Quality Management*. IFS Publications, Bedford.

Audit Commission (1992) *Citizen's Charter Performance Indicators*. HMSO, London, 80 pp.

Audit Commission (1994) *Staying on Course: the Second Year of the Citizen's Charter Indicators*. HMSO, London, 55 pp.

Audit Commission (1998) *Consultation on the Local Authorities Performance Indicators*. HMSO, London, 70 pp.

Babakus, E. and Boller, G.W. (1992) An empirical assessment of the Servqual scale. *Journal of Business Research* 24, 253–268.

Bailey, R. and Hall, E. (1998) Social and economic trends and their impact on the commercial leisure and hospitality sectors. In: Buswell, J. (ed.) *Guide to Good Practice in Leisure Management*. Financial Times Management, London, Section 4, pp. 4.5 01–4.5 13.

Bale, J. (1989) *Sports Geography*. Spon, London, 266 pp.

Barker, R. and Ward, P. (1999) Creating and sustaining quality culture. *Qualityworld* (May), 20–23.

Barnes, J.G. and Cumby, J.A. (1995) The cost of service quality. In: Glynn, W.J. and Barnes, J.G. (eds) *Understanding Services Management*. John Wiley & Sons, Chichester, pp. 178–202.

Beale, V. and Pollitt, C. (1994) Charters at the grass roots: a first report. *Local Government Studies* 20, 202–225.

Beard, J.G. and Ragheb, M.G. (1980) Measuring leisure satisfaction. *Leisure Research* 1, 21–33.

Becker, C. (1996) Implementing the intangibles: a total quality approach for hospitality service providers. In: Olsen, M.D., Teare, R. and Gummesson, E. (eds) *Service Quality in Hospitality Organisations*. Cassell, London, pp. 278–298.

Berry, L.L. (1995) *On Great Service: a Framework for Action*. Free Press, New York, 292 pp.

Berry, L.L. and Parasuraman, A. (1992) Prescription for a service revolution in America. *Organisational Dynamic* 20 (Spring), 5–15.

Berry, L.L. and Parasuraman, A. (1994) Lessons from a ten year study of service quality in America. In: Scheuing, E.E., Edvardsson, B.,

Laciness, D. and Little, H.C. (eds) *Proceedings of Quality in Services Conference*. International Service Quality Association, pp. 153–162.

Berry, L.L. and Schneider, B. (1994) Lessons for improving service quality – a customer's perspective. Unpublished Conference Papers, Managing Service Quality Conference, Manchester Business School, 68 pp.

Berry, L.L., Zeithaml, V.A. and Parasuraman, A. (1985) Quality counts in services, too. *Business Horizons* (May–June), 44–52.

Berry, L.L., Parasuraman, A. and Zeithaml, V.A. (1988) The service puzzle. *Business Horizons* (Septemmber–October), 35–43.

Berry, L.L., Zeithaml, V.A. and Parasuraman, A. (1990) Five imperatives for improving service quality. *Sloan Management Review* 31(Summer), 29–38.

Bettencourt, L. and Gwinner, K. (1996) Customization of the service experience; the role of the frontline employee. *International Journal of Service Industry Management* 2, 3–20.

Bitner, M.J. (1990) Evaluating service encounters: the effects of physical surroundings and employee responses. *Journal of Marketing* 2, 69–82.

Bitner, M.J. and Hubbet, A.R. (1994) Encounter satisfaction versus overall satisfaction versus quality: the customers' voice. In: Rust, R.T. and Oliver, R.L. (eds) *Service Quality: New Directions in Theory and Practice*. Sage, London, pp. 72–94.

Bitner, M.J., Faranda, W.T., Hubbert, A.R. and Zeithaml, V.A. (1997) Customer contributions and roles in service delivery. *International Journal of Service Industry Management* 3, 193–205.

Bogan, C.E. and English, M.J. (1994) *Benchmarking for Best Practice: Winning through Innovative Adaptation*. McGraw-Hill, London, 312 pp.

Bolton, R.N. (1998) Duration of customer's relationship with continuous service provider. *Marketing Science* 1, 45–65.

Boulding, W., Kalra, A., Staelin, R. and Zeithaml, V. (1993) A dynamic process model of service quality: from expectations to behavioural intentions. *Journal of Marketing Research* (February), 7–27.

Bradley, F. (1995) The service firm in international marketing. In: Glynn, W.J. and Barnes, J.G. (eds) *Understanding Services Management*. John Wiley & Sons, Chichester, pp. 420–448.

Brogowicz, A.A., Delene, L.M. and Lyth, D.M. (1990) A synthesised service quality model with managerial implications. *International Journal of Service Industry Management* 1, 27–45.

Brown, S. (1995) *Postmodern Marketing*. Routledge, London.

Brown, S.W. and Swartz, T.A. (1989) Gap analysis of professional service quality. *Journal of Marketing* 2, 92–98.

Brown, T.J., Churchill Jr, G.A. and Peter, J.P. (1993) Research note: improving the measurement of service quality. *Journal of Retailing* 1, 127–139.

BSI (1998) *Draft BSENISO 9000: 2000 – Quality Management Systems – Requirements*. British Standards Institute, London, 29 pp.

Buchanon, D. and Huczynski, A. (1997) *Organizational Behaviour – an Introductory Text*, 3rd edn. Prentice Hall, Hemel Hempstead.

Burca, S. de (1995) Services management in the business to business sector: from networks to relationship marketing. In: Glynn, W.J. and Barnes, J.G. (eds) *Understanding Services Management*. John Wiley & Sons, Chichester, pp. 393–419.

Burke, W.W. (1997) The new agenda for organisational development. *Organisational Dynamics* 26, 7–20.

Burns, J.P.A., Hatch, J.H. and Mules, T.J. (1986) *The Adelaide Grand Prix*. The Centre for South Australian Economic Studies, Adelaide, 221 pp.

Burton, T.L. (1996) Safety nets and security blankets: false dichotomies in leisure studies. *Leisure Studies* 15, 17–36.

Buswell, J. (1993a) *Case Studies in Leisure Management Practice*. Longman, Harlow.

Buswell, J. (1993b) *Customer Charters in Leisure Services*. Institute of Leisure and Amenity Management, Goring-Upon-Thames.

Butcher, H. (1994) The concept of community practice. In: Haywood, L. (ed.) *Community Leisure and Recreation*. Butterworth Heinemann, Oxford.

Buttle, F. (1993) *Quality Management: Theories and Themes*. Working Paper No. 257, Manchester Business School, Manchester, 25 pp.

Buttle, F. (1996) SERVQUAL: review, critique, research agenda. *European Journal of Marketing* 30, 8–32.

Cabinet Office (1991) *The Citizen's Charter: Raising the Standard*. Cmnd 1599. HMSO, London, 118 pp.

Cabinet Office (1998) *Service First: the New Charter Programme*. Office of Public Service, London, 75 pp.

Camp, D. (1997) Theme parks in Europe. *Travel & Tourism Analyst* No. 5. Travel and Tourism Intelligence, London, pp. 4–13.

Cantle-Jones, T. (1992) *Customer Service Pack for the Leisure Industry: Creating the Competitive Edge*. Longmans, Harlow, 48 pp.

Canziani, B.F. (1995) Integrating quality management and customer service: the service diagnostics training system. In: Olsen, M.D., Teare, R. and Gummesson, E. (eds) *Service Quality in Hospitality Organizations*. Cassell, London.

Canziani, B.F. (1997) Leveraging customer competency in service firms. *International Journal of Service Industry Management* 1, 5–25.

Cao, G., Clarke, S. and Lehaney, B. (2000) A systemic view of organizational change and TQM. *The TQM Magazine* 12, 3.

Caplin, R.H. (1982) *A Practical Approach to Quality Control*, 4th edn. Hutchinson, London, 356 pp.

Carlzon, J. (1987) *Moments of Truth*. Ballinger Publications, Cambridge, Massachusetts.

Carman, J.M. (1990) Consumer perceptions of service quality: an assessment of the SERVQUAL dimensions. *Journal of Retailing* 1, 33–55.

CCPR (1960) *Sport and the Community: the Report of the Wolfenden Committee on Sport*. Central Council of Physical Recreation, London.

Champy, J. (1995) *Reengineering Management: the Mandate for New Leadership*. Harper Collins, London, 237 pp.

Chandon, J., Leo, P. and Philippe, J. (1997) Service encounter dimensions – a dyadic perspective: measuring the dimensions of service encounters as perceived by customers and personnel. *International Journal of Service Industry Management* 1, 65–86.

Chaplin, R.H. (1982) *A Practical Approach to Quality Control*, 4th edn. Hutchinson.

Chase, R.B. and Garvin, D.A. (1989) The service factory. *Harvard Business Review* (July–Aug.), 61–69.

Chase, R.B. and Hayes, R.H. (1991) Beefing up operations in service firms. *Sloan Management Review* (Fall), 15–26.

Chebat, J.-C., Filiatrault, P. and Gelinas-Chebat, C. (1995) Impact of waiting attribution and consumer's mood on perceived quality. *Journal of Business Research* 34, 191–196.

Chin, K.S., Pun, K.-F., Leung, W.M. and Lau, H. (2001) A quality function deployment approach for improving technical library and information services: a case study. *Library Management* 4/5, 195–204.

CIPFA (1994) *Leisure and Recreation Statistics 1994–95 Estimates*. Chartered Institute of Public Finance and Accountancy, London, 89 pp.

Clarke, I. and Schmidt, R.A. (1995) Beyond the servicescape: the experience of place. *Journal of Retailing and Consumer Services* 3, 149–162.

Claxton, J.D. (1994) Conjoint analysis in travel research: a manager's guide. In: Brent Ritchie, J.R. and Goeldner, R.C. (eds) *Travel, Tourism and Hospitality Research*, 2nd edn. John Wiley & Sons, Chichester, pp. 513–522.

Clements, R. (1998) The birth of the new ISO 9000 baby. *Qualityworld* June, 22–23.

Clemons, E.K. (1995) Using scenario analysis to manage the strategic risks of reengineering. *Sloan Management Review* (Summer), 61–70.

Coalter, F. (1990) The politics of professionalism: consumers or citizens. *Leisure Studies* 2, 107–120.

Coalter, F. (2002) Warning: having fun can seriously improve your life. *Leisure Management* 22, 42–45.

Coleman, H.J. (1996) Why employee empowerment is not just a fad. *Leadership and Organizational Development Journal* 17, 29–36.

Collier, D.A. and Meyer, S.M. (1998) A service positioning mix. *International Journal of Operations & Production Management*, 12, 1223–1244.

Collins, B. and Payne, A. (1994) Internal Marketing: a new perspective for HRM. In: Armistead, C. (ed.) *The Future of Services Management*. Kogan Page, Cranfield, pp. 98–115.

Conaway, F. (1991) Segmenting will unleash mature market potential. *Public Relations Journal*, (May), 5.

Conrad, C.A., Brown, G. and Harmon, L.A. (1997) Customer satisfaction and corporate culture: a profile deviation analysis of a relationship marketing outcome. *Psychology and Marketing* 7, 663–674.

Cook, S. and Macaulay, S. (1996) Customer service training and development techniques. *Customer Service Management* (March), Issue 10.

Cooper, C., Fletcher, J., Gilbert, D. and Wanhill, S. (1994) *Tourism Principles and Practice*. Pitman Publishing, London.

Cooper, R. and Markus, M.L. (1995) *Human Reengineering*. Sloan Management Review, Summer, pp. 39–50.

Coulambidou, L. and Dale, B.G. (1995) The use of quality management self-assessment in the UK: a state of the art study. *Qualityworld Technical Supplement* (September), 110–118.

Counsell, R. (1999) Why change your culture? *Qualityworld* (May), 29–30.

Crilley, G., Murray, D., Howart, G. and Milne, I. (1997) The cost-quality relationship in Australian public sports and leisure centres: conventional wisdom revisited. In: Rowe, D. and Brown, P. (eds) *Proceedings of the Australian and New Zealand Association of Leisure Studies Leisure, People, Places, Spaces Conference*. University of Newcastle, NSW, Australia, pp. 42–47.

Crompton, J.L. and MacKay, K.J. (1989) Users' perceptions of the relative importance of service quality dimensions in selected public recreation programs. *Leisure Sciences* 4, 367–375.

Cronin, J.J., Jr and Taylor, S.A. (1992) Measuring service quality: a re-examination and extension. *Journal of Marketing* 56 (July), 55–68.

Cronin, J.J., Jr and Taylor, S.A. (1994) SERVPERF versus SERVQUAL: reconciling performance-based and perceptions-minus-expectations measurement of service quality. *Journal of Marketing* (Jan.), 125–131.

Crosby, P.B. (1979) *Quality is Free: the Art of Making Quality Certain.* McGraw-Hill, London, 309 pp.

Crosby, P.B. (1984) *Quality Without Tears.* McGraw-Hill, London, 305 pp.

Csikszentmilhalyi, M. and Kleiber, D.A. (1991) Leisure and self-actualization. In: Driver, B.L., Brown, P.J. and Peterson, G.L. (eds) *Benefits of Leisure.* Venture Publishing Inc., State College Pennsylvania, pp. 91–102.

Cumbria Tourist Board (undated) *Welcome Host at a Venue Near You.* Cumbria Tourist Board, Cumbria, 10 pp.

Currim, I.S., Weinburg, C.B. and Wittink, D.R. (1981) Design of subscription programs for a performing arts series. *Journal of Consumer Research* (June), 67–75.

Curry, A. and Monaghan, C. (1994) Service quality in local authorities: BS5750/ISO9000: friend or foe? *Local Government Policy Making* 4, 43–50.

Cutterbuck, D. and Goldsmith, W. (1998) Customer care versus customer count. *Managing Service Quality* 5, 327–338.

Dale, B.G. (1991) Starting on the road to success. *Total Quality Management Magazine* 3(2).

Dale, B.G., Van der Wiele, A. and Williams, A.R.T. (2001) Quality: why do organizations still get it wrong? *Managing Service Quality* 11, 241–248.

DTI (1995) *The Quality Gurus: What Can They Do for Your Company?* HMSO, London, 28 pp.

Dale, B.G. (1994a) *Managing Quality,* 2nd edn. Prentice-Hall, Hemel Hempstead, 600 pp.

Dale, B.G. (1994b) Quality management systems. In: Dale, B.G. (ed.) *Managing Quality,* 2nd edn. Prentice-Hall, Hemel Hempstead, pp. 333–361.

Dale, B.G. (1999) *Managing Quality,* 3rd edn. Blackwell, Oxford, 482 pp.

Dale, B.G. and Boaden, R.J. (1994) The use of teams in quality management. In: Dale, B.G. (ed.) *Managing Quality,* 2nd edn. Prentice-Hall, Hemel Hempstead, pp. 514–529.

Dale, B.G. and Lascelles, D.M. (1997) Total quality management adoption: revisiting the levels. *Total Quality Management Magazine* 6, 418–428.

Dale, B.G. and Shaw, P. (1999) Tools and techniques; an overview. In: Dale, B.G. (ed.) *Managing Quality,* 3rd edn. Blackwell, Oxford, pp. 280–314.

Dale, B.G., Boaden, R.J. and Lascelles, D.M. (1994a) Total quality management: an overview. In: Dale, B.G. (ed.) *Managing Quality,* 2nd edn. Prentice-Hall, Hemel Hempstead, pp. 3–37.

Dale, B.G., Lascelles, D.M. and Lloyd, A. (1994b) Supply chain management and development. In: Dale, B.G. (ed.) *Managing Quality,* 2nd edn. Prentice-Hall, Hemel Hempstead, pp. 292–313.

Dale, B.G., van der Wiele, A. and Williams, A.R.T. (2001) Quality – why do organizations still continue to get it wrong? *Managing Service Quality* 11(4), 241–248.

Danaher, P.J. (1997) Using conjoint analysis to determine the relative importance of service attributes measured in customer satisfaction surveys. *Journal of Retailing* 73(2), 235–260.

Danaher, P.J. and Mattsson, J. (1998) A comparison of service delivery processes of different complexity. *International Journal of Service Industry Management* 9(1), 48–63.

Davies, H. (1999) *Best Value. Research Seminar, Cheltenham & Gloucester College of Higher Education,* 12 May.

Davies, M. and Girlder, D. (1998) First impressions. *Leisure Manager* 16, 30–32.

Davis, J., Khodabocus, F. and Obray, C. (1996) Self-assessment: a path to business excellence. *Qualityworld Technical Supplement* (March), pp. 4–11.

Davis, J.C. (1962) Toward a theory of revolution. *American Sociological Review* 1, 5–18.

Deloitte & Touche (1998) *UK Visitor Attractions Survey 1998.* Deloitte & Touche, St Albans, 33 pp.

Deming, W.E. (1986) *Out of the Crisis: Quality, Productivity and Competitive Position.* MIT Press, Cambridge, Massachusetts, 495 pp.

DCMS (1999) *Tomorrow's Tourism* Department for Culture, Media and Sport, London, 80 pp.

Department of Trade (1982) *Standards, Quality and Competitiveness.* Cmnd 8621. HMSO, London, 32 pp.

DETR (1988) *Modernising Local Government: Improving Local Services through Best Value.* HMSO, London, 39 pp.

DETR and Audit Commission (1999) *Best Value and Local Authority Performance Indicators for 2000/2001.* HMSO, London, 178 pp.

Drew, S.A.W. (1997) From knowledge to action: impact of benchmarking on organisational performance. *Long Range Planning* 30, 427–441.

Driver, B.L., Tinsley, H.E.A. and Manfredo, M.J. (1991) Results from two inventories designed to assess the breadth of the perceived psychological benefits of leisure. In: Driver, B.L., Brown, P.J. and Peterson, G.L. (eds) *Benefits of Leisure.* Venture Publishing Inc., State College Pennsylvania, pp. 263–287.

East, J. (1993) *Managing Quality in the Catering Industry*. Croner, Kingston upon Thames, 296 pp.

Edvardsson, B.J. (1994) *Quality of Service: Making it Really Work*. McGraw-Hill, London, 270 pp.

Edvardsson, B. (1998a) Service quality improvement. *Managing Service Quality* 2, 142–149.

Edvardsson, B. (1998b) Causes of customer dissatisfaction – studies of public transport by critical-incident method. *Managing Service Quality* 3, 189–197.

Edvarsson, B. and Olsson, J. (1996) Key concepts for new service development. *The Service Industries Journal* 2, 140–164.

Ekinici, Y., Riley, M. and Fife-Schaw, C. (1998) Which school of thought? The dimensions of resort quality. *International Journal of Contemporary Hospitality Management* 10, 63–67.

Employment Department (1990) *Investors in People: 10 Good Answers to 10 Pressing Questions*. HMSO, London, 4 pp.

Employment Department (1992) *Investors in People*. HMSO, London, 14 pp.

Employment Gazette (1994) Table 1, labour costs by main industry sector. *Employment Gazette* (September), 314.

English Tourist Board (1998a) *How to Achieve the Rating You Want for Your Business: the New Harmonised Standards for Serviced Accommodation in England*. English Tourist Board, London, 26 pp.

English Tourist Board (1998b) *In Perfect Harmony: a Guide to the New ETB/AA/RAC Quality Standards*. English Tourist Board, London, 15 pp.

English Tourist Board (undated) *Introducing the Popular Welcome Family*. English Tourist Board, London, 10 pp.

Erstad, M. (1998) Mystery shopping programmes and human resource management. *International Journal of Contemporary Hospitality Management* 10, 34–38.

EFQM (1996) *The European Quality Awards 1996: Application Brochure*. European Foundation for Quality Management, Brussels,

European Foundation for Quality Management (1998) Bigger, better, improved? *European Quality* 4, 30–37.

EFQM (1999) *The EQFM Excellence Model: Improved Model (final version)*. European Foundation for Quality Management, Brussels, 43 pp.

Fache, W. (2000) Methodologies for innovation and improvement of service in tourism. *Managing Service Quality* 10, 356–366.

Feigenbaum, A.V. (1991) *Total Quality Control*, 3rd edn. McGraw-Hill, London, 896 pp.

Feigenbaum, A.V. (1999) The new quality for the twenty-first century. *The TQM Magazine* 11(6), 376–383.

Fick, G.R. and Brent Ritchie, J.R. (1991) Measuring service quality in the travel and tourism industry. *Journal of Travel Research* (Fall), 2–9.

Flanagan, J.C. (1954) The critical incident technique. *Psychological Bulletin* 51, 327–358.

Ford, R.C. and Heaton, C.P. (2000) *Managing the Guest Experience in Hospitality*. Thomson Learning, New York, 432 pp.

Fraser, D. (1998) Reel progress. *Leisure Management* 18, 42–43.

Freeman-Bell, G. and Grover, R. (1994) The use of quality management in local authorities. *Local Government Studies* 20(24), 554–569.

Frochot, I. (1996) Histoqual: the evaluation of service quality in historic properties. In: Robinson, M., Evans, N. and Callaghan, P. (eds) *Proceedings of Managing Cultural Resources for the Tourist, Tourism and Culture: Towards the 21st Century Conference*. University of Nottingham, Centre for Tourism and Travel/Business Education Ltd, Sunderland, pp. 48–59.

Gabbie, O. and O'Neill, M.A. (1997) SERVQUAL and the Northern Ireland hotel sector: a comparative analysis – Part 2. *Managing Service Quality* 1, 43–49.

Galloway, L. (1996) But which quality do you mean? *Qualityworld* (August), 564–568.

Garvin, D.A. (1988) *Managing Quality: the Strategic and Competitive Edge*. Free Press, New York, 319 pp.

Gaskin, M.P. (1991) The future of quality management systems. *Quality Forum* 17, 6–10.

Gaster, L. (1992) Quality in service delivery: competition for resources or more effective use of resources? *Local Government Policy Making* 19, 55–64.

Ghobadian, A. and Terry, A.J. (1995) How Alitalia improves service quality through quality function deployment. *Managing Service Quality* 5, 1–8.

Gillies, A. (1992) *Software Quality: Theory and Management*. International Thomson Computer Press, London, 208 pp.

Gilpin, S. and Kalafatis, S.P. (1995) Issues of product standardisation in the leisure industry. *Services Industries Journal* 15, 186–202.

Glancy, M. (1993) Achieving intersubjectivity: the process of becoming the subject in leisure research. *Leisure Studies* 12, 45–59.

Glancy, M. and Little, S.L. (1995) Studying the social aspects of leisure: development of multiple-method field investigation model (MMFI). *Journal of Leisure Research* 4, 305–323.

Glasford, R.G. (1987) Methodological reconsiderations: the shifting paradigms. *Quest* 39, 295–312.

Glynn, W.J. and Lehtinen, U. (1995) The concept of exchange: interactive approaches in services marketing. In: Glynn, W.J. and Barnes, J.G. (eds) *Understanding Services Management*. John Wiley & Sons, Chichester, pp. 89–118.

Goodale, T.L. and Witt, P.A. (eds) (1980) *Recreation and Leisure: Issues in an Era of Change*. Venture Publishing, State College, Pennsylvania.

Goult, R. (1995) ISO 9000 – no silver bullet? *Qualityworld* (March), 164–166.

Green, P.E. and Wind, Y. (1975) New way to measure consumers' judgements. *Harvard Business Review* 53, 107–117.

Griffin, A. (1995) ISO 9000 – a licence to trade? *Qualityworld* (Sept.) 622–624.

Grönroos, C. (1984) A service quality model and its marketing implications. *European Journal of Marketing* 18, 36–43.

Grönroos, C. (1988) Service quality: the six criteria of good perceived service quality. *Review of Business* 3, 10–13.

Grönroos, C. (1989) Defining marketing: a market-orientated approach. *European Journal of Marketing* 23, 52–60.

Grönroos, C. (1990a) *Service Management and Marketing: Managing the Moments of Truth in Service Competition*. Lexington Books, Massachusetts, 297 pp.

Grönroos, C. (1990b) Service management: a management focus for service competition. *International Journal of Service Industry Management* 1, 6–14.

Grönroos, C. (1990c) Relationship approach to marketing in service content: the marketing and organisational behaviour interface. *Journal of Business Research* 20, 3–11.

Grönroos, C. (1994) From scientific management to service management: a management perspective for the age of service competition. *International Journal of Service Industry Management* 3, 5–20.

Grönroos, C. and Gummesson, E. (1985) The Nordic school of service marketing – an introduction. In: *Service Firm in Service Marketing – Nordic School Perspectives*. University of Stockholm, pp. 6–11.

Grove, S.J. and Fisk, R.P. (1997) The impact of other customers on service experience: a critical incident examination of 'getting along'. *Journal of Retailing* 73, 63–85.

Guest, C. and Taylor, P. (1999) Customer orientated public leisure services in the UK. *Managing Leisure* 4, 94–106.

Gummesson, E. (1985) Applying service concepts in the industrial sector: towards a new concept of marketing in service marketing. University of Stockholm.

Gummesson, E. (1988) Service quality and product quality combined. *Review of Business* 9, 14–19.

Gummesson, E. (1989) Nine lessons on service quality. *Total Quality Management* (February), 83–87.

Gummesson, E. (1993) Service productivity: a blasphemous approach. *Proceedings of the Service Management and Marketing Conference*, Cardiff, (July), pp. 1–15.

Gummesson, E. (1994) Service management: an evaluation and the future. *International Journal of Service Industry Management* 5, 77–96.

Gummesson, E. (1995) Relationship marketing: its role in the service economy. In: Glynn, W.J. and Barnes, J.G. (eds) *Understanding Services Management*. John Wiley & Sons, Chichester, pp. 244–268.

Gummesson, E. and Grönroos, C. (1987) *Quality of Products and Services – a Tentative Synthesis Between Two Models*. Services Research Centre, University of Karlstad, Sweden, 18 pp.

Gunter, B.G. (1987) The leisure experience: selected properties. *Journal of Leisure Research* 2, 115–130.

Hales, C. and Klidas, A. (1998) Empowerment in five-star hotels: choice or rhetoric. *International Journal of Contemporary Hospitality Management* 10, 88–95.

Hamilton, J.A., Crompton, J.L. and More, T.A. (1991) Identifying the dimensions of service quality in a park context. *Journal of Environmental Management* 32, 211–220.

Han, S.B., Chen, S.K., Ebrahimpou, M. and Manbir, S. (2001) *International Journal of Quality and Reliability* 18(8), 796–812.

Handy, C.B. (1988) *Understanding Voluntary Organisations*. Penguin, London, 448 pp.

Harrington, D. and Lenehan, T. (1998) *Managing Quality in Tourism: Theory and Practice*. Oak Tree Press, Dublin, 302 pp.

Harris, K., Baron, S. and Ratcliffe, J. (1995) Customers as oral participants in a service setting. *Journal of Services Marketing* 4, 64–75.

Harris, S. (1999) Future gazing. *Leisure Management* 19, 45–47.

Hart, C.W.L., Heskett, J.L. and Sasser, W.E., Jr (1990) The profitable art of service recovery. *Harvard Business Review* 68, 148–156.

Hart, S. and Tzokas, N. (2000) New product launch 'mix' in growth and mature product markets. *Benchmarking: an International Journal* 7(5), 389–405.

Haywood, L. and Henry, I. (1986) Policy developments in community leisure and recreation.

Part 2: practice, education and training. *Leisure Management* (August), 21–23.

Hellsten, U. and Klefsjo, B. (2000) TQM as a management system consisting of values, techniques and tools. *The TQM Magazine* 2, 4.

Hemingway, J.L. (1995) Leisure studies and interpretive social enquiry. *Leisure Studies* 14, 32–47.

Henderson, K. (1991) *Dimensions of Choice – a Qualitative Approach to Recreation, Parks and Leisure Research*. Venture Publishing, State College, Pennsylvania.

Henley Centre (1996) *Hospitality into the 21st Century – a Vision for the Future*. The Henley Centre, London.

Henley Centre (1997) Future of the cinema. *Consumer and Leisure Futures* 2, 47–50.

Henley Centre (1999) *Consumer and Leisure Futures* 8, 17.

Hill, S. (1991) Why quality circles failed but total quality management might succeed. *British Journal of Industrial Relations* 28, 541–568.

Hines, S. (1998) cited in Giling, J. 'Sonic boom'. *Attractions Management* (April), 19–22.

Hjalager, A.M. (2001) Quality in tourism through the empowerment of tourists. *Managing Service Quality* 11(4), 287–296.

Hocutt, M.A., Chakraborty, N.E. and Mowen, J.C. (1997) The impact of perceived justice on customer satisfaction and intention to complain in a service recovery. *Advances in Consumer Research* 24, 457–463.

Hodgkinson, H. (2002) A shared strategic vision – dream or reality. *The Learning Organization: an International Journal* 9, 89–95.

Hoffher, G.D. (1994) *Breakthrough Thinking and Total Quality Management*. Prentice-Hall, Hemel Hempstead.

Holbrook, M.B. (1994) The nature of customer value; an axiology of services in the consumption experience. In: Rust, R.T. and Oliver, R.L. (eds) *Service Quality: New Directions in Theory and Practice*. Sage, London, pp. 21–71.

Holloway, J.C. (1998) *The Business of Tourism*, 4th edn. Longman, Harlow.

Honold, L. (1997) A review of the literature on employee empowerment. *Empowerment in Organizations* 5, 4 (electronic version).

Horovitz, J. and Cudennec-Poon, C. (1990) Putting service quality into gear. *Service Industries Journal* 10, 249–265.

Howard, O. (1999) Live the quality life: service with a smile. *Qualityworld* (March), 44–46.

Howat, G., Adsher, J., Crilley, G. and Milne, I. (1996) Measuring customer service quality in sports and leisure centres. *Managing Leisure: an International Journal* 1, 77–89.

Howe, C.Z. and Rancourt, M. (1990) The importance of definitions of selected concepts for leisure enquiry. *Leisure Sciences* 12, 395–406.

Hull, R.B., Michael, S.E., Walker, G.J. and Roggenbuck, J.W. (1996) Ebb and flow of brief leisure experience. *Leisure Sciences* 18, 299–314.

Hultsman, J.T. and Anderson, S.C. (1991) Studying leisure perceptions: a need for methodological expansion. *Leisure Studies* 10, 63–67.

Hurley, R.F. and Estelami, H. (1998) Alternative indexes for monitoring customer perceptions of service quality: a comparative evaluation in a retail context. *Journal of Academy of Marketing Science* 26, 209–221.

Hutchins, D. (1990) *In Pursuit of Quality*. Pitman Publishing, London.

Iacobucci, D., Ostrom, A.L., Braig, B.M. and Bezjian-Avery, A. (1996) A canonical model of consumer evaluations and theoretical bases of expectations. *Advances in Services Marketing and Management* 5, 1–44.

ILAM (1992) *Quality First: Quality Management in the Leisure Industry*. Longmans/Institute of Leisure and Amenity Management, Goring upon Thames, 62 pp.

ILAM (1996) *Customer Care. Fact Sheet 96/6*. Institute of Leisure and Amenity Management, Goring upon Thames, 4 pp.

ILAM (1998) *A Guide to the Leisure Industry – Some Key Facts. Fact sheet 98/8*. Institute of Leisure and Amenity Management, Goring upon Thames, 4 pp.

ILAM (1999) *Annual Report 1998/99*. Institute of Leisure and Amenity Management, Goring upon Thames, 34pp.

Industrial Society (1998) Ringing in the cultural changes. *Qualityworld* (May), 18–19.

Institute of Personnel Management Training (undated) *Information Notes*. IPM Library and Information Services, London, 6 pp.

Investors in People UK (2001a) *Overview of the Investors in People Standard*. Investors in People UK, London, 8 pp.

Investors in People UK (2001b) *An Introduction to Investors in People*. Investors in People UK, London, 4 pp.

Irons, K. (1994) *Managing Service Companies: Strategies for Success*. Addison Wesley, Reading, 246 pp.

Irons, K. (1997) *The World of Superservice*. Addison Wesley Longman, London.

Jeffries, D.R., Evans, W. and Reynolds, P. (1992) *Training for Total Quality Management*. Kogan Page, London.

Johns, N. and Tyas, P. (1996) Use of service quality gap theory to differentiate between foodservice outlets. *Services Industries Journal* 16, 321–346.

Johnson, C. and Mathews, B.P. (1997) The influence of experience on service expectations. *International Journal of Service Industry Management* 8, 290–305.

Johnson, M.D. (1995) The four faces of aggregation in customer satisfaction research. *Advances in Consumer Research* 22, 89–93.

Johnson, P.L. (1993) *ISO 9000 Meeting the New International Standard.* McGraw-Hill, London, 197 pp.

Johnston, R. (1995) The zone of tolerance: exploring the relationship between service transactions and satisfaction with the overall service. *International Journal of Service Industry Management* 6, 46–61.

Johnston, R. (1996) Achieving focus in service organizations. *Service Industries Journal* 16, 10–20.

Johnston, R. (1999) Service operations management; return to roots. *International Journal of Operations and Production Management* 2, 104–124.

Johnston, R. and Bryan, R. (1993) Products and services: a question of visibility. *Service Industries Journal* 13, 125–136.

Johnston, R. and Clark, G. (2001) *Service Operations Management.* Pearson Education, Harlow, 413 pp.

Jones, B. (1995) Quality awards. *Qualityworld* (February), 85–91.

Juran, J.M. (1988a) *Juran's Quality Control Handbook,* 4th edn. McGraw-Hill, London, 1872 pp.

Juran, J.M. (1988b) *Juran on Planning for Quality.* Free Press, New York, 340 pp.

Juran, J.M. (1989) *Juran on Leadership for Quality: an Executive Handbook.* Free Press, New York, 376 pp.

Juran, J.M. (1993) Juran's message for Europe. *European Quality* 1, 18–25.

Juran, J.M. and Godfrey, A.B. (1999) *Juran's Quality Control Handbook,* 5th edn. McGraw-Hill, London, 1872 pp.

Kalra, S.K. (1997) Human potential management: time to move beyond the concept of human resource management? *Journal of European Industrial Training* 21, 176–180.

Kandampully, J. (2001) Service guarantee; an organization's blueprint for assisting the delivery of superior service. In: Kandampully, J., Mok, C. and Sparks, B. (eds) *Service Quality Management in Hospitality, Tourism and Leisure.* Haworth, New York, pp. 239–254.

Karlof, B. and Ostblom, S. (1993) *Benchmarking: a Signpost to Excellence in Quality and Productivity.* John Wiley & Sons, Chichester, 208 pp.

Kawalek, J.P. (1994) Interpreting business process re-engineering on organisation workflow. *Journal of Information Technology* 9, 276–287.

Keehley, P. and MacBride, S.A. (1997) Can benchmarking for best practices work for government? *Quality Progress* (March), 75–80.

Kelly, J. (1980) Leisure and quality: beyond the quantitative barrier in research. In: Goodale, T.L. and Witt, P.A. (eds) *Recreation and Leisure: Issues in an Era of Change.* Venture Publishing, State College, Pennsylvania, pp. 300–314.

Kelly, J. (1983) *Leisure Identities and Interactions.* Allen & Unwin, London.

Kennedy, L. (1991) *Quality Management in the Non-profit World.* Jossey-Bass, Oxford, 169 pp.

Kerfoot, D. and Knights, D. (1995) Empowering the 'quality worker'? The seduction and contradiction of the Total Quality phenomenon. In: Wilkinson, A. and Wilmott, H. (eds) *Making Quality Critical.* Routledge, London, pp. 219–237.

Kettinger, W.J., Lee, C.C. and Lee, S. (1995) *Global Measures of Information.*

Kingman-Brundage, J. (1991) Technology, design and service quality. *International Journal of Service Industry Management* 3, 47–59.

Kingman-Brundage, J. (1992) The ABC's of service system blueprinting. In: Lovelock, C.H. (ed.) *Managing Services: Marketing, Operations and Human Resources,* 2nd edn. Prentice-Hall, Hemel Hempstead, pp. 96–102.

Kingman-Brundage, J., George, W.R. and Bowen, D.E. (1995) Service logic: achieving service system integration. *International Journal of Service Industry Management* 4, 20–39.

Kingston, N. (1998) Ready for a close-up. *Leisure Management* 18, 14–17.

Klassen, J.K. and Rohleder, T.R. (2000) Combining operations and marketing to manage capacity and demand in service. *Service Industries Journal* 2, 1–30.

Knutson, B., Stevens, P., Wullaert, C., Patton, M. and Yokoyama, F. (1990) LODGSERV: a service quality index for the lodging industry. *Hospitality Research Journal* 2, 277–284.

Kotler, P. (1996) *Marketing for Hospitality and Tourism.* Prentice-Hall, Hemel Hempstead.

Lam, T., Wong, A. and Yeung, S. (1997) Measuring service quality in clubs: an application of the SERVQUAL instrument. *Australian Journal of Hospitality Management* 4, 7–14.

Lapidus, R.S. and Schibrowski, J.A. (1994) Aggregate complaint analysis: a procedure for developing customer service satisfaction. *Journal of Services Marketing* 4, 50–60.

Largrosen, S. (2001) Strengthening the weakest link of TQM – from customer focus to customer understanding. *The TQM Magazine* 3, 348–354.

Laszlo, G.P. (1999) Implementing a quality management program – the three Cs of success: commitment, culture and cost. *The TQM Magazine* 11, 4.

Laws, E. (1999) Visitor satisfaction management at Leeds Castle. In: Leask, A. and Yeoman, I. (eds) *Heritage Visitor Attractions: an Operations Management Perspective.* Cassell, London.

Laws, E. (1995) *Tourist Destination Management.* Routledge, London.

Leach, L.P. (1996) TQM, reengineering and the edge of chaos. *Quality Progress* (February), 85–90.

Lee, Y., Dattilo, J. and Howard, D. (1994) The complex and dynamic nature of leisure experience. *Journal of Leisure Research* 3, 195–211.

Lee-Ross, D. (2001) Understanding the role of the service encounter in tourism, hospitality and leisure services. In: Kandampully, J., Mok, C. and Sparks, B. (eds) *Service Quality Management in Hospitality, Tourism and Leisure.* Haworth Hospitality Press, New York.

Lehtinen, J.R. (1985) Improving service quality by analysing the service production process. In: *Service Firm in Service Marketing: Nordic School Perspectives.* University of Stockholm, pp. 110–119.

Lengnick-Hall, C.A. and Hartman, M.G. (1995) *Experiencing Quality.* Dryden Press, Fort Worth, Texas.

Lentell, R. (1995) Missing services: leisure management textbooks and the concept of services management. In: Lawrence, L., Murdoch, E. and Parker, S. (eds) *Professional and Development Issues in Leisure, Sport and Education.* LSA Publication No. 56, Leisure Studies Association, Brighton.

Leonard, J. and McAdam, R. (2002) The strategic impact and implementation of TQM. *The TQM Magazine* 14, 51–60.

Levitt, T. (1972) Production-line approach to service. *Harvard Business Review* (September–October), 41–52.

Levitt, T. (1976) The industrialization of service. *Harvard Business Review* (September–October), 63–74.

Lewis, B.R. (1995) Customer care in services. In: Glynn, W.J. and Barnes, J.G. (eds) *Understanding Services Management.* John Wiley & Sons, Chichester, pp. 57–88.

Liljander, V. and Strandvik, T. (1997) Emotions in service satisfaction. *International Journal of Service Industry Management* 8, 148–169.

LIW News (1999) The Leisure Industry Report: International Leisure Industry Week '99, LeisureWeek.

Love, R. and Dale, B.G. (1999) Benchmarking. In: Dale, B.G. (ed.) *Managing Quality*, 3rd edn. Blackwell, Oxford, pp. 390–403.

Lovelock, C. (1991) *Services Marketing*, 2nd edn. Prentice Hall, Hemel Hempstead.

Lovelock, C. (1992) *Managing Services: Marketing, Operations, and Human Resources*, 2nd edn. Prentice Hall, Hemel Hempstead, 472 pp.

Lyon, P., Taylor, S. and Smith, S. (1994) McDonaldization: a reply to Ritzer's thesis. *International Journal of Hospitality Management* 13, 95–99.

Macaulay, S. and Clark, G. (1998) Creating a customer-focused culture: some practical frameworks and tools. *Managing Service Quality* 8, 3.

Macdonald, J. (1998) The quality revolution – in retrospect. *The TQM Magazine* 10, 5 (electronic).

Makinson-Sanders, J. (1996) Leisure's future. *Leisure Future* 4, 5–10.

Manfredo, M.J., Driver, B.L. and Tarrant, M.A. (1996) Measuring leisure motivation: a meta-analysis of the recreation experience preference scales. *Journal of Leisure Research* 3, 188–213.

March, R. (1994) Tourism marketing myopia. *Tourism Management* 6, 411–415.

Marshall, A. (1998) Hot seat. *Leisure Management* 18, 10–14.

Maxwell, G. (1997) Empowerment in the UK hospitality industry. In: Foley, M., Lennon, J. and Maxwell, G. (eds) *Hospitality, Tourism and Leisure Management.* Cassell, London, pp. 53–68.

Maylor, H. (2000) Strategic quality management. In: Moutinho, L. (ed.) *Strategic Management in Tourism.* CAB International, Wallingford, pp. 239–256.

Maynard, R. (1995) Investor in people: quality through people. *Qualityworld* (October), 697–702.

McDougall, G. and Levesque, T. (1992) The measurement of service quality: some methodology issues in marketing, operations and human resources insights into services. *2nd International Research Seminar in Service Management*, 9–12 June 1992, France, pp. 750–766.

McLachlan, N. (1996) Benefits of quality systems standards in the service industries. *Qualityworld* (April), 264–267.

McNamee, M., Sheridan, H. and Buswell, J. (2000) Paternalism, professionalism and public sector leisure: the boundaries of a leisure profession. *Leisure Studies* 19, 1–11.

McNamee, M., Sheridan, H. and Buswell, J. (2001) The limits of utilitarianism as a professional ethic in public sector leisure policy and provision. *Leisure Studies* 20, 1–25.

Mels, G., Boshoff, C. and Nel, D. (1997) The dimensions of service quality: the original European perspective revisited. *Service Industries Journal* 17, 173–189.

Meyer, A. and Westerbarkey, P. (1996) Measuring and managing hotel guest satisfaction. In: Olsen, M.D., Teare, R. and Gummesson, E. (eds) *Service Quality in Hospitality Organisations*. Cassell, London, pp. 185–203.

Mills, P. (1992) *Quality in the Leisure Industry*. Longmans, Harlow, 229 pp.

Mintel (1997) *Health and Fitness Review*. Mintel, London.

Mintel (2001) *Product: 2020 Vision. Tomorrow's Consumer*. Mintel, London.

Mosscrop, P. and Stores, A. (1991) *Total Quality Management in Leisure: a Guide for Directors and Managers*. Collinson Grant/ILAM, Goring upon Thames, 17 pp.

Mullins, L. (1996) *Management and Organizational Behaviour*, 4th edn. Pitman, London.

Naylor, D. (2000) Should western managers be encouraged to adopt JMPs? *Employee Relations* 22, 160–174.

Nisse, J. and Snobby, R. (1999) BSkyB aims to get onside with football clubs. *The Times*, 11 August, 25.

Normann, R. (1991) *Service Management*. John Wiley & Sons, Chichester, 185 pp.

Normann, R. (2000) *Service Management: Strategy and Leadership in Service Business*, 3rd edn. John Wiley & Sons, Chichester, 234 pp.

Oakland, J.S. (1993) *Total Quality Management: the Route to Improving Performance*, 2nd edn. Butterworth Heinemann, Oxford, 463 pp.

O'Hanlon, T. (1999) Change how you change things. *Qualityworld* (May), 10–12.

Oldfield, H. (1999) Quality awards: are they worth it? *Qualityworld* (January), 22–23.

Oliver, R.L. (1980) A cognitive model of the antecedents and consequences of satisfaction decisions. *Journal of Marketing Research* 17, 460–469.

Oliver, R.L. (1997) A cognitive model of the antecedents and consequences of satisfaction decisions. *Journal of Marketing Research* 17 (Nov.), 460–469.

Oliver, R.L. and DeSarbo, W.S. (1988) Response determinants in satisfaction judgements. *Journal of Consumer Research* 14, 495–507

O'Neill, M. (2001) Measuring service quality and customer satisfaction. In: Kandampully, J., Mok, C. and Sparks, B. (eds) *Service Quality Management in Hospitality, Tourism, and Leisure*. Haworth, New York, pp. 15–50.

O'Neill, M.A., Palmer, A.J. and Beggs, R. (1998) The effects of survey timing on perceptions of service quality. *Managing Service Quality* 8, 126–132.

Osbourne, D. and Gaebler, T. (1992) *Reinventing Government*. Addison-Wesley, Reading, 370 pp.

Oxford Economic Forecasting (2001) *Consumer Goods Industries Report*. Oxford Economic Forecasting Ltd, Oxford.

Oxford Partnership (1996) *The 1996 Cheltenham Gold Cup: Research Study*. Internal report.

Page, S. (1997) *Urban Tourism*. Routledge, London, 269 pp.

Page, S.J., Brunt, P., Busby, G. and Connell, J. (2001) *Tourism: a Modern Synthesis*. Thomson Learning, London.

Palmer, A. (1998) *Principles of Services Marketing*, 2nd edn. McGraw-Hill, London, 371 pp.

Parasuraman, A. (1995) Measuring and monitoring service quality. In: Glynn, W.J. and Barnes, J.G. (eds) *Understanding Services Management*. John Wiley & Sons, Chichester, pp. 143–177.

Parasuraman, A., Zeithaml, V.A. and Berry, L.L. (1985) A concept model of service quality and its implications for future research. *Journal of Marketing* 49, 41–50.

Parasuraman, A., Zeithaml, V.A. and Berry, L.L. (1988) SERVQUAL: a multiple-item scale for measuring consumer perceptions of service quality. *Journal of Retailing* 64, 12–37.

Parasuraman, A., Berry, L.L. and Zeithaml, V.A. (1991a) Refinement and reassessment of the SERVQUAL scale. *Journal of Retailing* 69, 420–451.

Parasuraman, A., Berry, L.L. and Zeithaml, V.A. (1991b) Understanding customer expectations of service. *Sloan Management Review* 32, 39–48.

Parasuraman, A., Berry, L.L. and Zeithaml, V.A. (1991c) Perceived service quality as a customer-based performance measure: an empirical examination of organisational barriers using an extended service quality model. *Journal of Human Resource Management* 30, 335–364.

Parasuraman, A., Berry, L.L. and Zeithaml, V.A. (1993) Research notes: more on improving service quality measurement. *Journal of Retailing* 69, 140–147.

Parasuraman, A., Zeithaml, V.A. and Berry, L.L. (1994) Reassessment of expectations as a comparison standard in measuring service quality: implications for further research. *Journal of Marketing* 58, 111–124.

Payne, A. and Clark, M. (1995) Marketing services to external markets. In: Glynn, W.J. and Barnes, J.G. (eds) *Understanding Services Management*. John Wiley & Sons, Chichester, pp. 322–369.

Peters, J. (1998) Why we need to bring TQM and HR development together. *Qualityworld*, 10–12.

Peters, T. (1987) *Thriving on Chaos*. Pan, London, 736 pp.

Peters, T. and Waterman, R.H., Jr (1982) *In Search of Excellence*. Harper/Collins, London, 384 pp.

Pike, J. and Barnes, R. (1996) *TQM in Action*. Chapman & Hall, London.

Pollitt, C. (1994) The citizen's charter: a preliminary analysis. *Public Money and Management* 14, 9–14.

Popham, P. (1991) The best of Oriental luck. *Management Today*, (May.)

Prior, D., Stewart, J. and Walsh, K. (1993) *Is the Citizen's Charter a Charter for Citizens? Belgrave Local Paper No.7*. Local Government Management Board, London, 30 pp.

QUEST News (1998) Benefits for everyone. *QUEST News* (December), 1–4.

Radbourne, J. (1997) Art of the matter. *Australian Leisure Management* (April/May), 14–15.

Randall, L. and Senior, M. (1996) Training for service quality in the UK hospitality industry. In: Olsen, M.D., Teare, R. and Gummesson, E. (eds) *Service Quality in Hospitality Organisations*. Cassell, London, pp. 164–182.

Reisinger, Y. (2001) Unique characteristics of tourism, hospitality, and leisure services. In: Kandampully, J., Mok, C. and Sparks, B. (eds) *Service Quality Management in Hospitality, Tourism, and Leisure*. Haworth, New York, pp. 15–50.

Richard, M.D. and Sundaram, D.S. (1994) A model of lodging repeat choice intentions. *Annals of Tourism Research* 21, 745–755.

Richards, P. and Le Grove, P. (1992) Delivering the citizen's charter. *Quality News* 18, 534–535.

Robinson, L. (1996a) An investigation into the use of quality programmes in local authority leisure services. In: *Proceedings of World Leisure and Recreation Association 4th World Congress, Free Time and Quality of Life for the 21st Century Conference*. WLRA, Cardiff, p. 77.

Robinson, L. (1996b) Barriers to total quality management in public leisure services. In: *Proceedings of World Leisure and Recreation Association 4th World Congress, Free Time and Quality of Life for the 21st Century Conference*. WLRA, Cardiff, p. 97.

Robinson, L. (1997) Barriers to total quality management in public sector leisure services. *Managing Leisure* 2.

Robson, A. and Prabhu, V. (2001) What can we learn from 'leading' service practitioners about business excellence? *Managing Service Quality* 11, 249–261.

Rojek, C. (1993) After popular culture: hyperreality and leisure. *Leisure Studies* 12, 277–289.

Rosenberg, J. (1996) Five myths about customer satisfaction. *Quality Progress* (December), 57–60.

Rosman, R. (1994) *Recreation Programming: Designing Leisure Experiences*, 2nd edn. Sagamore, Champaign, Illinois, 477 pp.

Rowe, K. (1992) Centre management: BS 5750. *Sports Industry Magazine* 96, 8–9.

Russell, R.V. and Hultsman, J.T. (1987) An empirical basis for determining the multidimensional structure of leisure. *Leisure Sciences* 10, 69–76.

Rust, R.T. and Oliver, R.L. (1994) Service quality: insights and managerial implications from the frontier. In: Rust, R.T. and Oliver, R.L. (eds) *Service Quality: New Directions in Theory and Practice*. Sage, London, pp. 1–20.

Ryan, C. (1997) From motivation to assessment. In: Ryan, C. (ed.) *The Tourist Experience*. Cassell, London, 235 pp.

Saleh, F. and Ryan, C. (1991) Analysing service quality in the hospitality industry using the Servqual model. *Service Industries Journal* 11, 324–343.

Saleh, F. and Ryan, C. (1992) Conviviality – a source of satisfaction for hotel guests? In: Johnson, P. and Barry, T. (eds) *Choice and Demand in Tourism*. Mansell, London, pp. 107–122.

Samdahl, D.M. (1988) A symbolic interactions model of leisure: leisure theory and empirical support. *Leisure Sciences* 10, 27–39.

Samdahl, D.M. and Kleiber, D.A. (1988) Self-awareness and leisure experience. *Leisure Sciences* 11, 1–10.

Sampson, S.E. (1996) Ramifications of monitoring service quality through passively solicited customer feedback. *Decision Sciences* 27, 601–622.

Sampson, S.E. (1998) Gathering customer feedback via the Internet: instruments and prospects. *Industrial Management & Data Systems* 98, 71–82.

Sandelin, T.E. (1985) Quality and performance measurement. In: *Service Firm in Service Marketing – Nordic School Perspectives*. University of Stockholm, pp. 20–24.

Sanderson, I. (1998) Beyond performance measurement? Assessing 'value' in local government. *Local Government Studies*, 4, 1–25.

Scarnati, J.T. and Scarnati, B.J. (2002) Empowerment: the key to quality. *TQM Magazine* 14, 110–119.

Scheuing, E.E. (1996) Delighting internal customers. In: Olsen, M.D., Teare, R. and Gummesson, E. (eds) *Service Quality in Hospitality Organisations*. Cassell, London, pp. 41–47.

Schmenner, R.W. (1992) How can service businesses survive and prosper? In: Lovelock, C.H. (ed.) *Managing Services: Marketing, Operations and Human Resources*, 2nd edn. Prentice-Hall, Hemel Hempstead, pp. 31–42.

Schneider, B. and Bowen, D. (1995) *Winning the Service Game*. Harvard Business School Press, Cambridge, Massachusetts.

Schneider, B., White, S.S. and Michelle, P.C. (1998) Linking service climate and customer perceptions of service quality. *Journal of Applied Psychology* 83, 150–163.

Schor, J. (1998) Beyond work and spend: time, leisure and consumption. In: Scraton, S. (ed.) *Leisure, Time and Space: Meanings and Values in People's Lives*. LSA Publication No. 57, Leisure Studies Association, Brighton.

Scott, D. and Shieff, D. (1993) Service quality components and group criteria in local government. *International Journal of Service Industry Management* 4, 42–53.

Seaton, A.V. (1996) The marketing concept in tourism. In: Seaton, A.V. and Bennett, M.M. (eds). *Marketing Tourism Products*. International Thomson Business Press, London.

Seay, T., Seaman, S. and Cohen, D. (1996) Measuring and improving the quality of public services: a hybrid approach. *Library Trends* 44, 464–490.

Seddon, J. (1997) Ten arguments against ISO 9000. *Managing Service Quality* 7, 162–168.

Segal-Horn, S. (1994) Are service industries going global? In: Armistead, C. (ed.) *The Future of Services Management*. Kogan Page, Cranfield, pp. 41–63.

Shewhart, W.A. (1931) *Economic Control of Quality of Manufactured Product*. Macmillan, London.

Shostack, G.L. (1984) Designing services that deliver. *Harvard Business Review* 62 (January–February), 133–139.

Shostack, G.L. (1987) Service positioning through structural change. *Journal of Marketing* 51, 34–43.

Smith, J. (1999) Spotlight – an assessor's view of the UK BQF quality award. *Qualityworld* (January), 24–26.

Smith, S. (1999) The branded leisure experience. *Customer Service Management* (January 30), 4.

Smith, S.L.J. (1994) The tourism product. *Annals of Tourism Research* 3, 582–595.

Sparks, B.A., Bradley, G.L. and Callan, V.J. (1997) The impact of staff empowerment and communication style on customer evaluations: the special case of service failure. *Psychology and Marketing* 14, 475–493.

Sports Council (1999) *Quest: UK Quality Scheme for Sport and Leisure*. Sports Council, London, 104 pp.

Stabler, M.J. (1989) Modelling the tourism industry: the concept of opportunity sets. In: Stabler, M.J. (ed.) *Leisure, Labour and Lifestyles: International Comparisons. Tourism and Leisure; Models and Theories*. Leisure Studies Association Second International Conference Proceedings 39, LSA, pp. 60–79.

Stabler, M.J. (1991) Modelling the tourism industry: a new approach. In: Sinclair, M.T. and Stabler, M.J. (eds) *The Tourism Industry: an International Analaysis*. CAB International, Wallingford, pp. 15–44.

Stebbins, L. (1990) *Quality Management in the Service Industry*. Ellis Horwood, Chichester, 178 pp.

Stewart, J. and Walsh, K. (1994) Performance measurement: when performance can never be finally defined. *Public Money and Management* 14, 45–49.

Stokowski, P.A. (1994) *Leisure in Society: a Network Structural Perspective*. Mansell Publishing, London.

Stravroulakis, D. (1997) Quality circle autonomy: evidence from a Japanese subsidiary and a western subsidiary. *International Journal of Quality and Reliability Management* 14, 146–159.

Stuart, I.F. and Tax S.S. (1996) Planning for service quality: an integrative approach. *International Journal of Service Industry Management* 4, 58–77.

Svensson, G. (2001) The quality of bi-directional service quality in dyadic service encounters. *Journal of Services Marketing* 15, 357–378.

Swain, P. (1999) Organizational learning: developing leaders to deal with continuous change. A strategic human resource perspective. *The Learning Organization* 6(1), 31–37.

Swarbrooke, J. (1995) *The Development and Management of Visitor Attractions*. Butterworth Heinemann, Oxford, 381 pp.

Swarbrooke, J. and Horner, S. (1999) *Consumer Behaviour in Tourism*. Butterworth Heinemann, Oxford, 463 pp.

Taylor, Lord Justice (1989) *Report on the Hillsborough Stadium Disaster: 15 April 1989, Final Report*. HMSO, London, 109 pp.

Taylor, S.A. (1997) Assessing regression-based importance weights for quality perceptions and satisfaction judgements in the presence of higher order and/or interaction effects. *Journal of Retailing* 73, 135–159.

Taylor, S.A., Sharland, A., Cronin, J.J., Jr and Bullard, W. (1993) Recreational service quality in the international setting. *International Journal of Service Industry Management* 4, 68–86.

Teas, R.K. (1993) Expectations, performance, evaluation and consumers' perceptions of quality. *Journal of Marketing* 57, 18–34.

Thatcher, I. (1998) The measure of pleasure. *Australian Leisure Management* (August/September), 60–61.

Tinsley, H.E.A. and Tinsley, D.J. (1986) A theory of the attributes, benefits and causes of leisure experience. *Leisure Sciences* 8, 1–44.

Titz, K. (2001) The impact of people, processes and physical evidence on tourism, hospitality and leisure service quality. In: Kandampully, J., Mok, C. and Sparks, B. (eds) *Service Quality Management in Hospitality, Tourism and Leisure.* Haworth, New York.

Torkildsen, G. (1986) *Leisure and Recreation Management*, 2nd edn. E. & F. Spon, London, 525 pp.

Torkildsen, G. (1992) *Leisure and Recreation Management*, 3rd edn. E. & F. Spon, London, 464 pp.

Torkildsen, G. (1999) *Leisure and Recreation Management*, 4th edn. E. & F. Spon, London, 592 pp.

Tourish, D. and Tourish, B. (1997) Assessing staff–management relationships in local authority leisure facilities: the communications audit approach. *Managing Leisure* 1, 91–104.

Tribe, J. and Snaith, T. (1998) From Servqual to Holsat: holiday satisfaction in Varadero, Cuba. *Tourism Management* 19, 25–34.

Tucci, L.A. and Talaga, J. (1997) Service guarantees and consumers' evaluation of services. *Journal of Services Marketing* 11, 10–18.

Varva, T.G. (1998) Is your satisfaction survey creating dissatisfied customers? *Quality Progress* (December), 51–57.

Vine, D. and Hele, J. (1998) There is less paperwork with the new ISO9000. *Qualityworld* (August) 32–33.

Voss, C., Armistead, C., Johnston, B.J. and Morris, B. (1985) *Operations Management in Service Industries and the Public Sector.* John Wiley & Sons, Chichester, 318 pp.

Wakefield, K.L. and Blodgett, J.G. (1996) The effect of the servicescape on customers' behavioural intentions in leisure service settings. *Journal of Services Marketing* 10, 45–61.

Walker, J.L. (1995) Service encounter satisfaction conceptualized. *Journal of Services Marketing* 62, 5–15.

Walsh, P.J. (1998) The use of quality programmes and services in local authority sport and leisure centres. MA Dissertation, The University of Central Lancashire, Preston.

Walt Disney (1998) Walt Disney World, Epcot welcome book.

Warner, F. (1977) *Standards and Specifications in the Engineering Industries.* NEDO, London.

Waterhouse, R. (2000) Are you experienced? *Sunday Times* 3 December, p. 21.

Wathen, S. and Anderson, J.C. (1996) Designing services: an information-processing approach. *International Journal of Service Industry Management* 6, 64–76.

Wels-Lips, I., Van der Ven, M. and Pieters, R. (1998) Critical services dimensions: an empirical investigation across six industries. *International Journal of Service Industry Management* 9, 286–309.

Wembley plc (1998) *Annual Report and Accounts.* Wembley.

Wheat, S. (1998) Profile of David Thomas. *Leisure Management* 18, 40–42.

Wilkinson, A. (1995) Managing human resources for quality. In: Dale, B.G. (ed.) *Managing Quality*, 2nd edn. Prentice-Hall, Hemel Hempstead.

Wilkinson, A. and Willmott, H. (1995) *Making Quality Critical.* Routledge, London, 240 pp.

Williams, C. (1997a) Quality management: a means of meeting customers' needs. In: Rowe, D. and Brown, P. (eds) *Proceedings of the Australian and New Zealand Association of Leisure Studies Leisure, People, Places, Spaces conference.* University of Newcastle, NSW, Australia, pp. 212–217.

Williams, C. (1997b) Quality systems and service delivery in the UK leisure industry. MPhil Thesis, University of Central Lancashire, Preston.

Williams, C. (1998) Is the SERVQUAL model an appropriate management tool for measuring service delivery quality in the UK leisure industry? *Managing Leisure: an International Journal* 3, 98–110.

Williams, S. and Parang, E. (1997) Using focus groups to match user expectations with library constraints. *Serial Librarian* 31, 335–339.

Wilson, A.M. (1998) The role of mystery shopping in the measurement of service performance. *Managing Service Quality* 8, 414–420.

Wirtz, J. and Kum, D. (2001) Designing service guarantees – is full satisfaction the best you can guarantee? *Journal of Service Marketing* 15, 282–299.

Wise, D. (1995) *Performance Measurement for Charities.* ICSA Publishing, Hemel Hempstead, 150 pp.

Woods, R.H. (1996) The role of organizational culture in service. In: Olsen, D., Teare, R. and Gummesson, E. (eds) *Service Quality in Hospitality Organizations.* Cassell, London.

Wright, L. (1995) Avoiding services marketing myopia. In: Glynn, W.J. and Barnes, J.G.

(eds) *Understanding Services Management*. John Wiley & Sons, Chichester, pp. 33–56.

Wyckoff, D.D. (1992) New tools for achieving service quality. In: Lovelock, C.H. (ed.) *Managing Services: Marketing, Operations and Human Resources*. 2nd edn. Prentice Hall, Hemel Hempstead, pp. 236–249.

Wylle, E. (1992) *Quality: Achieving Excellence*. Century Business, London, 256 pp.

Zeithaml, V.A. and Bitner, M.J. (1996) *Services Marketing*. McGraw-Hill, London, 608 pp.

Zeithaml, V.A., Parasuraman, A. and Berry, L.L. (1990) *Delivering Quality Service, Balancing Customer Perceptions and Expectations*. Free Press, New York, 226 pp.

Zimmerman C.D., III and Enell, J.W. (1988) Service industries. In: Juran, J.M. (ed.) *Quality Control Handbook*, 4th edn. McGraw-Hill, London, pp. 1–33.

Zink, K.J. and Schmidt, A. (1998) Practice and implementation of self-assessment. *International Journal of Quality Science* 3, 147–170.

Index